DEMOCRACY AND THE PUBLIC SPHERE

From Dystopia Back to Utopia

Hans-Jörg Trenz

BRISTOL
UNIVERSITY
PRESS

First published in Great Britain in 2024 by

Bristol University Press
University of Bristol
1-9 Old Park Hill
Bristol
BS2 8BB
UK
t: +44 (0)117 374 6645
e: bup-info@bristol.ac.uk

Details of international sales and distribution partners are available at bristoluniversitypress.co.uk

© Bristol University Press 2024

British Library Cataloguing in Publication Data
A catalogue record for this book is available from the British Library

ISBN 978-1-5292-3435-0 hardcover
ISBN 978-1-5292-3436-7 ePub
ISBN 978-1-5292-3437-4 ePdf

The right of Hans-Jörg Trenz to be identified as author of this work has been asserted by him in accordance with the Copyright, Designs and Patents Act 1988.

Cover design: Qube Design
Front cover image: Getty/Patrick Wilken
Bristol University Press uses environmentally responsible print partners.
Printed and bound in Great Britain by CPI Group (UK) Ltd, Croydon, CR0 4YY

FSC
www.fsc.org
MIX
Paper | Supporting
responsible forestry
FSC® C013604

Contents

About the Author

Hans-Jörg Trenz is Professor of Sociology of Culture and Communication at Scuola Normale Superiore in Pisa/Florence, Italy. He has held previous positions at University of Copenhagen, ARENA Centre for European Studies, University of Oslo and Humboldt University, Berlin. His main field of interests are the emergence of a European public sphere and of European civil society, European civilization and identity, migration and ethnic minorities, cultural and political sociology and social and political theory. Recent publications include *Solidarity in the Media and Public Contention over Refugees in Europe*, London: Routledge, 2021 (with Manlio Cinalli, Verena Brändle, Olga Eisele and Christian Lahusen); *Narrating European Society: Toward a Sociology of European Integration*, Lanham: Rowman and Littlefield, Lexington Books, 2016; and *Europe's Prolonged Crisis: The Making or the Unmaking of a Political Union*, Houndmills, Basingstoke: Palgrave Macmillan, 2015 (edited together with Virginie Guiraudon and Carlo Ruzza).

Preface

This is a book about the revival of democracy in the so-called age of post-democracy. It provides a thorough analysis of contemporary transformations in the public sphere and the media. Although its analysis largely supports the thesis of a decline of democracy, the book avoids jumping to the conclusion that democracy is coming to an end. There is overwhelming evidence that democracy is in crisis, with Colin Crouch (2020) referencing the acceleration of this process since the 2008 and subsequent crises. We have a rich account of the drama of democratic decline, but what succeeds democracy? We can diagnose the symptoms of post-democracy, but can we imagine a world without it? I argue that we not only lack the imagination to formulate a theory of a post-democratic world order but that we do not actually need such a theory in the first place. A core topic of public sphere theory is the co-evolution of modern society and democracy, and our sociological explication of the current crisis of democracy can gain much by drawing on this theoretical legacy. We can only make sense of post-democracy by continuing to write the theory of democracy and the public sphere.

My intention in this book is different from those authors who predict post-democracy as the future scenario of a world political order. Post-democracy is not the hypothetical endpoint of the current transition of our political regimes. At the same time, by arguing that democracy will continue to exist. I do not aim to raise counterfactual claims or engage in a normative debate about how democracy should be rescued. I instead take the challenges contemporary democracies are facing as my starting point to explore what happens after post-democracy. Hence I do not wish to understand how a utopia has become dystopian, but I depart from the discovery of dystopia and ask what remains of utopia. The encounter with dystopia is not some intellectual castle in the air: it is experienced by individuals and collectives, and such experiences are interpreted and trigger specific responses. Societal actors and groups might accelerate democratic decline or resist it and take corrective action. This leads me to base my book on the counter-intuitive assertion that our contemporary world of post-democracy is a golden age for democracy. The recent dynamics of contentious politics can no longer be adequately grasped as contestation *within* established democracies, or as contestation that aims at establishing democracy; they rather point at new forms of contestation *of* democracy. It is therefore worth taking a closer look at these conflicts not simply as practices that undermine democracy but rather as new and creative ways to support it. The contestation of democracy still takes the form of democracy and introduces new procedures of democratic legitimation.

Contemporary debate over the fate of democracy all too often focuses primarily on the symptoms of (dys)functional political systems and formal representative institutions of government. I wish to contribute to this debate with a discussion of the changing role of the media in democracy. There is much reason to be concerned by recent media developments in response to digitalization and globalization and their potential threats to democracy. A prevailing feeling of doom with the state of the media exists, yet at the same time we are becoming increasingly dependent on media use and content. The media world is seen to be on fire, and many of us predict that the worst is still to come. Such experiences of disrupted media landscapes also correspond to the widespread unease with the use of digital media and exposure to the dangers of the Internet. As media and communication scholars, we are more often fire detectors than extinguishers. On the one hand, we are expected to increase public confidence in the new media and produce knowledge of its risks and opportunities. We know the current state of the media all too well and can use this knowledge to make reliable predictions about trends in media developments. On the other hand, the prediction of an end to the public sphere and democracy is no longer a risk scenario but the consolidated state-of-the-art of contemporary media research, as corroborated by statistics of media consumption, probability calculations of media development and observations of media performance. Browsing through the pages of any media and communication journal will suffice as evidence of the bleak picture media scholars draw of the future media world.

Media and public sphere scholarship are rarely purely analytical. Many of us believe it is time to expose the precarity of the democratic public sphere through the findings of empirical research. The renaissance of critical media studies is partly demand driven, as society and politics increasingly depend on a critical assessment of media performance. There is a growing need to collect evidence and develop indicators for comparative analysis that allow us to assess media performance in relation to democracy.[1] The media crisis is quantified through data that illustrate, for instance, the drop in selected media companies' profits, the death of newspapers[2] or the loss of trust in news media and journalism.[3] However, such quantifiable indicators need to be linked to a 'normative assessment' of the 'state of democracy'. This is done through numerical ratings that quantify adherence to democratic norms such as media freedom, freedom of speech or the rule of law and thus allow for the scaling and ranking of entire regions and countries, visualized in world maps in green and red, illustrating the drama of democratic decay.[4] Such material in the form of graphs and maps of comparative assessment of democracy are again made available for public use and widely shared through traditional and social media diagnosis. In this sense, the diagnosis of a global erosion of democracy is constitutive for the emergence of critical publics that claim back democracy. In this sense, the diagnosis of a global erosion of democracy is a critical public sphere for the contestation of democracy. With this, I arrive at the main argument of my book that the path from the erosion of democracy to democratic renewal has already been laid. It is not a narrow path with restricted access but globally accessible. The search for democratic renewal is embedded in a global sphere of critique and linked to global practices of media and democracy monitoring, which can only exist because they are supported by the global media and because they resonate with a critical global public. The global space of media and democracy monitoring is also not just limited to some think tanks and experts but reaches out through popular media and creates specific knowledge and expectations in the performance of democracy that are shared by global audiences. There is a *world public* that critically monitors the *world performance* of democracy.

In this book, I wish to pick up and collect the various pieces of evidence about contemporary media and public sphere disruptions and their devastating effects on democracy and reconnect them to the evolving practices of democratic renewal. I not only aim to provide a picture of the current state of the media, the public sphere and democracy but also to discuss how we can know that the contemporary media and the public sphere have been disrupted. This leads to a better understanding of the analytical and normative dimensions of the public sphere and the interlinkage between empirical analysis (observation) and normative critique (assessment). In short, the argument runs as follows: in the modern public sphere, democratic disruptions and renewal are intrinsically related. Precisely because digital media technologies and the Internet are constantly blamed for undermining democracy, they also drive democratic reform. The dystopia of the disrupted public sphere is only thinkable through the revalidation of its utopian elements. In pragmatic terms: democracy is the inconclusive and never-ending process of criticizing its own insufficiencies. Through criticism of the public sphere, knowledge about the normative insufficiencies of 'real existing democracies' is accumulated. Yet critique is also a form of public intervention that calls for a more effective, egalitarian and inclusive democracy. The public sphere provides the communicative infrastructure, the normative substrate and the procedures that are needed to carry forward this struggle over the present dystopia and future utopia of democracy.

According to Habermas (2009: 135), public spheres are a 'demanding and therefore unlikely achievement of modern Western societies'. My book builds on this legacy of the modern public sphere but adds to the story the sociological insight that the decay of the public sphere must also be understood as a rather unlikely event (Trenz, 2021). As critique is the fuel that keeps the motor of the public sphere running, any critique *of* the public sphere also contributes to its reproduction. This is helpful for understanding the current talk about the crisis of the media and the public sphere from a new perspective. There is no lack of critical voices in the crisis–ridden public spheres of contemporary democracies. The basic linkage between criticism and public sphere transformation is therefore not disrupted but constantly renewed. My argument is that the modern public sphere needs to be analysed through the dialectics between disruption and renewal, between dystopia and utopia. The underlying norms of the public sphere open the horizon of democratization and social progress. Yet, the same norms are also constantly violated opening the space for public sphere criticism.

This leads me to my main argument that after dystopia can only come utopia. The critique of Enlightenment can only be put forward as a contribution to Enlightenment. If modern society is distinguished by describing itself as being in permanent crisis mode (Koselleck, 1973), it critically puts at test and revalidates its utopian elements. If we look at how contemporary forms of social movements and protest unfold through digital platforms and social media, we observe defiance of dystopia and resilient practices of public sphere renewal (Cammaerts, 2015; Jackson et al, 2020). Collecting evidence of disruptions to the public sphere and democracy is not simply an intellectual undertaking limited to the community of critical media scholars; it is a collective undertaking that draws on the daily experiences of critical media users and the creative ways they engage with the media. Whoever diagnoses the dystopia of the public sphere and democracy has already entered the spiral of critique that opens the potential for public sphere renewal.

My book is intended as a contribution to knowledge of the contemporary public sphere and democracy disruptions and the generation of this knowledge. I not only point the finger at dysfunctions of the media and democracy but also ask how public sphere disruption can be identified and its effects on democracy established. This is a meta-debate of contemporary public sphere transformations that combines media diagnosis and critique. What are the normative yardsticks and empirical indicators that allow us in our role as scholars and alert citizens to combine diagnosis and critique? Is our diagnosis of public sphere disruptions based on the normative critique of violations of public sphere principles, or is it based on analytical dimensions of a well-functioning public sphere? How do we know that the foundational principles of the modern public sphere have been violated or its procedures and infrastructures corrupted? And finally, what are the effects of the diagnosis of such disruptions of public sphere principles and functioning on the renewal of social order and the generation of democratic legitimacy?

The idea for this book originates from an effort to draft a programme for an interdisciplinary PhD school in the field of comparative media and democracy. We invited a group of scholars who shared an interest in the future of the public sphere and democracy to reflect on whether our existing knowledge of the functioning of democracy is still applicable to the digital media world. We were alarmed by the many insufficiencies and disruptions of contemporary media communications, which we had the chance to document and assess in our ongoing research projects (Michailidou et al, 2014; Cinalli et al, 2021; Michailidou and Trenz, 2021). At the same time, we were also attracted by recent developments in digital media communications and the opportunities offered to extend and renew the democratic project. Public sphere disruptions, giving rise to much concern, anxiety and trouble, are seemingly related to the way the idea of the public sphere resurges and its underlying norms are powerful reaffirmed on a global scale. How can we account for such a linkage between public sphere disruptions and resilience? And what are its manifestations, mechanisms and long-term effects for the future design of democratic society?

To approach the main challenges and opportunities of digital media communications and their impact on democracy, a synthesizing research effort is needed that reunites the rich data generated about specific aspects of digital media production, dissemination and consumption. Such an overview of the field of digital media studies might seem premature, as testified by numerous publications in the field which all too readily jump to fickle conclusions about the current state of the media or sound false alarms about alleged media impact and effects. A theory of the digital transformations of society is, however, not simply about predicting trends in media development. It needs to reflect on the possibility of critical social thought about media and its alleged effects on society and democracy. Such a critical theory of the media, communication and society is available in the form of modern public sphere theory. Is it still applicable? And how can public spheres, claimed to be disrupted by digital media communications, re-emerge?

Although a PhD school on public sphere transformations has yet to be realized due to the imponderables of EU funding, the drafting of this book nevertheless advanced and was facilitated by a series of unexpected writing retreats during the pandemic lockdowns of 2020–21. What a privileged and exceptional moment writing a monograph has been in my academic life. It required overcoming the restrictions that resulted from my various commitments to empirical research projects where targeted research outputs were expected. It also required broadening my readings, looking beyond the predefined teaching curricula of BA and MA education in media studies designed for young students, future digital practitioners who rarely experience opportunities for critical reflection. An escape from these routines of teaching was offered in the form of a fellowship during my sabbatical semester at the Weizenbaum Institute for the Study of Networked Society in Berlin in the winter and spring of 2020. The institute hosts a number of research groups from different disciplines working together to better understand the dynamics, mechanisms and implications of digitalization. As a guest scholar not committed to any empirical research project, I could easily switch focus and ask: How does digitalization research unfold, and what creates the conditions for a critical investigation of digital society and change? This is a question which is not limited to the conditions of scientific and academic research on digitalization. It is a question of how knowledge about digitalization is generated by the whole of society, how it is experienced by the members of society, how it creates expectations, hopes and fears, and how individuals make creative use of digital media technologies, giving rise to new forms of cultural expression and collective mobilization.

Digitalization, in short, should not be seen as something that happens to society but as a process applied, debated and critically assessed by society. The knowledge we have about digitalization is a critical form of knowledge generated by a society that describes itself as 'digital' and constitutes itself through operations and practices linked to the use of digital media technologies.

During my stay in Berlin, I experienced the Weizenbaum Institute not so much as a privileged place to think about digitalization but as an extension of what happens in society as a whole. My very much unexpected self-isolation during the COVID-19 pandemic in early March 2020 invited a thorough reflection on the simultaneity of public sphere lockdown and the accelerating pace of public sphere dynamics. Locked down in Berlin in the middle of the COVID outbreak, I experienced imposed privacy within the walls of a 25-square metre apartment in Prenzlauer Berg, and yet from my window I could observe that the public sphere of a big city cannot be shut down. The pandemic increased media dependencies and accelerated digitalization. The slowing down of public life was at the same time an invitation for the whole of society to go digital in the realms of politics, work and leisure, as well as private and even intimate relationships. The pandemic was also a powerful moment for the resilience of public spheres, which continued to thrive in the local neighbourhoods and made people engage in creative media practices. This is why I opted to make resilience practices prominent in both my theoretical reflections and empirical examples of public sphere transformations. There was no linear development, for instance, in the form of the degradation from a public to a private sphere. The conventional account of the decay of the public sphere and democracy did not fully grasp the dialectical tensions between disruption and renewal. Digitalization was related to new social practices and experiences, which still maintained old forms, like, for instance, solidarity (showing solidarity by social distancing during the pandemic), moral virtues such as compassion, or ethical responses, such as justice. The 'void' of the public sphere as a physical experience was counterbalanced by engagement in the virtual world and the occupation of digital spaces for information, debate and social exchange. The pandemic months were a time of constant communication and intensified social exchanges with friends and strangers. It was a moment of reflection that was very different from the mode of self-reflection in isolation chosen in previous times, for instance by monks. In important ways, personal involvement in digital society during the pandemic months remained bound to a renewed ethical commitment to the collective that took responsibility for its uncertain future. Through the intensification of digitally mediated communication, the normative project of modernity, Enlightenment and democracy was not dismissed but revived. These forms of recoupling of new digital models of communication and utopian visions of society are at the heart of this book.

This book delivers an account of the revival of the public sphere at the moment of its deepest crisis. There is life after post-democracy, which is seemingly still democratic. The research programme to be developed in the following chapters aims to investigate different forms of public sphere resilience and understand how the discovery of public sphere disruptions is systematically related to the conditions of the public sphere's resurgence. This goes significantly beyond the diagnosis of public sphere and democracy disruptions emphasized in recent research. I wish to indicate ways of democratic renewal not as a prescribed normative recipe but as inscribed into unfolding social practices. Public sphere renewal is not something to be projected into the future but something that is already happening, the limits and potentials of which need to be understood. The intention of the book, therefore, is not simply abstract, assessing how particular models of democracy apply in contemporary digital societies, but to test how the current infrastructure of media and communication enables democracy and continues to intensify or weaken the dynamics of societal democratization.

Digital transformations have arguably enhanced contestation of values within and across European societies. The increased salience of conflicts over values and identities in crisis-ridden Europe is often related to the rise of populism, regionalism and new nationalism, which fundamentally challenges the legitimacy of the European Union and the liberal-democratic systems of its member states. Against this account of a 'populist backlash' in Europe, which is related to public sphere disruptions, I wish to collect evidence and uncover mechanisms of democratic renewal and public sphere resilience. The main question is under which conditions digital transformation might generate constructive learning dynamics that improve rather than undermine democratic engagement and generate democratic legitimacy. Using examples from the social struggles against surveillance capitalism, the anti-populist mobilizations in the UK, Italy and Germany, and the revival of critical publics during the COVID-19 pandemic, I will discuss the potential of a broader transnational democratic movement that takes collective lessons from post-crisis Europe and seeks to modify how national and European governments are democratically designed.

In writing a book about contemporary public sphere transformations, it was not only essential to discuss the fate of democracy but to delve into a range of related topical debates about the design of the digital future of society. The book's sections can be read separately without the need for readers to engage in normative and theoretical debates about the public sphere. In particular, I wish to highlight my comprehensive review of the literature of digital sociology in Part III, which contributes to cultural study approaches in digital humanities on social practices of redefining privacy and publicity. Part IV expands on surveillance capitalism, which might be of special interest to social movement scholars seeking to understand the dynamics of digital protest and social media-driven resistance. Part IV also draws on current debates over populism as a form of (post-)democratic representation. As a matter of fact, understandings of the current challenge of populism often crystallize around modes of public communications and notions of political representation, both of which are at the core of the modern public sphere. The book provides a specific reading of populism as grounded in public sphere and media dynamics, combined with my interpretation of the public sphere as constitutive of the publics as 'popular subjects' of democracy. Analysing contemporary media and public sphere transformations leads us, therefore, to a new understanding of populism and the mechanisms through which it unfolds. Finally, I provide an updated and extensive discussion of the forms of crisis communication and the role of journalism in contemporary democracy, which links to ongoing debates about the struggle against 'fake news' and the future of (quality) media in post-truth politics. I draw here, in particular, on discussions within our Jean Monnet network on post-truth politics and democratic legitimation.[5] The chapter also profited from collaboration with colleagues at Freie Universität Berlin and the Weizenbaum Institute, resulting in the publication of two special issues for the journal *Javnost – The Public* in 2021.[6]

This book is also to be understood as a form of compliance with the expectation that sabbaticals should be used by academics to write monographs. Writing this book was a creative experience and a privilege. I was not bound by necessity to document specific research findings, explicate methods and display data for over-exacting reviewers. The book's different parts, nevertheless, went through several rounds of digital reviews. Many of the book's ideas were tested in debates in online workshops and seminars and critically scrutinized by my colleagues and research fellows. I owe a great debt of gratitude to my friends and colleagues at the Department of Communication of the University of Copenhagen, at Arena, Centre for European Studies in the University of Oslo and Scuola Normale Superiore, Department of Social and Political Sciences in Florence.

1

Introduction: Vanishing Publics – The Erosion of Democracy and the Public Sphere

The old public sphere is no longer. Not that it will be done any time in near future, it is done already. Digitalisation has triggered an all destroying explosion that has shattered the realm of human communication.

Eva Menasse, Ludwig-Borne-Preis acceptance speech, 2019[1]

Democracy has been disrupted. But to what end? So far, we appear to have no idea – beyond disruption itself.

Krastev, *Democracy Disrupted: The Politics of Global Protest*, 2014: 6

Hundreds of books have appeared since the early 2000 forecasting the erosion of liberal democracy in connection with what is identified as deep disruptions of media and communications in the digital age. Much collected evidence suggests that the best days of democracy are over, and that democracy might soon come to an end. Intellectuals have given up believing in the future of democracy, not because they embrace a better project, but because evidence speaks against it. But what binds democracy and the media so closely together? Why is democracy's destiny so intimately related to the health of public communication and the media?

The diagnosis of democratic failure does not start with a discussion of media infrastructures and dynamics but with political ideas and ideologies (Müller, 2011; Zielonka, 2018). The assumption that Western politics had witnessed the 'end of ideology' actually predates the fall of the Iron Curtain and of the ideologically divided world in 1989 (Bell, 1962) and relates to the sociological diagnosis of open societies shaped by secularization, individualization and enhanced reflexivity where collective projects lost their shine (Beck et al, 1994). Liberal democracy proliferated precisely because it did not require collective ideological commitments and allowed for the establishment of some sort of technocratic government with an emphasis on politics as 'problem-solving' (Giddens, 1994). Yet democracies are not simply made by individuals, and the 'neglect of the collective' has thus become 'ideological' in the way it has been promoted by some of the hardliners of neoliberal thought. In parallel, collectives began to be reshaped in the post-'89 counter-revolutions and search for new expressions of popular sovereignty in the form of ethno-nationalism and populism (Snyder, 2003; Wodak and Boukala, 2015; Zielonka, 2018).

In the 'new politics of extremes', democracy is seen as being crushed to death by neoliberalism on the one side and populism on the other (Zielonka, 2018). Yet neither neoliberals nor populists want democracy to come to an end. Neoliberals want to increase openness and the freedom of individuals as market citizens; populists want to regain control of the collective and enhance the popular sovereignty of national citizens and their exclusive belonging to confined nation states. If the end of democracy is not wanted, why is it taking place? Or is it simply not occurring, signalling that the current political struggle over democracy is just another form of democratic renewal? The 'new politics of extremes' are also a politics of non-reconciliation and polarization that is marked by a loss of respect and trust among political adversaries who perceive each other irreconcilable enemies rather than legitimate opponents. Liberals see the end of democracy as the victory of the populists; the populists see the end of democracy as the victory of the liberals. The two projects have become exclusive and incommensurable. Strong ideological polarization is back, and democracy is caught between hyper-individualism and hyper-collectivism.

At the same time, there is no alternative *to* democracy. There are, of course, alternative models *of* democracy, but it would be far-fetched to claim that democracy could be replaced by an alternative political order that seeks legitimation through non-democratic principles. We simply cannot imagine a stable political order that would be grounded in arbitrary rule, inequality, the denial of individual freedom and of collective self-determination. In Western societies, the trauma in the wake of fascism and communism fed into a deeply rooted popular belief in the prospects of liberal democracy (Giesen, 2004), while, in the non-Western world, the colonial past lingers and continues to inform political projects that are about emancipation and self-determination and call for global justice and responsibility. Nowhere are there any stable majorities that wish to replace democracy, and despite the authoritarian backlash in many countries, the founding principles of democracy are still held as valid, even by those regimes that propagate a new authoritarianism. The World Values Survey opinion polls demonstrate that democratic values are widely supported in most Western (and non-Western) countries, as well as in many places where large-scale mobilization takes place in defence of such values (Inglehart, 2003; Della Porta, 2005). Despite the more recent cultural backlashes (Norris and Inglehart, 2019), our present times do not know viable alternative principles of political order that could transcend democracy. Authoritarian regimes can sometimes gain stability and even popular support, but not legitimacy. They can temporarily build on the charisma of their leaders, but more often their authority can only be upheld through threats of violence and the repression of majorities by ruling minorities. Democracy remains an unfulfilled promise in any authoritarian state, and this regularly nourishes the surge of resistance movements that seek to overthrow arbitrary rule (which also holds true for non-Western civilizations, as the Arab Spring and protests in China testify).

Even though democracy as a principle of political legitimacy seems indisputable, contestations over democracy have increased. Since the beginning of the new millennium, dynamics of conflict have expanded in Western democracies from public contestations in democracy to contestations over democracy (Mair, 2013). Political parties increasingly engage in symbolic struggles over identities, values and the allocation of popular sovereignty, while government is taken over by unelected technocrats within national and supranational bureaucracies. Meanwhile, electorates feel increasingly alienated from political representatives, their electoral choice becomes more volatile and abstention is increasing during elections. The hollowing of democracy takes place not because people no longer believe in its superiority as a political system but because they have lost faith in the existing party systems and institutions of government to support democracy (Mair, 2013). This raises the intriguing question of whether democracies can de-democratize even though stable majorities wish to live in democracies and still believe democratic principles are valid. Peter Mair (2013) discusses de-democratization as an effect of the de-politicization of the representative arena of politics: national public spheres are no longer driven by party contestation over political decision-making, with 'mass spectacle' replacing 'mass involvement' in democratic politics (Mair, 1998). However, such a shift from 'representative democracy' to 'audience democracy' (Manin, 1997; Michailidou and Trenz, 2013) would still require a relatively unified public sphere of mass attention, where democratic politics can be staged for the mass audience. The Berlusconian-style TV[2] democracy is probably its closest realization (Sartori, 1998).

These critical assumptions about the de-democratizing effects of mediatized representative politics need to be qualified when applied to the new reality of digital media environments. For Philip Manow, de-democratization instead results from the drastic expansion of participation and the enhancement of political conflict, as facilitated by digital media. A democracy where voice is constantly expressed by all would be a democracy where representation of voice becomes impossible (Manow, 2020). If everybody challenges democratic values and identities all the time, contestation over democracy would be detached from the arena of politics and organized actors and institutions where such demands could be bundled and fed into the political system of decision-making. For Eva Menasse, this multiplication of voice has the same effect on the public sphere as the right for anybody to print money at home would have on the economy.[3] Contestation over democracy would remain 'void' and without value; it would continue 'ad aeternum' without generating any binding forces, or, in the words of Ivan Krastev (2014: 6), democracy would be continuously disrupted, but to no end – 'beyond disruption itself'. In this case, we could de facto speak of the *disappearance of the public sphere*.[4]

What comes after the public sphere? Philip Schlesinger (2020) describes the current accelerated transition with an unclear outcome as an unstable 'post-public sphere'. Yet it remains unclear why the current transition from the public sphere to post-public sphere and from democracy to post-democracy should be different from previous transitions of what Jürgen Habermas (1989 [1962]) famously analysed as the 'structural transformation of the public sphere'. According to this account, the public sphere is always subject to revisions that are driven by its own critical forces. However, such a critique as the driver of public sphere transformation has always been related to a further democratization of modern society and politics. Public sphere transformations were related to a progressive force of societal change in terms of modernization and collectively explored potentials for learning. If contemporary authors speak of a post-public sphere and of post-democracy, there is more at stake than first appears. The end of the public sphere would not simply mean a deep crisis of mass media, journalism and political communication. It would also be the end of utopia, or rather the end of modern society as utopia (which literally means a 'good place') of progress and betterment. After disruption comes dystopia, but dystopia is a question of survival not only for the media and the public sphere but for human society as a whole. In the context of digitalization, such dystopian visions have grown in popularity because they channel widespread fears and feelings of unease with the spread of digital technologies. Doomsday prophets, such as Yuval Noah Harari, have coined the slogan 'hacking humans', painting a scenario of artificial intelligence and algorithms taking control over us.[5] Such a nightmare scenario would be the end of humanity, replaced by a technology that will know you better than you know yourself and at some point will also replace the self.[6] The dystopian public sphere would thus be a knowledgeable technology that slowly expels humans as protagonists from the stage. Machines, not humans, would be the new carrier of knowledge. Protagonists and publics would no longer be needed to keep the machinery of knowledge production and application running.

How plausible is such a dystopian public sphere, one based on machinery without humans? For the time being, this dystopia is just another negative template for critique that exists because digitalization has generated its own utopian vision of society. There are alternative scripts of digitalization that drive public sphere transformation through the engagement of digital elites, their propagation (or rejection) of digital technologies for the betterment of society, and through critical publics that subject them to public scrutiny. In this sense, digitalization remains dependent on the infrastructures of a well-functioning public sphere through which a new utopia and its critique can be generated, channelled and take effect. The observation that both the utopian and dystopian public sphere scenarios have become elements of popular discourse can be treated by scholars as symptoms of the hopes and fears created by the spread of digital technologies. New public sphere protagonists, in their role as prophets or doomsayers of the future of digital society and democracy, are in search of new audiences. As such, these new audiences underlie the infrastructure of a well-functioning public sphere, which is, at the same time, put to the test by their critical interventions.

The public sphere is commonly approached through distinctions that allow both normative assessment and empirical analysis. The dimensions covered by these distinctions are, for instance, public–private, rational–irrational, true–false. Public sphere analysis often proceeds – in the form of a classification of communications – as belonging to the realm of the public or the private, or as having intrinsic values such as rational or irrational. To uphold such distinctions, we need to rely on communicative spaces as structured by norms that allow us to draw boundaries and decide about questions of validity. The public sphere provides the social and normative order of modern society. It further allows us to conceive social change as directionally channelled within the institutional and normative order, for instance in terms of learning and teleological planning. This constellation of society, as integrated by an encompassing public sphere of meaningful communication and reasoning, is specifically modern. Modernization is perceived as structured change within a given normative order. Modern society is defined through its capacities of self-criticism: it emerged as a society that found it necessary to constantly question itself and is based on a shared set of norms and an infrastructure of communication that allow such critical questioning. It is a society that observes itself through a mirror, to constantly question its own operations and the type of society it produces. This mirror of critical self-reflection can be called the public sphere. To unfold these capacities of self-criticism, modern society approaches and, in fact, often converges with democratic regimes of collective self-determination. Democracy combines these characteristics of affirmation and critical self-scrutiny. Criticism makes society intelligible and thus makes it possible to conceive of collective self-determination.

5

The response of the public sphere scholar to the 'after democracy and the public sphere' question is that there is no diagnosis of public sphere disruptions that is not at the same time expressed as a form of critique, once again filtered through the public sphere. The world after public sphere disruptions can only be imagined as long as we can presuppose that there is a shared infrastructure of communication for such an imagination to be given expression and find resonance. Public sphere and democracy criticism relies on prerequisites that only the public sphere can provide. In other words, the post–public sphere world can only be approached through public sphere criticism, that is, by critically examining the (dys)functioning of the media and of political communication in such a dystopian order. If this is the case, the question is why critique of public sphere disruptions should not, once more, be turned again into renewal. Breakup would not succeed dystopia; democratic utopia would.

Mirrored through the critical eye of the public sphere, the world after disruption takes shape as a possible world of renewed democratic forms and practices. One account is the powerful return of the public sphere and the relaunch of democracy through heroic actors and forms of political leadership. Such a new form of democratic entrepreneurship would be driven by progressive states and governments and by civil society in the promotion of a new world order. Nancy Fraser (2007) points out a possible direction to reconsider the meaning of the public sphere by taking its underlying norms seriously and interrogating their lasting impact on the transnational constellation of governance. This follows the main line of argumentation of Jürgen Habermas (2000), who identifies the EU and the UN as possible sources of authority that can be democratically addressed and legitimated by the constituents of global civil society and global critical discourse. Even though a democratic reconfiguration or constitutionalization of International Relations is not supported by contemporary political forces, it remains a utopia that drives public sphere criticism, and thus impacts on political legitimacy. In the following, I am interested in these internal dynamics of public sphere transformations that pick up and develop such new utopian elements.

Instead of the heroic and powerful return of a programme of constitutional cosmopolitanism that drives governments and integrates states, there are also more subtle ways of democratic renewal. As I will argue, the programme of democratic renewal is inscribed in the normal operational mode of the public sphere. The experiences of public sphere and media disruptions have nourished the notion of citizens being disillusioned with democracy, yet such a disillusionment is not simply individually experienced but has become part of collective interpretations. Disillusion with democracy is the breeding ground for the emergence of critical publics.

Democracy and its critics do not know their end. You cannot decide by democratic means to be non-democratic, but only confront existing democracies with their own insufficiencies. This means that there cannot be a scientific diagnosis of public sphere disruptions that does not simultaneously feed into the public sphere as critical input and pathfinder of democratic reform. Public sphere criticism is there as a form of remembrance of the solid old building blocks which might have been torn down but can also be rearranged and put back together to facilitate the construction of something new and even more solid. In this book, I will introduce the notion of public sphere resilience to refer to this eternal bouncing back of public sphere dynamics, which turns disruptions into a potential for innovation. The very fact that perceived public sphere disruptions become a public concern that is discussed and debated would be an indicator for public sphere resilience, as manifested in the collective will to overcome perceived deficits of media functioning and political communication. I will clarify throughout this book that such an elusive response to the inevitability of public sphere resilience does not remain hypothetical but, conversely, is driving contemporary dynamics of change in political communication and the media. The book, therefore, is meant as an invitation to further explore how public sphere utopia and dystopia propel each other.

By arguing that the public sphere is utopia, I do not wish to repeat a rather simplified criticism of the Habermasian notion of the (deliberative) public sphere as the dreamland of democracy. Rather, I wish to understand the public sphere as a field of contestation that is driven by the search for the formulation of the common good and the means of its realization. There is no paradise lost – like the good old times of critical journalism – that is not bound to a new horizon of improved media and communication capacities at the service of democracy. Public sphere criticism always bridges past and future visions. It builds history and narration. Past templates do not become irrelevant but are constantly revalued. What counts is how their validity is sustained and projected towards the future in such a way as to guide collective action in the present. The question of whether contemporary public spheres and media are disrupted is therefore closely related to the question of whether the principles, norms and values on which the public sphere was built are still valid today. It is not only communication infrastructures but also norms that need to be part of the diagnosis, which means, for instance, that even the complete collapse of public sphere infrastructures would not invalidate the norms on which they were built. The norms of the public sphere are a scaffold that can be used for different buildings. They are not abstract external projections but are concrete and real as part of the public sphere infrastructure and, hence, also inform the practices of individuals, as well as of the collective and institutional actors who populate the public sphere.

With its emphasis on the linkage between the diagnosis of public sphere disruptions in the digital age and public sphere renewal, this book contributes to our understanding of digital society. It takes a look at the greater narrative of digitalization, which is a public sphere narrative of utopia and dystopia. As such, and this is the central argument of the book, the narrative of digital society is a continuation of the narrative of modern society that constitutes itself through the public sphere. The narrative of digital society continues to facilitate critical self-reflection about the conditional factors of social order, its underlying norms and potentials. In practice, narratives of digitalization often tell the story of disruption of existing structures, invalidation of norms and loss of control. There is a dramatic element in the narrative of digitalization. The form this drama takes is well known: it is displayed as critique. And such critique has a specific function in the process of self-constitution of the digital society, not in the way of wilful design but of enabling individuals and organizations to work under digitalization, making use of digital technologies not simply in an instrumental way but opening up new horizons of collective action and projects for them (Süssenguth, 2015).

There is widespread agreement that society lacks an understanding of digitalization and its far-reaching consequences. So-called digital agendas of government and research programmes within universities have been set up to promote a better understanding of digitalization and societal transformation. Such calls are often instrumental, assuming that individuals need to improve their skills and learn to use digital media technologies while society or politics need to adapt to changing technological requirements. The so-called digital agendas developed by local, national and European governments mostly embrace such aspects of enhanced media use. Within science, new collaborative research schemes have been developed, as for instance between information and computer sciences and the humanities, to enhance empirical knowledge about evolving practices of media use and manifestations of digital culture and society. Such calls for a better empirical understanding of digitalization and its effects are not simply pointing at existing knowledge gaps but are also an indicator of the willingness to engage in critical discourse about the formation of digital society.

In this tradition, I wish to contribute here not simply by filling specific gaps of empirical knowledge but by responding to the need for critical assessment. My intention is not just to add another piece of empirical work to our existing knowledge of digital society but rather to engage in an extended exploration of critical discourse about digital society. This implies an empirical perspective of the field where such critical discourse is promoted and attended: the public sphere. The public sphere in this sense takes two forms in this book: first, as the empirical object of analysis in the form of critical discourse, its makers, distributors and audiences; and secondly, as the target of the critical debates the book analyses. The public sphere is the space where this contestation takes place and is the object of this contestation. Empirical descriptions of the effects of digitalization can be part of such critical discourse and, as such, can be taken as evidence for how digital society reflects on itself, about what it sees (in terms of selected empirical evidence about digitalization) and how it assesses these new developments. I will thus analyse the various modes and discourses, the many critical debates through which society reflects on the forms of digitalization and its consequences. Such narratives of digitalization become relevant as modes of societal self-description (Nassehi, 2019).

The substantive part of the book is divided into four main chapters. Chapter 2 traces the ideational dimensions of the public sphere. To validate the evolving form of public sphere criticism and to find evidence for how it relates back to the utopia of a possible new beginning, I will systematically approach the notion of the modern public sphere and trace its transformation. This requires us, first, to engage with the key texts of Jürgen Habermas and to reconstruct the legacy of European Enlightenment that formulated the linkage between publicity and reasoning. Secondly, I will identify the core normative dimensions of the public sphere and their interlinkage with democracy. Thirdly, I discuss degrees of erosion of democratic norms and public sphere principles. I investigate these accounts of democratic decay not as an empirical diagnosis but as a form of normative critique. As such, I am interested in what facilitates critique, who promotes it and what the cognitive prerequisites are for expressing critique in the form of specific knowledge about empirical facts and causalities. I call this a sociology of knowledge of public sphere critique. Chapter 3 delivers an empirical account of ongoing public sphere transformations in which I briefly recapitulate the research findings of disrupted media infrastructures and discuss their impact on existing democracies. Overall, my diagnosis supports and substantiates the intellectual critique of public sphere disruptions. In the third part of the book (Chapter 4), I will turn to the dynamic interplay between dystopia and utopia as a driving force of public sphere conflicts. The tense relationship between dystopian and utopian elements is traced in the collective search for truth and rationality, the difficult acts of balancing privacy and publicity, and in the struggle over democratic empowerment of the will of the people. From there, I proceed in Chapter 5 to the linkage between critique and utopia that is not simply postulated but empirically traced in the practices of resilience of collective actors. I will speak of public sphere resilience in the cases of identification of public sphere disruptions by collective actors in the form of critical discourse that refers to and at the same time renews the normative template of the Enlightenment public sphere. I apply these rather abstract thoughts by looking at manifestations of public sphere resilience in the context of digitalization and globalization: first, the rebalancing of private–public relationships; secondly, the populist backlash and the struggle over political representation; and thirdly, the COVID-19 pandemic public sphere.

2

The Legacy and the Future
of the Public Sphere

What is a public sphere?

Habermas and the public sphere

Before we can diagnose the disappearance of something called the public sphere, we need to find agreement on what it is that is disappearing. I should emphasize at this point that this book is not meant as a conceptual history of the notion of the public sphere in modern political thought and in theories of democracy.[1] Rather, I wish to make this notion of the public sphere fruitful as a tool for scholars from different disciplinary backgrounds (mainly media studies, political science and sociology) to understand challenges to contemporary media and democracy. I want to show that the public sphere concept is still indispensable to formulating a critical agenda and engaging in critical research of the rapid transformation of our digital media and communication environments. Through the analytical lens of the public sphere, we can identify the current trends of democratic society and politics: opportunities for democratization and threats of non-democratic backlashes.

Such a conceptual discussion needs to take as its starting point the voluminous work of Jürgen Habermas. If the ambition of this book is to combine the tools of structural analysis and critical assessment of contemporary media and communication developments, this design owes much – or almost everything – to the agenda of public sphere research that was set out in Habermas' book *The Structural Transformation of the Public Sphere*, published in German in 1962 (Habermas, 1990 [1962]).[2] Habermas did not invent the concept of the public sphere but rather located its origins in modern political thought and in the history of the Enlightenment. The first part of his book provides a conceptual history of the notion of the public sphere, while the second part lays out the agenda of critical research of media and communication. It developed a normative template of the 'modern bourgeois public sphere' and can be read as an invitation to the social sciences to make this normative template applicable to research with a critical intent (Wessler, 2019). The *Structural Transformation of the Public Sphere* is, therefore, not primarily a contribution to philosophy and conceptual history in that it has also contributed to the foundations of several disciplines of the social sciences, notably media studies, the sociology of communication, political theory and political sciences, for which it has become a standard reference. The reception of the book in English-speaking academia was, nevertheless, somewhat delayed. After the publication of the English translation of Habermas' *Structural Transformation* in 1989 (that is, 27 years after the German original), a collection of essays by scholars, mainly within the field of political theory, was published by Craig Calhoun (1992) and left an indelible imprint on future debates. The notion of the public sphere was made fruitful by these second-generation scholars, above all in normative political theory and in theories of democracy applied to the contemporary challenges of the transnationalization of government (Eriksen, 2007), of digital transformations (Dahlgren, 2005) and of individualization and privatization (Papacharissi, 2010).

In developing my argument further, I do not presuppose that the reader is familiar with Habermas' concept of the public sphere and its extensive reception history in social and political theory. Rather, I wish to emphasize the practical relevance of the concept of the public sphere and of its normative template for the understanding of contemporary media transformations and challenges to democracy. The concept of the public sphere is therefore not simply meant to be analytical or normative. It is made applicable as a critical template by social groups and actors who populate the public sphere and keep it alive and going. These everyday practices of claiming the validity of the underlying principles of the public sphere are certainly not informed by the work of Habermas. However, the 'bourgeois public sphere' identified by Habermas in early 19th-century literary exchanges and debates in coffee houses remains the framework within which these new public sphere actors continue to move and push their critical agenda forward.

This book offers a sociological reading of the work of Habermas as a contribution that was not only meant as a normative theory of democracy but as a theory of modern society.[3] The sociogenesis of the public sphere (that is, its emergence and inscription into societal dynamics and practices) reads as a reconstruction of modern society, which is distinguished precisely by its reflexive capacities to observe and critically test its own functioning. Critical discourse, which unfolds as a form of self-description and self-constitution of modern society, continues in contemporary practices of radical democracy (which includes the critique of deep ruptures in democracy and its normative foundations). Thus, the overall question is what happens if society applies critical standards to test itself? A sociology of the public sphere is a sociology of critique, which means that the philosophical undertaking to approach the concept of the public sphere can only be seen as part of this critical exercise. There is no theorizing about the public sphere outside of this framework provided by the modern public sphere, and no external view that could replace it.

Not presupposing familiarity with the oeuvre of Habermas might even be advantageous for developing my argument further. The reader can be invited to engage in a thought experiment and join me in a reflection about what we mean when we talk of the 'public sphere' and whether we can presuppose a common understanding of this key notion of democracy. In a seminar room where students and scholars of democracy meet for such a critical exchange, we would experience how understandings of the public sphere and its functions for media and democracy differ widely. Such differences relate to our scholarly backgrounds as scientists educated within different disciplines. Philosophers will associate the notion of the public sphere primarily with the process of Enlightenment and the writings of Immanuel Kant. Legal scholars would explain the public sphere in relation to the state and functions of law. Political scientists would relate it to the arenas of conflict and competition between political parties. Media scholars would focus on the role of journalists and newspapers and use the term almost synonymously with media systems. In democratic theory, the public sphere relates to processes of intermediation between political representatives and electorates, or to processes of public opinion and will formation. However, the notion of the public sphere has also been developed in a dynamic interchange between these different disciplines, and it is here that we can draw some initial lines of distinction regarding what constitutes a shared understanding of public sphere infrastructures, norms and functions.

Network, discourse, sphere?

The most obvious thing to say, and here all disciplines would agree, is that the public sphere has to do with communication. It facilitates discourse and connects individuals or a certain group of people through communication. The public sphere relates to discourse but also to connections or to social relationships facilitated by discourse. This is also what *networks* do, which is why, in later writings, Habermas indeed talks of the public sphere as 'a network for communicating information and points of view' (Habermas, 1996: 360). The notion of the public sphere as a network has a technical and a sociological meaning. It refers to networks as an organizing principle for the diffusion of communication, but beyond that also as a way for individuals to build connections as active/social members of the public (Friedland et al, 2006). Just like the public sphere, networks are not bound to particular places but are open and dynamic. Relations between the different nodes of a network are not exclusive but temporal and tentative. Loose connections allow for flexibility and invite constant recombination. As such, networks, just like the public sphere, offer potentialities for *real* exchanges, associations and collaborations among participants (Reckwitz, 2020: 204). They are a supportive infrastructure, but they do not materialize in a social structure that endures over time and is bound to stable patterns of interaction.

The empirical description of the public sphere as a network for communication nevertheless remains incomplete. Network theory is useful to describe the more technical aspects of bridging spaces, avoiding hierarchies and building loose connections among individuals and social groups while maintaining distance from others (Castells, 1996). Network relationships in the public sphere are loose ways of coupling to be distinguished from the close ties of family or community (Trenz, 2005). However, through a collective engagement in *discourse*, the public sphere does more than simply connect people through communication. Communication that is channelled through the public sphere has a specific scope and purpose. First, it is made visible and made accessible to others, which is different from secret exchanges, which, as in the case of the darknet, for instance, can also take the form of a network. Secondly, it binds people together with the purpose of seeking a common understanding. Communicative exchanges in the public sphere are not simply meant to be *instrumental*, for example by imposing my will on others through commands or the use of power. Communication that is channelled through the public sphere in the form of discourse is *social* and *normative* in the way it is meant to share meaning with others and seek common grounds of understanding. The public sphere for Habermas is therefore the realm of reasons, whereby 'reasons' are generated in pragmatic discourse and sustained by generalized claims of validity, and not just reduced to a 'reasonable disagreement' among 'reasonable people', as in John Rawls' theory of justice (Habermas, 1995). Sociologically speaking, public reasons sustained by pragmatic discourse constitute a shared world of meaning, which is *culture* and *society*, in the broad sense. Reasons refer to communication that is made meaningful, either by building on established structures of meaning such as 'known facts', traditions and norms, or by creatively bringing into play new information, rearranging existing knowledge or challenging taken-for-granted norms (Habermas, 1985: 102–40). The notion of *discourse* relates precisely to this unfolding practice of an exchange of arguments and reasons around selected topics to be considered as relevant (because they are controversial, for instance).

The specific group of communicators that engages in discourse around selected topics includes proponents (A) and opponents (B) of arguments, but also the position of a third party (C) that listens or is addressed by these arguments. We call this third position a *public*. Discourse is therefore always more than a dialogue or a talk that unfolds in private. Discourse is public in the sense that the arguments and reasons exchanged imply generalized validity, and therefore do not only need to be approved by A and B as interlocutors but also by any other person, C. The public sphere, just like a network, is a relational term, but while networks mainly connect speaker positions, the public sphere builds additional links between speakers and a present or non-present public.

In the most basic sense, a public sphere, then, is not simply about communication; it is about the observation of communication. It is about the transformation of a communicative space (A+B) into an observatory space (A+B+C). The position of C as the 'third' in a communication is decisive to situating a communicative exchange in the public sphere where it becomes possible for anyone to observe what is going on between A and B. The third position C demarcates the one who does not talk and does not need to respond but, for the time being, simply observes as the bystander of A and B. Still, the presence of C is known to A and B, and this knowledge of the presence of a bystander has an impact on the course of their communication. They say things differently than they would do in a private conversation. The notion of public discourse further presupposes that the validity of what is said in the conversation between A and B can be tested. Such tests rely on generalizability, which can be achieved either through an empirical test (is what has been said true?) or a normative test (is it right?). Validity is questioned in the conversation (B doubts what has been said by A), but only the presence of C adds the possibility of an impartial control mechanism and therefore a higher authority to decide about the validity claims contested between A and B. Rationality, therefore, requires public reasoning (Habermas, 1985: 8–43). The public sphere then turns from an observatory space into a space of rational discourse that is guided by a collective engagement in public reasoning.

The public sphere does not encompass all communication; it is about public communication, and public now means two things. First, it means *visible* in a way that communication can be observed and accessed by a third party. Second, it means *reasoning* in a way that the meaning of what is said is also explained and made relevant for a third party, including consideration of all possible or momentarily available points of view and perspectives. Public thus relates to visibility and 'generalized reason'. What is 'made public' can, therefore, claim a higher level of rationality than what could be achieved in a private conversation. In its most elementary form, this is attained by transposing a talk from the closed walls of a private home to the marketplace outside, which adds the component of passive listening and possible intervention by a third party in a private conversation. Such a transition from 'private' to 'public' presupposes the distinction of two separate spheres, or two separate social realms. However, this is not a constitutive distinction, but one that is only drawn through engagement in public discourse and upheld because it is claimed to be valid (for instance, when we raise the 'public claim' to protect privacy). It is only when a public sphere comes into existence that distinctions between public and private can be drawn. Without a public sphere, there is no private sphere, and those who live in authoritarian societies or absolutist states know what that means.

There is another frequently evoked notion of the public sphere as some sort of collective actor. Such a conception of the public sphere, or publics, as collectivities has been almost unanimously dismissed by public sphere and media scholars (Neidhardt, 1994b). A diffuse communication network does not share the attributes of a collective actor. Neither publics nor audiences are collective actors (Neidhardt, 1994a). Still, in common parlance, we often relate to the public sphere by ascribing some qualities of collective action, in terms of doing something together, or being held responsible for something, for instance when we say that the public sphere legitimizes or empowers some actors and delegitimizes or disempowers others. Language differences in the use of the notion of the public sphere matter here: in German, for instance, it is common parlance to say that *Öffentlichkeit* 'thinks' or 'has an opinion' or 'demands' something. As I will argue, the intuition that the public sphere *does* something with the content of communication can only be properly understood by elaborating the intersubjective rather than individual forces of speech acts that bind people together in collective reasoning. Public discourse *does* something, but how exactly it impacts other things cannot be understood through the intent of single actors. The public sphere is more than a communication flow that can be sufficiently described in technical or mechanical terms; it settles validity claims, shapes opinions of a group of people and coordinates collective action. To explicate exactly how this is done, Habermas developed a 'theory of communicative action' that overcomes a single actor's perspectives and instrumental reasoning.

Finally, as implied especially in the English translation of the term *Öffentlichkeit*, a spatial connotation also applies. The 'sphere' is sometimes simply used as a synonym of 'space' (such as in the French notion of 'espace public'); often, the public sphere is also described as an 'arena' or a 'stage' that can be physically located, such as a theatre or a parliament. Empirically, public spheres are often analysed as *national* public spheres, thus presupposing congruence between the public sphere and politically and territorially confined spaces, ideally distinguished by a shared language and culture. Yet at the same time, it is emphasized that this space or arena remains rather undefined and open and that borders are constantly shifting due to the restriction of the scope of public debates. The public sphere is therefore more accurately described as an open space, such as the market square or the urban realm, where access cannot be denied to anybody. However, this raises a couple of follow-up questions to be dealt with in the following, most importantly: How can it be that spaces are open? And what distinguishes such 'open spaces' from other spatial connotations of the political, such as 'the state' or 'the nation'?

At second sight, we can see that all these different connotations of the public sphere and of its position in social life are not mutually exclusive but substitute each other. The public sphere appears to be all of this: it is 'objective reality' either as an arena where people meet and exchange ideas or as a space that is territorially confined, or a virtual discourse that unfolds over space and time, or a network that is primarily defined through interlinkages. The public sphere is 'virtual' and 'real'. It is 'space' and 'sphere'. It is confined and open. Is it actor and discourse. We can reconcile these different notions by concluding that all these different elements can be reference points for the empirical description of the unfolding of public discourse and its effects. They can be auxiliary concepts that help us to approach the public sphere but that are inherently neither entirely correct nor wrong. Yet, if a public sphere can be all of these things, how can it be nailed down analytically?

The public and its problems

The term 'public' is used in a rather confusing and simplified way in media and communication research and in public opinion surveys, highlighting technical over sociological aspects of communication and, therefore, often missing its full explanatory potential. In media reception studies, the term *public*, if used at all, is largely held to be identical with the term *audience* (Livingstone, 2005). In public opinion research, publics are instead constructed as statistical aggregates: the sum of individual attitudes or the mean of the distribution of attitudes in a given population (Noelle-Neumann, 1974). Slavko Splichal (2012: 88–97) reminds us that publics are not audiences. There is a difference drawn along the lines of 'active and passive', 'critical and uncritical' and 'political and commercial'. In classical mass media, research audiences are simply conceived as passive listeners. In public relations, they are the target of communication that is strategically placed to 'reach out' with a message and impact on the opinions or attitudes of others. Publics, instead, are entities that generate and exchange opinions and that interact in discursive ways. As such, they also develop an idea of 'being' or 'belonging' to a public by virtue of sharing ideas or being concerned with the same topic of relevance. Publics not only receive content but also engage in communication, while audiences simply listen or consume. A public is then also 'thinking' or 'reasoning', while audiences are passively shaped through the efforts of others. Members of the public are citizens, while members of the audience are consumers. This also has positive and negative connotations: public is knowledge, while audience is ignorance; public is enlightened, while audience is manipulated.

The differences between publics and audiences not only matter as descriptive categories but also as normative scripts in ongoing communicative exchanges that allow us to distinguish different styles of politics, for instance in the way politicians address individuals either as citizens to be included in the public use of reason or as anonymous members of a mass audience. These forms of addressing either a public or an audience help to distinguish different levels of inclusiveness of public debates. It makes, for instance, a difference whether my intention is simply to transmit some particular information or a body of knowledge (as I do in a lecture), whether I also wish to engage my addressees in meaningful exchanges about this content (as I do in a seminar), or whether I want to provoke my addressees and mobilize them (as I do in a political speech). In a similar vein, if I design a blog page or a social media profile, I need to decide whether I wish to use this platform primarily to maximize visibility and reach out to the biggest possible number of people, which is often the case when I have a commercial interest, or whether I wish to use the platform to maximize user engagement through participation in meaningful exchanges with others, encouraging them to raise their voices or even to collaborate in joint projects or campaigns. In the first case, to be successful, I would need to reduce interactive features in the design of my platform to be able to focus attention and target users while avoiding distraction or uncontrolled user responses. In the second case, I would need to reduce generic communication, position myself lower in the hierarchy, and allow for frequent responses and interactions with others.

To further conceptualize this relationship between speakers and a public, we need to take into consideration the constant role shifts between these positions, which are facilitated or even encouraged by new technological means of communication. The presence of the public can be physical or virtual. The public can be in the room and follow an ongoing conversation (like in a theatre), or it can be spread across different rooms, which often (but not necessarily) implies that reception is postponed (like TV viewers). Even in the case of the non-physical presence of the public, their virtual presence is 'real' for the speakers, who know to perform for a public and need to take into account different patterns of reception. We can even think of the hypothetical (or in many cases not so hypothetical) case of a public that is only imagined by the performers in the public sphere. A mere belief in the presence of an audience, a hypothetical public, changes their course of communication. The case of factual non-attention of the public (the not-so-uncommon case that nobody listens, even if people should listen) creates a situation of public communication where the expectations and norms of the public sphere apply as constraints on the speakers who are involved in a communicative exchange. What is relevant is that a public could listen, not that it does listen. The virtual presence of the public, or even just the idea of the public's presence, is sufficient to leave an imprint on communication. I will change my mode of communication under the assumption that somebody is listening, even if my assumption proves wrong and nobody is interested in following what I am saying. In a similar way, the distinction between active and passive participants in a conversation allows for constant role changes. Members of the public are also entitled to speak out at any time and are free, or even encouraged, to switch roles.

Public discourse relates to all forms of communication where such a presence of 'the third' can be presupposed. In scientific discourse, for instance, whenever scientists exchange research results in a closed panel at a conference, 'the third' is presupposed as the broader community of scientists, that is, all those with the relevant competences and knowledge that give them the authority to intervene and test the validity claims in scientific communication (Nieto-Galan, 2016). In a theatre, a play is performed for an audience that, by way of clapping hands or booing, can give direct feedback on the performance, but through critical reviews the theatre performance also links back to the broader public sphere; there are, in fact, many cases where the whole nation talks about a theatre performance which provoked criticism or caused a scandal (Balme, 2014). In a parliamentary debate, the arrangement is similar to a theatre performance, with speakers' desks and an auditorium. However, speakers perform not only as members of parliament but also as representatives of the will of the people, addressing the whole of the nation (Manow, 2008).

In public discourse, 'the third' can relate not only to those explicitly addressed by the speakers (their targeted audiences) but to all those potentially affected by what is said or decided, or simply those who are casually listening, even without being addressed. The contingency of public discourse derives precisely from this uncertainty about 'the third' in public communication. Public discourse also operates over time: it not only allows us to speak to live audiences but to address past and future generations. References to past generations are frequently found in nationalist discourse when a discursive legacy gives authority to legitimate present choices (such as, for instance, the appeal to the authoritative voice of the 'founding fathers'). References to future generations become increasingly relevant when sustainability is considered as a public good, and when collective goods are negotiated that need to be preserved (Torgerson, 1999).

One persistent question in public sphere research is how the physical or virtual presence of the third, the public, changes the ongoing communicative exchanges among a group of speakers who engage with each other in direct forms of communication, such as a dialogue. The answer given by public sphere theory is that the presence of 'the third' impacts on the exchange of arguments and reasons by putting speakers under constraints of justification. The public has a controlling function on the rightness and legitimacy of a message. Its presence opens the possibility of intervention to correct what has been said, to add information or to adjust meaning. When one student confesses to a fellow student in private that she profoundly dislikes her professor, the other might share the same feeling. If she raises the same claim in the university cafeteria, she might be overheard by other students, who might intervene and ask for a better explication of the reasons for her feelings, share similar ideas or oppose hers. This increases the chances that speech has consequences and is followed by collective action (such as a protest against the misbehaviour of a professor). Justifications for what has been said by proponent A can of course also be demanded by opponent B. However, in a private conversation, such justifications remain detached from public reason, guaranteeing the generalized validity of a particular assertion. It is only when I am able to gather individual experiences and share opinions that particular patterns (like the constant misbehaviour of a professor) might show up and be recognized as a *public problem* that can be claimed to be of shared relevance. Such a process has been described by pragmatics like John Dewey (1927) as the recognition of public problems: no public without a problem. Habermas added a normative component to this pragmatic approach. According to his discourse theory of public reasoning, the emergence of a public through the identification of problems is only possible if particular norms apply to public exchanges of arguments. Most importantly: I can be held accountable for what I say – if the public listens, I can be reminded the next day or week or month of my commitment and may face consequences. These rules of accountability apply to public discourse and bind speakers together in their exchange of arguments. They are also meant to be inclusive, giving everybody the opportunity to listen and intervene on the basis of 'good arguments'.

The binding forces of public discourse

It is only from this angle that we can understand how the public sphere also generates what can be called a 'binding' or 'bonding' force. Speakers are bound together not only by their pragmatic exchange of arguments but also by the normative demands for justification raised by others. The public sphere binds people together who actively engage in communication and who passively listen. This is made possible through the power of arguments and through their collective engagement in the search for understanding (in the way the scientific community, for instance, is bound together in their search for truth, or the legal community in their search for the right interpretation of norms). In his *Theory of Communicative Action*, Habermas (1985) famously claimed that such a telos of seeking understanding is not limited to philosophical or scientific discourse but also guides everyday talk. The search for understanding is intrinsic in the usage of speech. This applies in the most basic sense to the presupposition of speakers that listeners have the ability to grasp the meaning of language. Even if I use speech in a purely instrumental way, for instance by shouting a command, I must make sure that 'other' understands me through the use of a shared language. However, in communicative action, such an understanding is not limited to the capacity of deciphering the language code (*Verstehen*); it applies also to the use of speech that convinces others of the validity of the arguments (*Einverständnis*). The public sphere is in this sense the realm where such validity claims can be raised and tested. Through such tests, the possibility of consent emerges, which is based on agreement about the underlying reasons why something can be claimed as valid (the 'correct interpretation' or the 'right thing to do'). Such agreement is by default very fragile, as new arguments might emerge at any time, once again challenging the validity of what has been established to be true or right in previous rounds of conversation.

Through the binding force of discourse, the public sphere can establish social order, but the communicative ties that bind people together over space and time are different from community ties. The public sphere does not create strong identities but binds an unknown group of people called *a public* that engages in the test of validity claims raised in discourse. Notions of the public sphere as based on collective identities, or 'thick cultures', are therefore misleading. As nobody can be excluded from the public use of reason, the public sphere is by default inclusive. This also means that members of the public will always strive for inclusion: everybody should be convinced by the truth value of an argument, or by the universal validity claim of a norm.[4] Discourses that unfold through the public sphere are measured against a normative template of rationality and inclusion. The way public discourse is built on a rational exchange of arguments and generating an informed opinion of the public will vary, but such variations may be subject to criticism. It is through public discourse that communicative power that can claim political legitimacy is generated. Norms, then, are not only a template of critique for the ideal functioning of the public sphere but are also a driving force for public sphere-induced change and as such have a palpable impact on the design of democratic institutions and procedures.

It is through such intersubjective practices of critique that unfold over time that we can understand how the public sphere indeed *does something* with communication and with actors involved in communication. In media and communication studies, we have developed several tools to help trace the effects of public communication. Most commonly, we refer to the 'input–throughput–output', or the transmission model of public communication, synthesized in the so-called Lasswell formula: *Who says what in which channel to whom with what effect?* (Lasswell, 1948). In public communication, and especially in PR-research, it is the output that particularly counts as a measure of the 'success' of communication. This output is commonly referred to as *public opinion*, which can be measured quantitatively (the distribution of attitudes within a population) and qualitatively (the process of synthesizing opinions through the exchange of arguments, and the value of these opinions when confronted with facts and norms).

The bourgeois public sphere: paradise lost or utopia?

Nancy Fraser (2007: 7) reminds us that the notion of the public sphere was primarily meant as a contribution to a normative theory of democracy. Habermas' *Structural Transformation* indeed provides a systematic reconstruction of the normative template of the public sphere and democracy. What is important to understand is that these norms are not simply postulated by philosophers but are inscribed into the practices of individuals who enter communicative exchanges to seek collective understanding. The notion of the public sphere is not just a normative template for democracy; it also refers to critical practices in the everyday interactions of individuals. More specifically, a public sphere is meant to be truth oriented and inclusive, giving public communication an epistemic value (in search of truth) and a democratic value (in search of collective self-determination). Individuals who seek understanding with others need to claim that what they say is true, that is, that it relates to facts, and that it is right, that it is supported by shared norms. They raise validity claims about the objective world and the social world, which again can be tested and challenged by others.[5] This process of 'seeking collective understanding' comprises key areas of personal and collective identities (who are we and how shall we live?) and of politics (what problems do we need to deal with collectively, and what could the possible solutions be?). In this last sense, the notion of the public sphere also contributes to a theory of social order and the normative integration of society (Peters, 2008).

In discussing the challenges of digitalization and transnationalization, media and communication scholars are often driven by public sphere nostalgia, reminiscent of the good old days of quality media and responsible journalism that promoted deliberative and participatory forms of democracy. Such an understanding of the bourgeois public sphere as a 'paradise lost' is also perceptible in Habermas' own account of the structural transformation of the public sphere, which reads as a history of decay, from the coffee houses of the Enlightenment period where the new bourgeois classes tested out their new freedom and capacities of reasoning to the mass-mediated public spheres of consumption of contemporary times. The historical origins of the bourgeois public sphere were sought in the unmediated and direct encounters of citizens of a city state in the agora (Arendt, 1998: 50–8). In the Enlightenment period as well, the first publics emerged as 'urban publics' through assemblies of citizens who claimed their 'civic rights' to work in professions of free choices, to engage in market exchanges and to influence local government. The idyll of the bourgeois public sphere was situated in an idealized past, and it was no longer clear how it could be rescued in late capitalist society.

Insinuating a kind of public sphere nostalgia in Habermas' structural transformation would, however, risk overlooking the main critical intention of the book that motivated the young Habermas to continue the tradition of the Frankfurt school of critical theory but at the same time to argue against the pessimistic outlook presented in Adorno and Horkheimer's (2002) *Dialectics of Enlightenment*. Habermas' main intention was indeed to give a positive impulse for the relaunch of democracy in the post-war context of the Federal Republic of Germany. For that reason, he went back to the idealism of Kant and not to the materialism of Marx. The critical template of the bourgeois public sphere was used to diagnose deficits and malfunctions of contemporary media, and to dare a prognosis of possible futures. In Habermas' account, the public sphere is not simply a paradise lost; it is a horizon for collective engagement. Enlightenment is meant as a project for the design of democratic society, and a public sphere unfolds in the form of a critique of its own insufficiencies.

This leads us to a second sociological reading of public sphere theory as a solution to the problem of the self-organization of society. The theory of the public sphere, apart from its critical-normative intent, has to be reconstructed as a contribution to the sociology of knowledge (O'Mahony, 2013). Habermas himself introduces the public sphere not only as a template for democracy but also as an explanatory model for individual socialization and for the institutionalization of social and political order. In his own words: 'A portion of the public sphere comes into being in every conversation in which private individuals assemble to form a public body' (Habermas, 1974: 49–50).

Early Habermas saw the bourgeois public sphere as an instrument of Enlightenment that was converted into social practices and political struggles for the building of a democratic society. Society relies on integration mechanisms and ordering principles that are different from the state. The public sphere offers an anti-Hobbesian solution for how social order is possible: not through the power hierarchies and social control and sanctioning mechanisms of the state but through collective engagement in public reasoning and the civic trust and solidarity generated through such practices. The public sphere facilitates solidarity among citizens, and thus social integration, through trust in institutions, is built and upheld through the free associations of the citizens (civil society). The democratic society is a daily conversation about the common good. As such, it not only relies on particular institutions and procedures for the division of power but essentially builds on the knowledge, competences and collective will of citizens to engage in practices of self-government. Such a notion of society is, however, not a deliberative community of like-minded citizens, nor does it presuppose pre-political consent. Through public reasoning and deliberation, the search for a possible consensus can be treated as a shifting horizon and projected towards the future. The bourgeois public sphere is not, therefore, a nostalgic past of a society that was still integrated through a consensual worldview, which has since vanished due to individualization and differentiation (as the sociological account of postmodernity sometimes reads). The public sphere is driven by the dynamics of enduring dissensus; it unleashes 'the anarchical force of saying no in public debates' (Habermas, 2021: 478), and it would cease to exist if consensus were reached. A society that could be based on an overarching and pre-established consensus would, in fact, no longer need to rely on public intermediation mechanisms. A consensual society is best preserved through silence, not through discourse. The contributions of the public sphere to integrating a democratically constituted society are therefore limited, as conflicts that are carried out through public debates have a 'principally agonal character' (Habermas, 2021: 478), and neither the truth nor the validity of arguments are eternally fixed and/or pre-established.

The bourgeois public sphere of Enlightenment historically emerged through the voice of free and autonomous individuals who broke with the silence around the core of political legitimacy. It was the voice of individuals who sought to reconcile individual and public autonomy by claiming their rights as citizens (Somers, 1993). Such a bourgeois public sphere continues to exist in the practices of citizens (today, it is mainly adopted by organized civil society) to communicate freely, criticize, control and engage in shared projects for the realization of the common good. In this sense, the bourgeois public sphere continues to be a utopian project for the self-constitution of society and a template of critique of the insufficiencies of the contemporary state, market and media that inhibit the free unfolding of reasons. Through such engagement in reasoning, a public body is formed as the anti-Leviathan, that is, not as an absolute sovereign body but as a source of critique, metamorphosis, evolution and, if necessary, revolution and rebellion.

The theory of the public sphere is converted here into a sociology of discursive democracy, which is not primarily meant as a template for the realization of the 'good and just society' but as a programme for sociological enquiry into the cognitive order of modernity, its formation as an outcome of societal learning and its dynamic transformation (O'Mahony, 2013). Whenever we talk about the media and the public sphere, we open a Pandora's box of the normative foundations of modern society and democracy. However, when we talk about the public sphere, we also mean very concrete and palpable processes of public communication linked to new ways of organizing media, politics and society. The public sphere has a material infrastructure and an ideational core. In approaching the public sphere empirically, we therefore need to take the dynamic interlinkages between facts and norms into account, for instance in the way new media technologies are used to promote critical discourse, or the way role definitions about the functioning of journalism are internalized by media actors and inform audience expectations.

A further shift in the conceptualization of the bourgeois public sphere of Enlightenment took place in the transition from assembly publics based on encounters in the urban space to reading publics based on a new infrastructure of social communication facilitated by print and, in particular, the press. Because of these developments, the *agora* or marketplace model of the bourgeois public sphere became increasingly insufficient and inadequate to describe the unfolding of communicative exchanges across space and time and within what is called a 'community of strangers'. The bourgeois public sphere of Enlightenment was distinct from the ancient publics in the Greek city states precisely because its constitutive relationship was that of communication between strangers. The visibility of the modern public sphere reaches beyond what is present. It links us to absent people and to spaces that we cannot reach. The modern public sphere, in fact, is both. It is still the space of presence, our shared space, but it is also the space of absence that is occupied by others, though still accessible to us.

One core function of the modern public sphere is to enable anonymous relationships among strangers. The members of the public are not bound together through personal acquaintance but through topics of shared attention. Individuals who constitute a public follow the same debates and share the same knowledge and information, but they will in all likelihood never meet and know each other in person. This does not mean that speakers and listeners need to be anonymous by default, but they *can* be. I can still talk to a good friend in the marketplace, but neither of us can exclude the possibility of somebody unknown overhearing our conversation and even deciding to interfere. 'Taking voice' is not only a possibility but an entitlement of 'other'. We cannot really prohibit 'other' from listening as we move around the marketplace. The interference of a third in a conversation opens a space of contingency of public speech (Strydom, 1999). If those who follow a talk or a conversation always moved within a confined space, were known to each other and could be fully controlled by the speakers, we would not speak of them as a public. The latter would instead resemble the traditional paternalistic role distribution in a private household described by Hannah Arendt in the *Human Condition*, where the head of the household is the caretaker of the personal needs of the other members and has control over what can be said and how it is said within the confines of the private home. Only in such a private setting can the principle of free speech be restricted: intruders are those who speak out differently, which is sufficient reason to expel someone from the home (Arendt, 1998: chapter 2).

Communication in the bourgeois public sphere of Enlightenment is mediated in the elementary sense that an external, non-present audience is entitled to listen and is also de facto found to be listening in a regular way. To talk of an external audience is at the same time misleading because the audience is always included. Apart from being addressed in the conversation, it can also decide to raise voice itself and through mediated or non-mediated channels 'talk back'. The audience becomes a 'public' in the more emphatic sense in that it has specific entitlements to raise voice and be included and develops competences to be knowledgeable and empowered (Splichal, 2012). This points to the central role of the media as a facilitator of the emergence of a public and of its empowerment. Historically, the bourgeois public sphere was constituted not simply by the right to assemble but also by the right to publish. It emerged in parallel with the press, which enabled public communication and public opinion formation processes to impact on government. Sociologically speaking, mass media infrastructures were needed to talk to strangers and to integrate an anonymous mass society.

The public sphere in democracy

Models of democracy vary, and the way people adhere to particular democratic ideals situates them as individuals and groups in the public sphere. Opting for a consensus mode, a participatory mode or a majority mode of rulemaking or supporting the ideas of liberalism, republicanism or communitarianism is not simply a question of hot philosophical dispute. The struggle over democracy remains inconclusive in established democracies and continues to divide populations. Adherents of different democratic ideals can typically be aligned along class differences, ideological cleavages or group-specific preferences of the population. Accordingly, it is also believed that public sphere models should be distinguished along the main types of democratic regime that have been established historically, and the specific groups of people empowered by it.

Normative models differ by making more or less strict assumptions about what the public sphere is expected to contribute to democracy and who should be empowered by it. Wessler (2019: 51–7) distinguishes between the liberal, the republican, the deliberative and the agonistic models of the public sphere. These models partly build on each other, with each model incorporating the normative demands of the previous one and adding new components. While liberals mainly emphasize individual freedom and promote equal participation and empowerment in discourse, republicans in addition wish to strengthen collective responsibility and highlight fairness and public good orientation in discourse. Adherents of the deliberative model look at the media and public discourse as a promoter of rational debates and a reasoned exchange of arguments, with the aim of achieving informed consent. Last but not least, the promoters of an agonistic model wish to allow for the inclusion of marginalized groups and minorities, who often express themselves through more narrative forms of communication and emotional expressions.

In comparative media studies and sociology, the main ambition was to operationalize such normative models of the public sphere with the aim of developing empirical indicators for measuring the public sphere and media performance. The parameters used to distinguish these models were variation in degrees of inclusiveness, the dominance of either elite actors or civil society actors as drivers of public debates, processes of negotiation, interest mediation, deliberation or cultural narration and a different emphasis on outcomes in the form of compromise, majority decision, consensus and strong or weak identities (Ferree et al, 2002). The models can thus be designed as an analytical tool for the normative assessment of the empirical patterns of political communication in 'actually existing democracies'. Public sphere analysis cannot decide about the normative desirability of different models of the public sphere and the intrinsic value of their underlying assumptions (which model has most value for democracy?), but it can inform the philosophical dispute about the feasibility of these models and comment on their chances of being institutionalized and put into practice. Sociological research becomes applicable for the design of democracy by underscoring which types of expectations in the media and the public sphere are realistic and how media systems and government can be designed, respectively (Wessler, 2019: 56).

When looked at more closely, these models of the public sphere are intrinsically biased and scaled in terms of their assumptions, ranging from realism to utopia. On this realism–utopia scale, the models are classified in line with our experiences with media, established procedures of democracy and existing institutional arrangements. Empirical sociologists thus tell us about the feasibility of models that are already framed in terms of being more or less applicable to the reality of mass media. Their empirical contributions, in the form of a feasibility test of normative models of the public sphere, are not only limited in terms of what we actually learn about the 'existing public spheres' but also insufficient from an analytical perspective because they fail to recognize how this normative critique of the performance of the public sphere feeds back into media practices and politics. By arguing that normative models of the public sphere must pass a reality test, empirical sociologists overlook the assertive and constructive power of social norms. The distinction between 'factual' and 'non-factual' is far from trivial but in need of public justification (Scholl, 2019: 47). The normative reality is to be considered as part of the empirical reality of our shared social world, objectively embedded in both its limits and potentialities. This is fundamental for our understanding of contemporary media performance and its critique. It is precisely because we can criticize the insufficiencies of existing media that we are able to reconfirm or even strengthen our belief systems about the ideal functioning of media in democracy. The detection of media functions and dysfunctions is not sufficient proof of the validity of normative assumptions that tell us what people expect from the media and how they meaningfully relate to media, making individual and collective use of media content and communications.

This opens a different programme for sociological enquiry into public sphere functions and performance. Sociologists need to refer to the normative legacy of public sphere theorizing, not in the form of empirical reality tests but in the form of beliefs in the legitimacy of particular models and the way such beliefs guide the communicative exchanges among citizens and their expectations. Norms are the horizon for social practices of engagement with democracy, not the solid ground and building materials for such practices. It is therefore not our task as sociologists to call the normative legacy of the public sphere into question. Empirical sociologists do not *test* norms but willingly or unwillingly *contest* them. If norms are found to be held valid, inform individual expectations and guide collective action, they have already passed the empirical reality test, and any objection to the unlikelihood of their empirical realization by empirical sociologists becomes a political intervention.

The dispute about democracy and the public sphere oscillates between normative assessment and empirical analysis. Normative political theory and empirical social sciences have become separate branches, creating cleavages in academic departments and among scholars. What both sides seem to overlook is that this dispute about democracy is fought, above all, by society itself, with social groups adhering to different normative ideals and seeking their realization. The public sphere is in this sense neither fully grasped as a normative projection by political theorists nor as an external object of analysis, the contours of which need to be empirically delineated. The public sphere is the infrastructure for carrying out this dispute, and, as such, it is shaped by the commonly held assumptions about what democracy should achieve, and how it should be modelled. To explore this constitutive relationship between the public sphere and modern democratic society, it is therefore useful to first establish how the public sphere *functions* in channelling and filtering public opinions over time and crystallizing the collective will of democracy. A sociological-historical account of the public sphere needs to come before the normative and empirical analyses. It should not limit its discussions to the good reasons *why* a public sphere is needed for democracy (the normative account) or *what* is achieved by the public sphere (the empirical account) but should instead investigate *how* the public sphere has entered such a symbiosis with the emergence of modern democratic society.

There is, in other words, a third way to make sociological sense of the public sphere beyond the confines of normative political theory and empirical sociology. The initial paths for such an analysis are once again found in Habermas, who discusses the transformation of the public sphere in relation to the evolution of social order and its contestation through competing legitimacy demands. In Habermas' socio-genesis of the public sphere (Habermas, 1989), the four functions are inscribed in the structures and institutions of public intermediation that facilitate norm-guided processes of communicative exchange among collective and institutional actors. In the democratic process, the public sphere is best described as a filter, but it is also an amplifier of public opinion and thus a catalyst of collective will formation (Habermas, 1996). It allows us to (a) detect and identify problems, (b) convincingly and influentially thematize them, (c) furnish them with solutions and (d) feed them into the political system. In his late work, Habermas thus delivers a more technical description of the public sphere as 'a network for communicating information and points of view' (1996: 360) and as 'an intermediary structure between the political system, on the one hand, and the private sectors of the lifeworld and functional systems on the other' (373).

Speaking of these filtering functions of the public sphere, we should not assume an ontological worldview where social problems are simply out there waiting to be detected and thematized. The public sphere is not a mirror or a telescope that allows us to uncover the 'nature of public problems', describe them in an accurate way and make the 'right' choices. The communicative structures of the public sphere rather remain rooted in the lifeworld and the shared beliefs about what is held valid and normatively desirable. In an *ontological world*, presupposing a pre-interpreted and holistically structured background of meaning, a public sphere would simply become unnecessary. The functions of the public sphere are therefore not to 'discover' social problems out there, but to name and interpret them in the light of the norms that are held valid, the observatory tools that are available and the language and scripts that are mutually understandable.

To function as a filter, the public sphere nevertheless needs to be related to particular outcomes that are identified as efficient solutions to social problems. The efficiency of solutions depends on the strength of the arguments used to establish a causal link to the underlying problem that is normatively framed and agreed upon. The public sphere opens the possibility of arguing for such a causal relationship in a way that convinces others of the relevance of the problem and the adequacy of the solution provided. When we talk, for instance, of the control function of journalism, we assume that, over time, a professional group of journalists has established a response to the problem of containing arbitrary political power. By following this line of reasoning, we treat the underlying problem, in this case 'arbitrary political power', as a dependent variable and use the underlying norm, 'autonomy' and 'self-determination', as an independent variable. We can ask: What is the problem with political power? In response to this question, we can provide evidence and solid arguments to conclude that arbitrariness is the problem with political power. Only after such a normative framing of the problem can we draft possible solutions to the problem of the arbitrariness of power, for instance in the form of strengthening the professional status of journalists.

The discourse model of the public sphere is built on the premise that both problems and solutions are contingent, and that they are related not out of necessity but because connections have been tried out, selected and made plausible to others. We do not see solutions because we have identified a particular problem, but we see a particular problem–solution constellation because we move within the public sphere that makes it visible for us and allows us to relate to it in a way that becomes meaningful for others. This problem–solution constellation is part of the social structure of the public sphere, not its purposeful outcome. At the same time, contingency does not mean complete randomness, precisely because the 'sluice' of the public sphere pre-selects particular connections for us, makes them more viable, more normatively desirable or more preferable than others. The public sphere structure is in this sense also a preference structure for making such selections about what we wish to see or ignore. Journalism as an institution, for instance, was not simply established in response to the need to control government. Through its institutionalized working practices or rhetorical devices (such as ready-made schemes of interpretation or 'frames'), journalism allows for the identification of public problems. The critical function of journalism, therefore, is not simply to detect abuses of power but to put government under permanent suspicion of being arbitrary, malfunctioning or insufficient and thus to impact on the daily routines of government. The theory of news criteria provides us with a perfect toolkit to analyse how such selection processes of public attention, as points of orientation for both critical publics and government, are organized.

Thus the sociological and the normative accounts of the public sphere are no longer separate approaches but are intrinsically related. A theory of the public sphere explains the self-constitution of modern democratic society in relation to processes of norm-setting and application. In more practical terms, the programme for public sphere research comprises all communicative practices and routines that are organized in a way to allow for the identification of shared problems and their possible solutions. As already emphasized by Dewey (1927), the public sphere emerges in response to the need to formulate a 'common interest'. A public sphere is a response to the problem of a society that cannot rely on external sources of legitimacy (like the 'divine'), and that has been emancipated from the 'Leviathan' as the Hobbesian solution to the stability of political order. The public sphere refers to the process of the self-organization of society that engages in problem solving through the collectively binding forces of reasoning. 'Indirect, extensive, enduring and serious consequences of conjoint and interacting behavior call a public into existence having a common interest in controlling these consequences' (Dewey, 1927: 126).

While constitutive to social order, the public sphere simultaneously introduces an element of restlessness in the double sense of an unfulfilled utopia and of critique. The public sphere allows society to build on an excess of critique. Critique is always to be expected, and never absent. There is always too much critique, as everything can and will be questioned, and consensus is broken up all the time. The uncommon is not what is criticized but what escapes critique and therefore has a special aura. To be the target of critique is a common experience, whereas the absence of critique points at possible malfunctions or public sphere pathologies. The idea of critique is further related to the notion of progress and social betterment. This applies the project of Enlightenment to the whole of society: the critique of reason drives collective learning. The template of scientific progress through critical questioning of existing solutions and replacement by better solutions applies to the model of society as a whole, detailed in the work of Bruno Latour (1999). This means, in turn, that collective learning would come to a halt in the absence of critique. The progression of society depends on keeping the machinery of critique going. Critique is ultimately also expected in the relationship of individuals to themselves, in the form of self-critique that is learned and exercised so that the success of individuals in society can be measured, rewarded or punished and their individual careers established.

The digital public sphere

A new structural transformation of the public sphere?

Contemporary debates in public sphere theory focus on the question of whether we are witnessing a new structural transformation of the public sphere, as manifested in the proliferation of new digital modes of public communication and networks (Dahlgren, 2005; Papacharissi, 2009; Trenz, 2009a; Seeliger and Sevignani, 2021; Habermas, 2022). In approaching this digital transformation of the public sphere, we can distinguish three lines of thought: (a) a new sociology of the public sphere, where transformation is driven by changing modes of communication and socialization; (b) a political economy of the public sphere where transformation is driven by market forces; and (c) a political theory of the public sphere where transformation is driven by norms. In the following, I will briefly summarize the main line of argument, as well as the limitations and inherent contradictions of each approach. I will then discuss the performance of digital and social media in the way they undermine but concurrently contribute to the re-imagination of the political community of democracy, in addition to how they subvert and constitute new critical publics and threaten and renew existing structures of mass media.

a. A new *sociology* of the digital public sphere postulates a fundamental change in the way new media are constitutive to a new kind of society. One important empirical observation is that hierarchies of public communication, as sustained through national media systems and the prominent role of public broadcasting, are increasingly replaced by *network* structures. The public sphere as "a network for communicating information and points of view" (Habermas, 1996: 360) adapts to the new reality of a network society (Castells, 1996). In the course of this new structural transformation of the public sphere, a virtual element of communication is introduced. With regard to this virtuality of the online public sphere, it must be remembered that the modern notion of the public sphere has always been grounded in anonymous relations among non-present strangers. There has always been some element of virtuality in the mass-mediated public sphere, which can no longer be conceived as an assembly of citizens. There is no reason to assume that online or digital public spheres are by default more virtual than offline mediated public spheres; on the contrary, there is evidence that social media often facilitate more communitarian and less anonymous interactions among citizen-users (Couldry, 2012). It is therefore far from certain whether the sociology of the public sphere needs to be rewritten. As I will argue, the patterns of sociability that are emerging through the networked public sphere are not fundamentally opposed to the anonymous publics of mass society but rather attempt to renew the linkage between the public sphere and the self-constitutive dynamics of democracy.

b. A new *political economy* of the digital public sphere approaches the changing market logics of the Internet from a perspective of power (Fuchs, 2016, 2021). It analyses the production and distribution of digital content in relation to the inequalities of access to information and the accumulation of knowledge and resources that might lead to domination (Aytac, 2022). The concentration of ownership of social media platforms, and the inequalities of empowerment through the use of digital technologies, result in new digital divides (Dahlberg, 2015) and forms of surveillance by large companies over individual users (Zuboff, 2019). The numerous cases where digital economies exercise public power to control private lives, and interfere directly in the democratic process, do not necessarily point to a structural transformation of the public sphere but rather to the inherent deficits in the institutional set-up of digital platforms and their regulation. The democratic affordances of the Internet, therefore, continue to be discussed as a question of the design of the democratic

31

public sphere (Forestal, 2021). A new political economy of the digital public sphere renews an old critique of the alienating effects of (digital) media and the call for taking back control of unbound markets.

c. A new *political theory* of the public sphere assesses the conditions for the democratic functioning of the public sphere in the digital age. This regards the question of whether digital citizens can still engage in informed opinion-making in a way that holds their government accountable and responsive (Cohen and Fung, 2021; Trenz, 2021). The public sphere, as Habermas (2022) has recently reminded us, cannot be approached solely in terms of media markets, new technologies of media production and distribution and changing habits of media consumption. Empirical indicators become pointless if they are not also discussed in terms of the normative requirements they are obligated to satisfy in democracy (Habermas, 2022: 147). A political economy of the digital transformation of the public sphere should not, therefore, be interpreted separately from a political theory that critically puts to the test the norms that apply in a digital democracy. The democratic performance of digital media is generally qualified in empirical research with reference to the principles of truth orientation and civicness of public debates. A clear symptom of post-democracy would be if both principles were either no longer held valid or were simply not applicable in digital communication worlds. Such a post-democratic scenario of norm decay would, however, conflict with political and market logics of digital media and their commitment to a world of enhanced information and participation. The capacities to discriminate between facts and fiction, and between civic and uncivic, remain central to social media affordances and continue to inform critical publics who *resist, regulate and recode* digital platforms with the intention of rescuing democracy (Muldoon, 2022). The dangers to the democratic public sphere might thus have less to do with technological changes that require a normative reorientation of society than with actors who violate these norms (Chambers and Kopstein, 2022). Public sphere disruptions would be a question of accountability, not of structural change. The problem of bad actors is serious enough as a threat to democracy, but it should not embrace normative or techno-dystopian defeatism (Chambers and Kopstein, 2022: 2).

There is thus a triple challenge of digitalization that is seen as undermining, yet at the same time reproducing, bolstering even, mass culture and society, capitalist modes of media production and distribution, and the communal characteristics of democracy. In contemporary discussions about the design of digital democracy, it is important to keep in mind, however, that *the public* is constituted as being against the mass commodification of culture, as well as against the closeness of community life. Users become digital citizens by engaging in alternative modes of production of media content and by expanding their horizons of communicative exchanges with strangers (Isin and Ruppert, 2020). The publicness of the Internet is wrongly understood as a restitution of the lost community. Publics are there to challenge the closeness of communities, question their taken-for-granted truths and correct their biased interpretations of the world around them. The viability of digital democracy depends, in this sense, on the fate of the public that leaves behind the privacy of the protected community.

The fate of the public in the new era of digital communication

Digital media are often characterized as media of convergence (Jensen, 2012). In its initial years, Web 2.0 was mainly script based, and users had to turn to writing as a way of self-expression and communicating with others. This was seen as a major rupture with the visual mass media culture of TV (van Dijck and Poell, 2013, 2015). Some would go so far as to sustain that the new script culture of interactive media was a democratic innovation, as writing in the form of text messages required a more active engagement with content (Diamond and Plattner, 2012). In more recent years, the Web 3.0 of enhanced connectivity brought about another change from more stable (and thus mainly script-based) content for collective use to more portable and short-lived content for individualized use through smart technologies based on new visual formats. The web is described in terms of media convergence which relates to forms of media use and practices (such as hierarchical and interactive) and to technologies. The network is constituted by both material and immaterial infrastructures, and it allows for specific forms of interactions between the subjects and objects that populate it. Such interactions between humans and material artefacts are part of what is described as 'creative media use'. Following the assumptions of Actor Network Theory (Latour, 2005), we can identify such material artefacts, for instance, in the servers that are technologies for bundling information but at the same time, as the name says, *serve* particular community purposes. As described by Halford and Savage (2010: 947), the web is 'the outcome of a network of heterogeneous actors – servers, protocols, users, websites, fiber optic cables and so on – none of which has an independent existence outside the networks of which it is part'.

The Internet further moved from a sharing culture of text based on open-source content to a more community-based culture of protected spaces with limited and controlled access to content. This facilitated the return of the visual through the popularity of video-sharing platforms and the technological advancements that allowed users to produce their own videos and images. Visuals, which are traditionally seen as more manipulative (Veneti et al, 2019), have been linked in various ways to a new participatory culture that engages users with content and political opinions, for example through new formats such as memes and gifs (Gubrium and Harper, 2016).

In light of these rapid changes in the development of the Internet, it does not come as a surprise that the 'fate of the public' in the new era of digital communication has been the subject of some controversy in the literature (Splichal, 2012). The search for the conditions of a digital public sphere starts from similar premises to the possibilities of adapting the structures and core functions of the modern public sphere to the Internet. The future of the public sphere does not solely depend on the digital media's performance as 'communication networks' but also on their capacities to generate *publicity*, that is, some form of 'societal visibility' coupled with claims for generalized validity that remain meaningfully related to the legitimation of democratic politics and the expression of the popular will. As with the emergence of television, the critical question is whether online media can still offer a platform for societal visibility that supports the emergence of a civic and participatory culture and thus establish the legitimacy of the democratic polity, or whether the new political economy of the Internet is simply endorsing people as apolitical consumers.

On the one hand, scholars have emphasized the democracy-enhancing potential of the Internet not only as a new and open space for the exchange of information and the facilitation of new modes of public speech but also through digitally enhanced democratic innovations such as e-voting, e-participation or digitally enhanced transparency of state institutions (Dahlgren, 2013). Media convergence could thus be seen as supportive of public sphere functions and open up the democratic potentials of access, deliberation and engagement among online publics. The digital public sphere of media convergence should be expansive, making flows of content more dynamic and empowering individual users and publics to express themselves and reach out through plural forms, languages and channels. Another tendency is to interpret online civic engagement as new expressions of literary or cultural public spheres. These would include, for instance, social network activities, entertainment and fan communities as a sort of pre-political phenomenon (Jenkins, 2014).

On the other hand, critical media research has outlined the democratic hazards underlying the commodification of the new digital conversational modes of public speech which are attached by mainstream media organizations to new business models in various ways (Fuchs, 2014b). The fate of the public is discussed with regard to a number of empirical challenges.

1. *The challenge of open content and disinformation*: regarding the most basic publicity function of the public sphere, 'publishing' content has become a widespread practice that is open to anybody. Social media 'sharing' can be interpreted as a more interactive and participatory form of content

production. Yet it also constitutes a modality of economic production at the level of mass communication, and users are elements of a newly emerging mass audience (Bruns et al, 2015). It is thus important to see how the expectation of 'sharing' and 'liking' and other forms of citizen participation are embedded in new business models for creating mass publicity (Bruns et al, 2015). 'All participation on the net, even the most radical political kind, feeds data into the commercial system that is its infrastructure' (Dahlgren, 2013: 58). Related to these new sharing practices, we observe global challenges to the independence of the press and journalism and the informative value of news. Digitalization and globalization have transformed the ownership and operation structures of media industries and changed the boundaries of the public and the private through hybrid modes of online interactions (Splichal, 2018). The big data industries develop as a form of surveillance capitalism that impacts on civil rights, limits political and personal freedoms, and is used for the manipulation of public opinion (Aytac, 2022). There is also increasing concern regarding the quality of online political information and debates. Misinformation, 'fake news' and populism are the symptoms of a more fundamental change within the public sphere, namely the cultural logic of big data, whereby no frame is accepted as reliable or trustworthy, and all frames, particularly those of journalists and other public actors, are treated by definition as flawed or suspected of biases (Andrejevic, 2018). Because the exposure to political news online is increasingly dependent on the consumption choices of individual users, who make use of personalized news formats to steer the filtering process and design their own news worlds, the Internet is seen as an echo chamber in which users reaffirm their pre-existing views (Flaxman et al, 2016).

2. *The challenge of fragmented opinion-making*: digital and global communication has led to fundamental changes in the way voices find expression and political opinions are formed. Biases in opinion are facilitated by targeted campaigning and propaganda but also through parallel processes of polarization and the radicalization of news audiences (Fletcher and Nielsen, 2017). The fragmentation of user communities takes risks by promoting monologues in segregated blogospheres but not dialogue in an integrated public sphere (Gripsrud et al, 2010b: xxvi; Splichal, 2012: 106–16). The pivotal question for online public sphere research, therefore, is how enhanced user activism and online communities can be related back to the spheres of public opinion and will formation that encompass the political community at large. The democratic significance of users' discussions and political engagement depends on their capacity to feed generalized debates around the formulation of the collective will and the possibilities for its political enactment (Fraser, 2007). In all consolidated democracies, this includes the gatekeeping and filtering function of

journalism that speaks to the whole of the political community and can credibly claim to articulate the voice of the people. The challenge for future public sphere theory lies in critically discussing digital and social media's modes of participation, networking and self-representation, without dismissing the public sphere's original functions of all-inclusiveness and facilitation of public opinion and will formation.

3. *The challenge of (mis)trust*: the delicate balance between trust and mistrust in representative government has been challenged by the advent of digital media. In the digital democracy, the work of journalists as trust mediators loses its significance, while political actors and parties as public communicators have been empowered to reach out through social media and build immediate relationships with their electorate (Haleva-Amir and Nahon, 2016; Stier et al, 2018). Trust relationships would thus, at least in appearance, become less mediated and unfiltered by journalists. Political trustees could develop their own media competences and apply them strategically through the use of Twitter and other social media. The sheer volume of information available to individuals, coupled with the democratization of participation in the public sphere through social media, discussion platforms, participatory journalism, personalized/curated news feeds and blogs, results in increased scrutiny of the traditional knowledge-producers, mediators and gatekeepers of the public sphere (journalists, experts and politicians). While public scrutiny of political and intellectual elites is welcome, if not necessary, in a democracy, the hyper-scrutiny taking place in the digital public sphere may have the unwelcome effect of weakening a commonly accepted benchmark for normative critique and moral standards (Mancini, 2012). Thus, the mobilizing function of digital communication means that while political representatives no longer rely on the mediating function of journalists to reach out to their constituents, they also face the challenge of being constantly mistrusted in their role as representatives of the people's will, predominantly by digitally empowered, formerly passive audiences.

4. *The challenge to social cohesion and identification*: digital and global communication has enhanced fundamental conflicts about values and collective identities, which shatter the normative underpinning of the modern public sphere – the rise of illiberalism, political extremism and post-democracy. Enhanced conflicts about values and identities are often related to the rise of populism, regionalism and new nationalism, which threaten the internal cohesion of European states and challenge the expectation of a convergence around democratic values. A new politics of identity is often characterized by deep disagreement and antagonism between social groups that escape established procedures of conflict management and solution. As a result, the digital transformation of the public sphere pushes the boundaries of the political community, often

leading to confrontations between communitarian-nationalists and cosmopolitans (de Wilde et al, 2019).

Evidently, despite the wealth of research on the democratic prospects of the digital public sphere, the results are inconclusive. The so-called cyber-optimism/cyber-pessimism divide remains ideological and, as such, cannot easily be settled by empirical research. The utopia of the cyber-optimists encounters the dystopia of the pessimists, which points to a divide that is inscribed into the structures of the public sphere and drives political contestation.

Instead of asking how public spheres are transformed by the Internet, we need to raise the more fundamental question of whether the co-constitutive dynamics between the public sphere and democracy still apply in the digital age, or whether we are witnessing an ultimate rupture. While a public sphere of mass media played a socially integrative role in the way it gathered information, aggregated opinions, controlled government and formed collective identities, the political economy of digital media 'disconnects' individual media users from the resources of a shared lifeworld and culture that are the basis of public understandings and interpretations. Such a logic of 'digital disconnect' is at work in the way the Internet contributes to the diffusion of information and facts and disaggregation of opinions, turning against democratic government and dissolving collective identities (McChesney, 2013). I will follow this line of argument from public sphere functions to public sphere dysfunctions and disruptions in the next chapter. For contemporary scholarship, it is not enough to underline that we are in the middle of an ongoing revolution but rather to point out the multiple paths such a revolution can take and the various actors and social struggles that drive it. Whether the digital revolution stands for the rupture of the constitutive link between the public sphere and democracy, or for a global democratic renewal, is not to be decided in a debate among critical communication scholars but is, first and foremost, a matter of ongoing public contestation.

3

Public Sphere Dystopia:
A Diagnosis

A sociology of knowledge of media and public sphere critique

The malfunctions of the contemporary media and the public sphere, and its destructive effects on democracy, social order and individual well-being, is among the most frequently discussed and controversial topic in political communication research. In this book, I am not so much interested in advancing a further diagnosis of the current malaise of the media and the public sphere but instead aim to understand how we as researchers, and in parallel also as members of a public, translate this knowledge into critique. I am taking the view of how critical knowledge about media and its effects is generated and used. How and by whom is such knowledge produced, how does it feed into public debates or trigger political mobilization, and what impact does it have on the functioning of the public sphere? In other words, what happens to the public sphere if it gains knowledge about public sphere disruptions? Thus, this book is a sociology of knowledge pertaining to contemporary media and public sphere analysis and critique. In examining the world of contemporary (digital and global) media, and the public sphere and democracy, it seeks to address the following questions:

- What do we know about contemporary transformations of the media and the democratic public sphere?
- How can we know?
- Who knows? And who produces that knowledge?
- What follows on from that knowledge? How is it received by users and critical publics, and what do they do with it?

The following pages will provide a systematic overview of our stock of knowledge about media and public sphere disruptions. I will turn to the process of knowledge production and dissemination that leads to such a diagnosis within critical media studies. Such an assessment will allow me to identify the social carriers of the discourse about public sphere dystopia: the knowledge producers and their recipients. I will then show how the producers of knowledge about public sphere disruptions are at the same time promoters of critical discourse. Their knowledge is not confined to academia but becomes common knowledge that is taken up by other social carriers and translated into forms of political mobilization. We thus observe a translation process of critical (dystopian) discourse into new utopias for society and democracy. In Chapter 5, I will illustrate that public sphere resilience and resistance do not simply remain a postulate of abstract theoretical thinking but actually underlie the motivations of critical citizens and progressive social movements. In approaching such broad movements for democracy, I am not interested in the emergence of protest, the strategic use of social media platforms for mobilization and the functionality of digital and social media for building identities and mobilizing collective resources.[1] Rather, I wish to depart from the constitutive dynamics of new forms of publicness that allow individuals and groups to critically address perceived shortcomings in digital media markets (surveillance capitalism), in political representation (anti-populism, as exemplified in the Remain campaign in the UK and the Sardines movement in Italy), and global justice and sustainability (as in the cases of #FridaysforFuture and the 'Yellow Vests'). This shifts the attention from considering the new media as an arena of claims and strategic political mobilization to the digital public sphere as the principal arena for the contestation of democratic legitimacy (see also Kavada and Poell, 2020).

What do we know?

Malfunctions and disruptions of the public sphere, media and democracy

The conclusions of contemporary public sphere diagnosis is quite dramatic. Established public spheres are currently seen as being undermined by two major challenges: the challenge to the unity of the nation state as the cradle of democracy, and the challenge to the quality of discursive exchanges among the members of that community and its modes of self-government and empowerment. This poses critical questions about the possibility of the constitution and empowerment of a transnational and digital public sphere that still adheres to democratic principles. In short, the following matrix for critical debates applies:

- National–post-national: transnationalization – the demise of the 'national public sphere': *How can a transnational (European and global) public be constituted and empowered?*

- Offline–online: digitalization – the demise of the 'discursive public sphere'. The distorting effects of online communication on democracy: *How can a digital public be constituted and empowered?*

The *transnationalization challenge* refers to the geographical scope of public communication and the possibility of confining public debates to a particular political space for the empowerment of the will of the people. In the so-called post-Westphalian order, questions have been asked about whether a nationally unified public sphere that is served by a national mass media in the control of national government is still feasible, and, if not, what this means for democracy (Fraser, 2007). The public sphere has historically established as the national public sphere that constitutes a system of representative democracy that is supported by the mass media and journalism to reach out to the whole nation (Gerhards, 2000). Transnationalization inevitably leads away from this ideal model of a unified public sphere of democracy. In the post-national constellation, we cannot presuppose any congruence between the political–territorial space of the state and the cultural–identitarian space of the nation (Klein et al, 2003). The prerequisites for building a public sphere of democracy would simply not exist, and hence to talk of a transnational public sphere would be an oxymoron, according to Nancy Fraser (2007). Only when we can argue theoretically for the possibility of a transnational public sphere, and show empirically that public sphere relationships and practices unfold beyond the national, can the notion of the public sphere be rescued.

The *digitalization challenge* refers to the formation of publics through online, digital media and the possibilities of their democratic empowerment. The new media challenge our understanding of how publics are constituted, and how public opinion is given expression (Papacharissi, 2002). This raises the question of whether new media still support the constitution of publics and their functioning in democracy, and, if so, how these new publics can be empowered, or indeed if they should be empowered (McNair, 2009; Papacharissi, 2009; Gerhards and Schäfer, 2010; van Dijk, 2012a). The assumption here is that traditional public spheres have a centripetal force and condense communication to shared opinions and beliefs. The public sphere proliferated in the coffee houses, which combined the consumption of media with real encounters that facilitated face-to-face exchanges in the form of dialogue. Consumption was further conducive to a relatively unified audience that demanded the same products. The very structures of the public sphere were built on analogue communicative exchanges. Digital communication and new media technologies instead unfold through centrifugal forces and dispersion rather than concentration. A digital network of information that flows with humans as nodes is not a public sphere as long as centripetal forces are also at work bringing humans together as publics of shared attention (Castells, 2009).

Transnationalization and digitalization are often seen as being directly responsible for a series of malfunctions of the media and public sphere infrastructures with regard to their capacities to inform, build shared knowledge and guide processes of public opinion and will formation. The diagnosis of these malfunctions points to the following pathologies:

1. *The pathologies of journalism*: in the realm of journalism and the news media, we observe: (1) a surplus of information, which overloads legacy media institutions' ability to verify the accuracy of content distributed online and challenge governments' policy-making ability; (2) the hybridity of content and data that flows in semi-public and semi-private spheres, with both content providers (for example, cultural industries or news industries) and individual users losing control over the flow of data; (3) the freedom of access and openness of digital media content and services that often comes at a price, namely pervasive surveillance, which may limit individuals' freedom and narrow their sources of information, as well as empowering businesses and states vis-à-vis citizens; (4) the rise of 'alternative news', which has undermined the authority of journalism as well as of experts and scientists and contributed to the spread of post-truth discourse, the generation and mass propagation of 'alternative facts' and a general reduction in the informative value of news (Michailidou and Trenz, 2021). The public sphere, digitalization and globalization have enhanced publicity by multiplying and facilitating access to information while at the same time transforming the ownership and operation structures of news media institutions. On many digital platforms, there is an abundance of information, but information stays before the gates, is unfiltered and is therefore inaccessible to most citizens (Bruns and Nuernbergk, 2019). Due to the wide accessibility of news online, the gatekeeping role of traditional journalism has lost its importance, making distinctions between fact-checked news and opinion difficult to uphold (Groshek and Tandoc, 2017). At the same time, the spread of news through social media channels is often limited to the semi-private interactions of particular communities. WhatsApp groups, for instance, can create their own news environment, often served exclusively by specific news providers (Resende et al, 2019; Boczek and Koppers, 2020). Disruptions take place at the level of news-making and news reception. Media fragmentation is a particular challenge to journalism as an institution with a distinct identity, established working practices, positions of power and market shares. News-makers lose their professional role models, and the professional field becomes blurred as anyone may lay claim to the title of 'journalist', while the criteria for the quality control of its various products are no longer applied or start to be questioned. Audiences access information randomly or turn away from news altogether. Critical publics disappear from the stage or become

marginalized as their feedback no longer finds its way to the public sphere or, if it does, is met with silence. Journalism, as some have claimed, has entered a death spiral, with lower circulation meaning lower profits and diminished quality, which again damages the reputation of journalism (McChesney and Pickard, 2013).[2]

2. *Digital divides and biases*: transnationalization and digital transformations have multiplied voices and opinions that are channelled through a plurality of media. Public spheres have become more inclusive and participatory, but at the same time, new digital divides have emerged, and media competences are distributed unequally. The development of digital media technologies and industries has further blurred the established boundaries between the private and the public realm. As a platform of global interconnectivity, the Internet has commercialized private and intimate relationships while at the same time privatizing public activities and restricting the realm of democratic politics. Through digital media, individuals can use the same platform or the same technology to expand both their private and public relationships; they can become information rich and more connected, but they can also more easily withdraw from public life. The retreat from publicness is, however, not necessarily compensated for by privacy gains, as companies and states can also more easily penetrate the private lives of individuals. New sources of biases in opinion have emerged through targeted campaigning, stealth propaganda, inauthentic online expression and unaccountable algorithmic filtering, which may potentially result in the manipulation, polarization and radicalization of substantial numbers of citizens. While these challenges have led scholars to express concern about audience fragmentation across several digital public spheres, studies do not corroborate the extent of the 'echo chambers' effect (Flaxman et al, 2016; Fletcher and Nielsen, 2017; Dubois and Blank, 2018). Instead, the no-less-damaging effect that emerges from empirical analysis is radicalization and even tribalization of political exchanges online, with opposing factions of contributors meeting on the same platforms not to exchange views, but insults. Moderate voices thus risk being drowned out across digital platforms.

3. *Loss of trust and support in journalism and democracy*: global and digital transformations make governments more vulnerable to public scrutiny and, in the long term, may undermine trust in democracy. The sheer volume of information available to individuals, coupled with the democratization of participation in the public sphere through social media, results in increased scrutiny of the traditional knowledge-producers, mediators and gatekeepers (journalists, experts and politicians). More specifically, digitalization and globalization undermine trust in the professional mediation of journalism and trust

in democracy that is built through journalism (Michailidou et al, 2022). Trust in journalism exists to the extent that the work of journalists is constantly put to the test by distrusting audiences, by the scrutiny of other journalists, and by other institutionalized or non-institutionalized forms of control (Ryan, 2001). This delicate balance between trust and mistrust in journalism is currently challenged by the advent of digital media. Trust in journalism is declining worldwide, according to the Reuters Digital News Report 2019.[3] There is further a growing body of literature indicating that news media and journalism carry responsibility for the decline of trust in democratic institutions and government, or for the decline of trust in science and expertise. The argument that news media erode trust has been most powerfully put forward by Patterson (2011) in his influential book, *Out of Order*. Based on extensive news media content analysis, he demonstrates how 'good news' stories have become marginalized while 'bad news' coverage has become the general norm across the news media spectrum, from print to television. In a similar vein, Cappella and Jamieson (1997) have argued that there is a spiral of cynicism at play in the way industrial news production and consumption have developed in Western societies: market pressures to conform with news values such as scandals, corruption and violence have pushed journalists and news organizations to select primarily negative news and frame it in a way that enhances public cynicism. Growing public cynicism due to negative news exposure, in turn, has fundamentally changed the expectation of news readers. Cynical news stories create cynical audiences who increasingly lose trust in democracy. Along the same line, Robert Putnam (1995b) argued that TV consumption led to the erosion of social capital and civic engagement. These findings were, however, controversial. Pippa Norris (1996), for instance, argued that watching news programmes overall proves beneficial to the health of democracy.

4. *Enhanced identity and value conflicts*: digital transformations have arguably led to an increasing contestation of values within and across European societies (Eigmüller and Trenz, 2020). The increased salience of conflicts over values and identities is often related to the rise of populism, regionalism and new nationalism, which threatens the internal cohesion of European states and challenges the expectation that European integration will lead to a convergence around democratic values. Public sphere transformations have, on the one hand, contributed to a 'silent revolution', a long-term process of cultural change that marks a shift towards liberalism, with political competition confined to mainstream parties (Fukuyama, 1999). Norris and Inglehart (2019) argue, on the other hand, that this development has reached a turning point, as new political parties and leaders have emerged in all Western societies that

mobilize electorates along a new cultural cleavage, pitting adherents of liberal values against adherents of illiberal or authoritarian values.

Zeitdiagnose: *A crisis of democracy?*

Taken together, these pathologies in the development of the contemporary public sphere and the media are embraced in the *Zeitdiagnose* of crisis (Streeck, 2014; Merkel, 2018). There is a historical dimension to the diagnosis of crisis in that a particular period of time needs to be distinguished from the 'normal state of affairs'. A crisis is commonly seen as triggered by a shock, such as the bankruptcy of Lehman Brothers in 2008, the Greek deficits in 2009 or the outbreak of the COVID-19 pandemic in 2020. As the crisis must start at some point in time, it must also come to an end. Some already speak of a post-crisis Europe that needs to move forward and define new narratives and political projects (Jones and Papaconstantinou, 2020), but others also claim that events since 2008 have had a cumulative effect, and that democracy and capitalism are entrapped and entering a permanent state of crisis (Blokker, 2014; Streeck, 2014; Offe, 2015). The analytical dimensions in the diagnosis of crisis are not clear cut, especially when what distinguishes 'crisis' from other forms of malfunction and disruption remains unclear. Crisis commonly denotes deep rupture: not transformation, but a rapid and dramatic departure towards something new and still unknown (O'Connor, 1981). In the case of a crisis of democracy, for instance, we do not mean frequent deficits in the application of democratic principles, such as participation or representation, but a change in the underlying democratic logic (Castells, 2018; Merkel, 2018). A crisis is a moment of uncertainty, where established models no longer work or collapse. Crisis-induced social constraints and conflicts would call into question the capacity of the public sphere and the political system (nation, state and beyond) to generate legitimacy. Economic crisis and the crisis of democracy are further seen as interrelated and affecting each other in particular ways. Economic malfunctioning and market failure challenge the recognition of political authority, for instance in the way crisis undermines trust in the problem-solving capacities of government, or in representative institutions, such as parliament. A crisis does not, therefore, simply affect the functioning of capitalism or the state but also the subjective feelings and experiences of the members of society who perceive such malfunctions as critical for their continued existence and feel their identities threatened (Habermas, 1975: 3). In this last sense, crisis is always to be understood as a legitimation crisis. It is not simply systemic but always collectively experienced, interpreted and filtered through the public sphere. As such, it puts social integration at stake; that is, it impairs the 'consensual foundations of [the] normative structures' of society (Habermas, 1975).

If the analytical dimensions of the crisis diagnosis often remain ambiguous, so is empirical evidence that indicates crisis. The economic and financial crisis of 2008 can be described in terms of objective factors, such as the effects or repercussions it has had on various sectors, for instance in the way it impacted on media revenues or caused the bankruptcy of media companies (de Mateo et al, 2010). Crisis nevertheless remains a matter of interpretation and experiences, which is also acknowledged in part of the literature that analyses crisis perceptions and contestations (della Porta, 2012; Guiraudon et al, 2015; Michailidou and Trenz, 2015; Smith, 2015; Trenz et al, 2015).

A legitimation crisis that translates into enhanced levels of public contestation is also diagnosed in the way legitimacy of the state and national unity are challenged in some parts of Europe by secessionism and a loss of trust in government. Although it would be an exaggeration to claim that there was a crisis of legitimation and democracy in a Scandinavian context, it is an everyday reality in many countries in Southern Europe (Keating, 1996; Armingeon and Guthmann, 2014; Duerr, 2015; Wodak and Boukala, 2015; Foster and Frieden, 2017). The dismantling of states as an indicator for a deep legitimation crisis is, however, rarely brought together with the fundamental questioning of democracy, but as in the cases of Catalonia or Scotland, is linked to new democratic movements. Even in failed nation states, public sphere dynamics are, therefore, still constitutive to democratic legitimacy and do not fundamentally undermine it, as is sometimes believed. Another frequently mentioned indicator for the current dissatisfaction with democracy is the rise of populist parties across Europe and the world. Such parties have been seen as 'anti-system' actors, challenging the architecture of representative democracy and its established modes of generating legitimacy. As such, they are seen as part of a historical counter-revolution, targeting liberal democracy and putting its institutions under direct attack (Zielonka, 2018).

The diagnosis of a crisis of liberal democracy and the public sphere would be incomplete if only discussed in light of the counter-revolutionary strategies of the political opponents of states and liberalism. Delegitimation is not just a political strategy of anti-liberals; it also results from the internal contradictions of crisis-ridden liberal capitalism, which has fallen short of its promises of equal chances and wealth for all. The diffuse evidence that liberal democracies have entered a deep crisis of legitimation needs to be discussed, therefore, in relation to the critical question of whether public sphere dynamics are still constitutive to the generation of democratic legitimacy. The liberal vision of democracy has not simply lost credibility; it may no longer be applicable to our contemporary world. In this last sense, the mechanism of democratic legitimation through debates that inform a process of public opinion and will formation would be fundamentally questioned. The crisis of democracy would not simply refer to temporary disruptions and malfunctions in democratic practices; it would be a crisis of paradigm. Political legitimacy would increasingly be built in a way that bypasses the public sphere. The challenge to liberal democracy would not just be external, confined to the new authoritarian forces or populist parties at the fringes of the political spectrum. Crisis would be inscribed into the structures of liberal democracies, with states failing to perform, unprepared to meet global challenges. Public sphere dystopias point to the possibility of a fundamental transformation of our communication infrastructures in the way public and private distinctions are redefined; the formation of publics is blocked, and opinion and will formation processes redirected. Dystopia would result in the fundamental questioning of the validity of the norms and values on which the modern public sphere was based. The newly dystopian infrastructure of communication could no longer be described using public sphere vocabulary, and a radical paradigm shift would become necessary to describe the newly emerging communication environments.

The end of democracy in the current constellation of media communications remains a threat scenario, but it is not a final verdict, nor a confirmed diagnosis. How, if at all, will it be possible to interrupt the chain of legitimation and delegitimation that characterizes the modern public sphere of democracy? Or do we not also experience here the ambivalence between disruption and renewal? By collecting empirical evidence of public sphere malfunctions and disruptions from different sectors and countries, I will argue in the following that the underlying norms and principles of the public sphere, such as freedom of speech, independence of the media, truth orientation and openness of public debates, have not been dismissed or replaced by new norms and principles. Instead, they continue to be inscribed into practices of democratic renewal and guide the interactions between media, political institutions and audiences not only in our well-protected Western societies but on a global scale. A post-democratic regime that has sorted out these normative issues and established alternative legitimation standards to guarantee stability and the consent of the population is therefore out of sight in the current constellation.

In conclusion, it seems that diagnosis of public sphere disruptions in the current context of a legitimation crisis is torn between two readings of crisis: first, as a period of transition where existing paradigms are shattered but reform is sought to overcome crisis; and secondly, as 'paradigm lost', where existing belief systems and practices are no longer applicable, and critical intervention becomes untenable. The diagnosis of public sphere disruptions thus remains incomplete, not to say confusing. It seems that we cannot think and describe public sphere disruptions without relying on both the infrastructures and scripts of the public sphere, and that the long-term processes, which we see as undermining the public sphere, are at the same time processes that have always been constitutive to public sphere development and transformation.

In order to get out of this conundrum and further develop the argument in this book, it will be useful to clarify the public sphere premises for both diagnosis and critique of the malfunctioning of media and democracy. If public sphere disruptions stood for a 'paradigm lost' situation, and democracy would cease to exist, critique would also be muted, and public sphere disruptions and their normative consequences could no longer be named or drive efforts at political reform. Public sphere scholars therefore not simply accumulate empirical knowledge about media disruptions, but also reconstruct the processes through which such knowledge is accumulate, interpreted and assessed in its consequences. The question about public sphere disruptions is no longer 'what do we know' but 'how can we know?'

How do we know?

In the previous chapter, the diagnosis of public sphere disruptions was found to combine empirical knowledge about contemporary media production, content and reception with critical knowledge about media performance, effects and impact. The functional analysis of public sphere disruptions, therefore, rests on the normative template of the modern public sphere. The four core functions of the public sphere that are necessary to make knowledge and information generally accessible (publicity), to make public use of knowledge (public opinion formation), to hold public institutions accountable (legitimation) and to form a political community (identification) are, at the same time, the normative yardsticks for a well-functioning democracy. Knowledge about public sphere disruptions is, in this sense, closely linked to agreement about a template of democratic legitimacy from which we can identify deviating practices. To reach such an agreement not only among scholars but also among the members of a critical public is a demanding task that presupposes the very public sphere infrastructures that have become the object of critique. Norm violations are not simply verified through empirical fact-checking but through the public use of reason. In other words, we need to engage in public communication and filter our empirical knowledge through the infrastructures of the public sphere, to formulate our conclusions about public sphere disruptions as a critical intervention within the public sphere. When confronted with the interpretation of our *times as crisis of* democracy or post-democracy, one must suspect that such a diagnosis is not meant to be simply diagnostic but rather needs to be understood as a contribution to critical discourse with its own normative presuppositions and justificatory requirements.

In the following, I wish to map out such an analysis of the way we diagnose the state of contemporary public spheres and the media: How can we know about public sphere disruptions and their devastating effects on democracy? The short answer is that we know about public sphere disruptions when we agree on normative yardsticks of public sphere critique and apply these to our own analysis. My aim, therefore, is not to establish the criteria that allow us to decide whether public sphere dynamics are disruptive or not. I rather wish to understand practices of critique, and how such a critique combines empirical indicators with normative yardsticks. Ultimately, I wish to show how our scientific diagnosis of public sphere disruptions is turned into a public sphere intervention with critical intent. Knowledge about public sphere disruptions paves the way from dystopia back to utopia.

Knowledge about media: analytical and normative

How can we know that media functions and public spheres are disrupted? Before we engage in any type of research on media performance, we need to establish assessment criteria, which remain disputed and can only be settled by entering a broader dialogue with science and politics. Knowledge about media combines empirical indicators for the observation of media performance with normative yardsticks for the assessment of media impact on individuals and society. Here, we come back to the guiding theme of this book: whenever we talk about the public sphere, we have opened a Pandora's box of the normative foundations of modern society and democracy. The public sphere is the empirical substrate and the normative horizon of the communicative exchanges that constitute modern (democratic) society. It denotes very concrete and palpable processes of communication among individuals and groups and ways of organizing media, politics and society. At the same time, it accounts for internal divisions and conflicts about what constitutes a 'good society' and what values, norms and future projects should be embraced by it. This means that we cannot really separate our diagnosis of public sphere disruptions from public sphere critique. Whenever we accumulate knowledge about media malfunctioning or failures, we do not simply describe media effects that can be reduced to analytical indicators or quantifiable measurements. As media and communication researchers, we inevitably *qualify* our observations of media operations and transformations. To come up with a *valid* assessment of our research findings, we rely on shared values and norms, the validity of which is put to the test whenever we measure public sphere performance.

The scientific study of public communication has always been driven by the ambition of producing reliable and objectifiable knowledge about media functioning in society. Such knowledge was often derived from the empirical observation and mathematical calculation of communication flows, their directions and deviations (Shannon and Weaver, 1949). The functional school of early media scholarship, as represented in the work of Harold Lasswell (1948) and Paul Lazarsfeld (Katz and Lazarsfeld, 1966), laid the foundation for a sender–receiver model and distinguished between different stages in the process of production, dissemination and reception of media content. This allowed for the application of causal models for the explanation of media effects through mainly quantitative methods. Later theorists added the possibility of a feedback loop (Berlo, 1960) to understand the ways senders receive information from the audience in response, or as a reaction, to their original input. Cultural study approaches, in particular, have contributed to our understanding of the reception context of communication and the creative practices of decoding messages developed by critical audiences (Hall, 1973).

Contemporary approaches to the study of media complexity have come a long way from considering media reception as a simple mechanical reaction to a message. There is a general understanding of the active process of interpretation that would allow publics to reject messages and build critical capacities over time. We wish to understand, for instance, not only whether some specific information sent out is received but also how it is understood and interpreted, and how such interpretations feed back into the process of public communication. We further wish to understand whether this information is true or false, whether it has damaging effects on the receiver, or whether it supports or enables the receivers to engage in 'constructive' media use.

As argued previously, the distinction between a functional and a normative account of the public sphere has been introduced as a division of tasks in media and communication studies: it is a point of orientation for researchers to approach their research topics in an 'orderly' way and structure the sequence of their scheduled analytical tasks to explain media functioning and role, first in society and then in democracy. By following these routine working practices, the processes of knowledge production about the media and the public sphere, and the processes of normative assessment and critique, should be kept separate. This is also reflected in the disciplinary divisions of an analytical, and thus scientific, approach to media and communication and the normative agenda of public sphere research and democracy, entrusted to political theory and philosophy.

The 'ordered' sequence of a sociological approach to media and communication is to first analyse media performance and effects and only secondly turn this knowledge about media into a normative assessment of the media. Empirical analysis should be the basis of normative critique. To do this, the functional account relies on the sender–receiver model of linear communication that triggers measurable effects. It answers the question: Why do we need the media, and how can we use it for the organization of social life? The normative account, instead, relates the media to the public sphere of democracy. It answers the question: How can we build a 'good society' with the help of media?

The democratic public sphere is the normative reference point for media and communication analysis, as well as for its critical assessment. The ideal functioning of media and communication is measured mainly through quality indicators, but it is also often quantified and metrically ranked (such as freedom of speech and democracy indices). Public opinion surveys are used, for instance, not only to measure the distribution of attitudes across the population but to gauge the success of public intermediation as well: governments constantly adapt their communication strategies in response to observed opinion changes. The established measuring instruments of public sphere performance offer tools of critical assessment that are used professionally by a range of actors and institutions, including individual media users, as in popular tests of self-performance (like checking their own social media rankings). Public sphere analysis thus allows the whole of society to become *analytical*, that is, to measure the success of their communication efforts (in reaching its targets, transmitting knowledge or achieving mutual understanding, for example) and, at the same time, to become *critical*, that is, building on this 'analytical knowledge' to respond to the question: How can our performance be improved to reach shared goals (like, for instance, participation, deliberation or simply democracy)?

In a linear model of public communications, the disruptive effects of media communication are only of interest if they can be attributed to a certain cause, if responsibilities can be established and, where necessary, corrective measures can be taken. This is the old line of attack of critical media studies: identify actors with bad intentions, corrupted media and misled audiences. Malfunctions, or normative violations, are thus identified at either the input, throughput or output level of public communication. As indicators, media scholars refer to either the intentions of actors who wilfully place content in the media, or the performance of media institutions and organizations to transmit that content, or lastly the attitudes of audiences who selectively pay attention and interpret that content. At all three levels, we need to make causal assumptions about intended media effects: that the bad intentions of the senders of information indeed shape the attitudes of receivers, that news selection and framing by journalists explains the agenda of democratic politics, and that audiences exposed to particular content behave in predictable ways, with desired or undesired consequences for democracy (negativity in the news, for example, leads to public cynicism; Cappella and Jamieson, 1997). But this does not yet provide the response to our initial question of *how* we can see these effects, and whether these effects can be ascribed to media or causally related to media malfunctions.

The new problems with the linear-functional account of media communications are the old ones. Public sphere transformations cannot be explained by single factors, causalities or logics (Bennett and Pfetsch, 2018: 246). One such ambiguity that came to the attention of scholars of journalism early on is the conflicting demands that are placed on public mediators to meet the functional requirements of democratic society (McNair, 2000). Lasswell (1948) himself distinguished between the needs of information, education and guidance, which shape three different types of journalism oriented towards a neutral-mediating function, a socializing function and an advocacy-critical function (Harcup, 2015). Media should be neutral transmitters that allow for unbiased information, but media should at the same time be educators and a critical voice. On the one hand, media should mirror social reality and not distort it; on the other, media should select and highlight aspects of social reality according to societal norms and should uphold moral standards and be devoted to the promotion of critical thought for the advancement of society. To be able to cope with such conflicting demands, journalism practices are found to be more ritual- and routine-driven than directional. Journalism production takes place within a field that is not externally modelled or steered but rather follows its own internal logics (Benson and Neveu, 2005; Bourdieu, 2005; Cook, 2005; Becker and Vlad, 2009; Hanitzsch, 2016). The practices and routines of news production are, therefore, in eternal tension with the expectations of what journalism should do and how journalism should behave.

Lasswell's transmission model of a linear and one-directional communication flow has, of course, always been based on simplified assumptions, which have been highly successful for building marketing strategies within the industries that offer media services (like PR) and attract clients. A simple model was needed to make people believe in media effects and to keep the whole machinery of media production and dissemination running. Also, from a normative perspective, assumptions about the linearity of public communication were desirable, as they allowed us to rationalize the functioning of democratic procedures of will formation. Corrections to this model were sometimes needed, but the underlying paradigm was rarely challenged within strategic communication and PR studies. Embedding political communication or advertisements within the public sphere was, for instance, found to be helpful to emphasize the contingency effects of public communication and the complexity of multi-directional communication flows. The task, then, was to re-model strategic communication by taking into account complexity and a growing number of intervening variables (Bentele and Nothhaft, 2010).

Within media and communication studies, a paradigm shift was proposed by James W. Carey (Carey, 1975, 1992), one of the pioneers of the new cultural approach to media. Beyond the causality of media effects, cultural study approaches have emphasized the ritual forms public communication takes and the ways such media and communication rituals produce, maintain and transform culture and society. Against the linear transmission model, media communication is not isolated and analysed as an instrument to achieve strategic goals, but rather understood in a specific socio-cultural context. This relates to a different understanding of society as not simply operating through communication, but as communication, or as Habermas would put it, as being self-constituted through communicative action (Habermas, 1985). Instead of failing or being successful, communication simply takes place. Yet, as has been explained by linguistics and semiotics in the tradition of de Saussure and Peirce, the way it takes place is explained by pre-existing structures of meaning, conventions of language use and routinized practices of conversation in the everyday exchanges of information (Garfinkel, 1967). The question of what effects public communication might or might not have depends therefore on what the participants want to see and what they selectively highlight in their ongoing communication. The instrumental use of media as a tool to achieve particular goals is, in this sense, embedded in the ritual of media practices that establish the rules of media use and the means of linguistic expression in a particular context.

Cultural approaches to the study of media rituals and public sphere approaches thus coincide in a way that does not dismiss the functional accounts of media's role in society but rather considers media functioning as embedded in the cultural background knowledge and interpretative context of society, which at the same time is shaped and transformed by the media. Instead of distinguishing *a priori* particular media functions as an external regulative principle of media performance, the way the media functions or should function is always (pre)defined by media practices and rituals. Media interpretations and assessment are part of an ongoing media performance and take shape in rituals of media critique, which confirm commonly held assumptions about media's role and functioning in society. In line with this approach, the critical-functional analysis of media performance and role in society has, in itself, become a ritual performed through the media, involving various actors and institutions who professionally deal with the media. As such, it is constitutive to a public sphere, as outlined in Chapter 2, that combines the possibilities of transmission of communication with the possibilities of its critical assessments. The public sphere is, then, so to speak, the institutionalized form of established procedures for the critical assessment of media performance.

The transmission model of public communication has, in this sense, become idealized as a normative template of critique, such as in current debates about the future of journalism and struggles against 'fake news' and misinformation. Media practices are indeed difficult to conceive if the sender of a message is not guided by the belief that messages can be strategically placed to convince audiences in specific ways. If people lose faith in media effects, they lose the motivation to engage with the media.

Professional communicators also learn to deal with the contingency of public communication over time and adapt their communication techniques pragmatically to media realities without giving up their guiding assumption that they exert certain degrees of control over communication flow.

The public sphere of criticism not only constantly puts the linearity assumptions of mediated communication to the test but also provides the reflective tools for questioning the underlying binary distinctions between media functions and dysfunctions. In facing the complexity of media and communication and its contingent effects, public communicators struggle with ways to uphold such distinctions, like, for instance, the one between information as constructive and unifying, and disinformation as disruptive and divisive. They also experience the constant failure of such distinctions, as information can be deeply divisive, and propaganda can unify and promote peaceful living. To say that the opposite of a disruptive public sphere is a public sphere that is constructive or supportive is tautological if no normative reference point is provided about what is to be constructed and supported. In the same way, you cannot misinform without generating new information. Distinctions between information and disinformation, between connection and disconnection, integration and disintegration, inclusion and exclusion, can only be drawn in a context-bound way, when normative reference points are established and agreed on by the participants. Modern public spheres have therefore been described as being unified through internal differentiation along functional and territorial lines (Gerhards and Neidhardt, 1991; Gerhards, 1994). But when does differentiation turn into disruptive fragmentation? These are questions that cannot be answered analytically and need to be decided in normative debates. As I will argue in the next section, the public sphere itself generates its own responses to the question when it is considered to be disrupted.

To talk of public sphere disruptions combines a form of diagnosis with critique. As such, it relates to an old topos of public sphere research: to advance knowledge about media functioning combined with criticism of media performance in democracy. The public sphere provides the normative template and constitutes the forum for the expression of critique. Accordingly, there are two yardsticks for the identification of public sphere disruptions, both tested out in Habermas' historical analysis of public sphere transformations (1989): (1) adherence to democratic norms and procedures, and (2) deficits in the performance of the available media and communication infrastructures. In the first case, the validity of the underlying norms is put to the test. Indicators for public sphere disruptions are found in democratic struggles or conflicts about values that question the normative underpinning of the modern public sphere. In the second case, compliance with underlying norms is put to the test. Indicators for public sphere disruptions are found in the behaviour of particular groups of actors, or in the performance of the media that do not comply with the underlying normative requirements. The identification of public sphere disruptions is, therefore, either a question of the validity of public sphere principles, or a question of the application of norms and the functioning of communication infrastructures and media institutions that support such principles. The public sphere would become redundant, or even collapse, if democratic norms and procedures were no longer held valid. The public sphere would become self-defeating if democratic norms could no longer be put into practice.

Knowledge and critique

As argued in the previous section, the analytical distinction between media functions and dysfunctions has always been meant as a critical intervention. Normative and functionalist accounts of the media converge in their intention of facilitating assessment of media performance and criticism. Their advantage is that ambivalence can be reduced, and clear-cut responses can be provided, whether media function or not or have integrative or disintegrative effects. The functionalist-normative account of media specializes in generating precisely this kind of critical knowledge that enables us to decide whether, for instance, a new media technology is supporting or undermining free speech, rational debate or community values. Functionalist and normative-critical accounts of the media thus converge in their neat and categorical distinctions that put order to the world of media communication and its effects. We need functional parameters or normative standards to be critical, and we need to be able to decide when and by whom such parameters and standards are violated.

What does this all mean with regard to our problem of how to identify public sphere disruptions? In general terms, it makes a difference to our understanding of public sphere disruptions as intentional, structural or systemic. In the first case, disruptions would be brought about by some actors who undermine media functioning or democratic values. In that case, we know of public sphere disruptions where we see the villains and can name them. Disruptions would result from deviant behaviour. This would be the case of corrupt democracy. In the second case, public sphere disruptions would be grounded in the malfunctioning of established democratic institutions and media markets. Institutional performance or market dynamics would be deficient, and thus no longer in compliance with public sphere principles. This would be the case of a dysfunctional democracy. Finally, public sphere disruptions could be systemic in the way the normative principles underlying the public sphere are no longer held valid for the building of political legitimacy. This would be the case of post-democracy.

In all these instances, we accumulate knowledge about public sphere disruptions by not simply diagnosing media effects and possibly quantifying them. There is a qualitative element as well, which has to do with the underlying norms that we hold as valid and wish to uphold when we measure public sphere performance. This means that we cannot explain public sphere disruptions by referring to a simple media transmission model of communication. We cannot simply say that public communication is disrupted if sender–receiver transmission fails, or if there is a technical interference or rupture between sender and receiver. Disruptions do not only refer to the mechanical process of transmission of information. Even in everyday talk, we not only want to make sure that the given acoustic conditions make our speech understandable. When we assess our interlocutors, we wish to understand, above all, whether the information sent out is true or false, accepted or rejected, or whether it supports a moral cause or undermines it. The transmission model of communication basically informs us (a) that communication happens at one point in time and between two fixed entities of sender and receiver and (b) how it happens (unmediated face-to-face communication, through the use of interpersonal media such as a telephone or channelled through the mass media or social networking media). Both are insufficient for the identification of public sphere disruptions, for which we would need to rely on information about why communication happens, and what specific significance or value it has when it does. Beyond the input–output model of communication, we therefore need to take in additional assumptions that tell us about the legitimate or illegitimate motivations and intentions of senders and receivers, the information value of content, the integrity and reliability of media, or the desirability of communication and media effects. Content can be illegitimate, such as violence or hate speech, speakers can be dishonest about their intentions, media can be distorted and media effects can be unwanted. In all these instances, the identification of public sphere disruptions relies on a form of critical judgement that classifies content, qualifies the intentions of interlocutors or assesses the desirability of media effects.

My argument is that a particular form of critique is already inscribed in the linear model of public communication. The linearity assumptions of public communication sustain critique in the form of an attribution of causal responsibility: whenever communication fails, either senders made the wrong calculations about reception, media amplifiers and filters failed, or receivers lacked the prerequisites of understanding. In addition to causal responsibility, the identification of public sphere disruptions relies on the possibility of an attribution of moral responsibility. Senders can make the right calculations on how best to place content to achieve particular effects, but content can be manipulative, thus restricting the choices of receivers in undesired ways. This latter would be the classical manipulation model of political communication or advertisement. In such a linear communication model, responsibility for public sphere disruptions can be attributed: wrong content, wrong actors, wrong media or wrong audiences. The attribution of causal responsibility in combination with moral responsibility is the prerequisite for public sphere interventions, that is, the translation of critique into corrective measures, as through regulation or legal intervention. Actors can be excluded or punished, distorted media can be redirected, and inaccurate content can be corrected.

To understand public sphere criticism, we thus need to investigate how causality and linearity assumptions are culturally inscribed, informing belief systems and normative expectations of public sphere actors and audiences in their daily media practices. The ritual of public sphere criticism can be seen in the application of common good criteria for the assessment of media content and performance. Legitimacy is attributed to media that enhances society or democracy through knowledge, education and/or Enlightenment. Illegitimate use of media is denounced in the way particular actors pursue private interests at the cost of others through advertisements, deception and/or manipulation.

The ritual of media critique is regularly performed by media scholars in their professional work of assessing the success or failure of media communication, media strategies and media functions. For the understanding of the potential of public sphere criticism, it is however important to diagnose how the ritual of media critique also becomes part of regular media reception and, as such, involves audiences in struggles over the legitimacy of media. The competences needed to develop a critical understanding of media are not only part of the programmes of media literacy and, as such, learned in schools and during the lifelong process of socialization with media. Critical news readership is also a central requirement of citizenship through which audiences constantly question the trustworthiness of media (Dahlgren, 2013). The ritual of testing media functions is triggered whenever a receiver of a message takes a reflexive stance that makes her think about the conditions of transmission of the message, the credibility of the sender or the reliability of the messenger through which it is channelled. Reading news, for instance, is a ritual of critically assessing the trustworthiness of the news source and the performance of the journalist who delivers it. Such rituals of critical news reading are popular themes in everyday political talk, for instance when we question the newsworthiness of a particular story, when we find reason to complain about the dumbing down of news quality, or when we are disillusioned by the editorial line of our favourite newspapers or the evening news on TV. Critical reflection can be a singular moment initiated by a literate news reader, but more often, it is a collective practice that involves (or even constitutes) a public. Whoever finds news untrustworthy still cares about the truth orientation of the public sphere (Chambers and Kopstein, 2022: 4). Media critique is, in this sense, always a renewal of the normative yardsticks of the public sphere that are applied collectively to assess media performance and content and the trustworthiness of news.

How can we perform the ritual of media critique? Boltanski and Thévenot (2006), in their sociology of critical judgement, refer to so-called orders of worth as a common resource of knowledge for critical judgement. Such orders of worth are a cognitive repertoire for justifications that can be used in critical discourse. In an adaptation of Kant's critique of judgement (Kant, 2000 [1790]), we can distinguish between forms of instrumental reasoning that underlie the linear-functional account of media communication, forms of moral argumentation that link media content and performance to shared values and democracy and various forms of aesthetical judgement that apply criteria of taste or feelings of inner harmony, beauty or identity to media content and performance. Instrumental and moral reasoning distinguish what could be called a political public sphere of critical judgement, and aesthetic reasoning helps to narrow down the cultural public sphere (McGuigan, 2005), even though the boundaries between these two spheres are (increasingly?) blurred.

For simplicity of argument, in the following I focus on the critique of instrumental and functional performance and the normative critique of media. Both have developed in parallel, establishing rituals of media critique that are internal to the discipline of media studies (in the tradition of what is called critical media studies), transdisciplinary (in the tradition of cultural studies, as well as approaches of political economy), or external, as a universal template for the critique of media content and performance that is applied by public intellectuals and political actors, as well as by members of the audience. The ritual of media critique is thus both an element of critical theory and part of everyday practices of media use and consumption.

As an example of how the discipline of media and communication studies developed as a ritual of instrumental and moral reasoning, we can think of the field of journalism studies (McNair, 2000). Critique is either performed as a judgement of news-making in relation to common, set goals or functional requirements, or as a judgement of news-making in relation to compliance with democratic norms and values. The first judge news according to criteria of instrumentality: if news media should inform, its performance is measured in the informative quality of content, or the knowledge gains of the receivers; if news media should entertain, its performance is measured in users' gratification, audience rates and popularity. The media industries themselves often have an interest in promoting instrumental criticism in the form of judgements of scale that serve as a point of orientation for users and audiences to make their choices of consumption. Rating systems are used to rank media products and brands, such as movies, bestseller lists or charts. Similar forms of ratings include web rankings of content by popularity, for instance in the form of blog rankings and recommendations of films and movies by commercial providers. Such rankings have also become popular in media and communication research, for example rankings of information value in journalism research or scales used in audience and media reception studies.

Judgements of moral and aesthetic reasoning often lack this binding force and the authority of science and cannot refer to systematic measurements of media effects. Instead of scales and rankings, we often find categorical statements about the value of media content as either right or wrong, as trustworthy or untrustworthy, as beautiful or ugly, or about the prognosis of desired or undesired effects. In such instances, the ritual of media critique is practised as a form of decoding of media content that opens spaces for the creative interpretation of audiences who might affirm moral or aesthetic judgements, but who might also correct or subvert them (Hall, 1973). Critique in the form of moral reasoning, therefore, typically correlates with audience divides or polarizations of opinions and unfolds in the form of controversial debates and exchanges of opinion as they are, for instance, carried out among public intellectuals and in media commentary (Jacobs and Townsley, 2011). Apart from moral judgements, other types of ethical or aesthetic judgement of media content and performance (like, for instance, content that is meant to provide pleasurable experiences, or to enhance community bonds) fall under this category of rituals of critical judgement that are carried out in public controversies.

The critique of media and public sphere disruptions often meets with the individual everyday experiences of 'broken media', the non-linearity of communication flows, the insufficiencies of knowledge and understanding, and the distorting effects on individual and collective reception. Most would probably agree that there are indeed disruptions at all three levels of public intermediation: too many malicious actors populate the democratic public sphere, whose democratic mindedness remains uncertain; too little effort is made by existing media organizations to provide accurate information; too many distractions divert audience attention. Attributions of causality are, in this sense, not only the domain of critical media studies; they are internal to the communication flows and, as such, constantly produced by the participants themselves as part of their interpretations of media (Luhmann, 2000). There is, in other words, a common knowledge about media functions and dysfunctions that binds people together and drives, at the same time, public discourse about media content and its effects.

We could then say that public spheres can think about their own disruptions and can attribute malfunctions or normative violations to the input, throughput or output level of public communication in such a way as to blame individual speakers, mediators or receivers. Such attributions become part of the common knowledge about media. The yardstick for identifying such disruptions would be to either study the strategies and goals of actors who wilfully design media content, the performance of intermediaries in selecting, amplifying and interpreting that content, or lastly, the attitudes of audiences and their guided or misguided choices in relating to media content. At all three stages of the communication flow, causalities about undesired media effects need to be attributed and individual responsibilities established, for instance that the pursuit of illegitimate goals by public sphere actors does indeed have intended effects, that media selection and framing shape attitudes and opinions, and that receivers' attitudes and behaviour is influenced by patterns of media consumption (for example, that exposure to violent content results in violent behaviour).

In discussing the scope of a sociology of critique of the media, the intention can therefore not be (as this is done in normative political theory of the public sphere) to establish such criteria for normative assessment of media disruptions, or to evaluate whether the criteria used in media critiques and by public intellectuals are suitable for such an assessment. From a sociological perspective, we are instead interested in the operation of building a commonly shared critical knowledge about media and public sphere malfunctions. In line with Boltanski and Thévenot (2006), we can assume that these capacities for critical judgements are collectively generated attributions of meaning and causality. They construct what could be called a *shared world of meaning about media functions and effects*.

At this point, we would need to enter a discussion about our human capacity for critical judgement, which is not simply a personal trait or cognitive skill (as derived, for instance, from the intellect), but a social skill that follows rules and conventions (Boltanski and Thévenot, 1999; Blokker, 2011). As I have argued in this chapter, critical judgements can be defined as a form of human reasoning that combines a causality judgement with a morality judgement about specific aspects of our shared social world, highlighted and made relevant. Such judgements attribute causality as a way to attribute responsibility. The 'ought to' of the critical judgement applies to our shared social world, not to nature. I cannot criticize a volcano for destroying a city; I can only criticize the volcanologists for their poor predictive skills. Critical judgements indicate the potential of social change to improve the conditions of social life, and 'do things better', collectively.

The sociology of the public sphere has invested in the development of a research programme that allows us to analyse how these capacities of critical judgement are collectively learned and socialized (Eder, 1985; Strydom, 2011). Unlike the ancien régime that relied on external authorities like the church to distinguish truth from falsehood, the public sphere trusts in individuals' critical capacities to make their own judgements and engage in reasoning. The public sphere further provides motivational incentives for individuals who are encouraged to build their cognitive capacities, strive for truth and become 'critical minds'. Public spheres, therefore, have historically proliferated in symbiosis with capitalist market developments and citizenship (Somers, 1993). In a free market, developing these capacities is paired with rewards in the form of influence, reputation and profit. Enlightenment was not meant to be just a moral demand (you should enlighten yourself) that has turned into a normative project (a democratic society). It unfolded as a social mechanism for the construction of social order and the self-constitution of society that operates through public communication. This process of democratic self-constitution of society is fundamentally *cognitive* in nature: it produces the knowledge that is needed for society to represent itself. At the same time, it is fundamentally *normative* in nature, and thus political in the way it symbolizes collective knowledge and power and critically puts its legitimate usage to the test (Strydom, 2000; O'Mahony, 2013).

Knowledge about public sphere disruption and its critique always requires, in this sense, a 'well-functioning' public sphere and presupposes the existence of a critical public that holds public sphere principles valid. The 'true' crisis of the public sphere would be silence: the unimaginable situation of the absence of critique, or the incomprehensibility of the languages through which critique is given expression. But would this be possible? We can criticize a society where the capacities of utopian thinking are seriously curtailed, but a society that is not driven by the motor of critique is beyond our imagination. It seems that even dystopia cannot lose its utopian reference point. Consequently, the critique of the dysfunctions of the public sphere, as I shall argue in the following, always bears the fruit of public sphere renewal.

Public sphere critique and renewal: from post-democracy to neo-democracy

The interplay between media diagnosis and critique has informed media and communication studies since its inception. This also included the radical questioning of the foundations of our knowledge about media and the public sphere. Back in the early 20th century, the American political scientist Walter Lippmann (1927) famously argued that the public exists merely as a phantom that haunts democratic theory, and that it becomes a dangerous illusion as a guide for democratic politics: 'For when public opinion attempts to govern directly, it is either a failure or a tyranny' (1927: 64–5). Members of the public are both ignorant and uninterested: '[T]he citizen gives but a little of his time to public affairs, has but a casual interest in facts and but a poor appetite for theory' (1927: 14–15).

As Lippmann himself worked as a journalist, he knew how to frame his book as a critical intervention in the form of drama and provocation. Lippmann wrote against democratic utopia and defined himself as anti-Kantian with the intention of rescuing American democracy from the fervour of the idealists. At the same time, his book raised numerous empirical claims in its 'diagnosis' of the dystopian elements of American democracy. From a contemporary perspective, the book presents an early but recurrent account of public sphere disruptions that are used as a critical test case to discuss the adequacy of democratic theory. It postulates the end of utopia and of the normative age of politics, and this at a time when the democratic promise was yet to unfold in most parts of the word. The book also provoked a public controversy and critical responses that resonate to this day. If Lippmann's intervention became the template for public sphere critique, the response it provoked from John Dewey (1927) became the template for public sphere renewal. Against Lippmann, Dewey famously argued that publics are not just there as an entity with a given interest or predisposition. Publics only come into being by applying the 'methods of debate and discussion' (1927: 142). There is no public without a correlating democratic process that identifies problems of shared relevance. The democratic process is not just political in the sense of facilitating collective decision-making and allocating power. It is also sociological in the way it reveals society to itself, giving meaning and form to the shared social world in which democratic citizens can recognize themselves as collective actors that shape the world in which they live and make it transparent and understandable. Democratic politics is in this sense the constant effort to make society and social life visible (Nassehi, 2002; Rosanvallon, 2008: 310). This visibility is never to be taken for granted in an essentialist way or rooted in stable symbols or cultural roots: it instead requires constant engagement through critical judgement that produces temporary political visions and projects.

There is an important lesson to be taken from this controversy: we can learn that there is a routine interplay between public sphere criticism and renewal, between dystopia and utopia that characterizes public sphere transformations. The public sphere constitutes what could be called 'critical sovereignty' (Rosanvallon, 2008: 122). It questions power and mistrusts government, yet such an exercise of critique becomes, at the same time, the reservoir for building trust in a civic community that engages in a collective project. The identification of dystopian elements of the public sphere can only take place through critical interventions in the public sphere. Any diagnosis of the dysfunctioning of government is, at the same time, a critical oversight of its possible functioning. The critical intervention questions legitimacy by confirming the principles of a well-functioning public sphere and democracy. Such critical oversights rarely, therefore, remain within academia but have the potential to inform democratic procedures and impact on democratic institutions. As such, they are part of what Rosanvallon (2008) calls 'counter democracy' and are carried by an intellectual counter movement in defence of the utopian vision of the public sphere, its possible reform and renewal. The public sphere and democracy can be criticized but not easily dismissed. The lessons of the Lippmann–Dewey debate are precisely these: that intellectual public sphere critique regularly feeds into reform, and even the radical denial of the validity or applicability of public sphere principles only contributes to their sustenance.

The idea that critique as a form of denunciation of the violation of norms also reaffirms and deepens collective norms and values is an old insight from Durkheimian sociology (Durkheim, 1973; see also Rosanvallon 2008: 41–52). Critical judgement, as this was also envisaged by Kant, not only creates bonds among individuals but also renews public virtues, thus strengthening the very norms it denounces as being violated. These insights have important implications for the contemporary debate on post-democracy, which is diagnosed within democracy. In such a new constellation of post-democracy, the constitutive linkage between government and the public sphere would be broken, and legitimacy would be generated through communication dynamics and infrastructures that are fundamentally different from those established by the free press and critical publics. Yet, how would this be possible? How can democracies claim to be or become post-democratic, if such a diagnosis is necessarily bound to the reconfirmation of the validity of the acclaimed democratic principles? How (if at all) can we conceive of a post-democracy as a novel regime *beyond* the public sphere, and not just as another form of critical intervention *within* the public sphere with the potential to contribute to democratic reform and renewal?

Our ideational, historical and empirical contextualization of the public sphere and democracy controversy invites us to make a more careful assessment of the claim of an epochal change of contemporary society entering the new age of post-democracy (Crouch, 2004; Agamben et al, 2011). Scenarios of decline seem to belong to the history of democratic theory, in the same manner as the public sphere has always been told as a story of decline (Schmitter, 2015; von Beyme, 2017). Post-movements are, however, frequently converted into *neo-movements*, as Klaus von Beyme (2017: 3) argues, referring to examples from art history (such as neo-classicism or new romanticism). In analogy to these phases of renewal in ideational history, von Beyme proposes the term *neo-democracy* that comprises all these progressive and constructive searches for a relaunch of the classical notions of democracy. Neo-democracy, as I understand it here, is not so much an attempt to rescue democracy and protect it from its enemies. Nor is it to be understood as the search for new models or new notions of democracy. Neo-democracy rather comprises different movements and practices to claim democratic values and the application of procedures of self-rule against disruptive forces. As such, neo-democracy is not a desperate fight for the survival of democracy in a post-democratic constellation. It is rather manifested in the resilience of democratic institutions and procedures, and the claims for the validity of democratic norms and principles raised in a public sphere that has never ceased its production of critical discourse.

There are at least two reasons why it might be premature to claim we are entering a post-democratic age. First of all, there is an inbuilt paradox that, in order to identify violations of public sphere principles in a post-democratic constellation, we need to rely on these very principles and test their validity. Just like Lippmann back in the 1920s, we engage as media and public sphere scholars in critical debates (and often rely on the publishing means and media techniques to 'sell' our critique on the market of public attention as particularly provocative, original or politically relevant). Our diagnosis of post-democracy becomes, in itself, a form of democratic practice: we *perform* media critique with the purpose of singling out malfunctions of media performances and claiming their negative effects. The analytical and scientific identification of public sphere disruptions is only possible as part of the operations of the democratic public sphere and thus also opens the path towards reflexivity and self-correction. Secondly, we can draw a historical line to argue that public sphere and democracy criticism (since Tocqueville) has always unfolded not to fundamentally question its foundational structures and principles but to reconfirm and renew them. The critique of performing actors and institutions *within* the public sphere (like a critical assessment of the achievements of government or political parties) is therefore intended as a reconfirmation of the integrity of the public sphere and the validity of its underlying principles.

Critique is conceived here as the machinery of the modern public sphere and society (Trenz and Eder, 2004; Eder and Trenz, 2006). The machinery can at times slow down and at other times accelerate. The public sphere and democracy can switch back and forth from crisis to routine mode. Critique is a principally unfinished process that keeps democratic society in a permanent state of alert, and confronts it with its own insufficiencies (Eder, 2006, 2013). If critique is the machinery for the unfolding of the modern public sphere, the norms and critical standards are the road signs that allow us to navigate the turbulent streets of public debate and controversy. This idea of the modern public sphere as an 'unfinished project' (Habermas, 1990) is closely related to a communicative undertaking of critique that is not only carried by intellectuals or elites but always involves, and also addresses, the general public.

If modernity, through its capacities for critical self-observation, unfolds as an unfinished project that nevertheless gives collective orientation and drives collective practices, the distinction between democracy and post-democracy falls apart. Public spheres are the driving forces for processes of modernization which coincide with democratization and, by default, are incomplete and inconclusive. Corrupt democratic or authoritarian regimes can try hard to avoid confrontation with critique and to suppress public sphere infrastructures, but the critical minds of the people cannot simply be disabled, and competing validity claims cannot be resolved by authoritarian decisions. In countries with authoritarian governments, there are frequent occurrences of violations of the principles of free speech and of the independence of the press are abundant, however, such occurrences are not hidden but brought to light and hotly debated. The spread of digital media and the Internet has intensified voices that call for free speech in authoritarian societies and trigger social and political unrest. It is often young people who fight for media freedom through uprisings such as the Arab Spring movement, or dissident movements in authoritarian countries like China or Russia (Salvatore, 2013). Dissidents from these countries become global icons for a critical public.

The idea of an epochal change of democracy adds to the existing accounts of public sphere criticism. As such, it can hardly be sustained by quantifiable empirical data but needs to be made *publicly relevant*. In the field of journalism studies, for instance, the diagnosis of media crisis and failure is backed by numbers such as the drop in newspapers sales or the decline in newspaper readership. Such numbers do not tell us about public sphere disruptions unless they are collectively interpreted in such a way as to become meaningful and possibly even to 'disrupt us', wake us up and raise our concerns. Whether the death of a single newspaper is detrimental to the public sphere or not is debatable. Closing down a newspaper might even enrich the remaining news landscape, especially if the newspaper routinely undermined the quality criteria of journalism and audiences punished it by cancelling their subscriptions. Normative assessments of media trends and media performance become essential to building expertise in media scholarship and are in high demand as critical input in public debates. Media science as a discipline has never been simply descriptive of the way media functions *in* democracy and has always added in important ways to our understanding of *how* media contribute to democracy. Without such a critical intent, media and communication studies lose their contours as a scientific discipline, embedded in the normative infrastructure of the public sphere and democracy to which media contribute. There is, therefore, no diagnosis of a disrupted public sphere that does not engage in a discussion of these normative questions of media's role in democracy and does not, at the same time, intervene in democracy.

In the empirical chapters, I will lay the focus on these re-coupling processes in terms of the resilience of the public sphere. Illustrations will be given for the conversion from post-democracy to neo-democracy in the context of the digital transformation of the public sphere. With reference to the struggle over privacy, the new representative politics of populism and the limits of post-truth politics during the global COVID-19 pandemic, I will trace the linkage between the identification of public sphere disruptions, the activation of critical discourse and the re-validation of democratic principles and procedures. This is important when discussing the contingent and non-linear effects of public sphere disruptions on democratic government: at first sight, they often mean serious malfunctions of democracy, exclusion or irrationality in decision-making. Moreover, such disruptions bear the seed of public sphere revival and resilience, with the possible effects of a reaffirmation of the validity of its paradigm and the strengthening of its principles and procedures.

Who knows?

The public sphere is only insufficiently described as a space of knowledge production and distribution if it does not open possibilities for the critical use of knowledge. In the following, I therefore discuss different groups of knowledge holders in the digital public sphere with their potential to enhance reflexivity in the use of knowledge in the form of critical debate.

The haves and have nots of critical media knowledge

The traditional holders of knowledge about how to express public sphere criticism are public intellectuals. The role of public intellectuals as gatekeepers of elite public discourse has broadened in the digital media world. A newly emerging group of what Peter Dahlgren (2012) calls 'civic intellectuals' has entered the scene who have the necessary knowledge to make creative use of multimedia text, audio and video formats to spread their messages. Through blogs or social media profiles, they create communities of followers to reach out directly with their targeted messages and opinions. If we define public intellectuals more broadly as those who link critical thought with a utopian vision of society,[4] we can locate a relatively broad group of protagonists in the online public sphere, among them many academics on Twitter and YouTube who promote critical agendas and reach out to relatively large, but frequently also fragmented, groups of followers (Jünger and Fähnrich, 2019).

Knowledge about public sphere disruptions is also closely related to knowledge about how to disrupt the public sphere. This know-how of manipulation has traditionally been a privilege of the demagogue. The manipulation of truth is an old power game (Arendt, 1967), and whether the digitally and globally transformed public sphere has fundamentally changed its rules and premises is open to question. On the one hand, new populist leadership styles develop based on new skills of truth manipulation through social media that establish direct links of unfiltered communication between the political representative and their constituents. Misinformation is not simply a systemic effect but all too often results from targeted campaigns by powerful providers and related consumption choices (Chambers and Kopstein, 2022: 3). Knowledge about truth manipulation can be exclusively managed by the leader, often assisted by syndicated news and opinion websites, such as Breitbart, that specialize in the spread of 'fake news' or conspiracy theories. In the post-truth debate, power has been accused of becoming 'postmodern'. For the new populist leaders, 'everything goes' in the creative ways they seek to subvert established truths and construct alternative facts (Newman, 2022). The postmodern knowledge of truth relativism and constructivism thus becomes of instrumental use for power holders. On the other hand, through digital media, the know-how of manipulation has multiplied as even ordinary Internet users are able to use technical means to fake photographs or feed targeted audiences with partial information. The Internet has also enhanced the capacities of ordinary people to check the truth value of information, which can be used, for instance, by citizens in authoritarian countries to resist their governments' attempts at manipulation. Individual users constantly risk becoming victims of manipulation, but mass manipulation, through ideological infiltration by the powerful, actually becomes more difficult. Precisely because the knowledge of strategic communication through media and public sphere techniques is no longer exclusive and anybody can develop these skills, truth manipulations multiply and diversify and thus might lose their power and impact. If the technical means for truth manipulation are in the hands of everybody, the knowledge-power game, described by Arendt (1967), has democratized in the sense of being equally available to everyone.

A further group that accumulates knowledge about strategic media use includes various professions that increasingly work under constraints of publicity. Through processes of mediatization, professionals who work with media extend far beyond the media business (Hjarvard, 2013). As a university teacher, for instance, scientific excellence is increasingly measured in terms of my capacity to reach out with research outputs and argue for their public and societal relevance. Scientists from different disciplines need to build media knowledge and competences, which often become part of their training through tailored courses designed to teach skills that can be used to improve outreach performance. As a consequence, scientists who depend on public visibility to build their career are also more frequently targeted by the media and become objects (and all too often also victims) of audience attention.

Knowledge about public sphere disruptions, therefore, can no longer be considered a kind of specialist knowledge that is reserved for public intellectuals, power holders or media experts. It is widely spread and reaches out to various groups of media producers, practitioners and audiences. As such, it nourishes unease with democracy and accounts for a loss of trust in media. If increasing numbers of people in contemporary democracies no longer trust the media, their changing attitudes, at least partially, are based on informed opinion in the sense that people also know much more about the media and have acquired critical capacities to assess media functioning

(Broersma, 2013; Trenz, 2021; Michailidou et al, 2022). Knowledge about media and public sphere disruptions is of instrumental use for many professional groups to plan communication strategically, place content and reach out to specific target groups. In a similar way, knowledge about media functions and dysfunctions is of practical use for media audiences to find orientation in complex information environments. Knowledge can be built strategically as a way to improve media performance and is generalized, as for instance in the way it enters education programmes. This reflects the new expectation that people *should* be informed about media, with an emphasis on media literacy, as part of school curricula. Digital citizens accumulate media knowledge from early childhood through tailored pedagogical programmes as much as through life-long learning by doing.

In the digital age, knowledge about media functioning is no longer reserved for power holders, media and communication experts, spin doctors and PR strategists. The public sphere infrastructures instead encourage citizens' involvement in creative media usage and engagement in critical discourse. The Internet is, in this sense, best described as a huge repository of knowledge and information. As the spaces of publicity are enhanced, the availability of information, through rudimentary mouse clicks, becomes the norm. The idea of creative media use has been relaunched with digital media applications or software developments in the form of individual production for expressive or creative purposes, for political participation or for the organization of collective work processes (Kress, 2003; Livingstone et al, 2005). Such an empowerment of individual users is not new but part of media history, as demonstrated, for instance, in the wide use of photography or print techniques in the early 20th-century public spheres. Engagement with media, and experiences of media use and consumption, relate to everyday processes of knowledge production that involve ordinary citizens in their private, family and community lives. Despite the technological optimism of previous generations of media users, this raised awareness early on of the possibility of negative media impact, dependencies or media malfunctions.

As big data producers, the cultural industries are also big knowledge producers about various aspects of media production, dissemination and reception. In the field of digital media knowledge production, we increasingly observe that companies, users, civil society and states have entered a battle over access to data that relates to inequalities and privileges of the use of related knowledge. Some of this knowledge is exclusively aggregated and used by the data owners, some is sold, for instance for the purpose of targeted advertisements, and some is shared with users on demand (like, for instance, through Google Analytics). Social media companies face increasingly conflicting demands, such as protecting private data from public knowledge on the one hand while making data that is considered to be of public interest accessible on the other, for instance by granting access to their APIs. Facebook, for instance, implemented an almost complete data lockdown in 2018 in response to the public outcry following the Cambridge Analytica scandal.[5] However, this created collateral damage for the possibility of conducting scientific research and acquiring knowledge about the dynamics of debates and user exchanges taking place on public sites. The privatization of Facebook data threatened to reduce public knowledge about social media communications that could be considered of high societal and democratic relevance. In 2020, Facebook reacted to demands to reopen API access for data retrieval by third parties. In an attempt to overcome the emerging divide between data-rich and data-poor research institutions, Facebook established Meta Research,[6] that should grant free access to content and user statistics from public sites to every researcher or journalist with a legitimate interest (such as independent research or investigative journalism).

Google were pioneers in developing a business strategy based on the accumulation and commercialization of private data, but, at the same time, the company has become a very rich and open information source, gathering knowledge about media and about what people are doing with it. Google wants you to use media for the price of receiving information about what you do with the media. Over the 2010s, Google have established a huge repository of media knowledge, which includes information about content, reach and individual users' needs and preferences. Google do, however, also share this knowledge and encourage its use as a mode to increase traffic on their websites. Google services are meant to facilitate the acquisition of knowledge but at the same time require users to build competences and know-how regarding navigation of the Internet. Google have contributed much to our understanding of the free Internet as a space of knowledge exchange by expropriating the holders of exclusive rights of information and their publishers: open access to libraries, to science, to news, to maps, but also to open services for the production and dissemination of knowledge such as free translations, free storage, free office programs and so on.

Individual media users are therefore not just raindrops washed away by the flows of big data. The infrastructures of the Internet require competences and knowledge to manoeuvre through the sea of big data. The value of big data and digital information sources is calculated in the way the data is used. This requires the application of technologies for the spread of data and the involvement of users in learning tools to enhance their capabilities. If online providers talk about the creativity of digital media use, they do not mean this as a slogan, but as a business mode. Like in any market, the commercialization of products cannot be exclusive. Digital markets depend on growth, which is measured in the expansion of traffic and use based on affordances and facilitating big data usage for everyone (Fuchs, 2014a). Social and interactive media are, therefore, indeed more demanding than classical mass media like television, used mainly for passive consumption. They require knowledgeable users to find content, engage with it or even produce it.

In the end, all users need to make their own private data management plans and need to know how to implement them through constant monitoring of their own patterns of consumption. Knowledge about managing one's own private data is part of our professional and personal life planning. This does not exclude power discrepancies between the data haves and the data have nots. Yet, there is a mutual dependency, and those who are rich and powerful in the possession of data can only profit from it by throwing it out and encouraging usage by others. Knowledge implies, therefore, something more than simply accumulated data. Knowledge relates to collective practices of interpretation and use of big data. To participate in the flow of digital data, media users need to be knowledgeable themselves. Building media knowledge and literacy has become essential as an individual survival strategy but also to keep the whole digital economy running. Knowledge about digital data use, functions and affordances is knowledge about the functioning of digital society and, as such, a key element of individual life planning, education and social orientation of individuals. We are not simply users of knowledge and information but are meaningfully engaged in the production of knowledge affecting all aspects of social life. This implies that we can also acquire critical knowledge of the clash between data-rich elites and the blind masses. We can identify the exclusive holders of knowledge who play off their specialization to extract data and information from the uncritical masses.

The renaissance of critical media studies

In facing the challenges of contemporary media transformations and disruptions, critical media studies have experienced an unexpected resurgence, and this despite the fact that the ideologies on which critical media studies were traditionally based are no longer in demand (Fuchs, 2016). The advent of digital media is a chance for critical media studies to redefine itself as a popular science rather than a niche academic discipline upheld by Marxist scholars (Taylor and Harris, 2007; Ott and Mack, 2020). The knowledge produced by critical media studies is practical knowledge that can be used for political mobilization and the development of resilient forms of public sphere resurgence, which we will analyse in Chapter 5.

The discipline of media and communication studies was a latecomer that was never fully embraced as an independent discipline in social science faculties. Even today, many universities still consider media studies to be part of humanities with a focus on media aesthetics and genres, but with minimal attention to the study of the material conditions of media production and the social and political implications of media use and reception. In our contemporary mediatized world, this struggle for emancipation as an independent discipline within the social sciences is probably lost. Media scholars cannot claim a monopoly of expertise in the analysis and explanation of media functioning and effects. In the analysis of contemporary media dysfunctions and disruptions, they rely on collaboration with other disciplines, since *all* social sciences have begun to investigate media functioning and effects. Knowledge production about media and its effects has become more than ever an interdisciplinary field. The dramatic scenario of enhanced impact of media, and the urgency of the social problems posed by media, are becoming the guiding narrative of the contemporary analysis of politics, society and culture.

Evidence for the centrality of critical media expertise can be found in the development of study curricula in psychology, economics, sociology and political science programmes at our universities since the early 2000. Within psychology, knowledge of critical media studies has become essential for understanding socialization processes, the addictive use of social media and gaming, new forms of psychological disorders and mental health (Wallace, 2016; Bian et al, 2019). In psychiatry, no therapy could be done without critical consideration of personal media use, which requires that practising psychologists acquire detailed knowledge of media content, patterns of media consumption and media effects. Within sociology, media consumption patterns explain transformations of family life, work, leisure and recreational activities. In the ninth edition of their widely used sociology handbook, Giddens and Sutton (2021) dedicate one separate chapter to the media but at the same time acknowledge the growing impact of digital technologies and social media in other chapters when dealing with the classical subfields of sociological research.

As these examples demonstrate, in much of contemporary sociology, media studies are no longer a niche of micro studies of individual user behaviour and consumption but offer a macro-sociological perspective of new media communications as a main structuring element of what is called the digital society (Lindgren, 2017). There is a growing demand for media expertise, not simply in the form of knowledge of technologies needed for the production or dissemination of content but increasingly in the form of skills of critical assessment of media effects and impact. Media competences are redefined in a way to also include capacities of risk assessment of media effects. This does not necessarily mean that our tools of analysis have become more sophisticated to better understand media effects and predict media development. There is an overall agreement that media are gaining in importance, but there is also growing uncertainty about how to study them. The disruption of public spheres has also disrupted the mainstream paradigm of mass communication studies and 'media effects' research (Mancini, 2012; Lang, 2013). Critical media studies promote a diagnosis that does not stop with the identification of disrupted media communication and predict chain reactions of disrupted identities, politics and democracy that cannot be understood by single disciplines. Under the assumption that media have ever more far-reaching effects, 'media effects' research has, at the same time, entered into a deep crisis that not only concerns the methodologies to be applied but also the underlying epistemologies of media studies, which have abandoned simple assumptions about causality. The more media are expected to have an impact, the less we as media scholars seem to be prepared to understand and explain media effects through simple causal analysis. This puts critical media studies under constraint as the complexity of its model's assumptions can no longer meet the growing public expectations, namely that media effects should be understood, predicted and attributed.

Ironically, we have less and less certainty about media effects in the digital age, and still our predictions about the expected impact of media communications are more far-reaching than ever. The diagnoses of contemporary society and democracy are all based on some extrapolated assumptions about media effects and impact, but at the same time, accountability and causality cannot be established, which might be one of the reasons why we frequently recur to vague formulas such as postmodern society, post-democracy, illiberal democracy, flawed democracy, post-factual democracy, the post-truth or post-reality society.

Critical media studies have always been understood as a form of empowerment: the tools of assessment of media performance give the power back to critical publics, enabling them to turn media production and the media performance of their representatives into constant objects of evaluation. Critical media studies' main contribution would thus consist of spreading such skills and capacities of critical media evaluation. Critical media studies as a widespread practice would thus add to the accountability of government in the sense of what Rosanvallon (2008: 33–56) analyses as institutionalized forms of distrust and counter-democracy through the media's watchdog function. Critical media studies are ultimately nothing more than an engine for the formation of critical publics. They allow individuals *through* the media to become vigilant citizens, critical *of* the media.

The everyday use of media knowledge: media literacy, fear and resistance

Digital media developments are accompanied by the call for more media literacy that is needed to emancipate individual online users and raise awareness of opportunities and risks of digital media use (Kress, 2003). Media literacy education is defined as a priority, serving the double purpose of risk prevention and skill enhancement. As such, the target groups of media education are, on the one hand, vulnerable persons in need of protection from the perils of digital media usage, including manipulation, misinformation, prejudices, sexualization, cyberbullying, loss of privacy and cyber-criminality. On the other hand, media education programmes are meant to build a civic culture of media literates who develop capacities to engage in creative media production and usage to compete on global markets (Jenkins et al, 2009). What is often overlooked in these pioneering programmes of media education for future generations is that media literacy has already been enhanced at unprecedented degrees, involving fast-learning individuals and entire groups of the population. Never before have media users been exposed to such a stock of accumulated experiences and information. Their socialization with media has turned them into knowledgeable users engaged in life-long learning through ever-changing media formats and content. Knowledge and expertise about digital media use are, for instance, shared among generations (Lee and Kim, 2018). Older generations will often consult their grandchildren for advice on technology, placing the younger generation in the role of IT and social media experts. In higher education classes, instructors may rely on the specialized knowledge of their students to discuss the functionality of new apps, or to understand the impact of digital innovations. It is equally misleading to assume that media expertise is secreted away within particular niches, or that it only develops within very narrow areas of specialization. On the contrary, we observe that knowledge is widespread, covering different aspects of media production, diffusion and reception. To be able to navigate the web, single media users must often accumulate experiences and knowledge, not only about the application of particular digital technologies but also about modalities of usage, possible audience responses and expected media effects.

Such accumulated media knowledge becomes, in other words, part of everyday knowledge. It is an everyday knowledge that is not only based on individual experiences paired with intuition but results from processes of collective interpretation, shared sources of information and life-long learning. Knowledge about the contours of the digital public sphere is essential for successfully navigating the web and for orientating oneself in this shared social world, as well as being a condition for successful life planning, personal development and success. We are all cartographers of the digital public sphere.

The use of digital media technologies often presupposes knowledgeable media users. There is a demand for media knowledge and expertise, and media users need to develop individual and collective strategies to meet this demand. Media users themselves produce knowledge about media, engage with content and collect experience with media use. The challenge of media literacy becomes a personal challenge for those many who, in one way or another, work with media. As the boundaries between media professionals and non-professionals are increasingly blurred, the passive media consumer is replaced by creative users with capacities to build their own strategies of distinctive media use. Schools and educational institutions adapt to these new market demands by educating young adults as media experts and raising media competence and media literacy as part of the education canon of the new middle classes, who define social status through distinctive media practices.

Learning by media users also takes place in reflecting about their experiences – their own incompetence and loss of power. The way society as a whole talks about the public sphere and media disruptions is, in fact, an effect of enhanced knowledge about media. Only those who know about the possible impact of media can diagnose the deficits of media performance and functioning. These inversed effects of media knowledge and literacy can also have a bearing on people's trust in media. The global trend of growing mistrust in media institutions would thus not simply be irrational but, on the contrary, reflect the growth of knowledge about media (Trenz, 2021). People know why they should mistrust the media, and people also increasingly learn to fear the media and collect selective evidence that confirms their fears. Media literacy programmes might, in this sense, not only have the desired effect of educating people to safely use the media but might also increase their feelings of unease regarding their personal use of the media (Koltay, 2011).

We need more research on the processes of how media users, through intensive processes of socialization with media, accumulate critical knowledge about media functions and malfunctions, and how this knowledge not only shapes patterns of trust and mistrust in media or has effects on personal well-being but is also turned into collective forms of mobilization and contention that can help, for instance, to articulate demands for media policies and regulation. Media knowledge and literacy are a necessity, often even a survival strategy, in the digital world. At the same time, various forms of user-generated knowledge have become an essential part of the functioning of media institutions and, as such, are increasingly used for the production and dissemination of media content. Apart from the possibility of collective mobilization, the growing mistrust in media can also be read as a form of democratic oversight of critical news readers engaging in democratic counter-politics by insisting on the use of public reason by media industries who mainly sell news for entertainment and scandal (Rosanvallon, 2008).

From a user and audience perspective, resilience often means developing techniques to navigate the new media. Entering the new, complex world of digital media is often combined with experiences of disorientation (Carpentier et al, 2013). This not only requires building media literacy and capacities to 'read media' but also 'learning to fear' the media, an essential part of the process. Digital users generate knowledge and critique that is born out of their fear of media. The experience of dependency on media knowledge and content creates ambivalent feelings of love and hate, of embracing particular media products while fearing, at the same time, the power of the tech giants over us: 'Who's Afraid of Google? Everyone', asks the American business journalist Kevin Kelleher.[7]

Feeling a sense of unease with media has become an everyday concern of many people. The more people make use of media, the more they find reasons to fear the media. What does 'media fear' imply? Media have been found to contribute to 'cultures of fear', for instance in the way they cover crime as a social problem (Altheide, 1997). On a more personal level, fear might be related to lack of knowledge about media operations and the opacity of media organizations as an anonymous power that takes control over private lives. For most people, such existential fear might be grounded in experiences of the negative impact of media content or use on their own lives or social environments. People might feel that media content is inappropriate or media use excessive, damaging their own life, professions, families or communities. Such fear in relation to new media and their unknown effects often gives rise to generational conflicts, for instance in the ways youngsters make use of a new media technology that their parents suspect can have damaging effects. In other instances, the widespread fear of new and social media is itself mediated and informed more by negative headlines about new media scandals or abuses of power than direct personal repercussions of negative effects or repercussions of media use. In other instances, fear of media becomes 'existential', related to diffuse feelings of loss of control or loss of orientation. FOMO (Fear of Missing Out) has been described as a social stress and disorder factor among social media users (Roberts and David, 2020). However, the opposite might also be true in that digital media users *learn* to fear the media, and that fear results from accumulated knowledge of media use and enhanced media literacy. We could speak in this case of an 'informed fear' that is shaped by individual and collective learning processes. Such learning of media users takes place in the experiences of dependencies and the loss of power that are reflected, thematized and rationalized, for instance through risk assessments and studies of impact. The more average media users become media literate, the more they find reason to feel uneasy about their own media use, culminating in learned fear of the media.

Fear as a motivational factor of social media use and experiences can thus be variably linked to knowledge of media functioning (and lack thereof). Fear is not simply irrational but can be rationalized and used in collective mobilizations. As such, fear is directly related to the control and surveillance logics of the digital world and of the many new dependencies it has created. There is, in other words, a correlation between the intensity of media use and media fear. The comfort and the commodity offered by digital media are at the same time nourishing feelings of unease with media. Some people might be literally lost in the media and collect increasingly direct negative experiences of media use. For others, such anxieties are rather the indirect effect of felt dependencies of media tools. This new ambivalence in our everyday relationship with digital media resembles the clinical diagnosis of schizophrenia: the more we are dependent on digital media functions and services, the more we suspect them of having malfunctions and disruptive effects on our well-being. The more such suspicions are expressed, the more they are confirmed. The more there is an 'objective need' to use the media, for instance in our professional life, but also in the way we build successful social relationships, the more we develop subjective fears of media failure. The more we need to trust the media and their services (in all their utilities and affordances), the more mistrust is created. The current unease with digital media is thus more than a vague feeling that something could go wrong: it is an outright fear of being confronted with an enormous giant that is suddenly everywhere, taking control over our lives and social environments.

It warrants mentioning that the focus of this book is not on personal disorders, but on public sphere disorders and their remedies. The development of a media psychology that could further explore this relationship between intensity of media use, dependencies and fear is not on our agenda. To carry the debate on public sphere dystopia forward, however, it is important to consider how personal experiences of digital media use are again feeding into public debates, thus laying the basis for a shared stock of knowledge and collective interpretations about digital media affordances, risks and opportunities. The needs of individual media users, and the expectations they have of digital media affordances, are not just private sentiments or individual dispositions. They matter as elements of critical discourse about digital media. From a public sphere perspective, the question, therefore, is not what type of psychological distress is created by digital media use and how individuals experience media disruptions, but what happens if people start evaluating and sharing their experiences in such a way that everybody is suddenly convinced that media and public communication are disrupted. Experiences of public sphere disruptions are not individual but discursive dispositions. They exist to the extent that they are expressed in a vocabulary that connects to the discursive repertoire of public criticism. The discourse of public sphere disruptions can only exist inside the public sphere; there is no 'outside' where such a discourse could find expression and be given shape.

Digital media usage has thus led to an expansion of critical scrutiny of media performance as an everyday practice of media users. We therefore need to understand the interlinkage between scientific and everyday knowledge production in the construction of the digital media reality (Berger and Luckmann, 1966). Both modes of objectified scientific observation, and everyday observation of public sphere disruptions, share the commonality that they are only made possible because they are increasingly filtered through the digital and social media infrastructures of the public sphere. There is an underlying process of digitalization of the process of knowledge production and diffusion. Put bluntly, we need digital media to be able to talk about our personal disruptive experiences with digital media, and we rely on digital media to share our expectations, concerns and anxieties. We further need to assume that there is a universe of meaning that connects us to digital media. The whole idea of a sharing culture is based on the assumption that we can shift roles as producers and recipients of media content and thus attribute shared meaning and interpretations to such content and consider it of shared relevance. This puts limits on the assumptions of a fragmented or deeply divided digital media world, where such divisions could no longer be marked as dysfunctional and disruptive. We always need to move within a shared world of collective interpretations, normative expectations and values about the ideal functioning of digital media. As digital media users, we need to take the position of critical observers who can expect, reasonably assume or even demand that the codes, scripts and programmes of digital content production are in congruence with this normative template. The difference between scientific observation and everyday observation of digital media disruptions is then only a technical one, not one that defines a fundamentally different epistemological status for our observations of public sphere disruptions.

Digital media technologies are a wonderful affordance for such everyday observations of public sphere disruptions in the way that they constantly engage ordinary users to become critical observers of media performance. Critical scrutiny of digital media performance and functioning is not only an optional feature of 'more sophisticated' media usage but is also an essential skill and requirement for successfully navigating the web. Social media users are, for instance, encouraged to rank themselves – 'applying tools' to improve their media performance and compare themselves with others. The scientific tools of media criticism become a common tool, which also means that the privileged position of scientific observation of the construction of media reality becomes a common good. If there is an equalizing and democratizing effect of digital media affordances, it may well lie in this facilitation of everyday critical observation of media content, usage.

4

Between Dystopia and Utopia: The Social and Political Field of Public Sphere Criticism

How to be critical in a digital media world?

The argument in the previous chapter was that public sphere disruptions are not part of an abstract knowledge that is reserved to media and communication experts but are experienced by members of the audience in everyday media use. The dystopia of the public sphere is a lived experience of those individuals and publics who populate the public sphere. The question I will address in the following is what media users do with this type of media knowledge. This means that I will need to approach the social field of public sphere criticism as a field of political struggle. The task in this chapter will be to identify the positioning of actors and their motivations to become involved in political struggles about media. Such struggles can be about: media content and representations, media policies and regulation, and access to and participation in media.

By raising this question of the social and political field of public sphere criticism, I depart from the narrow confines of media research to explore the full potential of public sphere research as a theoretical foundation of digital society and its rapid transformation. Within communication studies, we traditionally perceive of audiences as receptacles of media content. In social media research, for instance, online audiences are often seen as manifestations of public sphere dystopia, blind followers of the populists, echo chambers, bubbles and originators of hate (Pariser, 2011; Helles et al, 2015). Such a notion of audiences is incongruent with the notion of the public, which is not distinguished by reception but by critical reflection (Splichal, 2012). Whereas disrupted audiences are often quoted as evidence for dystopia, the public is a driver of utopia. A public can also engage in subversive practices or undermine values; yet, in so doing, it is norm-guided and recouples to a utopian vision of society and democracy. A public is constituted by reacting to the troubles to which it is exposed. It is not disruptive, but corrective, otherwise it ceases to be a public.

In the positioning of audiences and publics, we again find the interlinkage between dystopian and utopian elements as a driving force of public sphere transformations. Digital media users and audiences, can, as is often done, be seen as manifestations of dystopia, as for instance in the way their privacy is taken away, or how they are manipulated through disinformation campaigns and often react in irrational ways through expressions of hate. This overlooks how audience members can also experience dystopia, thematize it, raise it in public debates and thus become critical publics. Digital media users and audiences, in this last sense, are also drivers of utopia. Media critique is something that has become widespread and common. It binds people together; it is a practice of collective interpretation. We should turn the field of media and public sphere critique into our research topic: How do ordinary people live and experience public sphere disruptions? How do they thematize and debate them, and what makes their critical judgements possible, and with what kinds of political effects?

I have argued that the digital public sphere needs to be understood as being shaped by contradictory developments: there is no linear, one-directional transformation of the traditional public sphere based on legacy media. We can rarely draw neat distinctions between functions and dysfunctions, since digital public spheres are found to be fluid, transitory and hybrid. The digital public sphere is also not a second degree or higher degree public sphere. Digitalization is rather inscribed into the very infrastructure of the modern public sphere and democracy, not something new and revolutionary that challenges it from the outside (Nassehi, 2019).

While all this is well known, we tend to overlook how these contradictory developments are also a structuring element of the social field of public sphere criticism. Digital media enable and disable critique; they empower and disempower users; they are experienced as opportunities and as constraints for the satisfaction of personal and social needs. The critical debate about digital media, and its pervasive effects on society and democracy, is not taking place outside the digital sphere in an external and autonomous space; it is inscribed into the digital media infrastructures and dynamics. There are no sharp distinctions between dystopia and utopia; instead, there are constant overlaps. There is a great diversity of democratic practices in which the old and the new, the dystopian and the utopian elements constantly overlap. There is an inbuilt ambivalence between creative and disruptive media content and use, which is translated at the same time into civic activism and disillusionment with politics. This raises the principal question: How can you be critical of digital media if this critique is at the same time expressed through digital media?

In confronting this uncertainty about media effects, the parameters of critical discourse about the public sphere are determined by the need to

(a) establish the value of information, (b) balance the privateness–publicness of information and (c) enhance the possibilities of empowerment of individual media users and collectives. The struggle is about truth, access (inclusion) and affordances.

I intend to describe the field of social and political struggles of digital media criticism through the ambivalence of dystopia and utopia as manifested in three paradoxes that distinguish contemporary public sphere transformations. A paradox is understood, in the classical sense, as an argument built on two contradictory premises that can both claim validity, but at the same time, invalidate each other (Sorensen, 2003). In the struggle over the formation of digital society and democracy, I can make two opposing statements about the properties of digital media technologies and their impact and provide reasoned arguments to show that statement 1 holds true without invalidating statement 2. Accordingly, I can claim that digital media technologies inform and misinform, weaken and strengthen publicity and privacy, and empower and disempower users. In the following, I will discuss the *information–disinformation paradox*, the *privacy–publicity paradox*, and the *empowerment–disempowerment paradox* as three manifestations of contradictory developments that shape contemporary digital media and public sphere transformations.

The information–disinformation paradox

Digital media technologies account for a general information surplus paired with net-information losses. They build on the premise of open information, that is, information made accessible for everybody. Still, information remains a scarce resource. Digital media are meant to enhance transparency yet at the same time are found to be untransparent. The amount of information increases, while its value decreases. An abundance of news is available, but news has become increasingly unreliable and non-accessible for practical use, exposing media users to the risk of disinformation.

Digital media technologies are constant data providers. They collect and bundle existing data from all kinds of sources but also produce data in large amounts that would not exist without them. This is done in such a way as to turn the world into an observable place, but it also adds to the world in specific ways. The information universe of the digital media world is expansive, not simply in the way it explores existing places and turns analogue into digital data. The ambition is clearly to turn the entire analogue world into a digital format, like written texts, books or music, but the digital world is potentially larger and more expansive. Through digital data generators, online data archives are growing exponentially, while the analogue world remains stable. A computer program can produce a Beethoven-style symphony 200 years after the death of the composer, and there exists very reliable text-generating software that produces news articles or even philosophical essays.

Digital data generators expand both reality and virtuality. Information that is shared on social media can relate, in the classical sense, to external facts or events, like for instance, a news article, be it written by a journalist or a machine. Yet, shared social media content increasingly also builds interlinkages to other social media content: hyperlinks provide interlinkages between digital data points, and hashtags are used to connect to social media topics and debates (Jackson et al, 2020). To be able to navigate the web, users increasingly rely on information about what happens online. The social world as an observable place is constantly expanding through digital media, while the physical world as an observable space remains restricted. This means that digital media technologies do not simply retrieve data from existing sources but open up new sources of self-generated data that is used, found relevant and made profitable. On social media, for instance, news can be shared about external events, such as an earthquake, but increasingly news also refers to social media events, such as online firestorms or 'shitstorms'. Digital media technologies retrieve information from different sources, and it becomes more and more difficult to establish whether the location of these sources is external or internal to digital media. The difference between the operation of data retrieval from external sources and data production through internal proceedings becomes increasingly blurred. Digital media technologies are applied social constructivism. The social world through the gaze of digital media is no longer simply an object of observation; it is constituted through observation. You can no longer take an external social media observatory position and retrieve data from specific online places; you can only enter these places as a user who intervenes and constantly adds data that constitutes and perpetuates these places. Such observation-intervention applies to physical places: through a live webcam, the physical reality of a town square becomes digitalized, but at the same time, the digitalization through the webcam changes the physical space in particular ways, adds to it by expanding social experiences or takes away by limiting, for instance, the sense of smell (all depending on the observatory perspective).

Similar to the way physical places are observed by visitors, single media users in virtual spaces are also turned into objects of observation. A user is taken as a unit of data that has a specific value for digital media companies. The way this data is turned into value is in itself a form of media usage that feeds back and intervenes in shaping the user's personality, private life and social context. The effects of such interventions on user behaviour again become important objects of observation, and thus of new data retrieval. The various ways information is retrieved through digital media generate new information that becomes relevant for digital media operations.

If the whole world is turned into an observatory space, the world inevitably suffers from information surplus. Marres (2017: chapter 1) speaks of a digital deluge: a wealth of data that can be used, but is not necessarily used. The datafication of social life leads to an overproduction of data that reaches beyond social life, that is, beyond what is manageable by the data retrievers to be processed, interpreted and given social meaning in a particular social context. Ever more selective mechanisms need to be applied to sort through what is being observed. At the same time, because the whole world is observable, it is also always potentially observed by someone, which becomes part of the individual awareness of users. They know that by retrieving data from digital media, they constantly contribute to the generation of new data. Their data reception generates new valuable information. This does not necessarily hold exclusively for companies who track user behaviour through cookies. In a much more elementary sense, this holds true for all forms of social media usage which primarily consist of 'lurking' in other people's profiles to get an update about other users' activities. Social media proliferate through observing what other people do on social media, and social media companies are keen to share this information with other users, for instance by listing liked pages, recent activities or highlighting comments by others. All traces left on social media can be turned into content to be shared with others. The transparent user, nevertheless, remains non-transparent and only visible as a digital personality that is shaped by platform content and affordances. The consumer of digital pornography or the participant in video gaming shapes a digital personality with specific preferences or patterns of behaviour that would not exist without digital media and are constantly transformed by the platform with all its content and affordances. It is therefore inaccurate to say that digital media turn the world into an observable place because it is the observation of a place that constitutes the shared social world in the first place.

To understand how data is shared, it further needs to be pointed out that observation is not only performed by individual users but is a genuinely social observation. My observation is embedded in a shared observatory space. Take, for instance, the example of GPS and location apps. Through Google Maps and Google Earth, I can find information about remote places, but I can also access and experience them, receive updated pictures or, through a live webcam, participate in street events. Or take the website for my university, which informs users about academic staff, research, publications and courses. In addition, academic events are offered as live events, teaching takes place on interactive platforms or the library through online access opens to the world of books. The online university also expands, and academic publications are made available through open platforms and apps such as ResearchGate, academia.edu or Google Books, which store world knowledge and make it openly accessible.

The Internet can be described as a self-generating data machine (Nassehi, 2019). This holds true, in particular, for the smart technology of the 'Internet of Things' and its machine-to-machine communications (Greengard, 2015). A smart phone app retrieves data from a toaster and uses it as information that helps other gadgets in the household become smarter. Not only in the Internet of things but also in everyday social media activities, the usage of data is at the same time the motor for the generation of new data. The Facebook timeline is set up for information updates about the social environment of individual users, their participation in cultural and political life, their belonging to a neighbourhood, an urban community, a nation and the globe. For the average user, what counts is not solely daily updates, but minute-by-minute usages to satisfy a broad range of information needs, from professional activities to public life or private entertainment. At the same time, the use of this data and the various activities linked to data usage (such as clicking, liking, sharing, commenting or chatting) produce endless flows of new data that is of potential use for the Internet provider, the social media platform, third parties linked to it (like advertisers) or individual users and their friends' networks (Bossetta et al, 2017).

The abundance of information is often said to increase the risk of disinformation. Yet, there is some confusion about what we mean when we say that digital data, or modes of data processing, inform or disinform. As we cannot say that data is void of information, we need to establish the difference between information and disinformation by its modes of usage. Using data means connecting it to the communicative exchange of meaning about the shared social (and intrinsically, also physical) world. In terms used by Niklas Luhmann (2000), we can say that information is a form that results from observation. Such observation is not a single event, limited to time, space or a particular individual, but the ongoing operation of a social system. A family, for instance, establishes routines of close observation among its members, including their intimate relationships. At the same time, a family is observed by others (other families, friends, schools, welfare systems, the state) as being more or less intact, closed and persisting over time. Through digitalization, a social space becomes constantly observable through data that is automatically generated, can be retrieved remotely through binary, digitalized codes, and can be stored. Digital data provide a universal language for observation, yet to establish the 'value' of information, of such raw data, and to turn it into meaningful observation of something, digital media remain embedded in processes of cultural interpretation and normative evaluation.

In the following, I propose differentiating between digital data that conveys information, non-information and disinformation (Trenz, 2023). *Information* relates to any digital data that is turned into an object of observation about the social world. As such, it is typically followed up by communication. *Non-information* relates to data generated by digital media with a potential to be observed. This relates, for instance, to the accumulation and endless recombination of data that are facilitated by digital media technologies, but that, for the time being, are not activated by any social system and connected to ongoing processes of communication. Not everything that digital media technologies do is observed and talked about. A webcam can produce infinite amounts of digital data about what is going on in a particular physical space, but these data remain non-information as long as nobody picks them up. Only if someone with access to these data asks what happened at a particular time at that location is information generated. *Disinformation*, finally, is neither non-observation nor non-communication. On the contrary, it can only result from previous observation, and needs to be communicated. As such, it can best be approached as a specific form of information that is valued with regard to shared cultural patterns and normative standards. The standards used are those established by the modern public sphere, as codified, for instance, in ethical guides of journalism, or in the discourse ethics of communicative rationality. Disinformation is qualified information. This qualification process is a public sphere test of validity. It is information that is confronted with claims of generalized validity.

Let us first turn to the case of non-information, that is, the case of the non-usage of data. Digital data is constantly produced and recombined by machines, but it is not necessarily picked up and used by someone to mark a distinction and denote something. Digital data contain the potential of usage. There is always a potential that existing data could inform about something. This potential is activated by turning data into information about something, that is, marking them as an observation of something in ongoing communication. If non-information relates to all potentially available data, we need to face the logical impossibility that we cannot see it without turning it into information about something. When we start looking for it, and search for non-information in the endless flow of data, we continuously produce information. As soon as we identify something as non-information, it starts to inform about something (even in the minimal sense that it does not inform). The idea that digital data contain 'unused' information is, in fact, widespread in the public discourse about big data, and implied in the call to explore it as a potential source of knowledge that can drive economies, empower citizens and improve government (Lupton, 2014: 95).

The second case of information, therefore, relates to all kinds of data usage. Usage means turning data into information. In information science, this process is referred to as 'making data intelligent': information is generated in the transfer from 'raw data' to 'analysed data' (Räsänen and Nyce, 2013). Forms of data usage, however, are not restricted to the analytical operations of specialized data processers. For Niklas Luhmann, information results from any kind of communication as a selective reference to the social world (Luhmann,

1992). Data need to be attached to observation, and such observation can be activated by anyone, at any time. The act of observation takes away the neutral and indefinite character of data and demarcates a space of relevance: a distinction for what type of observation this data stands for. Digital data simply collect potential points of demarcation of the world; information, instead, is a specific demarcation of the world. Observation would, however, be wrongly understood as an operation that simply picks up available data or recombines it in a particular social context. Observation simultaneously generates new data through its forms of activation and recombination. We can observe how information is generated and what people do with information. We can observe how other people observe the social world by making use of particular data sources and selecting information as relevant or non-relevant. Digital media platforms offer, in fact, numerous possibilities for such meta-observations. The attraction of social media lies precisely in the possibilities it offers to observe people observing the social world. The facilitation of this form of meta-communication, which allows for societal self-observation, has always been a key to the understanding of public sphere dynamics (Trenz, 2005). The social media public sphere only amplifies these possibilities, and, as such, becomes the meta-public sphere for societal self-observation. It is based on multiple observations by users that constantly generate infinite amounts of new data. As such, it is imploding with data that inform about observations performed by its own users. Whatever information is retrieved by a user is turned into new information for other users. My Google searches, or my Facebook clicks to access content, even gain economic value and can be traded by companies for profit.

Let us now turn to the case of disinformation. As information can only relate to other forms of information, disinformation must also be considered as a form of information; it is not non-information (Nassehi, 2019: 99–107). This means that disinformation relates to the usage of data in ongoing communications that observe and interpret the social world and contribute to shared knowledge and meaning. Disinformation is the specific case of information that is identified as wrong. It results from a meta-observation that information which is retrieved from the flow of data is connected by users in wrong ways or misused. Disinformation thus implies an attribution of responsibility for the wrong use of information. It is a form of usage of data that is interpreted as wrong because of being non-factual or truthless. Such a 'mistake' can be attributed to particular people who make 'wrong' usage of information either because they lack the capacities for correct usage or are morally corrupted and have wrongful intentions. This interpretation of *wrong* information usage in the form of disinformation is thus used to remind us of the *correct* use of information. Disinformation, in this sense, is intrinsically linked to corrective measures, such as the call for truth or the right use of data.

The possibility of distinguishing between correct and wrong usage of information is thus intrinsically social and not in any way pre-established by the world of facts or science. These distinctions are meant to order the flow of information, to steer it and give it direction, and to focus attention on what is considered to be of relevance. As such, the meta-distinction between information and disinformation is a basic public sphere operation which is not simply in need of scientific proof but of public justification (Scholl, 2019).

This does not yet explain why the impression prevails that digital media have increased the risk of disinformation. The Internet public sphere no longer informs but confuses and implies serious risks of disinformation. In the digital information economy, the overflow of information decreases its value. The more information becomes available and accessible, the higher the risk of disinformation, that is, the possibility that information is taken up and used in social contexts that are experienced as disruptive and disconnecting. Analogue public spheres build on an economy of scarcity of information that is made available through approved channels at a controlled price. A filter applies in the application of the distinction between information and disinformation that is collectively identified and interpreted. Digital public spheres build on an economy of information overload that is constantly retrieved from endless flows of data through multiple channels and at fluctuating prices. This often makes the distinction between information and disinformation ad-hoc and contested. No filters apply that would allow us to sort out what has been approved and what has not.

The realm of observation is by default larger than the realm of communication. Observation takes place all the time, and data are produced, but communication does not necessarily follow. Observation therefore always leaves us with data overflows, potential information that could have been selected as relevant and can still be turned into meaningful communication at any time. Such data overflows are a missed opportunity and a potentiality. Digital media technologies function as potential information providers in the form of data that can be retrieved by others in often open and accessible ways. Information providers need to confront the problem of the insufficiencies of existing information processers and receivers. To make digital data manageable for personal use, providers rely on algorithms or filtering machines to manage big data flows. As our reliance on information filters increases, the amount of information that is filtered out also increases. This means that digital media technologies do not simply inform but also create non-used spaces of information. These spaces of non-information are filled up with all the data that could potentially inform about something, but for whatever pertinent reason, are filtered out as irrelevant. A digital video camera that monitors a public space, for instance, creates a space of potential information that can be, but is not necessarily, retrieved by someone. In a similar way, many aspects of social life are turned into quantifiable data, like our friendships and interests on social media, our casual conversations on chats, our search operations on Google and even our emotional responses to content in the form of liking or disliking. All this creates parallel spaces of information and non-information. These spaces are overcrowded with data that are never fully explored but not necessarily ignored. Even as data that are momentarily not used, and therefore do not inform, they still *could* be used by someone at any time for communication about the shared social world.

The increase of information correlates with an exponential increase in non-information. Digital media technologies produce ever-expanding surplus amounts of observation data but reduce the likelihood that communication follows. The rule seems to apply that in digital data processing, information is produced at a higher speed than it can be processed. The more data is generated by machines, the more the filters that decide what momentarily informs and does not inform need to be narrowed down. As content providers, digital media platforms have become our principal information sources and main channels for the dissemination of knowledge about the shared social world, yet on the receiving end, capacities of information management remain restricted. As the data sources multiply, the flow of data diversifies through multiple channels and platforms. This does not exclude the possibility of mass reception of some content, but it still leaves us with a great deal of other content that escapes the attention of the public. Large amounts of digital data that are processed by machines make the world of selected data that are experienced and found relevant appear smaller. In the case of traditional mass media, a shared information space and a common worldview were essentially formed by the selection of a handful of designated information providers. The construction of social reality was still heavily biased, as critical media studies continued to emphasize, but there was a socializing community effect in the way the same selective bias applied to (almost) everybody. In the case of digital media, not only do the selective biases of information providers multiply; information is further filtered by data receivers and their personalized schemes of data management. Depending on reception, the same data will inform some and not inform many. The size of those who are not informed by digital data is, by default, larger than the size of the few who retrieve particular information from data. There is always a surplus of digital data, increasing the risk of missing out on something for those who seek reliable information about what is to be considered as relevant knowledge about our shared social world.

The multiplication of selection biases in the processing and reception of digital data is one side of the coin. The other side is the enhanced contestation of the information value that decides on the relevance of the data for the shared stock of knowledge of the community at stake. Digital media users and related groups tend to disagree about the way information 'informs'.

The claim for information is no longer exclusive but becomes competitive. Competing claims about what informs, or should inform, are confronted with counter claims about data that disinform, are abused, retrieved in the wrong way or misinterpreted. Such contestation typically takes place in the paradigm struggles between different epistemic communities that link knowledge of science back to political power to inform political decision-making, as for instance in world politics when governments and NGOs discuss the effects of climate change or the risks of nuclear energy (Antoniades, 2003). Digital media have a tendency to expand such paradigm struggles to intergroup conflicts in a way that is increasingly detached from debates within science (van Dijck, 2014). By devaluing news, the information surplus of the digital age accounts for the contestation of the criteria of newsworthiness. The new uncertainty about what informs and what disinforms is linked to political struggles among opponents who discredit certain news sources.

The information–disinformation paradox is best illustrated in recent trends of journalism and news-making (Humprecht et al, 2020). Digital transformations mean changes in the political economy of news distribution. There is an *abundance of news* that is accessible to all. At the same time, there is no parallel increase in the *demand for news*. It is not that people necessarily turn away from news – they still demand to be informed, but as news is on offer almost everywhere, this demand can be mostly met by free supply, for instance through news apps such as Google News. The larger the information supply, the lower the market value of news (Picard, 2010).

In facing the digital transformation, quality journalism loses its monopoly as a provider and gatekeeper of news (Tandoc, 2014). The current crisis of journalism is not explained by the shortage of news but rather by its abundance (de Mateo et al, 2010; McChesney and Pickard, 2013; Newman et al, 2015; Wahl-Jorgensen et al, 2016). The multiplication of news puts established journalism under constraint because news selection is increasingly de-institutionalized and diversified. For individual news readers, this can mean a gain in autonomy over news, one that is paired, however, with decreased feelings of belonging to a shared newsroom. Algorithms select news in a much more reliable way than journalists do when it comes to the satisfaction of individual needs and preferences. Such decisions about news selection taken by algorithms are, at the same time, decisions about newsworthiness. The value of news is established in correspondence with individual users' demands and in disregard of shared values and criteria of relevance. Gains in individual autonomy come at the price of losses of collective bonds and liability. Algorithmic news selection remains, therefore, a poor replacement for professional quality checks of the value of information by journalism. It further violates core public sphere principles, which are established in the creation of social bonds and generalized validity through engagement in shared discourse. The information value of news not only has significance for the sustainability of journalism (both in economic and symbolic terms); it is also coupled with the idea of shared values and the collective commitment of a community of news readers who identify as citizens of a democratic polity.

The changing political economy of journalism ultimately explains changes in the working routines of journalism to deliver quality news products. The devalued product of news needs to be economized through processes that reduce the costs of news-making. Content that is delivered at high speed and low cost informs in different ways from content that is the outcome of deliberate editorial choices and quality checks. The *information value* of news is thus increasingly detached from the *validity* of news as a product that has been tested by the authority of journalistic standards of fact-finding, proof and argumentation. Individual news readers increasingly experience news as unreliable and untrustworthy, which again reinforces the trend for readers to turn away from news (Alexander et al, 2016). Journalism responds by spreading news through multiple platforms, which is often not the creative solution out of this dilemma but rather a form of 'creative destruction', as it leads to a further loss of control over distribution, and thus a further devaluation of news (Schlesinger and Doyle, 2015). In journalism studies, there are many accounts of how the professional work of news-making has become increasingly precarious. Many newspapers, for instance, have cut funding for investigative journalism or reduced the number of foreign correspondents, which has had serious repercussions for the availability of foreign news (Terzis, 2014). Critical media scholars speak in this regard of the death or download spiral of journalism, meaning that the structural and economic crisis of news organizations reinforces the aversion of audiences and further reduces the demand for journalistic products, with even fewer people ready to pay for quality news (McChesney, 2016). As a result, while news distribution and consumption spaces are opened up, the spaces where quality news is made and exchanged have been further restricted.

In the political realm, the information–disinformation paradox is paired with the enhanced transparency of democratic governments. The democratization and digitalization of government (or governance) are mutually reinforcing processes in the generation of information surpluses (Boehme-Neßler, 2020). The more governments become transparent, the more they send out information. The more governments become digitalized, the more information is generated and made available, in an unfiltered way, through direct access from online government platforms. Information about governmental activities or legislative processes is abundant, and interested citizens can search on any ministry or parliamentary website for proceedings, reports, briefings and minutes that are made available for public use. Facebook democracy has been described as an 'architecture of disclosure' (Marichal, 2012), where political representatives all too readily share information about their public and private lives (Stanyer, 2013). Spaces of secrecy become restricted, and activities are defined as public and open by default and, as such, are richly documented through textual and visual material.

Despite the enhanced transparency of democratic governments, electorates do not necessarily gain in knowledge and understanding of democratic processes. The political world remains an arcane one for those who do not experience closeness or meaningful involvement in political decision-making. The enhanced transparency of democratic government, therefore, produces first and foremost non-used spaces of information. The new transparency of democratic government is not enhanced by journalism or professional mediators either, but through self-publishing activities. The hugely enhanced transparency of democratic government remains largely unnoticed, as the publics that invest their time in, or have the specialized knowledge necessary to follow this constant flow of information, remain very small. Publishing no longer takes place on demand but is unsolicited. As such, the data that are produced about the activities of democratic government do not pass the hurdle of news. They remain non-information in a space of non-attention to democratic politics.

The unfiltered information abundance about democratic governments not only results in data redundancies. It also increases the risks of disinformation, that is, of the disruptive use of information in the democratic process. Such disruptions can be observed, for instance, in the randomized processes of news selection. Reach and attention is amplified to unprecedented degrees with hyper-attention for some highly selective news stories shared through social media among hundreds of thousands of readers, while many other stories go unnoticed, or mainly come to the attention of niche audiences. Users here face a double risk of disinformation: first, they risk missing out on something that could be of potential relevance but is not shared through any of the platforms they are using or highlighted by their personalized algorithm. Secondly, they risk journalistic standards not being met by their information providers and being served up 'false' news. In the 'fake news' debate, critical media scholars are typically concerned with this last aspect of an unfiltered amplification of unchecked news, namely lies and conspiracies (Broersma, 2013; Hendricks and Vestergaard, 2018). However, this 'fake news' threat not only results from the malign intentions of some selected new providers; it is also linked to the information overload and the de-institutionalized process of news aggregation.

In the traditional public sphere of mass media, processes of news selection and interpretation of a shared world of knowledge were highly centralized and steered from above. This led citizens to become dependent on journalism as a trusted and reliable institution that organizes news selection for the whole of society under the assumption that only a few content producers serve the needs of the great majority as information receivers. People were still exposed to the risks of journalists 'missing things out' or 'getting things wrong', but these were largely compensated for by the democratizing effects of mass media, which equalized the reception of knowledge and information with a potential to enhance cognitive capacities for all. Such an enlightened public sphere was never perfect, yet existing hierarchies and social divisions in the production and distribution of knowledge could be spotted and, wherever possible, remedied. The system of mass media communication was driven by critical internal and self-corrective forces. In the new digital public sphere, such a critical impetus survives with the promise to flatten the hierarchies between the information rich and information poor. However, this ongoing democratization of our information landscapes has had the reverse effect of loosening rather than strengthening the binding forces of public discourse. Through open sources and online sharing of information, content becomes diffuse and diversified, and interpretative contexts for reception multiply. Individual media users are encouraged to pick up whatever they like and make it relevant for themselves. For producers of information, the risks increase that targeted audiences are missed, or that there is simply nobody out there to listen (a well-known fear of anybody who posts social media content). Receivers of information live under the constant threat that some information may not reach them, or that the information they receive is outright wrong. What has changed in the digital age is thus the awareness of the risks of disinformation, paired with a loss of trust in information providers and mediators. The digital society is still highly dependent on intermediation, but standards for establishing the value of information in a collectively binding way no longer apply. The (not-so-new) observation that news is not simply out there but the result of a highly selective process is no longer hidden, but visible to everybody. People lose trust in news because they actually know more about the media and experience news as unreliable and randomized.

This leads us to a final question: Who in a democratic society has the authority to draw the line between information and disinformation? One possibility is that states should be responsible for guaranteeing the 'correct' use of procedures for establishing truth. The truth value of information would turn into a legal category and, as such, justify regulatory interventions in the functioning of news media and journalism. Such attempts to gain state control over the truth value of news are prominent in the fight against 'fake news'. Authoritarian states defend their version of truth with vigour, while liberal–democratic states try to regulate news markets to prevent audiences from the negative effects of disinformation (such as possible health damage) and to hold information providers legally accountable for the accuracy of information (Klein and Wueller, 2017; Alemanno, 2018).

Another possibility is to recur to the authority of science and scientific modes of truth to decide about the truth value of information. The scientification of the public sphere, however, has destructive effects on democratic modes of will formation and ultimately risks increasing uncertainty and further undermining trust in democracy (Weingart, 1999). The call for making public debates more 'scientific' and fact-based also disregards the possibility of the politicization of science and collides with conflicting calls for measures to re-establish democratic means of control over the functioning of science (Brown, 2009). The public sphere can, at best, establish an arena for science and democracy to enter into a dialogue; it can be used to enhance public participation in science, for instance, in the form of 'scientific citizenship' (Bickerstaff et al, 2010; Olsen and Trenz, 2014), but it does not empower science over democracy to impose its version of truth in public debates and use it for the legitimation of democratic politics.

The third liberal solution is simply to leave the decision about the truth value of information open to be decided by the market space of ideas. The metaphor of the public sphere as a 'marketplace of ideas and opinions' goes back to John Stuart Mill in his essay *On Liberty* and has been used by communication scholars on the basis that news and information value can be established and agreed upon through fair competition (Mill, 1861; Steininger, 2007; Eisenegger et al, 2019). In a marketspace, information is not priceless but traded through exchanges that lead to floating prices, depending on supply and demand. The metaphor of the marketspace can imply pluralization of supply and competition, but it can also lead to trade wars and monopolization. The question is: What accounts for price differences on the market of ideas? One response would be that value is established by truth. Information that is accurate sells better than information that is misleading. Customers do not want to be cheated and are willing to invest in authoritative and reliable sources of news. Fact-checked and evidence-based information would thus have a higher price justified by the value of scientific inputs. The problem is that factual information is often and increasingly available for free. There is an ethics of 'open access' to scientific information to which we contribute as scientists through our publications. A second, related response is that information value is established by supply and demand. Traditional public spheres of mass media were able to impose the value of information based on the assumption of scarcity: the more privileged and informed the eye of observation, the higher the price of information. If scarcity establishes the market price, the demand for quality news can more easily be coupled with the exclusivity of information, the informant's expertise or the particular efforts of journalistic investigation necessary to 'uncover truth'. In the context of information and news abundance, such established price mechanisms of journalism collapse. If both information-rich and information-poor news is available for free, the price of information is uncoupled from supply and demand.

Free information markets, therefore, do not necessarily enhance the quality of democracy. If the competitive market of attention and the market of truth-seeking collide, the mere quantity of information needs to be balanced by introducing quality criteria that are normatively grounded and justified and allow the filtering and interpretation of information according to shared criteria of relevance. In short, the public sphere is not only needed for accumulating information but for qualifying it. Through the public sphere filters, every piece of new information is embedded in a web of formerly qualified information as the output of previous observations of the social world that has already undergone a validity check. We can speak of disinformation as a form of unranked information that results from the collapse of selective public sphere filters and its mechanisms of establishing the shared value of information in a collectively binding way. Disinformation, in this sense, is a form of disconnected information that still claims to inform about something without being bound by the critical force of discourse.

The privacy–publicity paradox

Digital media technologies enhance publicity and make it possible for everyone to publish worldwide, yet public attention remains a scarce resource, and 'being public' is increasingly detached from 'being visible'. At the same time, digital media revalue privacy in the way private or even intimate data is shared and exploited. Thus, digital media have a tendency to make the public invisible and the private visible. How can this paradox be explained?

The digital public sphere invites us to rethink the relationship between private and public in various respects (Trenz, 2023; Papacharissi, 2010; Splichal, 2018). The early Internet was still based on the false promise that the private and the public could be re-arranged as a zero-sum game in the sense that losses in privacy could be compensated for by overall gains in publicity. Internet communications would increasingly turn public as a new standard for information, to be shared with others in a way that individual users gain in terms of recognition, and the community at large gains in terms of transparency (Levmore and Nussbaum, 2010). In that way, private information disclosed to others would make private life and democratic life richer. What was not foreseen is that the Internet could also lead to the simultaneous loss of privacy and publicity. In the contemporary debate, it is often deplored that private places are pervaded by the public, but at the same time, that public places are found to be shrinking. Calling for publicity does not necessarily mean being public, as not all individual attempts to place themselves on the market of attention can be rewarded to the same degree with attention. For many users, the lure of publicity is paired with the desire to escape from privacy, which is increasingly experienced as loneliness and social isolation (Fuchs and Sandoval, 2014). At the same time, users are exposed to aggressive promotion strategies by providers that constantly pervade their privacy.

In the modern public sphere, publicness-publicity and privateness-privacy relate, on the one hand, to two separate spheres of behavioural dispositions and modes of social interactions among individuals and groups, and, on the other hand, to fundamental rights and ethical principles of behaviour (Splichal, 2016). Private spheres and public spheres define the legitimate use of information and content in a given context. In a society based on private ownership, this is often defined in terms of rights of usage. A public ground can be used by all, as is implied, for instance, in the notion of *allemansrätt* (right of public access) in Sweden. A private ground can be fenced off and access can be denied and regulated. Enhancing the value of publicity means extending the use of something, which, for obvious reasons, is easier with resources that are abundant. There are no restrictions to the use of the air we breathe, but can there be restrictions to thought? The public and private distinction helps to uphold the idea of freedom of thought while at the same time regulating what should be spoken and unspoken.

For conceptual clarification, I will talk in the following of *publicness* as the situational context, in which social transactions and relationships are visible and observable. Observations are performed and communicated. *Publicity*, instead, refers to the act of making something visible, observable and accessible to others. Conversely, I will refer to *privateness* as the situational context in which social transactions and relationships are hidden, and thus not observable. *Privacy*, instead, is the act of protecting something from being observed and talked about by others. The relationship between publicness and privateness is one of shifting boundaries that reflect power relationships, conventions, bargains and agreements among groups and individuals (see also Splichal, 2018: 2). The acts of privacy and publicity are in need of empowerment and authorization. As such, they are typically regulated by the law, politics and the rules of the market.

The enhanced publicness of the online public sphere can be said to lead to a reversion of the value of privacy and publicity: the more publicness is enhanced, the more the value of publicity decreases, while, conversely, as the value of privacy increases, the more it is pervaded by publicness. In the traditional public sphere, publicity was a scarce resource that had a high public value and status. This put the single author, who was able to talk to the many, in a privileged and often powerful position. In digital public spheres, privacy becomes a scarce resource, a 'luxury commodity' as Zizi Papacharissi (2010: 46) puts it, and consequently gains in individual value. Taking measures to protect one's privacy typically comes at a high cost, as individual users lose affordances that are made publicly available and do not necessarily gain in social status or influence. Privileged Internet users are the ones who are able to protect their privacy without renouncing the public affordances of the web. What adds fuel to this is the change in media market logic. Traditional mass media rewarded privacy as they targeted consumers as isolated individuals, watching TV in their private homes, or buying a newspaper that was not meant to be shared with others (except within the confines of the family). Digital media business models, conversely, tend to punish privacy instead of rewarding it. Private user data is the raw material for social media companies to make profit, but in order to accumulate private data, social media need to enhance publicity as an affordance that is attainable for all and, as such, rewarded with public attention and recognition. The digital and social media markets price attention and turn individual users into private competitors on the public attention market. Public attention is the new currency that makes social media run as a competitive market, not only open to celebrities but linking visibility rankings to social status for every individual user (Webster and Ksiazek, 2012; Reckwitz, 2020). Individual consumers are meant to go public and to click and share content that invites public usage. Paywalls or secured login credentials are not primarily meant to protect privacy but are often used by the providers as tracking tools of personal data and usage. Once such attention markets are established, individual users are found to be willing to pay high prices (like giving up their privacy) for rewards in terms of recognition by their peers or the general public.

Digital data gain in economic value when they contain private information about media usage that is made exclusively available for business. The richer the data, that is, the more private information it contains, the higher its economic value. This can only apply when ownership over private data can shift: whenever Internet users agree to the terms and conditions, they release personal information for collection and use by companies. Private data become goods that are traded and merchandized. Following the new commercial logic of digital media markets, money is made out of users who sell their privacy. Privacy is turned into market goods, with private companies buying and selling private data. Privacy is only a question of the price paid on the market, and according to a comparative study conducted by the US-based think tank Technology Policy Institute, if the price is high enough, a company like Facebook would need to 'pay consumers a monthly $8.44 to share their bank balance information, $7.56 to share fingerprint information, $6.05 to read an individual's texts and $5.80 to share information on cash withdrawals'.[1] The price also varies according to country, with German users, and their notorious privacy concerns, requesting the highest reward.

The private data market is based on the assumption that private data can be commodified as goods that have a market price, and thus a public value. It is in everyone's interest that users share private information, and the more people collaborate in sharing private data, the more the collective proliferates. There is a public good ideology underlying the social media sharing culture, making sharing of private data a social norm. There is thus an attempt to define a legitimate use of private data by private companies who claim to serve the public good. An example of this would be Facebook or Google, which claim to have created rich information worlds that empower individuals and collectives.

Digital markets would not be *markets* if they followed the logic of the commons as was believed in the early days of the Internet. By following market logics instead, they are primarily profit-oriented, and do this by offering particular products for sale. Trades for goods on the digital market do not, however, necessarily involve direct payments through financial transfers; the market logics often go unnoticed. In other words, users do not know that they are 'buying' products, and providers can hide their profit orientation. To function as a market, the Internet needs to facilitate deals that satisfy both sides: providers take profit through financial gains, and users gain through specific affordances that enrich their private life and individual experiences. The specific form of deal that is established by digital markets is the one of trading private data. If you wish to entertain yourself, you need to agree to a transfer of private user data to the company that offers you the entertainment. If you wish to read news online for free, and do this regularly, the price you pay is that your online reading habits are tracked by the news provider (which is often not even the news organization but the platform that shares the news with you). In the liberal market Internet, even the protection of privacy is privatized. Individuals who wish to invest in privacy protection rely on private providers offering their paid services to protect against intrusion of privacy (Hoye and Monaghan, 2018: 358).

The premise required for this market logic to work is that individual media users agree to enter into a deal with a content provider. Instead of simply losing their privacy, individual users can negotiate their private data, either for gains of participation in public life or for the satisfaction of personal needs (such as information, orientation or entertainment) Such an agreement is even formalized in the way you need to confirm the use of cookies whenever you enter a website, or when you subscribe to the terms and conditions of becoming a 'user' of a specific platform. Based on this assumption of voluntarily using digital media, the personal autonomy of the media user is preserved, even if their privacy is lost. This works as long as the deal pays off for the company and the individual users. What this market model does not take into account is the psychological distress created by the loss of privacy, which is not necessarily equated with gains in publicity. The market treats individuals as isolated users and, as such, also curbs their public life in important ways. Instead of searching for publicness, individuals learn to avoid public exposure and move in an anonymous and hidden way in the cloud, fully visible to the provider who protects them from the public view. Web anonymity is part of the deal the users enter with their provider, which has the exclusive rights to collect private data while offering a safe environment protected from the unwanted intrusion of others (like one's personal social media account). This means, however, that individual user behaviour on the Internet is increasingly driven by fear of abuse by others, which might be partly related to real risks and dangers, like, for instance, data theft, malware or viruses, but all too often, it also relates to imagined threats. Once Google knows essentially everything, you also become a potential victim, and your whole personality is at risk. The public sphere is then no longer the realm of independence and autonomy but a hostile environment where private individuals are at constant risk of public exposure. Social media consumption results in schizophrenia and permanent frustration in the way individual efforts to protect privacy are not only minimal but also, by default, insufficient when referring to the insatiable appetite of social media companies for private data.

By turning publicity into a common resource, or even into a public virtue of social media behaviour (in the way Mark Zuckerberg defines the sharing culture as a vision of a more open and connected world), social media turn privacy into a scarce resource (Marwick, 2013). Privateness, which was the shared status of mass media consumers in the traditional public sphere, becomes a privilege in the digital public sphere and, as such, attains a higher value. This correlates with the devaluation of publicness, which is increasingly perceived as a threat to individual autonomy.

The relationship between privacy and publicity is commonly claimed to be symbiotic in the sense that, as Arendt maintains, there is no 'public realm' and 'private realm' as such, but only shifting public–private relations: public authority is needed to protect privacy, and only private individuals with protected status and rights can engage in public affairs (Arendt, 1998). As the 'public' and the 'private' rely on each other and cannot exist separately, they can also enter into a parasitic relationship. Public authority can easily become abusive and pervade privacy instead of protecting it, which is a constant temptation of power holders not only in authoritarian but also in democratic states. Political scandals in democracy are typically linked to such privacy transgressions by state authorities (Kepplinger et al, 2012). Protected private areas can instead be threatened by the 'tyranny of the intimacy' (Sennett, 1977), where public affairs are redefined as private and individualized in such a way that they mainly serve the purpose of individual self-fulfilment. According to Putnam's (1995a) commentary on American society in his book *Bowling Alone*, individuals would cease to be 'citizens' when they mainly seek entertainment in self-chosen isolation and opt to retreat from public space. Individualization would not only reduce the richness and dynamic aspects of public life but also change the very meaning of privacy, which is established in symbiosis with, and not in sharp contrast to, publicity.

In the public sphere, publicity, not privacy, is the norm. For the whole duration of the 19th and 20th centuries, publicity has claimed superior value over privacy. Publicity was discovered as a principle of societal self-organization of good government for a good society. In his essay 'Of Publicity', Jeremy Bentham famously gives the following three reasons why both individuals and governments should yield to publicity (Bentham, 1838):

1. The tribunal of the public: the public is a supervisory body that constantly assesses the exercise of political power. It might be incomplete in judgement, but it continually tends to be enlightened and, as such, 'unites all the wisdom and all the justice of the nation'.
2. The public secures the confidence of the people. People will trust each other if they experience that public reasoning becomes the basis of self-government. The habit of reasoning and discussion will slowly penetrate all classes of society. People involved in public deliberations are not only more educated but also more social- and open-minded.
3. The public enables the governors to know the wishes of the governed. In the same way as the people supervise government, publicity also allows the governors to know the wishes of the people.

The publicity principle, according to Bentham, is ultimately used to qualify public opinion as being grounded in 'public reasoning', which offers a critical yardstick against 'private opinion' that has not passed the test of publicity, or against 'false opinion' that upholds contrafactual claims by resisting the test of publicity.

Bentham was also aware of the reasons against publicity, which he elaborates with reference to the risks that members of a parliament face in their daily exposure to public scrutiny:

1. 'The public is an incompetent judge ... in consequence of the ignorance and passions of the majority of those who compose it.'
2. 'The increase of publications ... will increase the number of bad judges in a much greater proportion than the good ones.'
3. 'Publicity may expose to hatred a member of the assembly.'
4. 'The desire of popularity may suggest dangerous propositions to the members; – the eloquence which they will cultivate will be the eloquence of seduction, rather than the eloquence of reason; – they will become tribunes of the people, rather than legislators.'

Interestingly, Bentham's idea was that the dangers of publicity cannot be countered by escaping to privacy but only by more and better publicity. In much of his writings, Bentham therefore expanded on the techniques for improving the quality of public control, especially tracking techniques, that modern states could use to impose a panopticon on society.

In line with the democratization of society, publicness was seen as expansive, and thus came at the cost of privateness, which had to be filled with the richness of public life (like the TV which brought world experiences into the living room). Escapes into the private then became necessary or desirable as a response to excesses of publicness. If publicness was the norm, privateness had a specific protective status that needed to be justified. If standards of openness and equality of communication apply, private spaces should become accessible. Privacy is an exclusive right and restricted as such, while publicity is a norm that can apply to all information. As a consequence, the borders of privacy are in need of justification by those who defend them as privileges and exclusive rights and are always challenged by the expansive logic of publicity that makes spaces accessible and visible for all. The very act of turning something public is effortless: it is its simple appearance in public, but once visibility is achieved, it requires specific efforts to restrict it again, like, for instance, the specific techniques of image control applied by celebrities (McNamara, 2009). Still, publicity, that is, the idea that information is a common good and not a property, was revolutionary, as traditional stratified societies are typically based on a complicated system of divisions of knowledge and restricted access to information, as, for instance, in the form of patriarchy and the way gender roles regulate access to public and private knowledge (McKeon, 2006). Societies of Enlightenment are emancipatory in the way they deconstruct such orders of stratified knowledge distribution, for instance by revealing that such restrictions to knowledge access are culturally specific and do not correspond to any natural order of separation or by applying an 'archaeology of knowledge' to reveal the whole system of power that is needed to keep the stratified information flows operating (Hall, 2001; Foucault, 2002). The publicity–privacy distinction does not, therefore, strictly apply to traditional stratified societies, since for the great majority of subjects, there was neither a private space of retreat nor a public space of access. Modern differentiated society, instead, is established so as to simultaneously enable solitude and complicate togetherness (Papacharissi, 2010: 33). Once the norm is accepted that information about common affairs should be uncoupled from exclusive ownership, privately owned spaces can be drawn and constituted as meaningful spaces of interaction in response to publicness. The norm to disclose information about common affairs corresponds to the 'call' for publicity, while the claim for exclusive rights over one's private affairs corresponds to the 'call' for privacy, the former constituting the bourgeois public life and the latter the separate realms of private family life.

At the same time, to distinguish between public and private implies the idea of a transition: I can cross the borders between public and private.

Sociology has evolved around models describing the complex systems of border management and the rules and practices of border crossing that apply in modern societies. While macrosociology has focused on the structures of power, norms and institutions that constitute and uphold this distinction of separate spheres of social interaction, like the economic system, states and families (Parsons, 1951), micro- or so-called ethnomethodological approaches in the social sciences were meant to describe how people engage in practices of border maintenance and crossing (Garfinkel, 1967). One well-known example is Erving Goffman's distinction between frontstage and backstage and his categorization of the various means of impression management individuals use to present themselves in public life (Goffman, 1959). The transition from private to public, however, is not to be understood as a linear and unidirectional process. One commonly held misunderstanding is that to 'publish' something simply means to turn something previously considered as private into something public. It is however also the case that the privateness of a particular kind of information can only be established if the publicness, that is, the general accessibility of information, is taken for granted. In a town without a market square where people can freely exchange information to be considered of public relevance, no private homes can exist where people decide to keep information secret. 'Publishing' means creating content that claims visibility: it does not mean taking up content previously considered as private. It means creating that content for the eyes of 'the many'.

Publicity, in this sense, is a call for public attention to something that is claimed to be of public value. I can, of course, also decide to talk about my private business, or to make my love affairs public. This is done in such a way as to test the public value of this information, a test that can easily fail if others do not find my private business to be of sufficient interest, or my love affairs exciting. Privacy, in turn, is a call for secrecy, which equally depends on the attribution of public value. The point is that both the claim for publicity (the decision to publish) and the claim for privacy (the decision to keep something to myself) presuppose testing the public value of information. In everyday life, we can experience this in the way the value of privacy often depends on the efforts that are needed to protect it. The very fact that such efforts are necessary indicates that there is a potential public interest in that particular type of information and that we therefore have good reason to keep it private. This public interest in the privacy of others often correlates with social status. The love affairs of celebrities incite more curiosity than the love affairs of an academic. Privacy, however, cannot be claimed to be prior or even superior to publicity, as both are embedded in a realm of publicness where the value of information is already established. The reason why privacy can claim protective status in recent debates about data protection is that it has gained in public value. Once this value is fixed, the counter claim, which insists on the exclusive private use of that information, will inevitably fail to turn the object of attention again into something private and, to the contrary, might even increase its public value.

The paradox, thus, is that the decision to consider something as private can, by default, only be taken collectively, which at the same time takes away its private character. The claim for privacy is in this sense disguised as an individual choice that only becomes meaningful if publicly communicated. The claim for privacy is not simply the counter claim to publicity but an alternative claim for public value. Privacy claims are public claims that need to comply with standards, critical tests and justification requirements. Only if the public agrees that the value of something is worth being protected from the view of the others can the protective status of privacy be established and constitutionally guaranteed.

Privacy and publicity are about possible extensions or restrictions of visibility of content and information (Brighenti, 2010). If publicity is a claim for visibility that is justified by public value, privacy is the decision to make something invisible because it has a value that could possibly draw public attention. As a private person, I am always free to revert this relationship and to make public use of the value that is attached to my privacy. I could publish, for instance, a private letter and thus change the status of particular content or information, or I could write or talk in a way that makes my private thoughts public. This is always done under the assumption that my private information is perceived as having value for others, and that I wish to test its worth by engaging in public communication. In all these examples, this worth does not exist as a property of privacy; it is, strictly speaking, a mere suffix of publicness: the privacy of the letter depends on the possibility (and sometimes also the threat) that its content could become public. This is the reason why public authority is needed, in the technical sense, to protect privacy, but also in the more elementary sense to establish privacy in the first place. Specific efforts need to be made by constitutions, states and individuals to protect postal secrecy, but it is also through such constitutional provisions that specific practices of private communication can develop and individuals can act 'in good faith' regarding being private. This is often done with a hidden agenda of *postponed publicity*, for instance in the widespread practices of archiving private correspondence or keeping diaries, which keep open the possibility of later publication. In particular, 'public figures' engage in private correspondence, aware that this will be preserved for the public and that privacy is only provisional and bound to temporary choices or preferences. In the same way, my private thoughts in a diary are expressed in a way that is both comprehensible and able to be communicated to a wider audience.

The public sphere, in this sense, is the stage for the representation and performance of both public and private life. As there is no natural border between the two spheres, both public and private life are in need of constant curation (Marres, 2017: chapter 2). The public and the private are part of the ongoing contestation of the social in the double sense that there is, first, the need to give a personal account of one's decision to draw the borders between the private and the public, and secondly, the need for public recognition of such private accounts of publicness and privateness. The implications of this double need of accountability and recognition are that publicness and privateness are not optional or individual but socially constrained. Just because it is called 'public' or 'private' does not make it so. Many individuals revoke publicness when deciding to withdraw to the private; however, to their frustration, this is often not sufficient to change their public status. The opposite is also true: when striving to gain publicity, competing for publicity is often in vain.

If both claims for publicity and privacy are dependent on recognition by others, there are different degrees to which such demands for respect of privacy or attention by others are satisfied. Authors get satisfaction if their strategy to publish is successful, that is, their claim for public value is acknowledged by an audience willing to reward book content with attention (which, according to the business model of a capitalist media market, is combined with financial payments). Claims for privacy are not rewarded to the same degree as publicity, and satisfaction instead depends on the respect of the borders of privacy by others, which relies on convention, good will and partially also legal enforcement. If their private life is respected, individuals feel safe and protected, yet this respect depends on a previous collective agreement, on established conventions or on public authority. The value of privacy protection can only be established in response to, or in anticipation of, possible infringements of privacy. Without the threat of intrusions into privacy, there would also be no need to claim a special protective status. Privacy is valued when specific effort needs to be made to maintain it. The value of privacy in this sense depends on the extension of the realm of publicness. In the age of mass media, when publicity was a scarce resource available to few authors, privateness was the shared destiny of the many. In the digital age, when publicity claims are multiplied, the enjoyment of moments of privacy becomes the luxury of the few.

Publicity, however, does not necessarily mean visibility, as it also embraces the cases of non-attention to content that is made accessible. In the same way, invisibility does not mean that something has a protected private status: it only means the momentary absence of public attention. As attention is a scarce resource, the realm of invisibility is by default infinitely larger than the few selected spaces in the limelight of public attention. In the public sphere, withdrawing attention is not a restitution of privacy but a suspension of visibility. Claims for privacy by celebrities, for instance, might even enhance their visibility. In the same manner, to publish something does not mean to turn something that was previously invisible into something visible and open for all. To publish, as Max Frisch (1967) once remarked, means to search for an imaginary partner in conversation and to expose oneself to the risk of observation. Publishing is to be understood as an offer for others to join, to share the value of information and to consider it to be of public relevance. Publishing strategies, however, often fail, and would-be authors are exposed to the fact that nobody wants to pay attention to what they claim to be of public interest.

The following will elaborate on how the enhanced publicity of the web all too often makes it appear transparent when it is not. It focuses attention on the accessible and observable content, on the observers and their creative ways of making multiple use of online sources. The net, however, is not simply a place of observation, and publicity is not everything that counts. There are many operations that are not watched by anyone, either because they are hidden or because they are not observable, and publicity all too often obscures forms of power and surveillance.

The empowerment–disempowerment paradox

Digital media users are empowered by content providers to make creative use of media and strive for independence from media institutions. Empowerment refers to 'individual human actors increasing their capacity to shape their own lives and to participate in the shaping of social life more broadly' (Dahlberg, 2015: 271). Through the use of digital and social media, individual media users gain autonomy in getting information from multiple sources and engaging in horizontal sharing networks. Yet, people are differentially empowered by various levels and types of digital media access and usage (van Dijk, 2012b). The empowerment of individual users goes hand in hand with the empowerment of independent content providers who can build direct relationships to targeted audiences. This is paired with the simultaneous disempowerment of traditional mediators, such as institutionalized journalism. Mass media institutions, which in the old days had a lock on information flows, lose control over content and audiences. The free flow of information comes at a cost, namely the loss of institutionalized channels of mediation. Communication is dis-embedded and de-institutionalized: it is still public, or claims to be of public interest, but it is taking place outside of the institutionalized channels of public intermediation.

In capitalist media markets, competition between media producers goes hand in hand with the disempowerment of individual users as targets for paid content in the form of news, arts or entertainment. Sharing economies through digital and social media undermine traditional business models of media companies by empowering users over established content providers (Stephany, 2015; Meikle, 2016). Sharing, however, is not exclusively, or even predominantly, driven by non-profit organizations or peer-to-peer bottom-up initiatives (Laurell and Sandström, 2017). Rather, it has become a profitable business of sharing platforms that provide intermediary services to facilitate peer-to-peer contacts. For example, the sharing of news through social media has undoubtedly had devastating effects on established news industry business models, but it has not necessarily empowered users. Platform algorithms all too often regulate content sharing by giving preference to commoditized mass media products and marginalizing reader-generated contents (Michailidou et al, 2014).

The empowerment–disempowerment paradox can be formulated as follows: individual media users have never been so empowered to make creative use of media that can be published to the world. Their empowerment through creative forms of digital media use (such as blogging, commenting, posting, liking and sharing) results in an abundance of public or semi-public, yet unchannelled information and content. The increase in disconnected forms of user content add to a general feeling of disempowerment and nourish fear of missing out or performing poorly in the media visibility rankings. At the same time, individual media users, like never before, are put under a regime of domination that tracks their individual choices and preferences, intrudes in their private lives and makes their behaviour predictable (Aytac, 2022). Internet and digital media technologies build their business models on the empowerment of individual media users and, at the same, turn these forms of empowerment into a panoptic surveillance. This explains why feelings of empowerment by creative media use often go hand in hand with feelings of disempowerment and loss of autonomy of individual media users (Reviglio and Agosti, 2020).

Related to these problems of intermediation are the new hurdles for aggregating public voice. The de-institutionalization of public communication, at first sight, leads to an increase in voice, and thus can be taken as an opportunity for both individuals and collectives to claim representation in public life. The Internet also involves ordinary citizens to a much larger degree in so-called counter politics, including activities such as vigilance, denunciation and political evaluation (Rosanvallon, 2008). The Internet user is in a constant 'state of alert' when voicing distrust against government. The experience that political representatives can be challenged at any time, and by anyone, becomes an empowerment motif (Dahlgren, 2013: 16).

Voice in the democratic process has an instrumental and an expressive function (Dahlgren, 2013: 55). It is used to create visibility for public concerns but also by the individuals and collectives that claim interests, rights and identities. Any increase in the plurality of voice reduces the chances of its overall visibility. Enhancing voice in public debates also increases the likelihood that voice remains unheard. The expressions of de-institutionalized distrust in representative politics remain unchannelled. The single voice of critique perishes in the noise of public debates. This leads to the paradox, as Hanno Rauterberg put it, that the more people are empowered to raise voice, the more voices are raised in complaint that freedom of expression/opinion is restricted.[2] Equality to raise voice in the digital public sphere is decoupled from justice to be heard and recognized. *Equality* in public intermediation means that all are enabled to make use of digital media affordances; everybody is entitled to raise voice and even encouraged to publish worldwide. *Justice* in public intermediation means that all voices are equally echoed with the same chance of being heard and being dealt with by those they address. While the conditions for enabling voice can be accommodated by simple technical solutions, the conditions for justice require political will but refer to technically impossible solutions. The increase in voice in purely physical terms creates noise. There are no technical means through which the unmediated and unfiltered plurality of voice can be translated into public opinion and collective will. For the many unheard voices, these unmet expectations of the promises of digital empowerment create an eternal chain of frustrations, which again is translated into public voice, for instance in the form of conspiracy theories, which, not by coincidence, are, in substance, often about real or alleged media biases (Lee, 2005).

Feelings of injustice regarding not being heard are also increasingly coupled with experiences of being cancelled, or with claims of being a victim of 'cancel culture'. The experience that content, which claims public status, can also be cancelled is not just the conspiracy of some, but relates to regular practices in public spheres distinguished by unequal opportunities of access and hierarchies. Users not only learn to select content or to befriend but also to cancel content, defriend or report what they consider inappropriate. As Gabe Ignatow (2020: 16) put it: 'Social media platforms don't just guide, distort, and facilitate social activity – they also delete some of it. They don't just link users together; they also suspend them. They don't just circulate our images and posts, they also algorithmically promote some over others.'

Never before have so many people expressed their opinions and at the same time complained that their freedom of speech is threatened. Democratic citizens, who know well how to make use of their rights of free speech, have also become particularly sensitive in detecting alleged violations of the free speech principle. In the struggle for free speech, even the most powerful persons like Trump and Bolsonaro regularly claim to be victims of political correctness and alleged censorship and the 'fake news' propaganda of mainstream media. Public opinion-makers, who make a living expressing their opinions, express the opinion that they can no longer express their opinions.

Apart from such power games, claims about the negative effects of so-called cancel culture are often taken up by groups who feel marginalized and, for whatever reason, see their worldviews threatened (Norris, 2020). As such, the alleged spread of cancel culture can become the agenda of groups as heterogeneous as populists and liberal defenders of free speech, both stepping forward as defenders of a free Internet that does not censor content. Populists feel marginalized by the so-called liberal mainstream, while liberals feel threatened by the imposed regulatory mechanisms of 'political correctness', as was claimed in a manifesto drafted and signed by 70 German university professors in January 2021.[3] The struggle over the empowerment of different user groups in the digital public sphere leads to a new polarization between two variants of liberal free speech claimants: 'protectionists' and 'free speech radicals'. For the 'protectionists', the liberal values of the public sphere need to be rescued through high moral standards and regulation to preserve the quality of information and public debates. For 'free speech radicals', the 'moral straightjackets' of state control are rejected, fearing that the realm of 'what can be said freely' is becoming increasingly restricted.

The fluidity and hybridity of public debates with changing issue agendas and shifting attention cycles can be exciting at times, but it can also be highly frustrating. Those who raise their voice in public debates frequently make the experience that their efforts to engage in argumentation are not rewarded. The enhancement of free speech has pluralized content and information, but it has also multiplied the contesting arguments that can be raised in public debates. Instead of being rewarded by dialogue, enhanced knowledge, learning, respect and recognition, participants in online debates are increasingly frustrated by monologue-like speech situations, disrespectful behaviour and intolerance (Ruiz et al, 2011; Rossini, 2020). Such frustrations at the individual level make people turn away from argumentative exchange. If we experience that arguments do not matter, we might as well insist on our categorical statements or emotions.

In the traditional public sphere, debates through argumentative exchanges had the double function of facilitating informed opinion-making and learning, and making publics sovereign (Habermas, 1993; Bohman, 2000; Peters, 2008). Members of the public were rewarded by access to knowledge and power. Apart from the possibilities of cognitive advancements, participants in public debates could also feel empowered by either being part of the majority view or by the possibility of challenging the majority view. The loss of the deliberative quality of public debates, from this perspective, not only undermines the shared knowledge base of society but also equates with a loss of feeling of being empowered as a 'sovereign citizen'. Being part of the public sphere is no longer an experience of gaining control over one's own life and finding orientation in public opinion. It increasingly turns into an experience of loss of control, which further contributes to the overall loss of trust in democracy (Lahusen, 2020).

The strange alliance, or rather, the simultaneity of empowerment and disempowerment, is often experienced by individual media users as alienation (Rey, 2012; Reveley, 2013). The Internet is like a house without doors, giving you shelter but trapping you at the same time. The search for a private place within that house is paired with the experience that all measures of privacy protection are futile since users are under surveillance anyway: passwords cannot really be protected, personal pages are transgressed by strangers or flooded with personalized ads. Dependencies and a feeling of being at the mercy of arbitrary power are typical of totalitarian states. Instead of states, the social media platforms catapult users into something that resembles a totalitarian market, where individuals are at the mercy of digital companies and their surveillance techniques. To be at the mercy of markets might prove, for many, to be even worse than to be at the mercy of the state.

Feelings of disempowerment are an important explanatory variable for understanding the radicalization dynamic that is inherent in the online public sphere (Alvares and Dahlgren, 2016). Frustrated individual users form angry publics who turn their anger against political representatives, or against other media users they encounter online and find reason to dislike. Hate speech and radicalization might be understood as compensation for the sense of loss of control. The last resort for disempowered citizens to feel empowered is the freedom to be radical. The single voice needs to radicalize in order to still be distinguishable in online debates. Expressions of hate and violations of netiquette might entail sanctioning, but even becoming the target of sanctioning mechanisms can contribute to short-lived attention and fame.

We have seen how digital and social media disrupt established markets for the production, distribution and reception of media content by empowering and disempowering different groups of content providers, mediators and users. The paradox of empowerment–disempowerment leads to disruptive experiences, which are again taken up and given collective meaning. Thus exposure to contradictory developments and paradoxes does not necessarily lead to a disruption of public sphere infrastructure and dynamics, but rather is encountered creatively.

From dystopia back to utopia: public sphere resilience

Paradoxes are commonly seen as a problem of philosophy. Formulating and discussing them is an intellectual pastime. As such, they need to be extracted from the contradictions of social life and formulated in an abstract and formalistic way, so as not to disturb the underlying social practices. However, the three paradoxes of digital communication, which I have tried to delineate, are to be understood more as a practical problem than one of analytical philosophy. They describe, first and foremost, the practical challenges that digital media users encounter in their daily online exchanges. The paradoxes of digital communication, therefore, are not just diagnosed but are lived and experienced in the way critical publics occupy digital public spheres. In everyday media use and consumption, the paradoxes can be linked to various disruptive experiences at individual and collective levels. This means that they also trigger specific individual and collective reactions in the form of preventive or reactive measures, critical discourse or new waves of political mobilization.

Disruptions at the level of audience reception have come to the attention of media psychology (Blackman and Walkerdine, 2017) but are rarely used as explanatory variables in political mobilization research. A great deal is known about negative media effects on personality, but we tend to disregard how people react collectively to media malfunctions. If disruptive experiences mark our individual encounter with media, they also shape our collective ways of interpreting media and its functions. Individual fears and feelings of unease with digital media would be hollow if not expressed as a public concern. The fear of a loss of privacy is given a public form, meaning that it is reintroduced into public debates and potentially also translated into collective struggles for the defence and reconquest of privacy. Disruptive experiences with media become a shared knowledge base of society in the way they are collectively identified, interpreted, framed and targeted as a social problem. Understanding this interlinkage between disruptive experiences *with* media, and social cognition *about* the media, is crucial for the analysis of new practices of digital media use and the formation of critical publics. This translation process, from ways of thinking about media to ways of reacting to and interacting with media (for instance, in defensive or confrontational ways), will now be analysed as public sphere resilience.

As media scholars, we should acknowledge that concerns with media and public sphere disruptions are not only expressed at academic conferences but that many of the disruptive processes we identify have become an everyday concern for ordinary people. This also dismantles the myth of a voluntary loss of private data, which underlies the capitalist logic of digital media markets. Individuals enter the privacy deals not as autonomous media users but from a position of dependency on the affordances of digital media. Such dependencies are also not just hypothetical but collectively experienced. These experiences are given a political form when we talk of dominance and oppression. Here, we return to the classical emancipatory vocabulary of the public sphere.

The mixed experiences people encounter in their daily media use are turned into a huge data and knowledge depository, and as such, also into a repertoire of collective action. More than relying on established collective action frames based on predefined goals, people engage in connective action to interpret shared negative experiences with media, or the negative consequences of media use, express ideas about possible causes and consequences, and come up with tentative solutions (Bennett and Segerberg, 2013). Such thematically focused connections and engagements in online exchanges are self-motivated and do not require formal organization. They are typically driven by the desire to share private experiences and ideas with others, and to receive community support and recognition.

One recurrent topic of such connective action frames is the experience of media dependency and the vague feelings of unease with media. People make increasingly creative use of media and feel empowered, but people are also afraid of media and learn to fear media effects on their lives. As well as their own vulnerability, people also encounter others they identify as vulnerable, asking for their protection, for instance in the way it has become commonplace to protect children from harmful media content or abusive online practices. In addition to a logic of connection, they might follow a 'logic of collection' (Gerbaudo, 2022), for instance in the way shared hashtags, such as #metoo, are used to gather personal testimonies. Reacting to perceived media disruptions collectively is a form of public sphere resilience. People who learn to cope with negative media effects are not just defenceless victims of anonymous market forces but re-appropriate digital media affordances, build critical knowledge and define their own approach towards creative media usage. Being exposed to undesired publicness, or being empowered or disempowered in the use of digital media, becomes more of a political question than a destiny. The political comes back in the way people identify media malfunctions, experience vulnerability, claim rights of media usage, seek individual protection or develop utopian visions of a more inclusive, safer, balanced and rational Internet.

Disruptive experiences with media content and usage can, in this sense, become a catalyst of public sphere resilience. Practices of resilience are not just limited to intellectuals or academics who learn to be media critical. Apart from the emergence of new critical publics, individual media users also develop coping practices to deal with the perceived negative effects of media. My developing argument, in short, is that this new agenda of public sphere resilience is not simply to be understood as a new variant of public sphere criticism (the 'heroic' or 'reflexive' account) but as also including a whole range of everyday and routine practices of adapting to the new media and learning to cope with its consequences (the 'banal' or 'non-reflected' account).

The notion of public sphere resilience adds to the history of the structural transformation of the public sphere, not so much understood as a history of decay but of constant renovation and evolution. Habermas' 'structural transformation of the public sphere' reads in retrospect like an early warning of disruptive media developments, while, at the same time, reintroducing and updating the Enlightenment's idea of the public sphere as a template for collective learning and the facilitation of democratic progress. Seen from this perspective, the driving force of public sphere transformation is critique. The identification of such disruptive developments often translates into political mobilization and resistance, like the hacker movement. Critique, however, is also raised in everyday communicative exchanges and media usages. Critical publics emerge, for instance, in the testing out of new mediating techniques (such as content sharing through social media), relating to new providers of content (such as 'alternative news'), or more accessible formats for the presentation and diffusion of media content. The yardsticks for the unfolding of such practices are the normative standards of the public sphere, the validity of which can again be critically put to the test and contested. Public spheres exist because people engage in critical judgement, and they persist as long as there is critique, but public spheres do not result in a linear development of societal transformation in the direction of progress or decay. A public sphere theory refers to what Boltanski (2011) calls a 'sociology of emancipation', stressing the ability of individuals to engage in critical capacities and practices, to rise up against domination and injustice and construct their own interpretations of the social reality in which they live. Resilience relates precisely to these critical capacities and practices that do not aim at social revolution but at interpretation, collective understanding and social intervention.

At this point, we only need to take the next step, which is to ask how critique feeds back into the democratic process. Here, we need to go beyond media psychology, which analyses resilience practices as developed by individuals and as strategies of personal adaptation to new media developments. When we discuss the effects of disrupted public spheres, we often tend to replicate a common blind spot of media reception research, which consists of putting too much emphasis on individual media use and media effects on personality. The user focus in digital media research has replicated this template of media reception analysis.[4] Yet, what makes the digital public sphere sociologically relevant is that it does not simply single out and atomize individual users but creates collectives and enables forms of collective and connective action (Bennett and Segerberg, 2013, Nassehi, 2019). Public sphere resilience, first, is about how disruptive experiences with media become sources of common knowledge about media. Based on their personal disruptive experiences, digital media users enter a form of group therapy where they connect and take joint action. Therapy commonly builds on some sort of diagnosis of cause and effect, gathering knowledge and building competences. The malaise that gives rise to shared concerns needs to be understood, classified and analysed. The therapy of public sphere resilience involves individual media users in the collection of empirical data and evidence. In assessing the perils and chances of their daily media use, they operate very much like media experts and professionals. They often collect similar evidence that is used to validate knowledge, generated out of empirical facts and experiences. Secondly, public sphere resilience is about the search for collective solutions to identified problems. Media knowledge is shared as popular knowledge that is found to be of practical relevance and used to inform collective choices. Ordinary people often tend to have informed opinions about the risks of media consumption, or the many pitfalls of news reading, such as, for instance, their capacities to recognize or avoid 'fake news'. Media literacy and expertise become important practical knowledge that can be used to cope and survive in the digital media world, to discuss viable solutions to the identified problems and to take corrective measures against media malfunctioning.

Experiences of media disruptions thus create demands for media literacy and expertise, and ultimately increase common knowledge about media. At the same time, disruptive experiences with media guide the discussion about possible reform and the experimental modes of testing solutions. Experiences of disruption can not only trigger future innovation as a reactive process but can also be embraced as therapeutical measures, like in the slogan 'disrupt yourself' or the use of 'disruptive innovation' in professions where individuals are requested to permanently re-invent themselves and apply the 'art of self-disruption' (Johnson, 2015).

Practices of media resilience are firmly anchored in a new generation of digital media users who grew up with media but also experienced media effects first hand and learned to interpret and cope with them. For the younger generation, media are not solely passively endured; media are studied and attempted to be made intelligible. Media literacy has become part of school curricula, of university education across disciplines, and there is hardly any form of professional education where media competences are not taught and disseminated. Despite the perseverance of significant knowledge gaps and the profound deficits in current education to meet the demands for higher media literacy, Internet users have become more experienced with often highly specialized training in the application of computer software, dealing with data packages, or using digital platforms. This often includes detailed knowledge about media functioning, working practices and the capacity to calculate media effects with accuracy.

Media reception analysis needs to monitor how users collectively make sense of new media affordances, how individual experiences of media use and reception are shared and interpreted, and how people react to media in progressive or protective ways. The story of the disruptive public sphere tells us that new digital media primarily disconnect and dissolve existing bonds, invalidate norms or undermine collective action repertoires. The problem with these accounts is that we tend to focus on individual user reactions: we individualize media responses and lose the structural context of media reception, as well as the reconstitution of critical publics out of sight. Disillusionment with media and public sphere performance is a shared experience that is interpreted collectively, is given cultural form and expression and is translated into specific critical discourses.

Disillusionment with media content and performance can take various forms: disillusionment with the promise of a free Internet, with the affordances of digital communication, with privacy violations or with the inaccuracy of content. At the individual level, disillusionment can result in alienation, measured in a loss of trust in media (Michailidou et al 2022). Dystopia as a collective experience, however, is predominantly a chance for taking corrective measures and does not necessarily end in a social anomaly, or even breakdown of society. More likely is the translation of disillusionment into critique and new practices of civic engagement. Traces of this new civic virtue will be described in the following as public sphere resilience.

Resilience can now be approached as the case of criticism that often remains 'non-reflected' and even unarticulated. It arises out of an experience of dissonance or disjunction that requires individuals to engage in practical problem solving. The 'resilient public' emerges out of the awareness of shared and enduring adverse effects and negative consequences in the sense of John Dewey (1927). We encounter such a condition for the emergence of resilience practices in the shared feelings of disillusionment and alienation with media. Resilience is not different from or an alternative to social criticism. A more articulated form of criticism might inform resilience practices, or it might ensue from resilience. Resilience is the pragmatic aspect of experimenting with problem solving, while criticism is the more abstract aspect of formulating social problems and their solutions. Applied to the public sphere, resilience can also be understood as a re-equilibrating force that seeks to balance, at least momentarily, the many contradictory elements that make up public communication (Ritzi, 2021).

In the social sciences, a similar pragmatic definition of resilience is the 'bouncing back' of individuals or collectives in a situation of distress or emergency. It is an adaptive response to the unexpected effects of crisis after they have become manifest. As such, it is linked to the capacities of organizations, collectives or individuals to face and master a single or a series of disruptive events (crises) through the use of its own resources:

A strategy of resilience requires reliance on experience with adverse consequences once they occur in order to develop a capacity to learn from the harm and bounce back. Resilience, therefore, requires the accumulation of large amounts of generalizable resources, such as organizational capacity, knowledge, wealth, energy, and communication, that can be used to craft solutions to problems that the people involved did not know would occur. Thus, a strategy of resilience requires much less predictive capacity but much more growth, not only in wealth but also in knowledge. (Wildavsky, 1988: 77)

The term *public sphere resilience* can accordingly be used to categorize a broad range of social practices of *coping* with adverse media content and effects that are developed through private initiatives within civil society (though variously linked to the state, local government or private enterprises). In contrast to *resistance*, which is manifested in the active mobilization, non-compliance or civil disobedience of particular groups, *resilience* is often seen as not strategically employed and not directional. Public sphere scholars are typically interested in forms of resistance and contentious politics, not resilience. While resistance, by default, is a public activity, resilience is often considered to be linked to private and non-political activities. One reason for this disregard of resilience is the dominant communicative approach in the public sphere literature, which analyses the visibility of public discourse but tends to overlook everyday, and often banal, practices of public engagement. Another reason is the focus on political activism, critique and forms of democracy enhancement such as participation, transparency or accountability. Resilience, instead, seems to be about the maintenance of community life. Social movement scholars, therefore, typically link resistance to disadvantaged groups (Bieler, 2011), while resilience is primarily used by those groups who wish to maintain the status quo, or re-establish a previous order. Against this, I argue that resilience often becomes political and, as such, is related in important ways to democracy and thus constitutive to public sphere dynamics. Resilience and resistance are not simply antonyms then, but can be seen as complementary, for example in the local initiatives which combine the initial help given with a voice for the protection of minorities and vulnerable groups.

Resistance and resilience are not sharply distinguished practices that draw from different political action repertoires but rather relate to different styles of political performance by individuals and social groups who suffer from hardship or injustice. Experimental settings for public sphere resilience are occupied by new counter-publics seeking to escape the over-politicization and the commodification of the political arena. They result from the displacement of democratic politics to private spaces in response to the overcrowded, confrontational and commercialized public spaces. Resilience takes place in the more 'intimate' sphere of the private, which might not offer visibility, but collectivity, while the commercialized public spaces suffer from hyper-visibility, which no longer offers collectivity (Papacharisi, 2010: 41). The agenda of public sphere resilience is thus explained by more fluid transitions between public and political actions and private engagements. Instead of a sharp distinction between the two spheres, new social movements have mobilized for the politicization of the private spheres ('the personal is political'), accompanied by the search for new forms of political expression in private places (Papacharissi, 2010: 38). These semi-private forms of civic engagement are often not explicitly political in the sense of seeking public voice and visibility; they tend to be slower, more personal, more direct, less aggressive, but also more sustainable. They are closer to personal and collective identities, which are often felt to be aggressively undermined, or threatened, in the open public spaces.

Examples of such practices of public sphere resilience, such as withdrawal from hyper-publics, can be found in the fields of privacy protection and the struggle against disinformation and 'fake news'. Escapes into privacy are often combined with attempts to 'turn off' the news, or to restrict news consumption to restricted paid subscriptions. In Denmark, for instance, the phenomenon of 'slow news' has gained prominence (Andersen, 2020), with groups of high-profile journalists allowing an exclusive community of news readers to subscribe to quality news stories to be shared and discussed within the community. Both news providers and consumers are driven by the motivation to escape from noise and propaganda. While the slow news movement mainly attracts news readers who are already engaged in news, programmes of media literacy aim to enhance 'cognitive resilience', the building of adequate knowledge to enable individual media users to recognize propaganda so that disinformation cannot take root. This is combined with 'physical resilience' that needs to be designed and implemented by providers in their hardware and software to filter out and stop the spread of disinformation, interrupting the network by disconnecting its nodes (Bjola and Papadakis, 2020). 'Cognitive resilience' in the form of media literacy, and 'physical resilience' in the form of intelligent news filters against 'fake news' and propaganda, are often used in a complementary way, a so-called medical approach to public sphere interventions. The underlying idea is that the public sphere and the media need to heal from infection by taking adequate cures. Resilience is a kind of vaccination against media malfunctioning that immunizes potential victims and protects them from negative influences. However, the idea of cognitive and physical resilience is not just a form of individual protection; the object to be protected is the public sphere itself against the threat of disruption and dissolution posed by the abuses of digital communications. From a resilience perspective, the public sphere requires enhancements that enable it to reliably validate truth-claims based on accurate information and rational engagement, contain the effect of emotional escalation, prevent the radicalization of unruly counter-publics and reinforce the integrity of the notion of the public good (Bjola and Papadakis, 2020: 10).

Public sphere resilience, therefore, needs to be understood not just at the individual or community level but also as a form of democratic bouncing back. In the following, I will present evidence for such practices of public sphere resilience in the form of democratic experimentations facilitated by digital media. I will approach such experimenting publics in various cross-cutting sectors engaged in the protection of privacy, seeking out new forms of political representation and fighting the negative consequences of a global pandemic.

Does All This Really Happen? The Experimental Setting of Public Sphere Resilience

Public sphere contestations in the digital age

Contemporary Western democracies have entered a new phase of enhanced public sphere contestation. In contrast to previous historical epochs marked by high degrees of political mobilization, we do not simply observe an increase in the intensity of contentious politics within the public sphere. The new quality of these conflicts can instead be seen in the way the media and the public sphere have themselves become a target of contention. In the new millennium, Western democracies have opened a field of social and political struggle over the utopia of the public sphere. What is at stake is the validity and the applicability of the underlying norms and principles of democracy in the context of digitalization and globalization.

The popular diagnosis of the presence (or diagnosis of our times) as post-democracy does not grasp the new dynamics of contentious public sphere politics. Post-democracy is commonly seen as something that is passively endured or structurally embedded. It is something that just happens to our societies, a shared destiny because democracies cannot last and encounter a natural death. However, the transition from contentious politics *within* the public sphere to contention *of* the public sphere is not silent. Nor is it a linear process with a predefined outcome. The new contentiousness of the digital public sphere is an open-ended game that is not taking place somewhere at the periphery but encompasses the whole of the political system and its interrelations with media, markets and society. The way media has dramatically changed our daily lives and our professions has left a deep imprint on our democratic systems of political representation. Deep concerns with democracy not only affect state functioning but also other sectors, such as the economy, education and science. The plot for this large social and political struggle is still in the making. There is no central stage for performing the play, but many interrelated local, national and international stages with shifting audiences. Among the protagonists we find:

1. The digital industries, among them the big global players of social media capitalism, who in their role as collectors and merchants of big data often become the targets of political mobilization but can sometimes also become allies in the struggle for Internet freedom.
2. Traditional media organizations, such as newspapers and public broadcasting institutions, which are often found to defend the integrity of the national public sphere and the functioning of state-bound systems of political representation.
3. States and governments, which are traditionally the target of social mobilizations but also offer protected areas for the unfolding of public sphere resistance and resilience and, at least in the European context, have increasingly become an ally in the political struggle for the defence of democracy.
4. Political parties, which make creative use of new digital affordances for political mobilization, platform participation and symbolic representation.
5. International and supranational organizations, among them and above all the EU, which can sometimes become the target of political mobilization and at other times an ally in defence of democracy.
6. Civil society and NGOs, which increasingly seek alliances with states and with the EU in their struggle for the protection of citizens' rights of privacy and data protection; at the same time, they remain independent and flexible in their strategies and at other times might even seek alliances with industries, as for instance when fighting against state regulations on sharing copyright content on social media.
7. Public intellectuals who rediscover the public sphere as a field of political struggle and often dramatize the new quality of public sphere contestations as the struggle for the survival of democracy.
8. Users and audiences as protagonists of social media struggles for Internet freedom and democracy, and as citizens, who, in contrast to previous epochs of mass-mediated consumption, are deeply involved in creative media usage and not simply enduring structural transformations of the media.

Resistance is a core element of the contentious politics of digital society. Apart from resistance, active involvement in public sphere struggles often takes less dramatic and less explicit forms. People show resilience by collectively engaging in practices of learning how to cope with the digital media in a way that ensures their lives and communities remain protected or can take advantage of digital developments. The protagonists of public sphere struggles face uncertainty; they develop awareness of both risks and opportunities of digital media affordances. In this situation, resilience is often a safer strategy than taking sides and mobilizing resistance. Resilience avoids drawing sharp boundaries or aligning along cleavages. It maintains flexibility, which is an advantage in an open field of political struggle, where actors' coalitions and agendas quickly change, and the stage is open for improvization and experimentation. Resilience is developed in the way these often very private and fragmented struggles are knotted together, not necessarily in the form of large protest mobilization but in the form of practices that are replicated over time and developed in local settings. These resilience practices are carried forward with a potential or with the intention not only to identify public sphere disruptions but also to ask for corrections, promote democratic renewals and improvise solutions.

Public sphere resilience does not challenge the core parameters and normative yardsticks of the public sphere but rather seeks rescue and recovery. It is not emancipated by setting new standards (which distinguished the political struggles of the 19th and 20th centuries, for instance the development of citizenship rights, famously depicted by T.H. Marshall [1950] or the revolutionary mobilizations examined by Charles Tilly [1978]). Public sphere resilience often takes shape through forms of 'connective action' (Bennett and Segeberg, 2013) performed by individuals who associate and join forces. The protagonists are side figures rather than appearing on the big stage. They are not driven by the desire for major change and long-term impact ('let's change the world'), but by flexible strategies of adjustment, short-term goals and incremental change ('let's build on what we have'). However, resilience is not simply status quo conservation, or sheltering from loss, or the perceived threat of rapid change. It is part of the civil sphere and, as such, is sharply distinguished from community struggles, which seek fortification and closure (Alexander, 2006). Resilience combines the experience of disruption with the search for sustainable solutions. As such, it does not oppose but continues the emancipatory social struggles for social opening, fairness and equality of rights. It recombines individual emancipation with collective self-determination. It embraces the realm of civil rights and personal liberties and the realm of representation and democracy.

Turning now to these fields of public sphere struggles in further detail, I will first discuss public sphere resilience as emancipation in the context of contemporary struggles over rebalancing publicity and privacy. Secondly, I will discuss public sphere resilience as related to new ways for expressing political will, popular sovereignty and the representation of the collective. Lastly, I will turn to the special case of lockdown during the 2020–21 pandemic, which put basic public sphere functioning to the test but also triggered experimental modes of publicness as an 'escape' from imposed retreats to privacy.

Rebalancing privacy and publicity

Contested borders between the private and the public

In the development of modern mass media, the dynamic relationship between publicity and privacy is driven by contest. The establishment of borders and the process of transiting these borders are related to social conflicts, competing positions and discursive contestation. What is considered to be of private value by some is often contested by others. One of the challenges of public sphere research is to understand the field of negotiation and contestation and the different ways of being public and private, or claiming public and private status. The way such transitory practices and conflicts between the public and the private unfold has important consequences for the constitution of shared societal and cultural spaces (Papacharissi, 2015).

Mass culture and mass society can be distinguished by establishing a relatively rigid regime of separate spheres for private and public interactions, with established routines and practices of transition. As was elaborated by early critical theory, such a separation was needed to uphold a bourgeois morality of individualism coupled with a capitalist market logic of consumption (Adorno, 2001; Fuchs, 2016). Rigid regimes of separation between the public and private spheres were thus seen as tools of power and control that blocked the emancipatory potential of the public sphere (Eder, 2013). Capitalist media markets for mass consumption triggered a competition for public attention that required novelty and constant updates of issue agendas for public debate. This led to frequent transgressions from moral rules and a disrespect of privacy, such as those practised by tabloid journalists, for instance (Gripsrud, 2000).

Digital public spheres instead introduce a new fluidity and frequency in the transitions from public to private. This is perceived both as a threat and an opportunity for authors and producers to go public, and for users and audiences to escape privateness. In the organization of capitalist media markets, invisibility as much as visibility becomes more fragile, and ownership over content is contested. Sharing economies, however, are not entirely based on public use (like a public ground or a public library), but on the facilitation of transfers between private individuals that can be made economically profitable for the providers of services. The media market's logics, therefore, change, and instead of monetarizing the publicity of the few celebrities, companies make money from the privacy of the many.

As I elaborated elsewhere (Trenz, 2023), in traditional media markets, the surplus of privacy has led to an increase in the value of publicity. Privacy was for the many and publicity for the few. In digital media markets, the surplus of publicity instead leads to an increase in the value of privacy. Publicity is for the many and privacy is for the few. This reversion of the logics of mass media markets goes hand in hand with a reversion of the logics of public sphere struggles over privacy and publicity (Splichal, 2018). In the traditional public sphere of mass media, publicity was highly selective and could guarantee visibility only for the few. Privacy was abundant and was meant to facilitate relaxation for the many. People rarely chose to go private; they were instead assigned to private places as passive media consumers. Private homes were often not much more than artificially created spaces of retreat from capitalist consumption (Blatterer et al, 2010), or they were confined spaces of exclusion from participation in public life, upheld by regimes of power and inequality (such as mechanisms that excluded women or minorities from the realm of the public). In digital public spheres, the capitalist logics of media markets require an investment into new practices of transition between publicity and privacy (Sevignani, 2015). Through the use of digital media, people are not only offered the opportunity to escape their assigned spaces of media consumption (what is emphatically referred to as *users' empowerment*); they are called upon to search for publicity themselves through new practices of media use and various online publication activities.

As a result of these individualized and diversified mass publication activities, digital media markets reverse the correlation between publicity and visibility and privacy and invisibility. In traditional mass media, publicity could guarantee at least some degree of visibility (even though selective mechanisms applied and resulted in visibility rankings), while privacy meant invisibility. In turn, the new digital media often uncouple publicity from visibility, and hence increase the risk of making privacy visible. On social media, the opportunities for publicity are enhanced, but highly selective mechanisms still apply on the public attention market, which restrict visibility for shared content. To publish is not a guarantee of being watched and listened to by the many. Instead, a new experience of private publicity applies where private data that is shared with others mainly serve the purpose of surveillance by industry. Publicity thus loses transparency, with which it was traditionally associated, and unfolds through obscure mechanisms of individualized practices of media use and social media consumption.

Privacy as a new public good

We often hear: the public is out, private is in. New political struggles are fought for the protection of privacy as a public good and the containment of publicity as a public vice. Privacy in the digital world is evoked as a public good, with the promise of individual autonomy, freedom and self-determination, while the threatening and damaging effects of excesses of publicity are emphasized in terms of loss of control and surveillance, either by states or by capitalism (Hoye and Monaghan, 2018). Yet, in their calls for privacy, many groups still claim public status, raise public voice and claim to represent the public interest.

From a history of public sphere perspective, it is somewhat curious to observe that public sphere struggles in the digital age have led to the rediscovery and re-evaluation of privacy (Splichal, 2018). The idea of privacy, as expressed in personal autonomy, has historically been facilitated by a change in the observer's position from an absolute authority that surveys the whole to the pluralization (one could also say democratization) of observation as the right of everyone. Such a notion of privacy was unknown to traditional society, as individuals lived under the assumption that they were constantly observed by God. Nothing remained unobserved. As God was an absent observer, however, the totality of divine observation was substituted by the absolute authority of the ancien régime. The place of the total observer was taken by the sovereign king with his absolute power to obtain any information from his subjects. In confronting public authority, secrecy was not only unavailable as an option; it was even punished as a crime. It was only by introducing the public–private distinction that modern society could renounce the position of a total observer and build on a dynamic of public observation that is open to all. This divided the world of relevant information (what deserved to be observed) into private and public information. The demarcation of information considered to be public or private, however, remained circular: 'Public is what does not remain private and can be shared in common. ... Conversely, private is that which does not become public' (Papacharissi, 2010: 26–7). Private and public information, then, are not essentially different, as the information status for both depends on public recognition. Public information obtains its information status through the recognition of shared relevance. Private information obtains its information status through the potentiality of being turned public and is thus worthy of protection.

The late modern turn towards privacy can, from this perspective, be interpreted as reversingthe early modern praise of publicity as the organizing principle of state–society relationships. In the traditional public sphere of mass media, progressive struggles were fought for the extension of publicity while restricting the areas of privacy to intimate relationships (Sennett, 1977). In the contemporary digital public sphere, progressive struggles are increasingly fought for the right to privacy, which no longer comes at zero cost but increases in value and thus is in need of protection (Splichal, 2018). Privacy, which was the destiny of the many in the mass media society (the masses condemned to passive TV consumption in their private homes), becomes the privilege of the few. As such, privacy needs to be redefined as a public good, accessible to all and guaranteed by state and law.

In the digital sphere, scholars speak of the liquefaction of the public–private distinction through the emergence of hybrid forms of communication and interactions, such as interpersonal chats on video platforms or remote cameras and microphones (Splichal, 2018). Still, border management between the public and private continues to play an important role, such as in the way the Internet is commercialized or individual users seek to protect their data. While borders between public and private become more liquid, they still matter for most people, and media users are ready to invest time and resources in border management. Privacy, in this sense, is increasingly individually defined. Playing with the border of privateness and publicness becomes part of creative media use, where users need to implement their own privacy policies.

The liquefaction of the public–private distinction is a challenge for capitalist markets, as profit depends on the possibility of making goods publicly available for private consumption. It also challenges a well-functioning civil society, which protects citizens' personal rights while at the same time providing them with opportunities for free association and public engagement. The digitalization of society is perceived by citizens and social movements as a disturbance to the established privacy apparatus, one of the pillars of Western liberal and democratic societies. Digital media uses made for a discrepancy between individual and social-institutional approaches to privacy (Becker, 2019). While individuals *privately* encounter the allurement of social media publicness and are more than willing to give away their privacy for the price of entertainment, free affordances and sociability, the *public* demands for privacy protection, at the same time, are upheld and even strengthened. This leads to a cognitive dissonance between widespread media habits and practices of disrespect of privacy and the normative value of privacy. Digital media users, so to speak, have a permanently bad consciousness that their media usage is in breach of moral demands and societal expectations.

The demands for privacy protection, in this sense, are not only raised against the digital industries but also affect individual users and confront them with their own weaknesses. Insufficient protection of privacy not only bears the risks of public exposure but also of damaged reputation and immorality. Control over one's privacy and autonomy as a digital citizen instead conveys social status and recognition. At the same time, there is a growing discrepancy between moral demands for personal autonomy and individuals' notorious disregard for privacy concerns in their daily Internet use. People experience the inevitable incompleteness of their privacy, which requires a constant rebalancing of the porous border between the private and the public spheres.

In this context, the perceived threat of digitalization has nourished the illusion that individuals can and should protect and regain full control over their privacy. As privacy can no longer be taken for granted but needs to be sought out, and publicity is no longer rewarding but risky, public concerns find expression in different ways. Struggles over privacy in the digital age renew the romantic ideal of privacy as authenticity and self-determination (Nassehi, 2019). The urgency of privacy protection is explained by new perceptions of risk that see public spaces as principally unsafe and in need of control. Public exposure is seen as making individuals vulnerable, whereas private spaces guarantee safety.

Privacy protection is resilience in the elementary sense that it aims at restoring individual well-being and safety, and not primarily at promoting a common good. The new desire for privacy often builds on the ideologies of individualization that deny society and public responsibility. Unlike publicity, privacy is, at first glance, deprived of utopian elements. While publicity in the tradition of Bentham could be seen as the motor driving an open and transparent society devoted to the well-being of all, individuals seek to protect the private sphere in an attempt to shield themselves from the political.

In classical sociological thought, the modern 'self' is seen as constituted through its public exposure (Mead, 2015 [1932]). The modern individual has acquired a public status of which the idea that you can safeguard and self-determine your own privacy is only derivative. The 'self' interacts with society to come into existence and to claim 'personal autonomy'. If the self is always constituted through public observation, the notion of 'informational self-determination', which in Germany has become a constitutional guarantee against the intrusion of privacy by digital media, is a logical impossibility. The political claim for 'informational self-determination' over what is to be considered as public and private information only makes sense if we presume that there are potential publics that would agree on the relevance of the information, and possibly even make efforts to observe and pay attention. Information that is to be kept private needs to be publicly valued and its importance of protecting it publicly recognized. Privacy thus depends on potential 'lurkers'; it is only when privacy is under threat of invasion that its value can be established.

The new individualized demand to build a self that is as much as possible detached from observation by society would instead be symptomatic of a disrupted public sphere relationship. It would reduce privacy to the case of a self that wants to be kept alone and not further bothered by society. In psychological accounts, such a 'self' would appear as 'pathological'. Such demands would further put individuals under pressure, as the self needs to be backed by societal information to be able to decide about the value of information as private or even intimate. Deciding for yourself what deserves to be observed by others is a logical impossibility. Whether someone or something 'informs' or not is not an intrinsic value of the subject or object that is observed but an attributed value that depends on observation by society. This means that we always rely on public observation to be able to classify information as private or intimate. If nobody observes, no information is generated, which means that a world of pure privacy would be a non-societal space, a world that is empty of any kind of information.

If struggles over privacy are primarily driven by nostalgia, they run the risk of becoming anti-modern and detaching personal from collective self-determination. If privacy struggles are understood, however, as struggles over social status and recognition, they can hardly be fought in private, but reconstitute the political. The late modern subject strives for 'informational self-determination' as a romantic ideal for the full realization of the self (Reckwitz, 2020); yet this new ideal of 'informational self-determination' is only *prima facie* meant to give back a somewhat 'lost privacy'. It requires engagement in new forms of connective and collective action, mobilizing individuals whose primary aim is to reconquer public spaces of voice in the digital age. Digital citizens have not simply 'lost' privacy but rather have gained publicity. Their investments in privacy protection are facilitated by the new digital spaces of public exchange. Claims for privacy protection, therefore, open up a digital public sphere of resilience.

The new privacy struggles in response to digitalization become political in the sense of fighting for public recognition of claims for privacy, raising critical questions against industries but also forms of self-critique and empowerment. The claim for 'informational self-determination' is intrinsically political, not only because state authority is required to guarantee privacy protection but also because the rights for privacy need to be publicly respected and their validity tested (Nassehi, 2019: 199). Privacy claims rely on public recognition and seek public affirmation. The scripts for this struggle were already established by public intellectuals in the romantic period of the early 19th century, teaching citizens how to ascertain their personhood and creative autonomy as part of a modern national identity (Giesen, 1993). As such, the struggle over privacy as informational self-determination is a classical normative struggle of the public sphere that is turned into well-known political programmes and ideologies, like, for instance, anti-capitalism, individualism and conservatism. Contemporary privacy struggles can be programmed as left-socialist, liberalist-individualist and as right-conservative and, as such, are carried by different groups of the population. Instead of sharply dividing these groups, digital modes of fighting for privacy allow for creative combinations and unforeseen coalitions. The privacy resistance movement unifies the public sphere. Struggles over privacy as a form of public sphere resilience, nonetheless, do not primarily end up in the restitution of privacy and the retreat from publicness, but rather in the reconstitution of publics of collective self-determination.

Behind the struggle over the protection of privacy is an ongoing struggle over the value of publicity, and ultimately, about the price a political community is willing to pay for the quality of its communicative infrastructure. The digital public sphere has not opened these normative struggles but simply continues and relaunches them, as for instance in the way the traditional institution of journalism needs to reinvent itself to survive in the online world in order to defend the worth of its products. Whoever wants to revalue privacy also needs to find new responses to the question of the value of publicity and give new responses to the old question of how to defend the quality standards of debates and the value of information that 'deserves' to be public. In fact, the question of how to revalue our private lives and protect them from the risks and possibly devastating effects of excesses of publicity can only be decided collectively, with norms and standards that need to be scrutinized in public and by publics. Without this intrinsic linkage to publicity, privacy would fall apart, and individuals would no longer be able to meaningfully relate to it.

The protection of privacy itself is turned into a public struggle, which is not only a struggle over how to balance the public and the private but also about redefining the public good underlying this distinction, and often not so much redefining or even re-inventing it but rather re-launching and re-introducing it into debates that are only about short-term (and often private) interests. In response to the logic of capitalist media markets and their exploitation of private social media interactions for profit, the 'lost privacy struggle' could be considered as anti-capitalist or even anti-systemic. The struggle over privacy thus further politicizes the digital public sphere and confronts private actors with demands for public responsibility. Private entrepreneurs on the digital market have long resisted such a change in status from private to public actors, such as when Facebook was asked to confront the responsibility of being a media company and introduce quality checks on information spread throughout its public sites (Reiman, 2012). Facebook or Twitter are not only forced into cooperation with states to regulate communication in line with public sphere standards of quality but have increasingly begun to act as a public regulator as well, modulating forms of communication that have an immediate political relevance, for instance when they set community guidelines or consider whether or not posts are important to the public interest before removing them for violating set guidelines.[1] Unregulated social media exchanges proved to be highly damaging for the reputation of the providers. The digital industries' long-term strategy to deny such public status failed because state and public pressure increased worldwide. This means that they need to show they are willing to adopt quality standards of communication and invest in effective public regulation to protect themselves. Once Facebook's public status is recognized, they also need to meet higher standards of legitimacy and become subject to control by states and publics. They now regularly cooperate with state authorities and established journalism institutions and are held accountable by government and parliaments, for instance in hearings by the US Congress. This also means a changing status for users, who are calling for inclusion, participation and the distribution of revenue. On other occasions, digital industries might also claim for public status, for instance when they wish to appear not simply as private lobbyists but as partners of civil society in struggles for the rights of freedom of expression, or on an equal footing with states to decide about the regulation of the digital infrastructures.

From social media chatroom to darknet: the expanding digital private word

Struggles over privacy are not only cultivated in the form of a new romanticism but also stand in the long tradition of anti-capitalism: the private strikes back against state domination and capitalist exploitation. Digital media markets not only regularly violate privacy; they establish a system of 'surveillance capitalism' that puts private observers in place of public authority in search of techniques for totalitarian control. The lurkers are no longer state authorities who might or might not have legitimate reasons to penetrate privacy, but private actors who gain power by accumulating private information on others. Surveillance in digital media markets is transversal as everyone can now engage in surveillance with relatively low costs of entry (Hoye and Monaghan, 2018: 355). This has changed the logic of profit-making and capitalist accumulation. While traditional media industries were mainly content providers for mass consumption, with only a very restricted interest in the private information of individual media users, the new profit logics of digital media markets is 'big data', rich in private information (Helles and Ørmen, 2020). Digital capitalism has opened a market for 'big data' in the form of private information collected and used by private individuals and companies. In early modernity, states were the main drivers of the development of tracking techniques as a means of totalitarian control of private individuals. With digitalization, states, at least in the Western world, withdraw from surveillance, while sophisticated tracking techniques are developed by digital companies. Markets turn out to be even more totalitarian than states in the sense of applying tracking tools that even encompass our health and body, like registering the heart frequencies of hundreds of millions of smart phone users. Unlike capitalist markets, states institutionalized and centralized legitimate forms of tracking, for instance in the form of the police and intelligence apparatus. This state monopoly of legitimate forms of tracking has now been replaced by the diffusion of tracking technologies and their widespread use by all kinds of private actors: not only Google, Facebook or Amazon but also my employer, my school, my university, my mobile phone, my smart watch, my car, my toaster and my local supermarket. In this sense, digital society continues tracking practices that are inherent in modern society while at the same time opening them up for public use. Tracking has even become a regular pastime of social media users lurking around the profiles of others, or investing in techniques such as mobility cameras that allow private individuals to track public life in the immediate neighbourhood of their private homes.

Under the conditions of the digital attention market, a new form of publicity without publics is generated. Tracking technologies constitute publicity for private use. The public sphere has never been so public with regard to the availability of information and the openness of digital spaces to be accessed from anywhere by anyone. The many excesses of publicness become disruptive if conditions are not met to filter and channel communication and make it applicable for individual use. This aggravates the threat of surveillance domination (Hoye and Monaghan, 2018) and contributes to the feeling of being lost in publicness, as well as a widespread desire to retreat from public life or experience alternative forms of publicness.

However, digital capitalism is woefully understood if only based on surveillance. Digital media platforms fundamentally rely on private interactions and for that purpose create private spaces of encounter, empowering private users in significant ways. While collecting private data for commercial and political use, they also relaunch privacy. To the extent that publicity is amplified and everything becomes social, the market of private exchanges is also revitalized. The often-raised expectation that digital and social media platforms would replace privacy by unbound publicity, therefore, is implausible. In 2019, Facebook, whose mission in the early years was to make the world more open and social, announced a turn towards privacy protection. This can be interpreted as a response to growing public scepticism, but it is also in line with the market logic of social media platforms to confine protected private spaces of media consumption where individual users feel safe and unobserved. In line with the logics of public sphere resilience, we can expect that once such an ideal of empowered media users is put into practice, it will also generate competent users who reinvent and reclaim privacy as part of their 'creative media use'.

Despite this shared legacy of a close linkage between privacy and publicity and personal and public autonomy in Western thought, practices of privacy protection vary widely, and exploring such variations is a playground for sociologists. One main finding relates to the many cultural, class and gender-related differences in the application of privacy rules and practices. In his essay 'Privacy: Its Constitution and Vicissitudes', Edward Shils (1966) writes about the idea of privacy as a 'public' and 'community' value, which has been used by the 'white Western bourgeoisie' in a political struggle against other cultures and working classes and their lower appreciation of the value of privacy. Cultural specifics of privacy assessments also persist between countries, ranging from highly sensitive countries like Germany to countries where privacy concerns still rank lower, as is the case for many parts of Southern Europe (Bennett and Raab, 2017). From a socio-historical perspective, such differences could be explained with reference to the Protestant ethic,[2] different degrees of modernization or simply differences of education and media literacy.

In the following, I will collect some examples of creative media use that reclaims privacy. My view on these unfolding practices of privacy resilience is not that of a psychologist who is primarily interested in the individual motivations for escapes into privacy but rather of a sociologist seeking to understand privacy claims as part of public sphere struggles that reconnect to notions of a common good.

The first field of privacy resilience encompasses *intimate relationships*. The intimate online sphere can be used for chats and personal relationships but also more explicitly for erotic relations, cybersex or the consumption of pornography. As such, it is massive, according to some statistics encompassing up to 30 per cent of the world's Internet traffic.[3] For users who move in the intimate online sphere, privacy protection is a main concern, as bad experiences with providers of cybersex in the form of aggressive ads, viruses and spyware attacks, and other forms of harassment, are frequent. Online pornography is a 'dirty business', a case of predatory capitalism that offers sex as labour and exploits lonely users (Saunders, 2020). Apart from the porn industry, porn sites also facilitate user-driven exchanges, including the uploading of harmful or illegal content, such as revenge porn or images of abuse. Anti-pornography campaigners have therefore called for enhanced state controls and regulation of this intimate sphere, citing pornography's 'contaminating' moral effects and more recently also the scientific authority of the alleged harmful effects of porn consumption on personality (Perry, 2021). Fear of pornography as a public menace (Perry and Whitehead, 2020) can be a driver of moral campaigns in the form of public sphere resistance. However, online pornography is increasingly turning into a creative and diverse economy (Wilkinson, 2017), which opens a new playing field for start-ups that offer 'alternative porn'. The intimate online sphere thus shows resilience in the sense of creating a more 'cosy and safer environment' for sexual relationships. As described by a successful start-up for online porn in Berlin describes: there is a high demand by users and subscribers not only for safety but also for a more ethical approach to porn. The start-up therefore focuses on 'ethical porn' that is produced in a 'fair way' to avoid exploitation of the female body and to show respect for women. A new understanding of online pornography is offered as 'joyful togetherness' that is responsible and politically aware in its representation of the full diversity of sexual practices and human bodies.[4] The anti-capitalist struggle against the porn industry is thus turned into an emancipatory struggle of adult users who creatively enter intimate relationships without renouncing public responsibility. 'True' privacy and intimacy are reclaimed against the commercialization of porn and are meant no longer meant to be a disinterested privacy, but a 'responsible' privacy that is aware of human diversity, equality and respect.

A second field of online privacy resilience relates to the open-source movement, the sharing culture and piracy culture. New practices of community sharing of copyright content spread in early 2000, with the invention of file formats such as MP3 or AVI for popular use. The undermining of intellectual property and copyrights was soon criticized as a new form of limitless and uncontrolled consumption that shows disrespect towards artists and is harmful for the creativity of a cultural public sphere (Arvanitakis and Fredriksson, 2016). Calling for open access of digitalized content, however, refers as well to the utopian elements of the public sphere, with claims for the free and unlimited flow of information. The struggle over authorship is also taken up by different consumer associations and trade unions, defending not simply the right to publish but the right to be recognized as the publisher, the author or the owner of copyrights. The sub-politics of online piracy unfolded as an emancipatory movement against private property rights and in defence of the civil rights of individual users, e-democracy, free speech, open content and net neutrality (Lindgren and Linde, 2012). While subverting private property, the pirates of the Internet reclaimed, at the same time, an extended right for consumer privacy in the form of free choices of consumption and protection from legal prosecution (Aigrain, 2012; Spilker, 2017). As such, they constitute new private spheres of informal online user exchanges that are guided by norms of individual autonomy and reciprocity. The cultural industries and states launched a crusade against the sharing culture and file sharing providers such as Napster for their infringements of copyright law. The 'open-Internet' or 'open-source' movement of self-acclaimed pirates is countered by the industries and states as defenders of intellectual property law and authorship rights. This contributed to a further politicization of the sharing culture in some countries, seeking coalitions with political parties or even founding their own Pirate parties, which in countries like Germany and Sweden gained electoral success with their demands for an open Internet (Jääsaari and Hildén, 2015). In more recent years, instead of peer-to-peer file sharing, the sharing economy has become commercialized, with providers such as Netflix and Spotify offering affordable subscriptions for everyone to access cultural content for private use. Cultural consumption has been re-privatized once again, and the 'participatory culture' of the early Internet has turned into an 'algorithmic culture' that sells cultural products, turning them into personalized content for private use (Klein et al, 2017).

A third field of privacy resilience is the deepnet or darknet, which consists of applications which allow users to navigate the net with enhanced privacy settings and encrypted communications connected to non-indexed content that is made invisible to governments and companies such as Google. The deepnet is commonly associated with all the content that is stored online but is not searchable via regular web browsers such as Google Chrome. It contains all content which, for whatever reason, is not made publicly accessible: content behind paywalls, intranet, password-protected sites or all kinds of hidden networks. The actual size of the deepnet is difficult to establish, but it is estimated that Google, the largest search engine, has brought to the surface only about 4–16 per cent of all web content (Rudesill et al, 2015: 6). Despite the potential for enhanced publicity, hidden or secret content thus largely prevails over content that is made publicly accessible online. However, not all of this content with restricted access is, strictly speaking, private. It is more accurate to speak of the web as stratified by privileges of access to content and information based on memberships and subscriptions.

The darknet is a small section of the deepnet, containing content considered to be illegal. In the early days of the Internet, the darknet largely overlapped with peer-to-peer file sharing networks. If file sharing is perceived as harmful, the darknet is often seen as outright dangerous, for instance in the way it facilitates drug trafficking or the sharing of child sexual abuse material (Owen and Savage, 2015). Yet the darknet has many uses. Besides establishing huge illegal marketplaces, the darknet also responds to increasing concerns with privacy and censorship. As Jardine (2017: 2825) puts it:

> Ordinary people can use anonymity-granting technologies to protect their privacy from government agencies, political opponents, trolls, data-hungry corporations and even Internet service providers. People in highly repressive regimes can also turn to anonymity-granting Dark Web technologies, such as the Tor Browser, to circumvent censorship, exercise a right of free expression and maintain their privacy in the face of an abusive regime (or even non-governmental vigilantes, trolls or bullies).

Darknet applications are especially popular in countries with higher levels of restrictions on Internet freedom (Jardine, 2017: 2825). Darknet cultures also unfold to undermine practices of government secrecy in the form of whistle-blowers and spies (Coleman, 2014), providing safe spaces for the expression of political opposition in oppressive regimes, or facilitating access to scientific publications for non-subscribers of journals and e-books in the field of academic publishing (Rudesill et al, 2015: 9).

A fourth field of online privacy resilience is found in the escape from open platforms, such as Facebook, into private digital rooms of peer-to-peer exchanges. Social media instant messengers, and chatrooms such as WhatsApp, Snapchat or Telegram, respond to the need of social media users to enter more private conversations. They are social media platforms that favour private conversation over public talk yet still allow public communicators through semi-private talk to reach out at mass level. They also respond to safety demands, for instance in the form of encrypted content as facilitated by WhatsApp. Their offer of enhanced privacy functions becomes attractive to users who are scared by the excesses of publicness on other social media platforms, or who see themselves as victims of the regulatory turn of Facebook and Twitter. Content regulation in the form of banning posts and comments, and sanctioning for misbehaviour in public groups, as increasingly imposed by Facebook and Twitter, can be avoided by turning to instant messaging apps, where speech remains largely unregulated.

The semi-private world of the chatroom is experienced as less conflictive and less contingent, and as a 'safer' place to speak out and seek confirmation for one's private views and opinions. This means, however, that the epistemic horizon is restricted to what is held to be true by a group of insiders, which risks becoming a breeding ground for conspiracy theories, as I will argue later in the chapter. Yet, these groups, even if operating in a secluded, semi-private sphere, raise claims of generalized validity, which they protect from contestation and argumentation by others. The private chatroom, in this sense, is not private at all. It is public because its private members claim public consequences and also wish to raise public awareness of their concerns and to discuss issues of 'shared concern'. It is therefore erroneous to assume that the chatroom has entirely privatized political speech and has suspended the public–private distinction. We instead observe different modes of transition between private and public. One such transition to publicness can be called 'the boiling over effect': discontent and rage breeds in private chatrooms until it boils over to the public (Rall, 2019). The chatroom also plays an important role of trust building by sharing feelings of mistrust. It is constituted by trusted members who can talk more frankly about things that bother them, and who are often 'united in mistrust' expressed against established media and institutions of the public sphere. The common sense they develop is derived from the suspicion they entertain against the world beyond the group. The intimacy of the closed group comes at the price of hostility towards the world of mainstream media. Such an attitude of distancing can be observed in the choice of stories that circulate within those groups, often picking up alarming messages of being threatened or betrayed by some anonymous outside forces.

The last and most political field of online privacy resilience are practices of anti-surveillance capitalism. Such practices are not a social movement in the traditional sense. They can but do not need to take shape in political mobilization. Resilience against surveillance capitalism is often based on individual choices, awareness of Internet risks raised in schools, families or other informal institutions, and incentives for changing user behaviour as facilitated by new apps or start-ups. Risk avoidance and critical awareness of surveillance results from learning and new creative media usage that challenges the monopoly of the tech giants. Practices of anti-surveillance capitalism are also wrongly understood if simply reduced to the dimension of privacy protection. There are many good reasons to express privacy concerns in the use of the Internet, and to enter a struggle over the re-conquest of privacy. By expressing these fears and turning them into political mobilization, the anti-surveillance movement targets the heart of the public sphere and the public use of media technologies.

This idea of a totalitarian subversion of the public sphere into a panopticon for the exposure of individual lives is actually an old topos of public sphere research. However, fear of surveillance is traditionally linked to states, not to private companies. Orwell's dystopian vision of 1984 is one of state totalitarianism. The question of whether the state is still the leading threat to privacy is open to debate. A new type of digital surveillance authoritarianism is indeed developing, building on the readiness and capacities of states to develop a digital surveillance apparatus. Some states, like China, are the most advanced in optimizing surveillance of their citizens through the use of digital media technologies. This is facilitated by the lack of constitutional guarantees of individual rights, while disposing at the same time of resources and technical know-how to build an efficient apparatus of state control. In Western democracies, the legal and constitutional hurdles that states need to overcome are higher. At the same time, state authorities under liberal ideology have a tradition of building legitimacy not so much through surveillance but through the protection of individual autonomy. In most Western countries, there is a stable majority believing that states should not be allowed to make use of new surveillance technologies, such as face-recognition software. Excesses of state surveillance are controlled by the critical eye of the public, the media and the courts. New digital technologies remain, nonetheless, a temptation for states to invest in surveillance, and when facing terrorist attacks or crises, they might quickly swap sides.

There is a noticeable shift of emphasis in the discussion of surveillance capitalism in Western societies from fear of states to fear of private companies. Despite a growing awareness of risks, individuals are still tempted in many ways to sacrifice their privacy for shared content with the social media companies. This is precisely what Zuboff's (2019) account of surveillance capitalism is: digitalization builds on business models to make profit from private data and to reward individual users who agree to the use of their private data. The value of private data is thus counted as a currency that can be traded and negotiated by private digital industries. Unlike the obtrusive surveillance techniques employed by states, smart surveillance in the private sectors often goes unnoticed yet is able to create new dependencies that fundamentally impact on private life. Private Internet surveillance not only runs in parallel to public state surveillance but often competes with and disempowers states. Jan-Werner Müller (2019: 151) has pointed to the linkage between the experience of new dependencies created by the use of digital technologies and individual and collective fears of moving in the digital world. Digital markets are built on surveillance business models that only function because people are simultaneously made dependent on affordances offered by digital media. The types of involvement and participation in digital markets can create deep dependencies, sometimes even addictions, as for instance when social media attention becomes a matter of individual well-being, or when online visibility is used as a measurement of social status. The constant checking of status updates through our mobiles is not simply an annoying habit but an addiction, which gives away new private data, of great value for the companies, with every click.

A market that turns surveillance into a business model and, at the same time, creates dependencies that bind people to the market, can be called totalitarian. Tech giants have become totalitarian in the sense that they not only deliver control technologies to the power holders but increasingly use this technology themselves to replace the state. Facebook is one often-quoted example of 'corporate totalitarianism': their main ambition is to control every aspect of their users' lives, and they apply the perfect tracking techniques to do so. What makes it worse is that this new form of totalitarianism does not remain confined to states but encompasses 2 billion users across the globe (Bode, 2019). Facebook's pretention is also totalitarian in the way it claims to solve world problems. Rather, it has become a world problem, which no single state and no confined public can cope with. The fear that drives anti-surveillance capitalism mobilization is that totalitarian markets might prove to be even worse than totalitarian states, as they cannot simply be overrun by a revolution or targeted by forms of local resistance (Keen, 2012). Facebook is also totalitarian in the sense that it even encompasses the forms of resistance and resilience against anti-surveillance capitalism, which unfold through its own platforms and communication infrastructures.

The privacy trap: misconceptions and glorifications of privacy in the digital age

Forms of privacy resilience, as I have argued in this chapter, are often based on misconceptions and glorifications of privacy in response to digitalization. From a public sphere perspective, such excesses of privacy can be conceived as harmful and as undermining the common good. Privacy protection can have perverse effects on increasing the non-transparency of online opinion-making and reducing the possibility of corrective public interventions in political debates. It risks disabling the control function of the public sphere that is based on openness and accessibility of information. Privacy romanticism is an escape from publicness, not a rational response to reducing risks and making life safer. Empirical evidence for the assumption that individuals are exposed to higher risks in the public domain, while being protected in the safe harbour of privateness, has always been lacking. Instead, the more value social media give to privacy, allowing users to apply techniques to protect their exchanges, the more a social medium falls into a privacy trap, where individual risks and losses prevail over potential advancements of security. The following evidence argues for the importance of such a privacy trap on social media:

1. *Absence of public control*: for a long time in history, private spheres have been the realm of uncontrolled violence and male domination, not of safety and protection. Even in our contemporary societies, violence in private homes is more frequent and also often more tolerated than in the streets (Decker, 2007). Digitalization has potentially even exacerbated this problem since users are more exposed to forms of harassment and abuse in private online conversations than on public sites. While it is beyond doubt that the widespread use of tracking software has multiplied harmful breaches of people's online privacy, the idea that publicity correlates with vulnerability, and privacy with safety, has probably never been so inaccurate as in the contemporary social media world. Publicity is needed, more than ever, to raise awareness of the risks of misconduct in the private sphere and to promote adequate measures of protection for vulnerable people as potential victims. Enhanced privacy on social media might, therefore, make social media users even more vulnerable. Moving in the deepnet and the darknet might be useful as a form of protection from unwanted public intervention, or from capitalist surveillance, but it does not protect against harmful interventions or abuses by other users.

2. *Unreliable information worlds*: privacy is also a potential threat to the reliability of information that is received without going through the test of public scrutiny. Private niches on the web enhance the risk of exposure to misinformation and manipulation and thus undermine the promise of the online public sphere to promote more and better publicity, to guarantee communication standards and to reach out to the world with plural and impartial information. Private information worlds are often upheld with the specific purpose of blockading plural information and opinion and demands for public scrutiny. If informational self-determination also implies determination over the value of information, this would risk tearing our shared information world apart. The private net would become dark, not enlightened. Information would mainly spread in the form of rumour, and tests of accuracy and control of information could not be conducted. Procedures for establishing truth in the reduced public sphere would be constantly torpedoed by arbitrary conspiracy theories launched by the private sphere, which would generate conspirators on social media, not informed groups.

3. *Spread of fear and anxieties*: private groups on social media are often constituted by more vulnerable persons, communicating their fears or expressing their anger. The more they do this in secluded spaces,

like chatrooms on WhatsApp or instant messengers like Telegram, the more their fear becomes contagious. Private social media spheres, in this sense, are significant facilitators of panic and hysteria, 'generating fear about social change, sharpening social distance, or offering new opportunities for vilifying outsiders, distorting communications, manipulating public opinion, and mobilizing embittered individuals' (Walsh, 2020: 840).

4. *Restrictions to free speech*: the semi-private online spheres are meant to protect free speech, but such protective environments can again restrict free speech in important ways. Apart from informal controls and sanctioning of what is said in the groups, the free speech principle also loses its ability to build consensus or enforce criticism when used in the private sphere. Algorithmically amplified 'free speech' in privatized social media spheres can be seen as speech that is deprived of its sociological functioning of commitment to a shared realm of discourse. People might feel safe to make use of free speech in such semi-public or private rooms among trusted peers, but, at the same time, they generate distrust with outsiders and thus undermine the trust resources of society.

In the following, I wish to uphold a distinction between resilient publics and private conspiracy groups as two possible outputs of enhanced social media privacy. The first draw on privacy as a resource to regain control over personal data and manage the flow of information in a way that reduces risks and vulnerability related to public exposure; the second infiltrate the private sphere, exploit uncertainty and spread fear and anxiety. We speak of resilient publics if privacy is primarily meant as a form of empowerment and emancipation of media users over mediators and elites who tell them the truth. Truth finding has been 'democratized' on social media platforms in the way that individual users and small communities are encouraged to resist official narratives, to claim 'alternative facts' and be rewarded with attention and visibility, and, in fact, also recognition and identity for their alternative accounts of truth (Vaidhyanathan, 2018). However, such claims for alternative truths often avoid public scrutiny and justification and thus place themselves outside the realm of public discourse. The enhanced privacy risks being turned into conspiracy to undercut public sphere principles, rather than supporting resilience. While conspiracies might be successful in reducing uncertainty at the individual level, at the collective level they contribute to epistemic uncertainty and, in addition, are also placed strategically so as to undermine epistemic consensus. As research on the spread of conspiracies has shown, they rarely result from community practices and rather can be defined as a strategy of propagandistic domination (Uscinski et al, 2018; Weigmann, 2018). The violation of discursive procedures does not happen accidentally but by default. As such, conspiracies are a possibility but not a necessary outcome of the new search for privacy. The line between resilience and conspiracies, however, is difficult to draw in practice. Private online spheres often fluctuate between the two, which can best be illustrated by looking at the story of WhatsApp.

WhatsApp enhances private communication in the form of encrypted chat communication. It exists in an invisible and thus non-public space that excludes all non-members from the communicative exchange. What is communicated within a room, and how it is communicated, is not regulated by public speech, cannot be scrutinized, and the value of information is not commonly agreed upon. Yet, at the same time, this enhanced privacy is powerful enough to create semi-public opinions with an impact on political views and attitudes that are held by individuals not as members of the public, but as atomized receivers of private messages. The semi-private message might be even more authoritative because the information is exclusively held. Membership in a private chatroom might thus become more appealing than adherence to the public. There is a psychological satisfaction to sharing information exclusively with people who care about you and to experience the intimacy of people with the same concerns, the same anger. As William Davies put it:

> The political threat of WhatsApp is the flipside of its psychological appeal. Unlike so many other social media platforms, WhatsApp is built to secure privacy. On the plus side, this means intimacy with those we care about and an ability to speak freely; on the negative side, it injects an ethos of secrecy and suspicion into the public sphere. As Facebook, Twitter and Instagram become increasingly theatrical – every gesture geared to impress an audience or deflect criticism – WhatsApp has become a sanctuary from a confusing and untrustworthy world, where users can speak more frankly. As trust in groups grows, so it is withdrawn from public institutions and officials. A new common sense develops, founded on instinctive suspicion towards the world beyond the group.[5]

The information value in the private chatroom is established by the value of privacy and exclusivity, and no longer through the test of arguments in an open exchange. This is an invitation for political leadership to build privileged membership groups and to reach out only to supporters through their targeted messages (Gil de Zúñiga et al, 2021). Public relations can be filtered through private networks, and political campaigns can establish seemingly privatized relationships between party leaders and their supporters. Even the party congress can become a semi-private event to celebrate 'exclusive membership' (Gerbaudo, 2019).

The flip side of the psychological appeal of privacy in social media chatrooms, as Davies continues, is that it 'inject[s] an ethos of secrecy and suspicion into the public sphere':

> A communication medium that connects groups of up to 256 people, without any public visibility, operating via the phones in their pockets, is by its very nature, well-suited to supporting secrecy. Obviously not every group chat counts as a 'conspiracy'. But it makes the question of how society coheres, who is associated with whom, into a matter of speculation – something that involves a trace of conspiracy theory. In that sense, WhatsApp is not just a channel for the circulation of conspiracy theories, but offers content for them as well. The medium is the message.[6]

To understand why closed groups risk becoming a breeding ground for conspiracy theories, it is helpful to look at the mechanisms of muting internal criticism. Anonymity only works towards the outside world, but among members of a secret group, the mask is taken off and a rigid system of internal rules of behaviour applies. The critical eye is directed towards the outside, whereas complacency becomes the group norm. The idea of the public is perverted by the closed chatroom, which claims its right to remain private but still insists on being heard in its judgement of public affairs. This can be successful for achieving higher levels of in-group trust and cohesion. Yet precisely this strength of in-group cohesion risks disabling the control functions of the critical public sphere, ultimately perceived as hostile, distant, anonymous, impersonal or even fake. The social media closed group culture thus rejects the original promise of the Internet in terms of openness, inclusion and connections, and is anchored in the privacy of like-minded people who react to the perceived threats of privacy through secrecy and seclusion.

In reaction to the privacy trap and its recognition as a *public problem*, public sphere resilience is about re-evaluating publicness and regaining democratic spaces of openness and contestation. Abuses of privacy are thus overcome by public visibility. The Internet needs to regain visibility of public communication, which inevitably compromises privacy and confronts individual users with public responsibility. Such confrontations rely on innovative ways of making the private public again, for instance by exposing excesses of privacy in public or re-politicizing private, or even intimate relationships. Lisa Ann Richey (2016) shows how users of Tinder, who post pictures of themselves engaged in humanitarian work, are exposed by other users and ridiculed on open Facebook sites as 'Tinder humanitarians'. Such breaches of privacy are political, with the intention of bringing to the surface immoral practices and regaining visibility. This is in line with experiments of social media political communication, namely that the more we know about individual users and the less anonymous their movements, the more they will behave in controlled ways (Taylor et al, 2019). Add a public e-mail address and a real picture to a user, and their social media behaviour will change considerably. Publicness of communication reintroduces a shared value orientation, establishes procedures of accountability by bystanders and triggers mechanisms of self-control. Visibility, not only to friends but to members of the same profession, the local community or the whole country, is not simply putting individual users at risk of exposure. Being exposed also means being connected, open-minded and responsive to the expectations and criticism of others. This critical self-awareness adds to the struggle over privacy as a new public good. The question regarding how to rebalance public–private relationships in the digital age is ultimately a question of Internet regulation, where civil society and states enter a new alliance against global digital capitalism.

The political struggle of privacy protection: A new alliance between state and civil society?

The question of what sort of regulation is required to protect privacy is a controversial subject not only at the domestic level between defenders of a free Internet and supporters of state control; it is also among the most contested issues in international relations, affecting EU competences and the relationship between states and global companies. Both call for and against Internet regulation, a new type of public sphere beyond the national and in search of a rebalanced relationship between privacy, ownership and freedom of the Internet. With regard to the EU copyright directive, for instance, protest was mobilized transnationally under the assumption that such regulation would affect the freedom of the Internet and freedom of speech with regard to the sharing of copyrighted content, such as parody (memes) or news articles. Such protest includes a plethora of actors: EU member states, the United States and other states potentially affected by the regulation; the European Commission and the European Parliament; social media companies, either as lobbyists or as campaigners[7] (YouTube, for instance supported campaigns against the EU directive); and civil society (both right-wing mobilization in support of free speech and freedom of the Internet and civic-libertarian movements).

The political struggle over the regulation of the Internet has given birth to strange alliances. An open-source Internet can curb the power of the tech giants but also threatens the intellectual property rights of creative users. The protection of copyright, therefore, is as much in the interest of big media companies, such as Hollywood film studios, as it is of independent authors and artists. The defence of free speech and a free Internet is not solely the domain of civic-libertarian movements but also backed by states and companies, while state and EU efforts at copyright protection are often denounced as illegitimate limitations of free speech. While there is a real concern that states and companies might use copyright enforcement, hate speech regulation or misinformation campaigns as a form of political censorship, the struggle for a free Internet at the same time polarizes the web community, which is increasingly being taken over by right-wing groups who fear that their content might be banned from social media.

The open and free Internet movement not only enters into conflict with authorship associations but also with the defenders of the quality of information. Here, it is not property rights and questions of intellectual authorship that are highlighted, but questions of the informative value of media content and truth of information. Ultimately, this is a struggle about the application of public sphere standards: a well-functioning public sphere is traditionally measured not just by the amount of information channelled but in the way content is qualified, information filtered and content made relevant for different societal groups and audiences. The struggle over intellectual property rights and the struggle over the quality of information and debates are in this sense interrelated, as both rely on selective mechanisms to reward creative content. The recognition of what can count as valuable communication needs to be coupled with reward schemes that distinguish providers of quality content over others. An open-source public sphere infrastructure cannot resolve the problem of how to establish the value of information in a way that is fair and acceptable for the majority of users. By granting equal access to content combined with equal voice and equal chances to be listened to, the free and open Internet would omit the filtering function of the classical public sphere. As such, it would be an incomplete public sphere; a liberal communicative space deprived of its epistemic dimension.

The debate about the regulation of free speech and intellectual property on the Internet, therefore, is not simply about the control of free market exchanges but touches upon core principles of civil society and the public sphere. Rather than dividing, it unites states and civil society in new alliances against the arbitrary power of social media companies that may interfere with citizens' choices and participation in the public sphere (Aytac, 2022). The struggle against surveillance capitalism is in this sense an opportunity to build a new alliance between states and civil society. Unlike states and their particularistic solutions to the problem of 'taming' capitalism, civil society holds the promise of 'universalistic' solutions. They can meet with states in a joint effort to seek market regulation and best-for-all solutions. If states stand for authoritarian rule over global flows of communication, civil society claims for a new common good orientation in the protection of privacy, individual autonomy and standards of truth. State surveillance against capitalist surveillance gains in efficiency but remains incomplete because it is bound to a particularistic agenda that often places states as interest actors in opposition to each other. Coordinated state interventions against surveillance capitalism, in this sense, can profit from civil society cooperation in gaining credibility and overcoming conflicts of interest, while civil society can profit from state cooperation in gaining efficiency of control through the advancement of international law and global standards.

Anti-surveillance state interventionism always bears the risk of a new authoritarianism. States which try to 'regain control' over digital communications through regulatory interventions often do so by limiting the anti-authoritarian and subversive dynamics of free speech. State authoritarianism is obviously a bad replacement for corporate surveillance, and protesters in Hong Kong clearly find digital Leninism, imposed by the Chinese government, to be a more threatening scenario than digital capitalism.

If state authoritarianism is a bad antidote to corporate authoritarianism, the only alternative states have is to take a progressive role as a protector of the democratic public sphere and its principles. The steering of the digital transformation is based on the premise of a public interest to be defended, and actively promoted, against private actors. Such a new state mandate requires civic partnerships and enhances international cooperation. As such, it is based on a typical European script of governance that makes states responsible for regulating a market of common exchanges. State actors are not only pushed by consumers and Internet users to take back control and protect privacy; they also have a self-interest in occupying lost terrain over global markets and building trust in their new role as a benign supervisor of media communications. The task ahead is to embed digital capitalism in a democratic public sphere that requires investment in political steering and the design of digital markets (Forestal, 2021). The regulation of digital markets is framed as a question of governance, not government, emphasizing innovative modes of management while also relying on legal rules and authorities. This requires collaborative schemes, networking, decentralized solutions, delegation of competences, involvement of stakeholders and sharing of responsibilities. In digital governance, networks do not simply replace markets and hierarchies but supplement their functions in such a way as to enhance the steering capacities of the political system over media and the economy (van Dijk and Beek, 2009; van Dijk, 2012a).

Raising the question of power and control over digital markets can thus be taken as an opportunity for state actors and regulatory agencies, such as the EU, to renew their political legitimacy. Especially when faith in government and democratic steering capacities has become fragile, political actors can seek to build trust by investing in their new role as protectors of citizens' rights and privacy against the digital industries. As such, the trump card over digital markets is not only raised by left-wing parties, who traditionally ask for the extension of state regulation over free-riding neoliberal economies. Claims for state sovereignty over globalized industries are also a fixed element of the agenda of right-wing or populist parties, who propagate their claims of 'taking back control' over the global media and their alleged liberal agendas.[8]

In the battle over the digital future, civil society becomes the wooed ally, not only for states but also for global companies. Tech giants, like Facebook or Google, have always propagated the image of 'being friends'. Their self-declared mission is not simply 'making profit' but enhancing technological progress combined with public welfare. They also regularly sustain liberal values, such as free speech and freedom of information, and the rights of their users for limitless access to content. To be targeted by civil society as 'evil' in the battle against surveillance capitalism, therefore, affects them in a particular way and directly undermines the credibility on which they base their business models. Once users have learned to fear the tech giants, their marketing strategy of propagating an open-access Internet increasingly falls on deaf ears. This again offers an opportunity for states to take the lead in the social and political struggle over the digital future, laying the political pathways for recoupling digitalization to social norms and the values of privacy and property.

Embedding the digital world in a world of social norms and values could become the major state task of the 21st century (Staab, 2019). More than ever, states that are willing to engage in this struggle will need to seek alliances with other states and with civil society. The regulation of the Internet is a task for the internal cooperation of states, private actors and civil society. Partnerships between state authorities, civil society and consumers will ultimately also need to get the digital media industries on board by appealing to their responsibilities and making use of their know-how for creative solutions.

Unrestrained digital markets, which have been claimed to be neoliberalism's greatest triumph (Starr, 2019), might also become the triggering moment for a powerful return of state regulation and multilateral international cooperation. Since the early 2000, the online economy has created monopolies that have powerfully pushed back against government and insisted on de-regulation as the best guarantee for economic growth and technological innovation. Digital industries have accumulated power but have failed to develop societal visions of how to use this power. They mainly targeted individuals to engage in social activities, but they did not define social forms, norms and responsibilities. What was emphatically called an online community was de facto used as an object of exploitation by predatory capitalism. The Internet, in this sense, is not politically neutral but aggressively protective of a liberal agenda. With the open society vision having been discredited, if not perverted by the Internet gurus and their neoliberal dogma, civil society and consumer associations once again embrace the regulatory state. However, states are not always benign regulators but can also follow their own agenda of surveillance. The dark side of digital capitalism, therefore, is state authoritarianism.

The renewed state authority in regulating the Internet has a symbolic and an instrumental aspect. In many countries, national executives play with the threat of regulation but lack credible means, or a willingness, to implement it. State regulatory efforts also remain symbolic in the sense of being based on false premises: they propagate national sovereignty and ignore the rules of network governance and shared sovereignty. The efficiency of Internet regulation is dependent on multilateralism and the application of international law, yet many governments prefer to take unilateral action while, at the same time, further undermining international organizations or supranational governance arrangements such as the EU. New authoritarian leaders are themselves often entangled with digital industries or seek to enter deals with them to their advantage. As shareholders, they are not anti-market, but rather competitors who seek to improve their own market positions through strategic moves, such as the threat of regulation. Symbolic and unilateral state activism against the media conglomerates might bring short-term gains in political legitimacy domestically but in the long term risks backfiring, as the authoritarian measures taken by states might not only be inefficient in curtailing the social media industries' strong market position but also help the industries to build their own legitimacy and gain credibility in their claims to defend the free Internet against state authoritarianism. In the fight against the EU's copyright regulations, for instance, the EU institutions promoted stakeholder participation but acted in a rather exclusive way towards non-expert citizen activists (Vetulani-Cęgiel and Meyer, 2020). Some of the digital providers instead supported grassroots protest. In March 2019, more than 130 European businesses signed a joint petition with free Internet activists demanding the European Parliament reject the directive.[9]

If new state authoritarianism has been facilitated by the failure of digital industries to develop a utopian vision of society, the same digital industries, who failed in the first round, could quickly catch up by propagating such a utopia against the new authoritarian state. It remains debatable, after all, whether the media industries are really Big Brother. Their hunger for private data might be insatiable, but their primary aim remains to make economic profit, not to accumulate political power. Becoming entangled in power politics might even be economically damaging, as has been repeatedly experienced by Twitter and Facebook during the American elections of 2016 and 2020.

States are therefore still more likely to turn into a Big Brother than digital industries. The mode and purpose of private data collection changes fundamentally if pursued by states: first, privacy intrusion is imposed upon individual users, and even their hypothetical choice to protect privacy is taken away. Secondly, the purpose of collecting privacy data becomes explicitly political and a question of control of individual behaviour that has real and palpable effects on individual users' lives, as well as their social, economic and political activities. While on the free Internet, individual users have room for manoeuvre to negotiate their privacy and experience gratification of their individual needs by entering a deal with the providers of content, the state-regulated Internet makes all users equal as involuntary suppliers of private data that are used to build and expand state authority.

China is the constant reminder that such differences between a state-authoritarian model of Internet regulation and a free market model actually matter, and that the horror scenario of a state-regulated Internet is not just fictional. In many respects, the United States stands for the other extreme of predatory capitalism and unrestrained power of private entrepreneurs that equally disempower users and threaten their personal autonomy. It is here that Europe, and the EU as a regulatory agency, take a special role in the struggle over the digital future. The EU has entered the regulatory competition over the Internet by offering viable alternatives to both the US model and its trust in private entrepreneurship and the self-regulatory powers of the digital markets, and the Chinese model with its search for authoritarian solutions. The regulatory Internet becomes a new utopian project for the renewal of the democratic public sphere. The focus is on users' privacy protection. The EU's open Internet directive is based on the principle of equality and non-discrimination, prohibiting Internet service providers from privileging the Internet access of private users. The Council of Europe strategy of Internet governance aims 'to ensure that public policy for the Internet is people-centred in order to build democracy online, to protect Internet users, and to ensure respect and protection for human rights online'.[10]

The way civil society embraces private data goes beyond the individual choices of withdrawal to privacy. Practices of resilience in response to the perceived threat of surveillance unfold not so much in the intimate private sphere but often include engagement in non-profit-oriented and community-based experimental modes of usage of private data. Thus, there is a debate within civil society between those who insist on privacy as an absolute principle and the individual rights of informational self-determination, and those who claim that big data should be viewed as a public asset and made accessible for public use (Lupton, 2014: 151). The anti-surveillance or dataveillance movement supports safety of digital communications through the development of alternative browsers and search engines, ad-blocking or anti-tracking software, and data encryption tools. This allows people to create safe spaces for individual and community interactions. As a result, people regain control over their personal data and at the same time restrict the amount of information that is given away for use by states and companies. Reclaiming private data is not simply about protecting one's privacy but rather about using private data in creative ways to advance the self and communities. This is a way to recognize the public value of private data and allow communities, friends or peers to use it in a more controlled way. Through the enhancement of media literacy and digital skills, increasing numbers of people are learning about the application of tools for gathering and interpreting their own data. Providers respond to this demand for private data use by allowing individuals to access their own meta-data, for instance by granting access to users' profile data and developing apps for profile analytics. This results in increasing amounts of home-made big data, which is available for personal or community development. 'Community informatics' is about the use of information and communication technologies to support social, cultural and economic development of communities, and to assist members of the community in handling their own data (Gurstein, 2007). 'Data philanthropy' is about companies who share their data with public research institutions, international organizations or governments to use the power of prediction for the benefit of society and global prosperity (Taddeo, 2017). 'Quantified Self' is a movement that supports every person's right and ability to learn from their own data.[11] Such learning not only implies self-development but also includes the possibility of aggregating one's own data with others' data to create broader insights into community life and society.

In reaction to privacy concerns, social media corporations have also implemented massive data access restrictions on their apps and websites. The data lockdown was meant as an attempt to protect privacy of user information, in response to the Cambridge Analytica Scandal, and the demands of many consumer associations and state authorities to take effective data protection measures. However, this emphasis on private data protection came at the cost of the public utility of the social media platforms banning other forms of admissible public or community usages of 'big data'. Data of public interest were declared private and withheld by private companies who claimed exclusive ownership. This contributed to the re-privatization of social media and the rejection of corporate responsibility for the manifold private activities of users whose engagement in speech was no longer qualified and/or publicly scrutinized. The Facebook data lockdown was seen as worrying, not only by developers but also by the research community, declaring in 2018 that 'systematic research on Facebook content is now untenable, turning what was already a worryingly opaque, siloed social network into a black box that is arguably even less accountable to lawmakers and the public – both of whom benefitted from academics who monitored developments on the site'.[12] What is more, the Facebook data lockdown is equivalent to a public sphere lockdown and, as such, has major damaging effects on democratic accountability. In practice, it means that Facebook, which has become one of the major forums of public debates for the formation of opinions and political attitudes, can no longer be scrutinized by critical journalists or researchers. Facebook has since responded to criticism and in 2020 facilitated collaboration with independent researchers with the establishment of CrowdTangle as a '*public* insights tool' for outsiders to have greater transparency regarding what is happening on Facebook and Instagram.[13] However, the parameters of the use of these data, and the all-important question of who gains access, are again set by Facebook. Future social media research will likely be concentrated and monopolized by some influential and resourceful research centres, with privileged access and capacities to deal with 'big data', whose task it will be to deliver knowledge for public use about the important question of the impact of social media on democracy.

Critique of the digital industries has so far been quite moderate, with consumer associations and states trying to formulate rules and re-establish public control. The success of such measures depends on the power of users and their political representatives to create sufficient pressure on companies to change corporate policies and seek collaboration. Users of digital media are far from being disempowered and can find effective ways to express their concerns and impact on the future design of the digital public sphere. Apart from moderate and collaborative forms of criticism, there is also a more radical critique of surveillance capitalism and the tracking economy that stands in the left-revolutionary tradition (Dyer-Witheford and Matviyenko, 2019). From this last perspective, anti-surveillance capitalism is carried by movements who are ready to enter a 'cyberwar' with the big Internet companies like Facebook and Google, not simply by boycotting their products but by doing damage to their business plans. While it is open to debate whether data hacktivism is a new form of civil disobedience (Delmas, 2018), these forms of radical protest often build on a form of public sphere Manichaeism, reclaiming for themselves the distinction between good and evil.

The political struggle over privacy protection in the digital public sphere is one of the examples of new ideational conflicts. It cannot be overlooked how these value-driven conflicts relate back to the material interests of particular groups, the industries or the power of states. Degrees of controversy can vary greatly. The struggle against hate speech, for instance, is highly consensual, as you cannot really oppose any good-minded person who wants to turn the digital world into a more civilized place. Struggles over authorship can instead be highly controversial and are linked to economic struggles of distribution, often hiding material interests behind ideational concerns. In the same vein, the often highly controversial struggles over the principle of net neutrality and opinion manipulation are linked back to power conflicts. Public opinion is meant to enlighten, but it also empowers, which opens a conflict over the illegitimate use of opinions in political struggles and a ranking of the quality of opinions as either informed and deliberated, or as formed and manipulated.

The sharp distinction between digital conflicts over privacy as post-materialist or ideational and old materialist and redistributive conflicts, therefore, is not sustainable. Sociologically speaking, there is no world of values that is detached from the world of material interests, and vice versa. The digital divides of values do not stand for a clash of civilizations (like, for instance, authoritarian China against the liberal Western world) but are fought internally at the heart of our democracies. If dichotomies no longer apply to international relations, as was still assumed by Huntington (1993), then domestic cleavage structures are often based on false dichotomies. National public spheres cannot be neatly divided between communitarians and cosmopolitans in the defence of democratic values (de Wilde et al, 2019), as positions are constantly shifting and values are either embraced or opposed by shifting coalitions. In particular, populists are often found to be opportunistic and not value-driven (Müller, 2016). They notoriously play with ambivalence and, depending on opportunities, have had no problem combining their frequent attacks on values at one point in time with the defence of the very same values at another.

Digital society has by now embraced the need for a rules-based Internet and social media that are common-good oriented, instead of being abused by private interests. The threat of anarchy if digital media markets lose control has created a consensus that regulation is necessary, even though the struggle over what type of regulation should apply on the Internet has just begun. This is not just a legal and political struggle but a struggle over the formation of digital society. Curiously, a rules-based social media is also what the big social media companies ask for, as their expanding activities depend on norms and infrastructures that cannot be provided by markets.

The regulatory turn has a symbolic significance as it defines a shared social responsibility, which digital industries cannot escape. After alliances have been sought between civil society and states, digital industries could become allies rather than enemies in the struggle for the digital future. In surveillance capitalism, industries are targets of social protest. At the same time, the anti-surveillance struggle contributes to the redefinition of their public responsibilities. That such public responsibilities exist was for a long time denied by the industries. Until recently, the Internet providers have insisted on web neutrality as an ordering principle of the digital public sphere. Facebook famously claimed to be only a neutral platform, and failed to take responsibility for content that was shared and social interactions that were facilitated on their platform. This is the old normative ideal of a liberal market-regulated media, which guarantees free speech and freedom of information but requires media owners and providers to remain politically neutral and to abstain from quality control of information. It is not the first time in history that such a denial of the media's social responsibility has proven unsustainable. The digital industries are facilitators of online traffic but also the ones with the technical toolkit to control the traffic. If traffic gets out of control, new roads need to be paved and old blockages removed. The owners of the road cannot simply deny responsibility for the flow of traffic on their roads. Web neutrality, therefore, is not some sort of natural state of media but an ideological stance that serves the interest of certain powerful players. It is revelatory that during the last days of the Trump administration, the principle of web neutrality was no longer upheld by Facebook and Twitter but by the US government, which denied the freedom of the providers to moderate content on their platforms. When web neutrality is imposed by states, it could, in fact, be used as a form of censorship against the partisan press, or any form of opinion expressed by journalists. A legal neutrality rule, therefore, does not support a free public sphere but would instead risk becoming a powerful state weapon against journalists.

In response to growing concerns about misinformation, conspiracies and echo chambers, industry strategies have shifted from denial of responsibility to embracement. If disruptive echo chambers are no longer seen as systemic, causalities about their triggering effects can be derived, responsibilities ascribed and adequate counter measures taken (Chambers and Kopstein, 2022). How serious the industries are about replacing liberal market logics with a new regulatory turn remains to be seen, though there are ample reasons to remain sceptical. Surveillance capitalism is still booming, with more sophisticated technologies and ever-growing databases. Precisely because they have accumulated this power, the big players, like Facebook and Twitter, can no longer claim to be just a neutral platform for the self-realization of users. They need to run advertising campaigns to fix their scandals and commit themselves to the fight against 'fake news' and hate speech. In response to the Cambridge Analytica scandal, Facebook launched a worldwide apology tour in 2018 under the slogan 'Here Together'. The campaign targeted individual users by showing a human face ('sorry, can we still be friends?') but was also used to promote a new brand identity, anticipating the will to cooperate with civil society and states on humanitarian issues and the definition of the common good (Hall, 2020). The major digital industries were also part of the EU anti-hate speech campaign, launched in 2019.[14] This was accompanied by new features to encourage users to support human rights concerns through 'slacktivism', or the temporary change of profile images (Vie, 2014).

This 'big tobacco moment' of the big techs (Chambers and Kopstein, 2022: 5) in recognizing their public responsibility raises the question: Who do they serve if they declare themselves to be public interest actors? The digital industries design a digital world, not a nationally confined market. As such, the underlying notion of publicness can only be defined in global terms. With this in mind, the digital industries have indeed become agents of a global public sphere. This is in line with the development of global

146

capitalism, which establishes, through international forums such as the Davos Summits, a network of powerful elites developing ideas about the global economy and responsibility (Ojala, 2017). At this critical juncture, the industries can be observed to be shifting between denial and embracement of global responsibilities, and the way they shift depends very much on the power of users and consumers and their growing capacities to make use of the same media technologies that are critically targeted to launch a new utopian vision of the public sphere and democracy.

The struggle over privacy, from this perspective, is to be understood as a struggle over the confinement of citizenship and democracy beyond the national. This might result in a new post-national form of *digital citizenship* as states and the Council of Europe have started to frame it.[15] The defenders of privacy, for this purpose almost necessarily, enter new state alliances and will need to seek collaboration with courts in order to decide about their cases of violation of privacy principles with the public authority of law.

To sum up, these insights about the dialectics of surveillance capitalism are an important corrective of linear thinking of public sphere transformations in terms of either progress or decay. By making the Internet part of their daily life, users also learn to deal with the ambivalences of online communications and to balance the risks and opportunities of the web for their own private, professional and public life. The key for successfully navigating the net is: do not think linearly; think dialectically. The Internet user is not simply a passive victim of surveillance capitalism but contributes to it in specific and creative ways. We use the net to increase knowledge, but by doing so, we need to realize that the net gets knowledge about us (Zuboff, 2019). Such experiences of the contradictions of digital capitalism are yet another form of knowledge. Experiences of disrupted communications are not just individual; they are collective. The digital society comes into being not simply through the creative usage of digital technologies but, as Dewey (1927) would have put it, from the awareness of 'important social consequences' of such usage. This includes the experience that resistance to digital capitalism and web surveillance cannot simply be bottom-up. It would be naive to trust civil society alone in its heroic fight against surveillance capitalism. Only by seeking new alliances with power and state authority can the tech giants be challenged.

Appeals to the people: the struggle over democratic representation

Claiming democratic representation

An important testing ground for contemporary public sphere dynamics is found in what I will investigate in the following as large-scale struggles over democracy, or rather over democratic representation. Political representation is to be understood as a *public* arrangement (Pitkin, 1967: 221). It is part of *public opinion*, which is built from the preferences and attitudes expressed by the voters, the rationales and justifications delivered by the representatives, and the norms and expectations enshrined in the political system. For a theory of political representation, it is important to note that the public is always at both ends of the process (Pitkin, 1967: 224). Representatives' pursuit of public interest, and responses to public opinion, cannot be overridden by pure self-interest, otherwise they would cease to be representatives. In equal terms, the readiness of the single citizen to vote for a candidate cannot be detached from the lifeworld of communication, exchanges of opinions and interactions with other voters, as it is only through such interactions that political preferences are shaped.

Thinking of political representation as a *public* arrangement is useful, first, to re-conceptualize representation as a triadic communicative act, and second, to approach the particular form and process of *democratic* representation. As a communicative linkage that needs to be claimed for, political representation is not substantial but ascriptive and thus relies on the persuasive power of public discourse that mediates between political agents (claimants), constituents and audiences (Saward, 2010). By defining representation as a claim to be representative for someone or something, the focus is not on the strategic act of claims-making but precisely on the dynamic and performative aspects of representative claims-making that operates through public and media discourse. From this perspective, political representation extends beyond the principal–agent perspective (Lane, 2009) to include 'the third' as a passive bystander, who is equally addressed by the claim for representation, even if not formally included. We encounter this position of the third, for instance, whenever political agents claim to represent minorities but use broader public mobilization to convince others of the necessity of minority protection. The 'third' or the audience becomes decisive as the wider resonance body of representative claims-making, which accepts (or rejects) a claim as being representative for something or someone. The process of representative claims-making thus needs to be studied in relation to its capacities to create publicity.

Understanding political representation as a *public* arrangement is useful, in a second step, to approach the particularity of *democratic* representation, both as a form and as a process. Democratic representation is not defined here in terms of formal aggregative procedures, or through its inputs or outputs, but rather grounded in the generalized validity of representative claims-making to stand for the public. As a form, democratic representation relates to any expression/symbolization of the collective will (Urbinati and Warren, 2008: 391). Democratic representation thus transcends the particularity of a representative–constituent relationship through its claim of generalized validity. It is made by the claim of a partial subject (individual, namely in the form of a representative claimant, or corporate, in the form of a parliament) to stand for the general will. As a process, democratic representation is about collective will formation. It is made by the public contestation of all who claim to represent the collective will. As such, it is processed through public speech that meets resonates with the audience. Democratic representation, however, is not simply generated at the input side of the legislative process through public discussions, elections and referenda but encompasses the whole process of 'law-making', its public salience and visibility.

Democratic representation – in contrast to simple aggregative mechanisms of interest representation – is further based on the assumption that the democratic contest is not only about the accommodation of particular interests but also about the validity of norms that apply to the process of collective will formation. The underlying norms are codified in the form of (a) equality (all can participate in the formation of the collective will), (b) rationality (the formation of the collective will is informed through substantive argumentative processes), (c) publicity (the underlying forms and processes need to be publicly visible and accessible) and (d) effectiveness (the expression of the collective will should have a chance to become effective and empowered).

The theory of political representation aligns here with the theory of the public sphere as outlined in Chapter 2. We encountered the position of the 'third' in the 'public', which is not simply a political community, or the electorate, or the constituent of a particular polity but the resonance body for generalized claims of validity. Crucial to the democratic representation of the collective will are the intermediary processes, that is, the question of how representative claims are channelled and made public. In this sense, the representative claim, as defined by Saward (2010), can also be understood as a claim to publicity. As Habermas observed in 1962: organizations and delegates 'display representation'. 'The aura of personally represented authority returns as an aspect of publicity.' Representation is less an element in the internal structure of an association 'than an expression of its claim to publicity' (Habermas, 1989: 200). Democratic representation requires such claims to be publicly raised, that is, made visible and accessible to the public. The point, already implicit in Hanna Pitkin, is that political representation is based on public speech through which the validity of the claims (or arguments) 'to represent' someone is publicly scrutinized and contested. Following John Stuart Mill's famous account, publicity is seen as a device to hold public choices accountable, both from the perspective of office holders in the act of representing and of citizens in the act of voting. This 'self-disciplining effect of public speech, however, is of no use unless the public is also empowered and qualified to form a "sound judgement"' (Mill, 1998 [1861]: 360). This latter function is performed by an independent self-steering mass media.

Publicity as measured in the public visibility and resonance of the representative claim relates to a neglected function of political representation, perceived as a triadic relationship between representatives, the represented and the audience. The focus then shifts from the normative quality of democratic representation to its sociological function in order to generate societal visibility. Democratic representation points to the part that needs to be held accountable for the whole. Representative democracy, therefore, needs to safeguard the visibility of the parts and their relationship to the whole. This points to a core condition of success for the establishment of a representative system of democracy, which can be measured in its capacities to generate communicative spaces, or to constitute a public sphere (Eder, 1985). Representatives are those with the capacities to produce and process publicly visible forms, arguments and discourses. In this way, the representative system of democracy reproduces itself as a visible unit and differentiates itself into positions that can be held publicly accountable.

Populism as a disrupted representative claim

New media and the Internet are not necessarily bad for representative democracy. The Internet does not replace representation by participation. By enhancing new forms of participatory democracy, the Internet has also multiplied representative claims, for instance by various civil society actors, or by global interest representatives (Trenz, 2009b). Social media struggles over democratic representation have a potential to unfold an all-inclusive dynamic and demarcate political spaces that reach beyond the national. While democratic representation has been opened up by digitalization and globalization, there are at the same time increasing efforts to reclaim representation in a way that re-establishes the linkage to territory and community. Such attempts to close the discursive spaces, within which claims for political representation can be raised by plural actors and groups, distinguish the *new populism* from democracy (Shaw, 2020: 181–222).[16]

The thesis I wish to test in the following is that populism can be explained in relation to such substantive changes of media and communication. Media and public sphere transformations have a profound impact on our ability to imagine political representation. Populist mobilization aims to regain a spatial dimension of political representation in its delimitation of claims for generalized validity raised in global digitalized public spheres. The spatial dynamics of claiming democratic representation are thus disconnected from the spheric dynamics of claiming universal rights and justice. With this, democracy is not regained, but split apart. This is why I wish to discuss populism not as serving a 'corrective' or 'redemptive' function in democracy but as being fundamentally disruptive to democracy and the public sphere.[17]

Populism as an invocation of a unitary representation of the people is neither new nor very original. Public sphere struggles have always been organized around such cultural repertoires of representations of the people and the popular will. Historically speaking, it should be restated, however, that the modern public sphere emerged in opposition to the representative publicness of the courts, and the bodily representation of the sovereign (as embodied by Hobbes' famous illustration of the Leviathan) (Habermas, 1989: 5–13). The public sphere disaggregated the body of the king and the claim for a unitary representation of truth. With the emphasis on the public use of reasoning, participation and deliberation always precede political representation, which comes in the form of the expression of a popular will that remains open to criticism. The collective of democracy has, in this sense, always been the chimera of democratic politics (Weale, 2019). The sovereign people are a myth that can be observed in action (Canovan, 2005). The people have a double space in democracy: as the constituent power and as an artefact of popular will formation. They underlie democracy and are constructed through democratic politics. Representation, on the one hand, is a demand raised by the people as the constituent power of democracy. On the other hand, representation is only made through democratic politics, which is why the people cannot exist prior to democracy, or constitute it. National representative systems accommodate this dual space of the people with reference to an imagined community of democracy, while at the same time upholding relatively inclusive processes of will formation with an emphasis on individual freedom and equality (Balibar, 2014). This framework served to limit demands for a unitary representation of the people.

As I elaborated elsewhere (Trenz, 2023), populism is the attempt to suspend the dual space of democratic representation. By insisting on the unitary representation of the people, populists do not simply continue the myth of the people as the constituents of democracy but close the discursive spaces through which popular sovereignty finds expression. Populism insists on the myth of the unitary representation of the people but does not allow for demystification. It thus truncates the articulation of the will of the people in favour of its original, fictious expression.

To understand why such a unitary representation of the people has gained in popularity, it is not sufficient to point only at the success of populist mobilization and the persuasive power of traditional nationalist discourse. The new salience of 'the people' in political mobilization instead needs to be explained with reference to a change in the communicative environments through which democracy is enacted, and the way publics, who *claim to represent* the people of democracy, are constituted. The return of representative politics is related to broader processes of public sphere transformations and the specific ways new globalized and digitalized media have contributed to the liquefaction of the collective. The anti-social and disconnected social media dynamics demystify the notion of the people, yet the Internet is still full of old and new myths that drive the collective imagination of democratic politics. Contemporary public sphere transformations have increased the demand for a unitary representation of the people while at the same time making such representations implausible. The new *populist struggle over democratic representation* can be distinguished along the following lines:

1. *The idea of the lost community*: one striking feature of contemporary struggles over democratic representation is the lack of a political project. Struggles over democratic representation are not forward looking but rather driven by the idea of a lost community. Instead of the utopia of a promising democratic future, the driving force of political mobilization is the nostalgia of a lost democratic heritage. Experiences of past struggles over the public sphere and democracy remain an important reference point in current debates, for instance when the golden age of the nationally integrated public sphere of democracy is taken as a yardstick. Such references to the past risk increasing uncertainty instead of directing present choices, since the 'glorious past' cannot easily be restored, nor can changing value orientations of society be reversed.

2. *The unifying logic of populist representation*: the struggle over populist representation follows a unifying logic. In the words of Canovan, the claim is 'to represent the sovereign, not a particular sectional interest or economic class' (1999: 4). This claim to represent the people in a unified way has far-reaching consequences for our common understanding of democracy and plural interest representation through elections. The claim for unitary representation of the people is anti-majoritarian and allows for the rejection of democratic procedures of will formation. By insisting on the unitary representation of the people, populists justify their disregard of the majority (Urbinati, 2013). The function of elections is no longer to aggregate the majority, or to accommodate plural interests and identities, but to arrive at a genuine expression of the will of the people. If populists are in the minority, they can still genuinely be 'the people'. If they happen to gain a majority, as, for instance, in the Brexit referendum, they do not simply form a majoritarian government but claim to establish a new regime that stands for the absolute will of the people in disregard of any minority or particular identities. The populist demand of unitary representation claims higher morality and superiority over the democratic demand of plural representation in the way it disregards plurality and diversity of positions that need to be equilibrated and deliberated. Populist representation stands above 'politics'. It adds a new quality to conflict, which is no longer simply about particular interests or ideologies but about the true people and their leader beyond parties (Urbinati, 2019). Such a claim for unitary representation of the people

does not simply continue democratic politics; it reverses democratic rules by interpreting the sovereign people as a legitimizing principle above any particular standpoint or elected majority.[18]

3. *The authoritarian shift*: the populist demand for the unitary representation of the people is authoritarian in the way it enforces the will of the people over others and restricts individual rights and liberties. The distinction of the true people implies the authority to rule over its enemies, to exclude them in a categorical way and deny their rights as equals. Populism is, by default, disrespectful to the rights of 'the other'. Claims of representing the people are therefore commonly accompanied by claims of who does not represent the people. Often our own people are only identifiable through such supportive claims that are meant to target those who are considered as *unrepresentative*, such as the elite or outsiders. As put by Jo Shaw, populism represents

> both a vertical challenge (by an insurgent 'people' against a dominating elite in order to work towards a 'true democracy') and a horizontal challenge against outsiders (that is, a group that may include those who legally 'belong' to the polity as citizens, but who diverge on some key vector, for example, of race or ethnicity). (Shaw, 2020: 186)

This implies that populism is authoritarian on the inside (the vertical challenge) and aggressive on the outside (the horizontal challenge). The renewal of the myth of the representation of the people implies a denial of recognition of diversity. Once in government, this disregard of all possible contradictions and ambiguities turns authoritarian. Populist parties can gain democratic elections, but it is against their ideology to lose majorities (Urbinati, 2019). A populist leader in government implements authoritarian rule that stands above the 'non-representative' (the internal enemies) and drives an aggressive foreign policy (the external enemies). As noted by Michel Wieviorka (2018), populism as an oppositional movement is only popular democracy in disguise, but what comes after populism is authoritarianism.

The claim for the unitary representation of the people is the strength of populism and explains its persuasive power and mobilization potential. Yet, it is also the weakness of populism. Calls for the people are strong in terms of their persuasive power but weak in terms of their conceptual vagueness and contradictions, which can easily be pointed out by political opponents. Populism is not an ideology that can give substance to the notion of the 'true people' but rather gains its mobilization strength from its constitutive ambiguity with regard to the question of how to affirm the will of the people (Mény and Surel, 2002). This 'constitutive ambiguity' is not simply a scholarly problem to nail down the phenomenon of populism. It is also a strategic move of populist mobilization to escape democratic control and critical judgement. Ambiguity serves as a protective shield against established procedures of democratic accountability and allows populist leaders to systematically ignore procedures of representative and parliamentary politics in the name of the direct or collective affirmation of the will of the people (Urbinati, 2013: 145).

The weak point of populism is precisely this lack of ideological strength and its reduction to a single claim. Whoever sees the people has created uniqueness but also risks seeing nothing else and occupying a single-edged agenda. The people can be evoked and mystified, but they cannot really be seized, which makes the mobilization *of the people* notoriously unreliable. The imposition of popular sovereignty can become a burden for individuals that are subsumed under 'the people'. The anti-populist claim results from such feelings of obtrusion by the populists. It demystifies the people and restores pluralism and diversity of political opinion. While the populist will insist on simple language and reduction, the anti-populist opponent reintroduces complexity. In the following section, I will explore how populism is challenged by democrats, and how the cultural backlash against democracy (Norris and Inglehart, 2019) can trigger a second democratic backlash against the backlash of populism.

The emerging populist and anti-populist fields of political contestation

The field of populist and anti-populist contestation is opened up by the media. Traditional (legacy) and new (digital) media do not necessarily provide a fertile ground for the amplification of the populist demand but can also erode it. Populism is performed through the media (Moffitt, 2016). New and old media, and not parliaments, are the main arena for populist parties to challenge representative democracy. Media logics are generally believed to contribute to the rise of populism, and its charismatic leaders can often be found to be innovative media strategists (Mazzoleni, 2003, 2008; Krämer, 2014; Alvares and Dahlgren, 2016; Esser et al, 2017). In political campaigning, the populist communicative style aligns with journalistic demands for personalized and conflictive news stories. News framing often follows a similar polarizing logic, for instance in the way foreign politics are framed in terms of 'our national interests' against the rest of the world (Neumann et al, 1992; de Vreese, 2004; Kim and Zhou, 2020).

Digital public sphere transformations and their far-reaching impact on the re-definition of publicness embrace populism more often than they seek distance. In particular, social media are ambivalent, allowing, on the one hand, claims for political representations to multiply while, on the other, facilitating a populist communicative style that escapes public accountability.

In claiming for political representation, a populist logic of belonging or not belonging to the 'the real people' has become dominant in social media campaigns run by populist leaders and parties. Their success in turning social media into a battlefield over political representation is remarkable, as social media analysts commonly assumed the opposite, that social media would mainly contribute to the fragmentation of the political space.

Conversely, and in a self-contradictory way, populists reject the idea of intermediation. The notion of populism as an immediate relationship between a leader and the people does not foresee the place of the mediator, which is the traditional role of journalism. The idea of the authentic people, evoked by populism, must be different from the audience of the mass media, which addresses 'masses', not 'the people'. The immediacy of populism seems anti-media, which is why many populist leaders prefer social media as their mouthpiece to talk to 'the people' in an 'immediate' way. This is commonly accompanied by the critique that mass media do not allow for the authentic expression of the popular will (Canovan, 2005: 90).

The emphasis on cultural closure by the populists can also be seen as contradicting the media's expansive market logic. As market actors, media institutions seek to avoid polarization and to find common denominators to reconcile different audience tastes and opinions to address the plural interests of their readers. In the historical development of journalism, broadsheets have replaced the partisan press (Donsbach and Patterson, 2004; Hallin and Mancini, 2004). Newspapers that openly support the populist parties' claim for unitary representation of the people would risk becoming niche products. The imposition of a populist media logic would require major structural changes to news markets and a return of the partisan press, which, according to critical observers, has occurred in the United States since the early 2000 (Levendusky, 2013). In Europe, tabloid journalism in countries like the UK and Austria has repeatedly been found to openly support populist mobilization, for instance in the Brexit campaign in the UK or campaigns that promoted anti-immigration and anti EU referenda in Austria.[19] In other places, journalism shows resistance to populist demands, especially the so-called quality journalists who more often than not sit on the side of the enemies of populism and are unlikely to become their allies. As populist leaders cannot rely on news media, they instead voice criticism against them, attacking the 'lying press' that has lost sight of the national interest and the people's genuine will.

As noted, the struggle over the representation of the people is fundamentally different from what is commonly referred to as 'representative politics'. The populist demand boosts partisan contestation and adds a new quality to conflict as a struggle over democracy. This discursive shift has important implications for the organization of democratic elections, where campaigning often takes a bipolar form between the 'true defenders of the people' (the populist leaders) and the representatives of plural democracy (the remaining democratic parties of the left and right). As could be observed, for instance, during the French presidential elections, or during the Brexit referendum, campaigning by both camps is no longer interpreted as competition *within* democracy but as a fundamental struggle *over* democracy. The populist camp rejects outright the idea that the poll serves the aggregation of the voice of the people and re-interprets it as the genuine expression of the popular will. The 'people' then become a catchphrase for the formation of a new political bloc to regain political weight and voice, even though, sociologically speaking, the populist voters form ad-hoc alliances of dispersed voices of frustration and dissatisfaction. Didier Eribon (2013) explains the success of Front National (renamed National Rally in 2018) in France precisely in terms of the radicalization of traditional class conflict. While parties of the political left were vanishing, their constituents remained disempowered and humiliated, seeking to find different symbolic expressions in terms of what is referred to as 'the people'. Democratic elections then become the opportunity to trigger the struggle over the people. Instead of seeking coalitions among the different parties that represent societal interests, the election polarizes, even to the point of becoming violent. The election is no longer a routine event that allows a government to form but follows an extremist logic where everything is always at stake. The populist electoral mobilization during elections serves the purpose of the self-construction of a new collective actor called the 'people'. Apart from this voice of protest during elections, these 'people' might not have much in common, but precisely for this reason, the populist leaders put so much emphasis on the 'unity of the people' that stands above majorities.

The logics of the formation of the 'popular will' constitute a new kind of symbolic struggle that is not simply different from representative politics and identity politics but also suppresses previous expressions of interests or identities. Eribon (2013) mentions the case of French women from working-class backgrounds who would never want to give up their right to a legal abortion yet still vote for the National Front party, which promotes precisely the opposite. Appeals to the people make such contradictions invisible and allow for the unification of diverse interests and identities of 'the people'. Each election is then staged like a popular referendum: you vote because you belong to the people, not because you wish your particular interests and identities to be represented. This means, in turn, that the political opponent is no longer seen as representing other interests or identities but is perceived as fundamentally different and not belonging to the same people. In the same vein, coalitions of diverse interests (which in representative democracies are the norm) are disqualified and delegitimized as elitist and hostile to the 'real people' as represented by the populist vote, which, even if still in the minority, is considered as the only legitimate outcome of an election.

My interpretation of the new quality of electoral contestation as a 'struggle over democracy' is different from the interpretation provided by political scientists, who talk of a new cleavage in the party landscape of Western democracies. Cleavage theory assumes a bipolar constellation of democratic politics, with a traditional ideological divide (left–right) that is increasingly replaced by a new identitarian divide, which is variably described as Green-Alternative-Libertarian (GAL) *versus* Traditional-Authoritarian-Nationalist (TAN), or cosmopolitan versus nativist (Kriesi et al, 2013; Hooghe and Marks, 2018; de Wilde et al, 2019). As argued by Eribon (2013), this distinction is problematic because 'identity politics' do not simply replace 'class politics', but rather hide it. By claiming that everything is about culture, cleavage theory curiously replicates the populist logics of political mobilization. Representing the struggle as a cleavage between cosmopolitans and nativists means adopting the moralizing language of political conflict, with cosmopolitans claiming higher moral authority over nativists and their 'particularistic' worldviews (which is precisely the attitude that nourishes the populists' anti-elitist resentment). In the moral framing of the political struggle over democracy, one typically asks what is wrong with these new representations of popular will, and how, from a majoritarian standpoint, they can be corrected. The bipolar framing of conflict is thus an imposition of power and hegemony of interpretation over the bipolar framing proposed by the populists themselves. Eribon, in his lucid analysis, challenges the political opponents of populism and invites them to raise the question of what the alternatives could be for the so-called supressed classes when conducting a political struggle in such a bipolar constellation, where the elites have already decided for them what their moral choices should look like.

Populist mobilization would, however, be wrongly understood as a struggle over recognition and positive self-affirmation that is self-driven by the needs of its supporters. To carry on the struggle over democratic representation, it is necessary to establish political representatives. The populist leader is a self-acclaimed representative of the people, who, at the same time, rejects the idea of being 'representative'. Their legitimacy is derived from the claim of a genuine expression of the will of the people, which is a form of legitimacy that is not available unless it is expressed as a 'representative claim'. The populist demand of unitary representation of the people requires, therefore, specific communication skills. The credibility and trustworthiness of the leader are dependent on media performance. Populist leaders are well known for their strategic and innovative use of old and new media, through which they run their campaigns and are often successful in building charismatic authority for themselves. Their media campaigning efforts are meant to re-unite various dissatisfactions and dispersed voices, in what Ernesto Laclau (2005) has described as a 'chain of equivalence'. The particularism of representative democracy is transformed into one single demand embodied in the figure of a populist leader. The people's voice is formulated with disregard to individual differences and group specifics. The political community is unified and not represented in its historically grown diversity. However, this unification remains dependent on the maintenance of antagonism, which is upheld through deeply polarizing public debates.

If we take this logic of populist reason by the word, it not only allows for the formation of the political subject of the 'people' but also implies the formation of the 'adversary' of the people. The same constitutive dynamics that give shape to populism as a political force also give shape to its political opponent. An important element of the populist strategy consists of the provocation of public reactions and in scandalization, needed to enhance the visibility of the populist claim. Its opponent should not simply endure the populist attacks to be 'non-representative' of the people; it should respond in a way that gives force to populism, recognizing the legitimacy of its claims.

My argument is that it is precisely this coupling of the unitary representation of the people with its targeting of political adversaries that makes populism deeply vulnerable to exposure and ultimately to being dismantled by public reasoning. The concept of the 'unitary representation of the people' is founded on the fallacy that 'populist reason' could simply replace 'public reason'. However, 'populist reason' is not independent of or superior to 'public reason' but remains fundamentally contested. At the same time, populism mobilizes through the public sphere and thus renews political competition and enhances democratic contestation. By following its own logics, it contributes to the formation of a democratic opposition, fostering the unification of this opposition in their struggle against populism. Public sphere dynamics are not only suspended but enhanced. It is a fundamental miscalculation by populist leaders to assume that they could control media and public sphere dynamics in a way that suspends the contestation over who represents the people. Political opposition, shaped as a unitary response to the populist challenge, at the same time escapes the logics of 'populist reason' by critically putting the populist demand and the performance of its leaders to the test.

If populism is distinguished as a 'style of communication' (Moffitt, 2016), we can also distinguish a communicative style for the performance of anti-populism (Trenz 2023). The political opposition against populism rejects the populist logics of acclamation through the use of argumentation and public reason. The 'adversary' of populist mobilization, then, is no longer a 'target' but a 'political agent' in the struggle over democracy. Through anti-populist mobilization, the debate about democratic legitimacy is re-embedded in the public sphere, where the question is not so much who is the most credible in upholding the myth of unitary representation of the people as who has the best arguments to defend the public interest.

Populist polarization is thus ultimately self-defeating. It contributes to the formation of a political opposition and gives voice to the various anti-populist forces that might have very little in common but find themselves united in the rejection of 'populist reason', which is denounced as non-representative, anti-democratic and ultimately authoritarian. The resilience of the public sphere against the populist challenge is measured in the indignation of the anti-populist voice, those who hold plural arguments, diverse identities and individual life projects against the hubris of the unitary representation of the people. The presumptuousness of the populist leaders to represent the people never really unifies but divides, while creating antagonism and ultimately exacerbating the divisions they claim to overcome. As the populist claim for the unitary representation of the people, by default, fails to unify the people, it can at least have the effect of unifying the opposition against populism. In the same way that the many potential minorities and fractions of society are targeted by populism as adversaries, they also feel reason to object to and oppose populism. Their visibility as a negative status group is the outcome of populist mobilization and the triggering moment for anti-populist mobilizations, groups that claim democratic rights but would not come into existence if not as a response to populist mobilization.

Anti-populism is responsive: it develops its distinctive communicative style in critical exchange with populism and through the mobilization of public reason to refute the populist demands (Moffitt, 2018). Anti-populism is a backlash against the populist backlash. It emerges out of a public sphere struggle of argumentative exchanges that does not simply seek confrontation with populism but convincingly argues to reject it. The populist and anti-populist struggle is not simply the antagonism of two opposing camps in a polarized democracy but a dialectic two-level game of anti-democratic and democratic forces. According to Hamdaoui (2021: 2), 'a stylistic anti-populism is made of formal and pro-institutional language, has a technical or intellectual approach to politics, encourages respect towards political elites and favours composure over exuberance' The language of anti-populism, therefore, is not just distinct and oppositional; it is the language of the democratic public sphere's resilience. The transmutation from a populist to an anti-populist style of communication is depicted in Table 1.[20]

Engaging in a discussion on the style of representative politics reveals why the backlash against the populist backlash is not just a contestation between two opposing camps but a more ground-breaking democratic movement. The political style and rhetoric of anti-populism does not want to put alternative choices on the table or to oppose single positions taken by populist leaders. It is instead meant as a 'corrective' of populism and a resurgence of the democratic public sphere against post-democracy. The democratic counter-mobilization is a public sphere corrective machinery that aims to

Table 1: Populist backlashes–anti-populist backlashes

Populist style (Moffitt, 2016)	Anti-populist style
Anti-pluralism →	Demand for plural voice and respect for minorities
Unitary representation of the people →	Individual citizenship, parliamentary and pooled sovereignty, discursive will formation
Simplified language that expresses general distrust of the complex machinery of modern governance and the complicated nature of policy solutions →	Slow politics over quick action, recognition of ambivalence and need for negotiations, compromise, consultations and expertise
Bad manners, political incorrectness and disregard for facts →	Emphasis on facts and arguments, political correctness and rational language

re-energize citizenship through the establishment and demarcation of new democratic spaces online, as well as in the public squares and in parliament.

To exemplify the dialectics of populism and anti-populism, consider the case of simplified language use that often characterizes social media mobilizations. If populists, through simplified language, emotional slogans and appeals to the people, try to reduce ambivalence and make the world explainable for their supporters, this escape from complexity turns them into an easy target for their political adversaries. The simplified language of populist campaigners makes them vulnerable by exposing them to criticism and indignation. The very diverse group of anti-populists is united through its distinct style of communication. It would be erroneous to assume that the anti-populist forces need to join a unified political camp with a distinct identity (like 'cosmopolitans'), as is sometimes assumed in political cleavage theory. The high-school climate activist and the Frankfurt banker are not united in their shared cosmopolitan mindset but by their reasons for opposing the populist claims of unitary representation.

The anti-populist strategy thus consists not only of making an alternative offer for political representation but also in changing the whole procedure through which political representation finds expression. This requires a different type of media use, not simply contrasting the populist demand with the enlightened truth of the anti-populist but re-introducing uncertainty and plural, open-ended procedures of truth finding. The reverse of populist post-truth is insurrectionary truth (Newman, 2022), which challenges established truth and is meant to reintroduce norms and procedures of truth finding. Against post-truth, which is authoritarian, insurrectionary truth is emancipatory and, as such, no different from the Enlightenment notion of truth finding as an emancipatory project that underlies the modern public sphere. Anti-populists, in this sense, are not re-inventing truth or introducing a new practice of truth finding, but rather are using new media to reinstall modern public sphere norms and rules.

The new digital media infrastructure is in no way hostile to such a project of insurrectionary truth. Anti-populists are not necessarily discriminated against by social media logics. As I will attempt to demonstrate, there is an audience demand for a re-differentiation of public opinion. In facing such demands for knowledge, trusted information and critical reflection, the promoters of post-truth or post-factual opinion are placed in a disadvantaged position because their calls for unitary representation of the people do not allow for the differentiation of arguments and the testing of validity claims that have become the new requirement in online debates. The demand of unitary representation of the people thus has a double unifying effect of facilitating populist mobilization and, in a dialectic mode, triggering a broad anti-populist movement, which is not simply counter-mobilization but a revocation of the populist demand. This offers a framework of research for the analysis of contemporary mutations of democracy, raising doubts about the idea of an epochal change towards post-democracy. The encounter between populism and democracy takes place within a resilient public sphere where public reason and principles of enlightened debate cannot simply be suspended and, at the same time, democratic disconfigurations create the conditions for democratic resurgence.

Democratic resurgence: the performative repertoire of anti-populism

The anti-populist movement positions itself in this battle over political representation not as an alternative to populism but as a form of democratic resurgence that takes up the challenge to redefine the role of publics as democratic constituents in global representative politics. In a first approximation, we can distinguish individual from organized practices of anti-populism. For many individual citizens, anti-populism remains largely unorganized and spontaneous. It is the attitude of enlightened citizens to remain sceptical and distanced and a civic duty to formulate critique, even if it remains private. Anti-populism, in this sense, is carried by the 'silent majority' and does not necessarily need to be articulated in broader public debates. We also observe how many users on social media recur to a 'civic mode' of language use, without necessarily engaging in political debates, but still moderate claims of exclusion, national sovereignty and demands of unitary representation of the 'will of the people'. Others might decide to reduce social media use or sign off because of frustration with the harsh tone of online debates. Their decision is intended as a rejection of the 'bad manners' of populism, seen as threatening their own values and identities.

In other instances, anti-populism becomes more organized. Individual criticism is turned into innovative ways of democratic engagement. In its organized forms, anti-populism can gather large majorities of social media users who express moral indignation against populist transgressions. Examples of such majoritarian anti-populist mobilizations include anti-racism or gender-equality campaigns. In all these instances, the claim for the unitary representation of the people is opposed through reference to universal values, plural identities and diversity. Such broad anti-illiberalism coalitions can become decisive and often account for the defeat of populist parties in national elections, as for instance in Emmanuel Macron's victory in the French presidential election in 2017.

My model of a dialectic revocation of populism implies that progressive democratic movements do not need to be explicitly anti-populist. Their struggle is not confrontational, but transitive. The populist leader is best ignored, and the agenda shifted by raising representative claims at a higher level of political aggregation, for instance in the form of the defence of the common good that claims a higher legitimacy than populists' particularistic claims. Through such universalization strategies, democrats escape the populist–anti-populist polarization. In the following, I will approach the performative repertoire of anti-populism with reference to four cases. The first is the Brexit 48 per cent campaign, which reinterprets the expression of the unitary voice of the people as domination over plural identities and life projects, and thus as a fundamental violation of democracy. In a similar way, the Sardines opposition in Italy seeks a representation of silent majorities who refuse to engage in debates with populists and claim a higher moral ground of democratic representation that considers individual plural identities. The Yellow Vest movement rejects political and union representation as a bottom-down call for social justice that is mainly anti-capitalist. Finally, the example of #FridaysforFuture is the representation of a new generation, which also escapes any categorization as 'people' and, at the same time, can hardly be opposed or targeted by populists as 'enemies'.

The 48 per cent: Brexit as bereavement

To illustrate resilience forces in the struggle over democratic representation, a closer look at the dynamics of the Brexit referendum in the UK offers useful insights.[21] A referendum is a preferred tool of populists for raising their claims of unitary representation of the people. With its pretension to unite the direct voice of the people, a referendum de facto divides and often polarizes the population (Iyengar and Simon, 2000). The appropriation of the majority vote as the will of the people regularly encounters fierce resistance. Instead of reconciling the population, a referendum, therefore, risks to polarize. In the Brexit case, remain supporters on the losing side of the referendum did not simply lose the vote in an election but found themselves emotionally shattered, deeply betrayed and dispossessed of their identities (Murray et al, 2017; Brändle et al, 2018a, 2021). Under such conditions, the claim of the 'Brexiteers' that the referendum would unify the country and become the foundation of a renewed UK turned out to be illusionary.

While the pre-referendum campaign was dominated by expressions of deep-seated Euroscepticism of British citizens, and the mobilization of strong emotions expressed in their desire for 'national independence' and anger against the political establishment (Vasilopoulou, 2016), the post-referendum period saw an unprecedented, largely unexpected and highly emotional pro-European mobilization, with street protests in London and other cities, as well as local pro-EU groups in towns and cities across the UK seeking to stop the Brexit process in the name of the 48 per cent (Brändle et al, 2021). The so-called 48 per cent became a political force and a unified actor only after, and as an effect of, the referendum. 'remainers' put substantial efforts into occupying alternative media spaces for mobilization and challenged the majoritarian pro-Brexit British tabloid press through highly popular campaigning sites on social media. Their enhanced social media presence was also used as a base for the organization of protest marches in London and other cities in 2017 and 2018 and local pro-EU groups in towns and cities across the UK seeking to stop the Brexit process in the name of the 48 per cent.

The post-referendum public sphere combined the resilience and resistance of the heterogeneous groups of 'remainers'. Resilience was expressed in the form of non-recognition of the referendum result by citizens who found their identities and life projects threatened. 'Our identities were taken away' and 'our life projects cancelled' were frequently expressed by participants in protest marches against Brexit during 2017–18 (Brändle et al, 2021). Such psychological reactions to a distorted and threatening event were, at the same time, used as an opportunity to confirm social bonds. Resilience was personal, but it was also connected through shared feelings and emotions. Indignation was not simply reactive in the form of a passionate and emotional response of losers in a game. It sought argumentation to dismantle the illegitimacy of the referendum campaign that, from the point of view of the 'remainers', violated core democratic principles of fairness and truth orientation of public debates. Such an engagement of citizens in debates does not need to be highly confrontational. It often does not confront the political adversary (the populist is a slippery target, anyway), but is rather inwardly oriented. The Remainer campaign was reminiscent of the practice of preaching to the converted. It was neither successful at re-establishing truth and fairness in public debates, nor at turning the majority in their favour. The campaign's social media sites were used instead as forums for exchanging personal experiences about Brexit, sharing fears of negative consequences and feelings of anger, sorrow and political disillusionment.

Such shared indignation can quickly turn into political mobilization, even though no clear line exists that distinguished post-referendum public sphere resilience from resistance. Political protest was often expressed in a way that did not directly confront the political opponent but rather tried to occupy the streets in alternative ways. In fact, the places for the protest marches were chosen in a way that made confrontation unlikely, and where the majority of the local population would meet the protesting crowd with sympathy (such as in the city of London). Another reason for this lack of political confrontation was the reluctance of political parties or trade unions to position themselves as supporters or opponents of the post-Brexit political mobilization. The 48 per cent, in fact, complained about the lack of parliamentary representation, with their causes defended by single MPs, not by a major political party. Subsequent elections testified to the failure of the 'remainers' to turn their protest voice into a unified vote for a political party that would support their cause. The three parties that opposed Brexit (the Greens, the Liberal Democrats and the Scottish National Party) remained marginal in Westminister system. The pro-Brexit marches instead created new ad-hoc forms of political representation of the 48 per cent as a political body that became visible in the streets but ephemeral in the political arena. The cathartic expression of indignation was insufficient as a repair mechanism of the disrupted public sphere.

Apart from such mass street demonstrations, the very heterogeneous group of the 48 per cent was held together through social media campaigning. 'Remainers' used social media campaigns not so much for amplifying their voice but for crying out with anger or mobilizing new supporters. Social media became, above all, an experimental field for testing out alternative political expressions and engaging in an exchange of facts and arguments. The campaigning site served as a corrective mechanism for the populist claim of unitary representation by building legitimacy through the force of better argument and justification. The aim was to keep a debate alive, something which Brexiteers denied opening up again after the referendum. It is thus noteworthy how resilience and resistance were employed interchangeably through everyday engagement in political talks and occasional mobilization, with a unifying effect on the formation of a democratic opposition to Brexit.

For the 48 per cent, the campaign did not continue by adopting the populist style of communication but rather by explicitly reverting it into a campaign against populism. The opposition was unified by the rejection of populist reason and the shared indignation about the presumptuous claim of unitary representation of the people. To approach these dynamics of anti-populist counter-mobilization, it is important to understand how the claim for the unitary representation of the people in the referendum was perceived as a threat of domination and authoritarian takeover of the winning majority over the minority (Fossum, 2019). The Brexit majority interpreted the referendum as the re-establishment of the 'real people' and the genuine expression of their will. Such a claim of the 'objective representation' of 'we the people' was an attempt to ban any legitimate opposition strategy. The populist logic was totalitarian. It did not foresee any space for plural representation, compromise or recognition of diversity but only categorical exclusion of the political adversary from the definition of 'the people'. As the losing minority of the 48 per cent was excluded from the space of political representation, the anti-populist response could not be given through the means of regular partisan politics. Instead of entering opposition, the anti-populist coalition needed to reinstall democratic procedures in a disrupted public sphere. Anti-populist mobilization, therefore, was not oppositional but corrective. The 'remainers' did not simply oppose exiting the EU. They entered a struggle over democracy to prevent domination and authoritarian takeover. In the aftermath of the referendum, the task was not only to oppose Brexit, or to seek compromise that would facilitate a 'light Brexit'. Their struggle also implied a change in the communicative style for the claiming of political representation, not as a counter-image of the unity of the 48 per cent but by actually recognizing that there is no such counter-image, and that there are only different procedures for the 'making of' democratic representation. Instead of insisting on an alternative notion of the people, the anti-populist style of communication introduced diversified procedures for claiming representation as a dynamic process during which identities of the citizens were only formed and given plural expression. Such creative ways of multiplying instead of unifying the oppositional voice were displayed on the occasion of anti-Brexit marches, organized mainly in cities that were distinguished by their multicultural and cosmopolitan lives. Protesters did not line up in the protest as a uniform mass but rather staged their diversity and the plurality of reasons to oppose Brexit through advocacy groups like Women for Europe, Students for Europe, Workers' Europe, Environmentalists for Europe, UK Indians for Remaining in the EU, and many more.

Such creativity is also found in the very different use of social media as a playground for different identities and interests. Against the populist provocation, the anti-populist opposition gains from its emphasis on fairness, procedural rules and political correctness. Against the demagogical exclamation and simplistic language typical of the Brexit campaign (Collins, 2019), the campaigning style of the 'remainers' is argumentative and fact-based. Their campaign does not operate within a polarized scheme of political struggle but with references to truth and reason. They do not seek confrontation but exchanges of information and opinion. The retreat to facts and reason is an effective way to shield themselves off from the antagonistic logics of polarization applied by the Brexiteers and their attempt to out the opposition as adversaries (Galpin and Trenz, 2022).

From a bottom-up perspective of grassroots democracy, we have analysed online campaigning in the aftermath of Brexit as 'digital acts of citizenship' (Brändle et al, 2018b), conceived as loosely connected forms of citizens' collective actions based on the expression of shared concerns, similar experiences of empowerment or disempowerment and advocacy for a common cause. Digital acts of citizenship can consist, for instance, in fact-checking and corrections of distorted images that are spread by Brexiteers and related media. Cyberspace was occupied by critical citizens to re-open the political struggle and to re-collect and reconstitute as political subjects. As digital citizens, 'remainers' articulate a plural political voice, express their shared concerns about Brexit and fight for their right to work, free movement and non-discrimination within the EU.

Instead of focusing on the pros and cons of European integration, 'remainers' thus opened a broader normative and identitarian debate that engaged in plural and diverse opinions about the impact of Brexit in re-shaping British politics, society and democracy. Commenting as digital acts of citizenship became a form of engagement, with factual argumentation a testing ground for the quality of arguments and a playing field for a diverse and plural democratic practice. While the populist style was rooted in an anti-pluralist approach that categorically excluded the 'other', the anti-populist style required activists to position themselves as anti-racist, pro-immigration or cosmopolitan, recognizing plural voices and respect for minorities and difference: 'the 48 per cent', EU-27 citizens, Scottish voters, the scientific community, middle- and lower-income families, or students. This was combined with concerns about EU citizenship and possible violations of rights as enshrined in EU law. The anti-Brexit opposition, however, was not only defensive but also forward-looking, with calls for positive action to reconcile British and European identity.

However, by positioning themselves in sharp opposition to the 'liars' of the Leave campaigners and the 'propaganda' of the Brexit-leaning newspapers, the 'remainers' could not entirely escape the polarization dynamics of Brexit. Their resilience practice responded to public sphere disruptions in a disfigured democracy, where a democratic voice could hardly be restored without 'naming' and 'blaming' the adversary. The debate was also meant to reinstall the 'remainers' as the 'enlightened', 'educated', 'rational' holders of the 'truth', which became yet another stereotypical element in the debate. The othering of the 'Brexiteers' included, for instance, a frequent demonization of the political opponent, often attributing essentialist characteristics to the other based on strong collective signifiers such as uneducated, stupid, evil or corrupt. The strong emotional targeting of the other as enemies needs to be interpreted as a recurrence of a populist style within the anti-populist campaign. In the end, the anti-populism style did little to bridge the deep divide of British society but rather reinforced a deeply polarized vision of the UK.

Il Popolo delle Sardine: the non-bodily representation of democratic politics

Italian cities are famous for their central piazza: a physical space for the spontaneous gathering of people, both citizens and foreigners. The piazza is a local public sphere that belongs to the community, and invites the world to visit, very much along the lines of the 'agora', described by Hannah Arendt (1998) as the nucleus of the modern idea of the public sphere. For most Italians, the piazza is a communal place that can be easily reached just by leaving the family home and is visited for business, participation in social life, the exchange of news and engagement in political affairs (Canniffe, 2008). In November 2019, this passion for street-level politics led young Italians to develop an innovative form of contestation of populism: Il Popolo delle Sardine (The People of Sardines). The idea for this new movement goes back to a flash mob organized by four friends to challenge the right-wing Lega party and its leader, Matteo Salvini, who held a party congress in Bologna on 19 November 2019. While the congress was attended by around 5,000 supporters of Salvini's Lega, the idea of the protesters was that an even higher number of 6,000 and more Bologna citizens should simultaneously gather on the city town square just to be present and easily outnumber the populists. The movement was thus initiated with the primary intention of rejecting the populist claim of unitary representation of the people, confronting the Lega with the local opposition of a city that stood in solidarity against it. Local resistance by an anti-populist majority was meant to reintroduce diversity into the debate. The protest also intervened in the ongoing regional election campaign, not by supporting any of the candidates for the mayor of Bologna but by denouncing the campaigning style of a single party, the Lega, as unacceptable and outside the spectrum of legitimate democratic representation. The debate was about principled aspects of the democratic process and about democratic style and aesthetics, leaving the choice of the voters for particular programmes, or candidates of the left or the right, open. The movement made a statement for the rescue of partisan politics by calling upon the people to align along the ideological left–right axis of the political spectrum and not to vote for the extremists. The particular form of protest chosen was unusual in the sense that it occupied the piazza in silence, thus abstaining from political statement and alignment.

The choice of this innovative form of protest can be explained by widespread fatigue with the media omnipresence of the right-wing Lega and its leader, Salvini: "We need to free ourselves from your oppressive omnipresence, starting with the web."[22] If populism is mainly a media show that seeks provocation and polarization (Moffitt, 2016), the anti-populist protest organizes peaceful encounters and reconciliation. If populism is 'loud, colloquial, and hateful', the Sardines are 'polite, formal and encouraging' (Hamdaoui, 2021: 3). The name chosen for the movement, 'Popolo delle Sardine', is meant to express this idea of an 'anti-body' (*anticorpo*) and not of a movement: to stand close and mute in the piazza like Sardines in a tin – 'no flag, no party, no insult'.[23] The physical square was chosen as a place of encounter instead of social media. As social media were already flooded with messages by Salvini, the new idea was to occupy media-free spaces. Noise should be replaced by silence: "You have chosen to drown our political content in an ocean of void communication. Of these contents, nothing is left." The aesthetics of silent protest in the piazza renounces political messages that could disrupt the harmony of a peaceful gathering. Instead of the usual banners from political groups, protesters brandished placards in the shape of a sardine: "No banners; we don't want symbols at such a beautiful gathering."[24]

In seeking direct and personal confrontation with Salvini, the Sardines are a movement that explicitly identifies as 'anti-populist'. Anti-populism is not simply an attribute but the main identifier for the movement. The movement exists because populism is *misrepresented* in the public sphere; its leaders monopolize the stage of politics and are everywhere in the media, without really speaking for the majority of the audience. More than a movement, the Sardines can be considered as a form of audience rebellion against a bad performance in the arena of representative politics. The viewers wish to leave the show but cannot switch channel. If the populist leader behaves like the torero in a bullfighting arena, he encounters in the Popolo delle Sardine an audience that does not judge the performance but opposes the deadly spectacle.

Opposition to the over-performance of populism required a change in the performative style of political opposition. Hamdaoui (2021: 8) describes the anti-populist communicative style of the Sardine people movement as threefold:

> Firstly, they seek to re-introduce politeness and respect in the discourse by contrasting with the exuberant style of Salvini. Also, they present a different aesthetics by delivering a clean and sober language that breaks with the Lega's noisy and talkative habits. Secondly, they intend to re-mobilise citizens as physical persons by organising peaceful demonstrations that counterbalance Salvini's visibility and ubiquitous presence on social media. Thirdly, they seek to put complexity back at the centre of politics, and to break with the simplistic and Manichean populist discourse.

The image of Sardines as a symmetry of silent citizens needs to be understood as a symbolization of the *body politique*. By seeking vicinity, the protesters send out signs of friendship and harmony to stand close together instead of being anonymous, confrontational and adversarial. This is a visual and physical representation of the people, not as 'voice' but as silent majority. It is an experience of an anti-mass that escapes the sociopathic domination and seduction of the leader.[25] The silent protest was meant as a reminder for the populists that their claim to represent the people was unsubstantiated and pretentious. Being present in the crowds, nevertheless, created a feeling of empowerment and solidarity for the protest participants. The silent crowd sent out signals of power as an electorate whose choices matter. As such, the anti-representative presence of the people in the square simultaneously expressed the readiness of the protesters to enter new bonds of representation, not by replacing partisan politics but by reminding political parties of their role in democracy.

The Sardines, therefore, stand for the revitalization of representative politics by civil society. They respond to the incapacity or unwillingness of the existing political parties, and particularly of the centre-left party, Partito Democratico, to lead the anti-populist opposition (Hamdaoui, 2021). The Sardines are a non-partisan movement, meant to support the partisan system. In their own words, they want to fill the vacuum of political representation, not by replacing the parties but by being their pathfinder. A bottom-up mobilization of citizens should give new impulses to democratic parties, encourage them to oppose populism and facilitate their reorganization. The ultimate aim is not the empowerment of the people through grassroots politics but a revitalization of representative politics led by political parties and political leaders opposed to populism.

Similar to the 'remainers' campaign in the UK, the Sardine people fight the exclusionary effects of populism through a defence of pluralism and diversity in the public sphere. The piazza is also the inclusive place that unites diversity, where different opinions can be expressed and where no agreement is necessary. The recognition of diversity goes hand in hand with the acknowledgement of the complexity of politics and the need for the specialized knowledge of professional politicians with expertise in problem-solving. As politics are complex, uncertainty can also be accepted, which is why the protesters abstain from formulating their own proposals for policy reform. They do not wish to occupy the field of politics but still encourage seriousness in professional politicians and experts against the easy solutions provided by the populists. In promoting their own agenda of democratic politics, the movement remains rather general. It is not explicitly left, but still regularly links to progressive issues such as feminism, defence of equality, social rights, pro-immigration and environmentalism. Through this emphasis on consensual issues, the movement escapes polarization and defends a form of value universalism, which is not partisan but cosmopolitan and thus feeds into different types of political parties (della Porta, 2021). As such, they often cross paths with the environmental protest group #FridaysforFuture, with whom they have organized joint events. Both movements stand for the uprising of a new generation in search of political representation.

The movement is not explicitly anti-party, but it shares and also amplifies a widespread distrust in political parties and does not wish to identify with party politics. Nor would any political party clearly back the movement. To distance itself from the Five Star Movement as a new organizational form of movement party (Conti and Memoli, 2015), the Sardine movement made it clear that they would not seek electoral competition but rather back traditional organizational forms of party politics. Against the rather elderly constituency of the Five Star Movement, the Sardines are made up of the younger generation, who protest against the excesses of movement and mobilization in Italian politics. The Sardines are an anti-movement movement, against the Five Star Movement and the Lega and their pretension to occupy the field of social movement politics. If political parties become movement parties, social movements become anti-movement. And if movement parties gain visibility through the omnipresence of speech and political talk (della Porta et al, 2017), the non-movement mobilization withdraws from speech and escapes from noise.

Similar to the 'remainers' in the UK, the Sardines are a movement in search of political representation, yet their demands to be represented are not satisfied by any of the existing political parties. The Sardine movement also shares the anti-Brexiters' diffuse fear of populism as an anti-democratic and authoritarian force: 'Here, we felt like we were being invaded by a political discourse based on aggression, show business and lies.' The denunciation of populists is mainly directed at the presumption of unitary representation of the people. This is combined with fear of hatred and extremism of the more radical forces of the Italian right. Fear sometimes also encompasses the alleged irrationality and incompetence of the populist leader who threatens to carry the country into economic recession or damage its international reputation. Populist politicians are depicted as immature, childish and ignorant, as dangerous charlatans, or as demagogues who lack logical understanding and need to be countered with knowledge and intelligence (Hamdaoui, 2021: 11).

As in the case of the 'remainers' in the UK, the question is whether the performance of anti-populism is possible without recurrence to populist elements of political representation. In the case of the Sardines, the street mobilizations have a clear target and identify a political adversary in the explicit mentioning of the Italian Lega, and the personalized way of confronting its leader, Matteo Salvini. The focus on Salvini can also become an obsession and reflect real antipathy and, in this sense, contribute to the polarization of the population. A similar ambivalence can also be found in the way the movement accuses traditional media and journalism of under-performing and being corrupt, and social media of over-performing and being a breeding ground for populist opinion. Such media-critical attitudes are widely shared by the Italian population.

Looking beyond Italy, the Sardine movement can be interpreted in the context of the application of cooling down techniques by media users and audiences against the enhanced publicity of the online public sphere (Pörksen, 2018). As I will argue in the following, such cool-down practices are often related to the new media fatigue of segments of the audience. As such, they should not be misread as a retreat into privacy, leaving the field of political contestation to the populists. The Sardines and similar movements in other countries instead align with other practices in the field of public sphere resilience and thus stand for a new impetus of democratic renewal and learning.

#FridaysforFuture: the power of global representative politics

#FridaysforFuture is an international climate movement based on the grassroots mobilization of young people. It became very popular in 2018 as a form of school strike, initiated by groups of students who skipped Friday classes to participate in local protests and ask political leaders to take action to prevent climate change, to save the planet and the future of their generation. #FridaysforFuture was initiated by Swedish pupil Greta Thunberg, who organized protests in Stockholm in August 2018, an example that was soon followed in other cities across Europe and around the globe, with more than 1 million strikers in 2,200 events organized in 125 countries on 15 March 2019.[26] As of today, the movement purportedly connects 14,000,000-plus people in 7,500 cities worldwide.[27]

Why is the climate movement a struggle over political representation? Within national electoral systems, children are only indirectly represented and have no personal voting rights. This makes school strikes an initiation rite for political activism in later life but not a form of political protest that is taken very seriously by the authorities. #FridaysforFuture, however, go significantly beyond such episodic protest events, making demands for the representation of the new generation of millennials. Protest movements that are carried by a new generation are not new (Rucht, 2019). Only recently, we have witnessed other international youth movements, such as Occupy and Pulse, raising a radical anti-capitalist agenda. While older generations regularly describe the upcoming generations as less political, these young activists explore new forms of political expression yet relate to old agendas of social justice and global solidarity. They fight the dystopia of political abstention and link back to the glorious times of social movements' grassroots mobilization back in the 1960s and '70s. #FridaysforFuture, however, is not simply a protest of the present generation; it also extends the representative claim to all future generations. Raising climate change as their top priority, the millennials combine their claims for generational representation with claims for common good representation. In this way, their representative claim is not only successful in bridging the space from local to global protests; it also bridges time from a dystopian present to an uncertain future, which can hardly be envisaged as utopian. The political struggle is about the rescue of the material base of the earth, and not primarily about political ideas and values. Unlike eschatological movements and their prediction of the apocalypse, the movement seeks alliances with science to calculate risk scenarios. #FridaysforFuture, nevertheless, contributes to the expansion of the utopia of the public sphere in the important way of revising the moral foundation of representative politics, demanding the inclusion of the voice of posteriority.[28] This extends the universe of discourse. While claims for social justice remain heavily contested, the claim for generational representation leaves behind the realm of value conflicts and argues with the need for the survival of humanity.

The claim that young protesters stand for a new generation, nevertheless, should not be taken literally. It is a representative claim that competes in the public sphere and that is contested by other young people who do not align with them (and support, for instance, populist or right-wing parties). Dieter Rucht (2019: 8) notes that the movement in Germany is present at high schools but not at other schools offering a less academic education. Also, protest does not diffuse to universities. It is ultimately only a minority of school children who participate in protest, and we cannot assume that their claims are shared by the entire generation.

The climate movement, however, does not simply claim numerical representation and, in fact, cares little about being outnumbered by majorities. The claim for generational representation is validated in combination with a related claim for the representation of the common good. Common good representational claims are used to justify the authority of global civil society against special interest representatives, such as states or economic actors (Trenz, 2009b; Pollak, 2013). 'Saving our planet' is of course a very material struggle that enters into conflict with the expansion of capitalist markets, property rights and the use of common resources. As a strategy of conflict avoidance, the ecological movement can reframe sustainability and redirect public debates by countering questions of redistribution with questions of political representation. Sustainability is then essentially about how to represent our planet, and by whom it is represented: the young generation standing for humanity and embracing all future generations (O'Riordan et al, 2020). In the way the struggle over the rescue of our planet is reframed as a representative and non-distributive conflict, #FridaysforFuture can also self-consciously suggest climate action as a solution to global conflicts. By introducing the idea of climate justice and equity, the climate movement seeks to broaden their agenda and build bridges to other global movement struggles, suggesting a possible consensus that is carried by a global community.

The movement, consequently, defines its adversary with reference to those who are made responsible for generational disparity, framed as breaches of value and injustice that can be personally attributed. In terms of generational conflicts, this adversary can be the past generations of their parents, whose immoral behaviour threatens their children's future. The older generations are seen as incapable of acting, and therefore as illegitimate; their voice is devalued, as they will not have to live with the consequences of their actions. The young generations' claim for political representation is thus sustained by a higher moral authority. Numerical representation and majority rule are rejected as notoriously insufficient and incapable of providing quick and sustainable solutions for the pressing issues of climate change. Majorities, even if constituted by democratic vote, can still be morally wrong. 'How dare you' is the outcry of indignation against the generation of climate polluters. #FridaysforFuture is a counter-public that uses public speech in the classical sense of holding the powerful accountable: "My message is that we'll be watching you. … You are failing us. But the young people are starting to understand your betrayal. The eyes of all future generations are upon you. And if you choose to fail us, I say: We will never forgive you."[29] Moral superiority is translated here in a language of contempt and condemnation of the adversary. Through religious connotations (blaming of sin and grace), the movement at the same time transcends the democratic public sphere of open debate. In facing the urgency of climate action, there is no time for scepticism. The protection of our climate is an absolute moral demand that does not allow for compromise ('There is no Planet B').

The climate change movement as a representative world public is thus sustained through an absolute moral claim ('save our planet'), which discredits any form of oppositional voice. At the same time, the environmental universalism is implicitly deeply anti-populist because it radically rejects any particularistic logic of representation in the political struggle. Instead of unilateralism and nationalism, the protest calls for multilateral action and political initiative, international cooperation and delegation of sovereignty. Anti-populism, however, is not a clearly defined political strategy that is applied in daily confrontations with a political adversary. In their daily political struggles, the environmentalists mostly decide to ignore the populists[30] or punish them through moral outing as a form of politics that does not listen to science, is not driven by facts and the consideration of the moral consequences of these facts. In light of the magnitude of the climate challenge, the populist challenge is only a side issue. For the climate activists, the political skirmish against populism should not distract from the main struggle of rescuing the world, which is why populist attacks against them are better ignored than addressed.

Nor do national populist parties seek direct confrontation with the climate change movement. The attacks against Greta Thunberg on right-wing social media forums are instead self-defeating, exposing the misogyny of the climate change deniers and contributing to their marginalization in public debates and the media (Gelin, 2019). Populist parties and their leaders seem to be clueless in their stance against the #FridaysforFuture Movement. They fear a political opponent that is similar in the way it refuses to engage in plural representative politics and moves beyond the left–right cleavage but occupies a new moral agenda, which populists also cannot really oppose, consider as irrelevant or openly deny. The moral superiority of the climate movement, in this sense, is a real thorn in the side of populism. Unlike partial interest representatives, #FridaysforFuture is an adversary that cannot be targeted. Like the populists, they do not want to reconcile, but to disrupt. Yet, the way they seek disruption is not meant to undermine the public sphere but to re-establish its common good orientation. Unlike the radical populists, with their often-ostentatious style of living, the climate change activists conduct the life of politically moderates, but by applying a radical and no-compromise-seeking morality against themselves and others (Marquardt, 2020).

Climate change radicalism is sometimes used by the political establishment as evidence to expose the immaturity of young and inexperienced protesters. The 'climate hysteria' of the activists is said to violate two central normative yardsticks of the democratic public sphere: the rationality of debate, and the readiness to build majorities and seek compromise. By pushing the movement into a minority position as 'young hysterical people', the so-called political establishments accept, at the same time, the invitation to enter into a generational conflict for which the climate activists have laid the grounds. For the young protesters, a reference to numerical representation in support of their calls for urgent action against climate change is unnecessary. #FridaysforFuture activism is prepared to counter the accusations of climate hysteria with facts and arguments in public debates. If necessary, they can easily support their arguments numerically. The representation of numbers has been brought back through successful ad-hoc mobilizations: the great majority of the scientific community that backs their gloomy predictions and the mass mobilization against the populist climate change deniers on social media in the streets. In Norway, a populist digital movement emerged in 2019 under the name of People's Uproar Against Climate Hysteria. It was initially successful in mobilizing more than 100,000 supporters on Facebook. A spontaneous counter-movement on Facebook was immediately established called 'People's Uproar Against Uproar Against Climate Hysteria', which mobilized mass support within Norwegian society within a couple of days, turning the 100,000 populist supporters into a small minority. This is a struggle over representation of the people in the very classical sense. It is a re-pluralization of the political space, showing that, by simple means, not everybody agrees with the claim by some to represent the people. The populist claim of unitary representation of the people is thus re-partialized. In most cases, it does not take much to expose populism on social media and to show that a populist movement's self-acclaimed leader does not represent the people, that there is no real people's uproar, or even that many of the followers of populism are de facto well-known troublemakers and supporters of right-wing extremism and xenophobia.

The Yellow Vests Movement: the shifting alliances between populism and anti-populism

The Yellow Vests Movement emerged as a spontaneous expression of popular discontent in reaction to the rise in fuel taxes announced by the French government in October 2018. After initial protest events, various online petitions were posted in November 2018 and widely shared through social media, covering a broad range of eclectic issues and calls for grassroots democracy, participation, fiscal and social justice, as well as the resignations of President Macron and the Philippe government.[31] Unlike the other three movements discussed here, protest was not primarily meant as a political struggle to restore a functioning democracy but as a social and economic struggle against marginalization and the exclusionary effects of market liberalism and globalization. The movement thus stands in the long French tradition of social upheavals, unorganized strikes and rural protests against Paris (Connolly, 2010). Such protests frequently turn violent: for example, the Yellow Vests Movement staged street riots and blocked roads and fuel depots, with their actions being met by a disproportionate police response.

The Yellow Vests Movement was, at the same time, trendsetting in the way protest of so-called social underdogs was symbolically expressed and institutionalized. One new trend is that waves of violent riots were triggered by seemingly insignificant government decisions. Such mass mobilizations were facilitated by the worldwide trend of a decline in trust in the democratic system (Norris and Ingelhard, 2019). In Chile, for instance, violent mass protests were triggered in 2019 by the government's decision to increase the costs of public transportation. In both the French and the Chilean cases, street mobilizations targeted single government decisions in order to express popular discontent with the system at large. The Yellow Vests Movement also received attention in other European countries, where protesters have used yellow vests as a symbol of solidarity with workers. Protests in all these different places were nourished by a sense of injustice that was related to the widespread feeling of not being represented but overlooked and silenced.

We observe a form of protest that does not seek to renew representative relationships with political parties and government but rather break the constitutive linkage through the expression of wider grievances and anger that cannot easily be remedied (Rouban, 2019).

To understand how these new radical forms of contestation of democracy were given expression, we need to analyse more closely the communicative infrastructure of protests. For the protesters, social media and the streets are not simply two separate realms, the one virtual and the other real, but are used interchangeably as places of encounter for the underdog (Chamorel, 2019: 59). Social media and street fights are struggles over visibility, in a very elementary sense, in a public sphere, where attention is a scarce resource and spaces of celebrity are already occupied. Social media and the streets also convey a feeling of inclusion where 'everything goes', and thresholds for the expression of voice and diverse opinions are low. This is the function of so-called subaltern counter-publics as discursive arenas that develop in opposition to the official public sphere (Fraser, 1992). They are formed in response to experiences of domination and exclusion from official discourse that legitimizes the existing economic and political order but does not allow anyone to address the injustices inherent in that order.

Through the combination of social media and street protests, the public sphere entered into an experimental mode, where political action was ad-hoc and localized. Such a decentralized movement with many local bases in rural areas can be considered as rather atypical in French politics. Social media groups were previously strongly anchored in local democracy (many of them continue until today, though at a much lower rate of participation). What distinguishes the Yellow Vests Movement, however, is the early institutionalization of new forms of protests, facilitated by the use of shared symbols and rituals that allowed for the identification of the movement and recognition of their concerns.

Many observers have classified the movement as populist,[32] but it is unclear on what basis a leaderless grassroots movement should take a populist form of mobilization. First of all, there are no significant overlaps between the Yellow Vests Movement and the constituents of the National Front as the major right-wing populist party that equally claims to give voice to popular discontent in France. The Yellow Vests Movement instead spans the political spectrum. As reported by Reuters, an opinion poll of 2019 found that a minority of Yellow Vests supporters had voted for Macron in the 2017 French presidential elections, but the majority had abstained, or had voted for either far-right or far-left candidates.[33] The anti-establishment messages spread through social media typically mix leftist and rightist themes. This is different from populist parties who need to stand for election, or populist grassroots movements like Pegida in Germany, where protesters clearly align with right-wing agendas.

Secondly, the attempt to reintroduce class politics and to realign along ideological cleavages is incongruent with populist politics of identity. If populism is to be understood as a form of identity politics, with their adherents identifying as 'true citizens' of the nation (Müller, 2016: 3), the Yellow Vests do not defend national interests or pride in France, but rather emphasize divisions within French society and the image of a 'broken nation'. They seek identification with working-class culture but do not claim that workers are the only legitimate representation of 'the people'. Class differences matter, but they divide the people rather than unify them. At the same time, the Yellow Vests are used as a symbol to bridge differences and invite other social groups to join their social struggle. The Yellow Vests flatten differences, such as ethnicity or gender, and highlight differences of class. Everyone can put on a yellow vest and participate, but it is unlikely that everyone will.

Thirdly, while populism requires central organization and leadership, the protests of the Yellow Vests Movement remain diffuse and often anarchic. Instead of promoting forms of personal leadership, the movement emphasizes grassroots participatory democracy and promotes internal plurality and diversity. On Facebook, several groups existed with partly differing agendas and competing calls for actions: in the banlieue of Paris, the local Yellow Vests groups were often recruited by young French people of Arab descent;[34] in rural France, protests were mainly carried out by 'angry peasants', identified, for instance, as Catholic *Gilets Jaunes* (Yellow Vests).[35] To accurately reflect this internal diversity, the populist demand for strong leadership and a unitary representation of the people was not an option. The movement chose to be diverse, not belonging to anyone, and covering a broad range of different identities.

With this emphasis on diversity and plural representation, the Yellow Vests Movement was initially successful in securing a relatively broad range of supporters. According to a November 2018 opinion poll, the movement had the backing of around 70 per cent of the French population.[36] After the first months of mass protests, the movement became more eclectic, and participation during 2019 and 2020 decreased considerably. Like the movement itself, its public appraisal remained ambivalent, one side seeing it as a progressive movement that encourages deliberative democracy, and the other as a populist movement close to fascism. Denouncing the Yellow Vests' populism and illiberalism, for example its anti-elitism and anti-intellectualism, was indeed the main response of the French political establishment, with various influential French intellectuals joining the chorus (Rouban, 2019). The protest against the fuel tax price was interpreted as anti-environmentalist and subverting a progressive agenda of global politics (Connolly and Antini, 2021). Evidence to back such accusations was found in provocative instances of violent protests or attacks by protesters against minorities. Alexander Hurt talks in this regard of 'the ugly, illiberal, anti-Semitic heart of the Yellow Vest Movement'.[37]

Acknowledging this ambivalence, the Yellow Vests Movement could be characterized as proto-populist, adopting an interesting mixture of populist and anti-populist rhetoric, and constantly shifting between the two. Connolly and Antoni (2021) called the Yellow Vests a 'messy action' and 'messy movement'. This is in line with what the French political theorist Philippe Corcuff (2021) has diagnosed as 'la grande confusion'. Of all the 'isms' that have historically informed democratic politics, only 'confusionism' is left. For new forms of social mobilizations, there is no longer a requirement of coherence of a political project. Discursive confusion corresponds to a kind of 'everything goes' in political mobilization: a movement cannot only shift constantly between left and right positions; it can also claim to be environmentalist or agrarian, popular or working class, rural or urban, anti-colonial and anti-immigrant, or it can raise demands for fiscal, social, economic and ecological justice in one sentence. The movement's messiness is related to the messiness of partisan democracy and democratic institutions. It reflects the difficulty of building a collective oppositional actor against populism, which is not itself contributing to the hollowing out of representative democracy.

The anti-populism of the Yellow Vests Movement, in this sense, is strikingly similar to Macron's 'En Marche!' that was mobilized in 2017 as a kind of emergency anti-populism in order to prevent the victory of the Front National candidate, Marine Le Pen, in the French presidential elections: 'Both are fuelled by social media, anti-establishment rhetoric, and distrust of political parties, labour unions, and the traditional media: They are the twin products of the crisis of political representation' (Chamorel, 2019: 59). To underscore their differences from Macron's 'En Marche' and to justify their strong anti-Macronism, the Yellow Vests emphasized their social movement character. Yet, ultimately, this claim of being a social movement stands and falls with the messiness of political protest. A protest movement that invites everyone to participate and bring their concerns can hardly convey solidarity among the protesters to fight for the same cause.

Populism and anti-populism: a no-win situation or democratic learning?

How can we make sense of the different performances of anti-populism as a practice of public sphere resilience? Anti-populism is not simply a political opposition strategy against the salience of populist leaders and their recent electoral successes. It is triggered by experiences of democratic decline and fear of the negative effects of disrupted public spheres and the media, of manipulation, polarization, radicalization and post-truth. The symptoms of post-democracy are not passively endured but rather reconstitute and reactivate publics that defend the common good and the plural voice of democracy.

Similar to populism, anti-populism is not an ideology, or a political doctrine, but a practice used by individuals and collective actors to engage in democratic values and claim legitimacy (Brubaker, 2017). As such, anti-populism is not an intellectual response that tries to invalidate populism but rather grows out of the experiences of daily confrontations with populists. The place for such encounters between populists and anti-populists is the public sphere, where both display their stylistic repertoires, routines and practices in the struggle over public attention and visibility. If populism is based on provocation, anti-populism could simply be seen as reactive. As a distinct style of communication, it reacts, however, not simply to the provocation by populists but also develops a critical response that transforms the populist claim, invalidates it and involves publics in argumentative exchanges that reach 'beyond populism'. It would be erroneous, therefore, to assume that there is an equivalence between populism and anti-populism, or that both are equal competitors in the public sphere. The symmetry of the populist claim of a unitary representative link between the people and its leaders is broken by an asymmetrical response. Anti-populism is not necessarily copying a populist style in its strong moral rejection of populism – because you exclude others, we now exclude you (Müller, 2016: 53). Anti-populism, rather, is distinct in its rejection of the categorical thinking of populism – because populists are exclusive, we are inclusive; because they are irrational, we are rational; because they show bad manners, we show respect. Such an asymmetric response is more the strength than the weakness of anti-populism. It might not always be the most popular, or highly visible, response in the media, but it corresponds to normative requirements and demands for democracy that are supported by a silent majority.

The four manifestations of anti-populism described in the previous section vacillate between what can be described as a *politics of cooling down* and a *politics of indignation* against the perceived threat of populism. A politics of cooling down underlies the anti-populist protests of the Sardines in Italy and, partly, also of the 'remainers' in the UK. Against the perils of a polarized public sphere dominated by hate, 'fake news' and the constant breach of discursive rules, there is a growing number of citizens that seek recognition, respect and authenticity. The constant campaign of the populists, and their omnipresence in all media channels, has resulted in the widespread media fatigue of the audience. The highly visible excesses of online debates by radicalized but ultimately marginal groups have a chilling effect on audiences that results either in their withdrawal from online media spaces or, because such a withdrawal often comes at a high cost, in demands for quality media and engagement in alternative media uses. Heated debate, constant indignation and resentment become a negative marker of a populist style. To be distinguished from the bad manners of the populists, the anti-populists seek to lower the temperature of public debates. In facing the growing irritability of the online public sphere, any expression of outrage over the outrage of the other would become indistinguishable from the populist style. Polarized and radicalized debates are meant to create fear and anxiety, but such fear can be redirected against its creators. The anti-populist turns the fear of the radicalized opinion and lie of the other into resilience, for instance by inviting reflection on preventive strategies to avoid radicalization of opinion and how we can escape online bubbles. Public sphere disruptions then fall back on individual media users and their choices regarding what to do with the media. This turns the plot of anti-populism into a story of strength and victory. Resilience means not falling into the trap of polarization or post-truth. Only the losers end up there, whereas winners develop successful strategies to prevent and overcome polarization. Young people have often internalized such anti-populist practices of media usage: being socialized with new media and learning to become literate, it is simply uncool to end up in hate-driven debates. Resilient media use and the capacity to cool down is a capacity that comes with status and recognition.

The widespread despair at the desolate state of publics brings people together and creates publics. These publics of despair, like the Sardines in Italy and the 'remainers' in the UK, are at the same time the publics of hope that raise demands for the quality of debates, for respect and truth against the disrupted populist communication cultures. Against hate, intolerance and lies, the key values of anti-populism – civility, maturity, deliberation – sound rather elegant. Their experiments with new languages of mitigation are part of the contemporary transformations of the public sphere and evidence for entering into a process of democratic renewal.

Withdrawal and cooling down, however, is only a partial response. The new democratic publics recognize, at the same time, the need for civic engagement and radical change in facing global problems. Fear of populists is also fear of uncertainty in a future world of capitalism, to which the populists provide inadequate responses. Media fatigue can go hand in hand with indignation fatigue, but it can also trigger new indignation. Anti-populism can be the side product of an alternative grassroots politics of indignation, manifested in new mass mobilization and protests, as in the case of the global #FridaysforFuture movement and the Yellow Vests Movement in France. These movements are seemingly close to the populists, directing their indignation primarily against the elites and the political establishment. Unlike the bipolar logics of popular interest representation, their protest is value driven and based on the inclusiveness of global solidarity and justice. By laying the agenda for a global politics of justice, and by claiming for truth, the populist opposition and their emphasis on particular interest representation and 'alternative facts' is left behind. Populist parties are thus not considered as equal competitors for visibility in the public sphere, but rather treated with disdain. The anti-populism of these movements is only a side-line of a major struggle for a world of justice and equality.

Anti-populism as a ritual of critique of the partiality of representative politics comes close to the intellectual critique of populism as a disfiguration of democratic politics (Urbinati, 2019). It is interesting to see how the scientific literature on populism combines elements of an actor approach, an institutional approach and a systemic approach in the diagnosis of populism. The rise of populism can be explained by the mobilization strategies of populist parties and the appeal of new forms of leadership, by the insufficiencies of existing democratic institutions to satisfy citizens' democratic demands and by the structural transformations and the general change of values in Western democracies.[38] These three types of diagnosis should, however, not be confounded, as they are based on quite different premises and bear different consequences. By following the first two explanations, public sphere norms and principles remain intact. They are violated, but these violations can be named and sanctioned. In a classical Durkheimian sense, the norm violation leads to the revalidation of the norm (Durkheim, 1964). Populism, according to Mudde (2012), would be a corrective to democracy (or any form of democratic disruption). By following the third explanation, democracy and the public sphere would risk being transformed beyond remedy. This is the post-democratic scenario where democratic values would be fundamentally called into question, and their validity subverted. Only with reference to this last case would we speak of a change of paradigm, or rather of a situation of *paradigm lost*, as, for the time being, there are no alternatives to democracy.

Benjamin Moffitt has recently raised the question of whether anti-populism is consistent and effective,[39] consistent in the way it convincingly opposes populism by defending the values of liberalism and democracy, and effective in the way that it actually has a potential to mobilize and conquer populism. In the discussion of our four manifestations of anti-populism, we found mixed evidence. On the one hand, anti-populism builds its success on the very idea of restoring public sphere rules and distinguishes itself through reasoned debate and fact-based arguments from post-truth politics. It is also remarkably successful in mobilizing 'silent majorities' that stand up in indignation against the spectre of populism. On the other hand, many expressions of anti-populism were found to be inconsistent, for instance in the way they oppose illiberalism but equally propose a no-choice policy that violates democratic values. There is also evidence that anti-populism can fuel polarization in the way it excludes the populists as 'anti-democratic', only to reinforce populist beliefs and strengthen their positions. Anti-populist backlashes would thus risk making populism even stronger and more radical. Or, according to the critique by Moffitt in the *Guardian*,[40] anti-populism is simply about re-branding the Third Way: it is a hidden form of TINA ('There is no alternative') politics. Some leaders and mainstream parties have also adopted what Moffitt describes as the 'good populism strategy': in order to win elections against populist parties, they imitate the populist rhetoric, for instance by being anti-immigrant in a 'more democratic' but still rather unfriendly way, like the Danish Social Democrats successfully did. Political parties who claim to be democratic, and disguise themselves as populists in an instrumental way to win votes, would become indistinguishable from populists. They would not restore democracy, but rather accelerate the deep transformation of democratic politics.

Looking at the various manifestations of anti-populism discussed in this chapter, these objections seem to be unwarranted: the anti-populism of Renzi or Macron and their defence of something vaguely called 'political stability' was explicitly rejected by the movements of democratic resurgence identified in the previous section – in the UK, the 'remainers', the 48 per cent of the electorate who voted to remain in Europe, turned the Europeanism of the economic elites upside down; the Yellow Vests movement's indignation primarily targeted Macron's government and its TINA-style politics; the Sardines' wish to re-establish the legitimacy of democratic institutions and their parliament, in their eyes violated by political parties; #FridaysforFuture is essentially about the reintroduction of political choice in democratic politics. As such, these movements contribute to the unmasking of the caricature-style anti-populism of European leaders, restricted to the defence of political stability or the 'return to normality' arguments. The official anti-populism of TINA-style politics leaves an ideological void that does not satisfy the voters' demand for political change and values. Populism is rightly understood not as the cause but as the response to the resurgence of undemocratic liberalism (Mudde, 2021). Yet, the voters will also feel the insufficiencies and contradictions of the populist response, which gives rise to new mobilizations of democratic resurgence. The democratic anti-populism of these movements targets the illiberalism of both mainstream representative politics and of populism. It is through this double struggle that democratic public spheres may be restored, reintroducing 'the common good' parameters as the horizon of democratic politics.

The struggle between populism and anti-populism is not a continuation of partisan politics between equal contestants. It is not a struggle that simply juxtaposes different styles of politics (such as a consensus style versus an antagonistic style), or one that competes over the best way to represent the people. The field of (anti-)populist contestation is not internal to democracy, but transformative *of* democracy. In facing the populist challenge, democracies are looking into their own uncertain future. Post-democracy is not an option, but a fate. Not even the populists choose to be post-democratic, but in their typical ambivalence, they claim to be the 'true democrats' over the enemies of the people. Democratic politics typically engage people in projects of societal self-realization, turning humans from passive subjects into active agents of history. The looming post-democracy would mean for many a downgrading from their acquired status as citizens, back to subjects deprived of civicness. Such experiences of a loss of status and alienation are underlying current public sphere mobilization in the form of an intensification of democratic politics. As post-democracy only becomes thinkable within democracies, it will not be realized by democracies. The winner in the controversy between populism and anti-populism could therefore well be democracy. The criticism that is practised by anti-populism is not simply an alternative argumentative style of democratic politics that develops in opposition to populism. It is *the* democratic form of politics among equal participants who enter an inclusive debate, the plural expression of opinion and the openness towards new horizons of collective self-realization. In facing the post-democratic scenario, such processes of re-democratization are accelerated, not blocked. A post-democracy, then, is merely a template for public sphere criticism that invalidates itself at the moment it is exposed to public scrutiny.

The COVID-19 pandemic: public sphere resilience in times of societal lockdown

The resilience of publics in a moment of societal standstill

The COVID-19 pandemic of 2020 and 2021 will be remembered as an unprecedented moment of societal standstill. Public spaces of physical encounters with others became inaccessible and were defined as risk areas.[41] The lockdown of public life radically changed culture, politics and markets, as people were banned from work, schools and universities. Privacy during the pandemic was not self-chosen but imposed by law and the authority of states. While individuals were forced into privacy, public concerns about the expected negative impact were growing. As the pandemic spread, the economy started to experience a recession, and unemployment increased. At the same time, trade-offs between public health and fundamental democratic principles became necessary (Engler et al, 2021). State of emergency orders were declared throughout the world, allowing governments to suspend civil liberties and to adopt sweeping measures such as strict confinements and quarantines, the monitoring of social distance and closures of national and even regional borders. Such protective health measures were recommended by the scientific community and the World Health Organization (WHO) as necessary to effectively contain the virus and protect the health of the citizens. The advice of scientists was embraced by governments, ordinary citizens and the media. While public spheres were physically closed, pressing normative questions were raised that required broad engagement in public debate about how to balance the obligation of states to maintain public health with the costs of disproportionate interferences and the rights and freedoms of citizens.

The COVID-19 crisis disrupted the 'normal' mode of public sphere functioning as an 'uncertainty reducing mechanism' (Trenz et al, 2021: 5). In this normal mode, knowledge is accumulated, shared and channelled in such a way as to facilitate informed public opinion and will formation. In the exceptional mode under the pandemic, public spheres operated under conditions of enhanced uncertainty: knowledge was not (yet) available, orientation was lost and information that can be used for political decision-making was not yet tested and/or can be contested. The kinds of social responses triggered by crisis are ambivalent. On the one hand, the pandemic risks intensifying existing trends of public sphere disruptions and social anomie as a form of social disorder, or normlessness. On the other hand, the forced isolation and privacy enhance practices of public resilience. Society bounced back and intensified a dialogue about its underlying norms and possibilities for engaging in solidarity. If physical places are closed down, the virtual society (has modern society not always been virtual?) not only continues but even intensifies its exchanges and reactivates collective modes of problem-solving, coordination, networking and mechanisms of learning. The sociological agenda of resilience, as a mode of collective reactions to crisis, derives from these insights (Hall and Lamont, 2013). Resilience is in this sense the opposite of social anomie, or rather its denial and avoidance. Public spheres become resilient through the reconfirmation of social norms in a situation of enhanced uncertainty, where routine ways of functioning are temporarily unavailable and need to be replaced by new, experimental modes of coping (Rampp et al, 2019).

Exposure to risk of an unknown disease, economic uncertainty and bad news bombardment in a situation of forced social isolation undoubtedly created unprecedented levels of distress on an individual level. By looking beyond these manifestations of personal distress, we need to understand how crisis is collectively experienced and triggers coordinated responses. Instead of a long standstill, we can expect that society recomposed and reshaped during lockdown. Society, as well as capitalist markets, cannot simply be frozen or brought to a halt. A crisis does not suspend public life; it disrupts and redirects it (Eastham et al, 1970; Holten, 1987). In retrospect, a crisis will be remembered as an axial moment of change, a moment in collective memory that allows us to distinguish between 'before' and 'after'.

This idea of crisis as a bifurcation of societal evolution, of course, is a very political moment. It puts the legitimacy of government under constraint (Habermas, 1975) and activates political decision-making to mitigate negative effects and to lay the paths of future development. Politics under crisis shift from routine to emergency. Decisions are necessary, but they are themselves risky, as they need to be taken quickly and under uncertainty. The crisis is a moment of consensus and solidarity about the shared experiences of disturbance, and the need to make collective efforts to overcome hardship. At the same time, it is a moment of conflict about the type of measures to be taken, and the sharing of the costs imposed by crisis.

To talk about the resilience of the public sphere relates to new forms of publicness and engagement in communicative exchanges as an escape from standstill and privacy as imposed by the lockdown. Such a search for publicness does not require physical movement by leaving the private realm and entering the public. Possibilities for escapes into publicness are linked to media devices that can be used within the walls of our private homes, such as the news media, the entertainment industries and, above all, social media. When social distancing became the new rule, it is no surprise that people sought new ways to connect online. Internet traffic went up considerably, with people not only seeking information, entertainment and social contacts but also suddenly becoming reliant on web services to work and learn from home.

The experimental modes of new publicness activated during the COVID lockdown took various forms. In the following, I will discuss three manifestations of public sphere resilience as they became salient in different contexts during the COVID-19 pandemic. They relate to innovative ways of using social media for the facilitation of (a) social encounters, (b) emotional expressions and (c) the sharing of information and facts.

A shared urban space: social encounters during lockdown

Metropolitan centres, where the diversity and density of social relations were suddenly and unexpectedly suspended, were hardest hit by the COVID lockdown. Restrictions of access and of activities during the pandemic, such as holding a political rally, are rather high barriers for the unfolding of public sphere dynamics. Urban spaces became a public sphere in the important sense that they allow individuals to leave their private households for public affairs. During the lockdown, the urban space could, of course, still be used as an escape from the private home into publicness, as could be observed in the number of people using their local neighbourhoods or public gardens for strolls. Legal restrictions on mobility and restrictions on public transportation in metropolitan areas thus led to an intensification of the density of social interactions and a revival of the local neighbourhood community as the last resort of public interactions during lockdown. When even a visit to another neighbourhood had to be justified, and remote places for travel were out of reach, freedom of movement was indeed literally restricted to the local neighbourhood. The metropolis that is defined as a space of flow by its global connections and movements of travelling in and out (Castells, 1996) became a real local space.

Escapes from privateness into publicness, however, are not only facilitated by physical movement (leaving the private space and entering the public) but through various modes of media usage. The lockdown of physical spaces of encounter did not affect the core of the modern public sphere, which is not so much a space to assemble as a sphere for the unfolding of discourse among anonymous members of the public (Neidhardt, 1994b). In this situation of seeming collapse, a reminder is useful that the public sphere, as I argued in Chapter 2, is mostly a virtual communicative space that applies to social situations, where face-to-face encounters and direct talk are unfeasible.

This means that in a situation of forced shutdown, when social contacts in physical spaces are suspended, virtual communication through the channels of the media can continue. The pandemic situation, and the forced suspension of encounters, intensified the needs of the audience to gather information and exchange news about this unexpected situation and the various risks involved. Constraints and restrictions of social life activate communication networks, and new and creative uses of the media in response to audience needs. Being locked down at home, you can still communicate with friends and strangers, you can engage in social media small talk, you can be political or show solidarity. The intensification of social media traffic, during lockdown, might be mainly explained by film and music streaming, online gambling or porn consumption, but social media platforms also hosted numerous social media neighbourhood support groups, facilitated online encounters, or online exchanges of goods and services. If it is true that public life is the pulse of the big city, then there is a chance for social media to become urbanized. Social media encounters gain in reality if the centres of the big cities appear surrealistic and unreal. When analogue social relations become a health risk, people go digital and build a safer online environment. When the open city is closed down, the Internet can open up. When your own home and neighbourhood become a prison, the digital world can become an escape.

The pandemic, therefore, inevitably led to a reappraisal of the digital public sphere, which thus far has mainly been made responsible for its disruptive and destructive forces in undermining local life and community. Never before had the distinction between real and human social exchanges and virtual exchanges seemed so inadequate. The closeness of real encounters became a peril, while the distance of digital networking became a virtue. Digital distancing was relativized in light of the experiences of social distancing. As noticed by many, the imposed lockdown of public life would have been unbearable without the possibilities for individuals, groups and economies to rely on the Internet, not simply as an escape but as a sustainable substitute to continuing social life and re-establishing links to locality. When social life offline is downloaded, the online social interactions are uploaded. Digitalization is then no longer a choice, but becomes essential for survival.

Many who experienced social lockdown in one of the metropolitan areas of our Western world were fascinated by the many creative ways the emergency situation was turned into a pushing factor for a bottom-up digital public sphere, which became progressive, supportive and, without exaggeration, life-saving. During my Berlin stay in one of the city's most vibrant local neighbourhoods (the famous Berlin *Kiez*) during the winter and spring of 2020, I could observe how local people developed the habit of visiting their favourite café's website once a day to say hello, exchange local news and support each other. Local life and neighbourhood contacts not only continued in digital form but in some instances even intensified. You could buy a virtual coffee to guarantee a basic income for the owner of a public space, or you could start planning communal projects. In all these different forms, you supported the maintenance of public spaces, even though they were closed and could not be physically accessed. The public space was reopened as a virtual space that was still available for economic transactions, like transfers of money, and for public talk. The Internet was suddenly no longer optional, a kind of useful supplement or playground for use in our free time. It turned from a toy into a tool for community building.

The notion of a *Kiez* as part of the metropole maintains some basic public sphere functions in the way it facilitates a lifestyle that is informal, creative and open. It invites guests and strangers, like tourists, not only for a visit but also to constantly interact with locals and participate in communal life (Till, 2005). Most importantly, the *Kiez* already builds on informal networks that link to other (local and global) spaces. Thus, the *Kiez* is more than a neighbourhood network; it is an urban space for global encounters. When hit by the COVID lockdown, the resilience of the urban space of neighbourhood is not coincidental but based on established practices and the availability of pre-established structures, networks and technologies that distinguish the local neighbourhood.

My interest here is not so much in the possibilities for a physical escape from private to public, like quarantined Italians singing to audiences on the opposite side of the street during lockdown, but in how the conditions for an escape into publicness were set by the creative use of digital media. Such creative uses are not restricted to virtual exchanges, protected by the anonymity of mass communication, but often include possibilities for 'real encounters' of friends and strangers. Platform IT developers were seemingly influenced by Habermas' public sphere political philosophy (Wynn and Hult, 2020), borrowing from public sphere vocabulary in the design of their software packages: 'Meets', 'Zoom' or 'Teams'. The way people 'gather' on such platforms typically combines all levels of publicness: private or semi-private encounters, purposefully organized groups, regular work meetings, public assemblies with open or restricted access with various modes of 'giving the floor', shifting roles between speakers and listeners, sharing information, running parallel chats and so on. While new platforms for encounter and assembly were designed in a way to minimize anonymity, facilitate group discussion and teamwork, the old social media platforms like Facebook or Twitter were increasingly used in anonymous mode, allowing individual users to hide as members of a mass audience.

The design of software, however, is but a poor substitute for a public sphere if the new places of public encounter do not also embrace the normative dimension that distinguishes the modern public sphere of democracy. As was rightly pointed out by Zizi Papacharissi, online exchanges, such as those facilitated by cyberspace, only open up a new type of public sphere if they also promote a democratic exchange of ideas and opinions: 'A virtual space enhances discussion; a virtual sphere enhances democracy' (Papacharissi, 2002: 11).

The new dependency on digital media technologies for public sphere resilience and survival, therefore, raises a number of critical questions: first of all, how sustainable online social, professional and political life can be in light of the many de facto limitations of the available infrastructures, its insufficiencies and restrictions in use. Secondly, how sensitive the new platforms are with regard to questions of justice and equality, and what effects of marginalization do they create, with new divides between the digital privileged and underprivileged. Thirdly, how much can we really rely on a digital public sphere that, in effect, is privately owned and controlled not by states, but by private companies. Such critical questions of sustainability, openness, equality and inclusion are not only raised by critical media scholars but drive public contestations about the design of digital public spheres.

To turn urban spaces into new public spheres, it is therefore important to verify that these urban spaces are not detached from criticism. As such, they should facilitate not only the physical escape from private to public, as was soon invented after the first lockdown in May 2020 through the development of apps that allowed users to regain mobility in the local space while allowing them to maintain social distance (Samuelsson et al, 2020). In all likelihood, cities will be places where demonstrators will reconquer the streets to protest against curfews, or to blame their local and national governments for mismanaging the crisis. The city is a place for reason and emotion. It will be populated by citizens with diverse needs, some of whom will opt for obedience with authorities, while others will find reasons to mistrust their government and oppose the restrictive measures taken during the pandemic.

A shared emotional space: collective sentiments during lockdown

During the pandemic, going digital was not only instrumental for the maintenance of work and social relations. Social media were also used in innovative ways for the sharing of feelings of distress and emotions. Isolation and loneliness were for many an almost existential experience, leading to high levels of psychological stress. Symptoms reported by health authorities were fear, anger, sadness, worry, numbness and/or frustration. These might lead to chronic health problems, worsening of physical and mental health conditions, eating disorders or drug, tobacco and alcohol abuse. Recommendations for healthy ways to cope with stress are to connect with others, talk with people we trust and engage with our community, even if online and through social media.[42]

During the pandemic, bad information and misinformation went viral throughout social media, which risked increasing people's anxiety rather than helping reduce it. High stress levels can correlate with more intensive social media activism. People with anxiety often express themselves through social media, which can contribute to their emotional well-being but can also increase stress. The state of heightened anxiety during the pandemic can correlate with partisan information processing, partisan selective sharing and exposure to extreme positions and misinformation (Freiling et al, 2021). Strong feelings, like fear and anger, can often work as a selective filter for people who only seek (mis)information that resonates with their state of emotion (Wiederhold, 2020).

Social media emotion management, therefore, is not only accountable for acquiescence but can also mobilize segments of the population and unite them in indignation. A combination of fear and anger is the emotional underpinning for protest. If protest is a legitimate response of emotionally mobilized citizens, the lockdown during the pandemic de facto closed available protest venues. Under such circumstances, social media can be used to stir up anger and despair in parts of the population, but they are a poor substitute for the public outcry of their emotions. This might be conducive to political mobilization that tries to reconquer the streets through engagement in violent forms of protest (Wollebæk et al, 2019).

Highly emotional debates often correlate with enhanced levels of politicization, a passion that translates into politics (Walzer, 2002). Emotions in politics go hand in hand with a particular sensitivity towards perceived transgressions of values, such as restrictions of freedom or violations of social justice. Such emotional debates can also easily turn against the transgressors: the government that takes away our freedom during lockdown, the profit orientation of the industry or some imagined conspirators. Surveys report that restrictions of freedom were accepted by the majority of the population under condition of equality. Many people expressed indignation about those who did not follow community rules, or tried to maintain privileges (Viehmann, 2020). If equality becomes the norm, the privileges of some are more difficult to defend, and levels of tolerance decrease.

Last but not least, the shared emotional space is also turned into an observatory space for monitoring and controlling the emotions of others. Participation in social media exchanges can give reassurance that others share similar emotions, for example that they are also fearful or angry. Digital affordances facilitate, in this sense, a new form of publicness in response to the global health crisis, which consists of mutual observation and comparison of societies and their different responses and emotional reactions to crisis across the globe. The emotions of others become newsworthy. Specific social media content is created that is used to communicate about human suffering in distant places, balcony singing in Italy, the drama of fear and public mourning, or the moral outrage of protesters. The media witnessing of the emotions of others remains ambivalent. In some instances, it can trigger compassion. In other instances, it triggers repudiation and calls publics back to reason against the perceived emotional overreactions of others. Emotional witnessing can be an invitation to share feelings (such as the imitation of balcony singing) in search of alternative ways to express feelings (for instance, by turning fear into support instead of opposition), or to make efforts to be less emotional and behave 'more rationally' than others. As part of the daily news package about how the pandemic was lived by others, emotions were thus more than sensational entertainment but an important foundation of knowledge and information about the pandemic and its impact on individual and social life.

A shared news space: information during lockdown

Journalism and the news media were considered to be an essential business during the COVID pandemic. As such, they contributed in various ways to the building of resilience capacities of society and democracy in lockdown. First of all, the pandemic was an opportunity for independent journalists to gain prominence and credibility in their claim to serve the public interest and help people to survive (Casero-Ripollés, 2020). When times are bad, journalism went back to basics, informing about risks, instructing and giving advice about how best to cope and survive. At the same time, journalism became more collaborative. Through their desks, journalists could still engage in international collaboration and work together with foreign colleagues to build stories that helped the public to understand the global pandemic.

Secondly, a global pandemic also created a global space of news production and diffusion. As journalistic production internationalized during the pandemic, news content also took a more global perspective. The global gaze on the pandemic and the suffering it created (Chouliaraki, 2010) was not simply an effect of enhanced social media diffusion of news but of the functioning of journalism and news organizations in translating personal concerns into collective issues (Schoenfeld et al, 1979). Global journalism is a distinctive news style that acknowledges the difficulties of applying sharp distinctions between domestic and foreign issues (Berglez, 2008). Through global problem framing, drama and news value can be increased (Lück et al, 2016). A global perspective is taken, for instance, in the way causes are sought and responsibilities ascribed for the spread of the pandemic, either through externalization (for example, by blaming China) or internalization ('what happens far away affects us', 'global problems require global solutions'). Another technique journalism uses to take a global perspective is international comparison and ranking, which requires the application of universally applicable critical standards, such as adherence to values, the availability of public health services or the application of metrics, such as infection and mortality rates. One recurrent practice of journalists was to compare and contrast how their own country performed in comparison to others, in order to discern good and bad practices, or to detect viable solutions as they were applied by governments and health authorities elsewhere. Apart from criticism, the international comparative view is often used for dramatization. Journalism issue framing of the magnitude of the crisis and its dramatic effects requires comparison: the problem needs to be put into perspective, and the risks need to be identified. The drama of the pandemic further related local victims to victims abroad, putting their suffering into perspective, and making their grievances relevant for local audiences.

By taking a global perspective, journalism further reassesses the prominence of actors as protagonists of news stories. As the pandemic related local with international politics, it also pushed the actors who had credibility in defending a global agenda to the forefront. This regards the authority of international organizations like the WHO or the Director of the US National Institute of Allergy and Infectious Diseases, Anthony Fauci. The new emphasis on 'responsible government' puts constraints on the mobilization strategies of populist parties' leaders, whether they are in opposition or in government. Their isolation, as international policy actors, reduced their visibility during the pandemic, as they were not part of the global chain of events that drove the crisis, allowing government executives, in many cases, to effectively marginalize the populist opposition. The new protagonists, instead, were state executives, governments and experts with power and legitimacy in international politics. In defending public health issues, national interest frames are insufficient, and credibility can only be gained through collaboration with international organizations. In this sense, the drama of the pandemic fashioned new heroes, like health experts and virologists, which are part of an international community, and villains, like inert leaders, who stand for the inadequacy of nationalist problem-framing.

Even though the pandemic opened a window of opportunity for global journalism in terms of news framing, it also challenged established working practices, and put news organizations under heavy financial constraints.

Working in isolation is not the ideal condition for the production of news. While information flows were heavily controlled by government, opportunities for journalists to put government officials under public scrutiny were reduced. A report prepared for UNESCO shows that press conferences were cancelled during the initial period of the pandemic in countries like Slovenia and the Czech Republic. Other governments introduced remote questioning during press conferences, which proved to be less effective, as no follow-up questions were permitted.[43] In many places, critical journalists were also exposed to assault and online mobbing and could not be properly protected.[44] In Germany, for instance, Coronavirus anger led to violence against journalists during protest rallies.[45] In addition, many news organizations struggled for economic survival. The European Journalism Observatory reported how news publishing faced a rapid loss of advertising revenue in 2020, and as a consequence, journalists were laid off. In many countries, the pandemic also increased political pressure on journalism, as emergency legislation often had an impact on free speech and freedom of the press. European countries were unequal to the task of ensuring that journalism survived. While local newspapers in Denmark profited from generous direct support payments by the government, newspapers in the UK made big losses.[46]

Some critical observers also expressed fear that the independence and freedom of the press was being put at risk by 'fake news' and state interventions during the pandemic. Reporters without Borders reported a wide spectrum of restrictive measures on press freedom on COVID-19 coverage.[47] However, in the absence of empirical studies, the degree to which news quality and independence of journalism was really corrupted during the health crisis is hard to establish. Instead of talking of an accelerated crisis of journalism, researchers should be aware of country-specific developments. Countries with strong public service media in Northern Europe were more resilient to disinformation than polarized countries in Southern Europe (Humprecht et al, 2020). Nevertheless, the governments of all EU member states, in a joint venture with the EU, took protective measures to guarantee the quality of information, and ban disinformation campaigns, often through foreign intervention.[48] Such interventions were meant to safeguard the truth orientation of public debates and guarantee the information value of the press.

Turning now from the production to the consumption of news during the pandemic, we need to ask how individuals face uncertainty by relating to news in order to access information, evaluate risk and find orientation. The global health crisis was paired with a surplus of global information about the dimensions of crisis. While social spaces were closed down, at the same time we were bombarded with global news. The existentialist experience of social isolation went hand in hand with excesses of news media consumption. By confronting the surplus of negative news about the pandemic, our relationship with news values changed. For many news readers, the question of the quality and trustworthiness of news was raised as a question of survival. It was raised in everyday situations, for instance by asking whether we can trust the information that was shared on social media, or whether the media experts, who interpret and translate this information for us, were credible.

What type of resilience can we expect with regard to emerging patterns of news consumption in response to the pandemic? The first possibility is that enhanced news consumption during the pandemic would enable people to access information that is essential to reducing risks. According to the classical theory of 'uses and gratification', news is accessed to decrease uncertainty, find orientation and give advice in situations that are experienced as stressful. Many news organizations, therefore, have increased their efforts to provide reliable information and quality news. They satisfied the essential needs of individuals who were left alone with the pandemic, and give quick responses to essential questions: 'How should I behave in order to remain healthy and reduce risks?' Furthermore, immersion in the world of news can offer security in the form of community bonds, affiliation and solidarity with others. Watching a news show on television conveyed the feeling of a shared destiny that 'we are all in the same boat', even though we were dispersed in isolation in our private homes. This is important for conveying some sense of solidarity that resources would be shared and the crisis managed by holding together as a community.

Secondly, the principled ambivalence of news consumption needs to be acknowledged, which can help as well as hurt. In psychological studies, a possible linkage between selective exposure to news and anxiety has been emphasized (Valentino et al, 2009). Excessive news consumption can increase anxiety, and anxious news consumers might either search for even more information through the news or withdraw from news altogether. In such a situation, we could also expect that withdrawing from news manifests itself as a form of resilience. Withdrawal becomes meaningful, in particular, in a situation of enhanced uncertainty, when knowledge and information as generated by journalism remain provisional and ambivalent, experts often contradict each other and governmental decisions remain contested. Moreover, the abundance of news, which is monothematic and negative, can create unprecedented levels of distress on both the individual and collective levels. Established techniques of reducing uncertainty might no longer work or become unsuitable for covering the complexity of the global pandemic. This again might challenge trust in established news sources and in journalism and increase fear of being misinformed by the news media.

What do we know about the dynamics of news consumption during the pandemic? As the pandemic unfolded, we might expect that practices of resilience in news consumption would develop over time, with information needs satisfied, especially in the initial phase, and saturation achieved in later weeks with people even turning away from news altogether or embracing increasingly 'alternative' and 'fake news' agendas. At first sight, it is without doubt that media habits changed dramatically as people faced COVID-19 and all its uncertainties and restrictions. In forced self-isolation, many people became news junkies, developing excessive patterns of news consumption, for instance by constantly checking updates of news websites, or by following live news threads on their mobile phones, possibly even while sitting on the sofa and simultaneously watching TV news. News media during the pandemic, however, was monothematic. For weeks, the pandemic was the one and only topic covered by journalists, since the whole political apparatus was reduced to dealing with COVID-19 emergency measures. The public sphere during the pandemic was a single topic public sphere. With this, the COVID-19 news coverage breached a central rule of journalism work to prevent issue fatigue through plural issue agendas and frequent changes of top stories. This single topicality of journalism during the pandemic can, in fact, only be compared to war coverage, and, indeed, journalists and political actors frequently resorted to war metaphors to frame the pandemic (Castro Seixas, 2021). Even though there is agreement among experts about the inappropriateness of this vocabulary, the use of such repeated statements like, 'we are at war against the virus' or 'killer virus' are not per se power-based and violent but can also be used to back moral justifications of the need to act together in solidarity (Castro Seixas, 2021). The COVID-19 news coverage was, in this sense, also unusual in the way it made strategies of media agenda setting through dramatization that was redundant or even counterproductive. The problem-framing of a global pandemic did not need to build on further stimulation through the journalism exaggeration machinery. If a news story, under normal circumstances, can never be bad enough, we experienced the opposite dynamic in the initial phase of the pandemic, when the spread of the virus was still restricted to the province of Wuhan, China, and the Western media largely ignored the foreboding crisis. News coverage of the pandemic was caught up in real events before journalists started to invent sensationalist news stories. The hyperbole became reality. In this new situation, news media were instead accused of playing down the seriousness of the pandemic and not uncovering facts that made for negative news as audiences began craving good news and signs of hope.

Patterns of news consumption during the COVID-19 pandemic largely confirm this process of an upgrading of journalism. News consumption in six Western countries went up, especially during the first weeks of the lockdown, with people turning primarily to unbiased news sources from governments or health organizations (Nielsen et al, 2020). In Germany, the most popular news was provided by public broadcasters, through TV, but also through their widely used news apps. A majority of people reported that they visited trusted news sources from public broadcasters several times a day. Not only was news read through apps but it was also shared through social media, or forwarded through direct messages to friends or groups of friends through WhatsApp (Viehmann et al, 2020). According to another study, 97 per cent of all Germans reported that they used at least one mainstream professional news source (TV, radio, print) a week, and 82 per cent additionally read news from non-professional sources such as social media sites. The smallest share of only 12 per cent used so-called alternative media, which are most likely to contain disinformation or 'fake news' (Frischlich et al, 2020). This already indicates that the risk of exposure to disinformation was reduced. Only a small minority of news consumers primarily used alternative news sites and almost nobody exclusively used non-professional and manipulative news sources. The same study, however, shows that even though purposeful selection of alternative news was low, a total of 36 per cent still reported that they encountered COVID-19 related distorted information, and 17 per cent helped to spread conspiracies through social media. This confrontation, though, also had obverse effects in the sense of increasing people's awareness of the risk of misinformation. Resilience becomes relevant here to prevent news consumers from confronting disinformation, or to refute the conspiracies.

From pandemic to infodemic

A global pandemic goes hand in hand with epistemic uncertainty. As Habermas put it: "Never before has so much been known about what we do not know."[49] There was an inbuilt insufficiency of knowledge in all news about COVID-19. Still, choices had to be taken by governments, which triggered other uncertainties that we were basing our far-reaching decisions on false information. These insufficiencies of knowledge pose a challenge to scientists and politicians regarding how to communicate 'uncertainty' without losing agency and trust. Epistemic uncertainty is also hard for political journalism to digest, especially when its main tenet is to reveal the truth behind power. One possibility for handling epistemic uncertainty is to reduce the level of political conflict: it is risky for mainstream politicians to position themselves in the absence of facts, with only partial knowledge and information from various types of experts to go on. In a political climate of emergency, the possibilities for the formation of a political opposition are restricted, and mainstream government and opposition prefer to suspend or postpone partisan contestation. As evidenced in opinion polls, such an all-partisan consensus enhanced general levels of trust, yet the absence of political contestation among elites was also a source of mistrust, and opened up an opportunity for the formation of new oppositional forces from the margins of the political spectrum to spread fear about the quality of the information on which these choices by government were based. De-politicized news and debates were an invitation for a bottom-up opposition. Such a politics of fear has always been the domain of populist parties, who became the main drivers of opposition during the emergency.

Lessons from past pandemics teach us that misinformation, conspiracies and scapegoating are recurrent phenomena in communities threatened by massive illness, death and economic disruption (Poos, 2020). The pandemic, with its increased demand for facts and news, offered an opportunity for the mobilization of public opinion based on the spread of 'fake news' and misinformation. If a pandemic enhances the risk of exposure to misinformation, it also escalates the possible negative effects of misinformation, which de facto become their own health risk, and not simply a symptom of disrupted public communication. It is precisely this exposure to higher levels of risk that triggers public sphere resilience.

The confrontation with 'fake news' during the pandemic does not need to have disruptive effects on the public sphere; it can also raise the awareness of news consumers, challenge their critical capacities, provoke reactions of disgust or indignation, and thus confirm public sphere values. Interpreting the digital information disorder as no longer the result of impersonal technological imperatives is a moment of political awakening (Chambers and Kopstein, 2022: 7). Resilience in such cases is driven by the fear of being misguided or following bad advice. The pandemic as a breeding ground for misinformation can also contribute to the building of some sort of immunity against propaganda and the restoration of truth orientation in public debates. Resilience becomes relevant here in the way news consumers learn to avoid confrontation with 'fake news' or prevent the spread of conspiracy theories.

The fight against the infodemic notably resembles the fight against the pandemic in the sense that both involve a kind of medical approach to restore public health. Since the Enlightenment, rationality has always been considered as an element of public health that can be dispensed like a dose of medicine. This ascribes responsibility to enlightened rulers to invest in education and science, as much as in medicine and hospitals. A healthy society is distinguished by its strength of devotion to truth and gains of knowledge that are measurable through indicators of individual and collective learning. By promoting factual information, societies can build immunity against superstition, long ago replaced by scientific methods of truth finding. Still, the public sphere can be infected, and diseases can return in the form of prejudices, propaganda or misinformation. The public sphere, therefore, needs to develop a repertoire of 'medicines' that can be applied to heal the infection. The fight against 'fake news' often stands in this old tradition of public sphere maintenance. Specific authorities, or professional competences of public sphere caretakers, are created that can provide medical prescriptions and subsequent cures.

By adopting this Enlightenment vocabulary of a medical approach to public sphere resilience, the proliferation of 'fake news' is seen as 'parasitic' on a well-functioning public sphere. 'Fake news' and conspiracies can spread because freedom of expression is principally guaranteed. States do not have the authority to impose truth but need to allow plural and competing interpretations of facts. The violations of rules of argumentation, justification and proof are intentional and as such can either be sanctioned by a higher authority or can be detected and contained by self-regulated media and public debates. This works well if proponents of 'fake news' and conspiracies are not banned *a priori* from access to the media to reach out but are filtered out only *a posteriori* from public debate. The free speech principle requires that they are given a fair chance to participate, and that their voice should be considered as a possible alternative expression of protest or legitimate concern, for example of marginalized people. 'Fake news' and conspiracy proponents themselves need to adapt to public sphere logics and subscribe to normative standards of public debate. Even if their primary aim is to undermine trust in democracy, they still need to use public sphere infrastructures in such a way as to make their own contributions appear trustworthy. In doing so, they not only rely on media infrastructures and channels to amplify and reach out to audiences; they also require critical engagement with news and presuppose audiences that take critical distance and question truth. 'Fake news' as part of bottom-up mobilization can become critical in the basic sense that it is used to question power and gain control. The protesting citizens as promoters of fake news are also children of the Enlightenment: they make use of their own mind, question what is taken for granted, express critique, control political elites and even invoke the authority of science in their claims for 'alternative facts'.

Research on the possibilities of cognitive resilience against disinformation remains episodic and case specific. One persistent finding is that capacities to recognize 'fake news' are actually widespread, but that news consumers, for a variety of reasons, still decide to engage with fake news (Reuter et al, 2019). 'Fake news' has become a 'genre' of its own that provides templates for producers and schemes of interpretation and engagement for users. News consumers, in this sense, are not necessarily cheated but might be attracted by this new genre, often for banal reasons such as entertainment, for instance. There is some evidence that 'fake news' might arouse curiosity, but not necessarily belief. The sensationalist style in which it is written is a lure to attract readers' curiosity and often has entertainment value. To consider fake news as funny news is sufficient motivation to minimally engage with it, which might include sharing or commenting. The fact that people share 'fake news' on WhatsApp without believing it was observed during the

Brazilian elections: WhatsApp chat groups were primarily set up for sharing curious or particularly funny news; the main purpose was entertainment, and the overall credibility was low (Resende et al, 2019).

The technical features of creating intelligent software and algorithms to reduce the risks of false information should not be discussed separately from the ways of enhancing the cognitive capacities of individual media users and publics to read news critically. In the fight against 'fake news', these individual capacities are often mistrusted, with maybe too much emphasis put on the cures prescribed from higher authorities. The medical approach to this fight against 'fake news' should also take into consideration the possibility that a body can develop auto-immunity. Examples are community interventions and prevention through media literacy programmes in schooling, designed to build resilience capacities in young adults. Soft interventions by teachers, experienced users or caretakers can also be institutionalized in the form of rule setting and moderation of groups on social media, creating safe and supportive environments that enable users to comply with the rules. The capacities of individual news consumers or reader communities to develop resilience practices autonomously are related to their self-understanding as enlightened subjects and sovereign citizens who need to hone their critical analysis skills in order to handle distorted information competently.

The development of cognitive resilience capacities against disinformation can be criticized as demanding and as excluding those who lack the respective skills to accumulate knowledge and process information. Factual information about the pandemic and the new prominence of experts might enhance the epistemic quality of debates but do not make the public sphere more inclusive. For those citizens who are neither networked nor news junkies/media literate, it is more difficult to decide about the quality of information received. The risks of being victimized by 'fake news' and disinformation thus increases for those who also suffer most from the negative effects of emergency in their social and professional life.

Among the winners of public sphere resilience instead is professional journalism, which has reorganized in important ways to confront the infodemic and 'fake news' pandemic and enhance its reputation. The 'fake news' hyperbole has helped journalists to brand their product as distinct and occupying a higher status. Professional journalism can support the development of resilience practices, but it is also performed as a practice of resilience, for instance in the way professional journalism establishes working practices of quality control, reformulates ethical standards or promotes new constructive news formats (Hermans and Drok, 2018). Paired with this, experts gain prominence in the news. Levels of trust in scientists is found to be consistently high in all countries. The news industry became an 'essential business' for scientists, used by the WHO and national health authorities who inform and reach out. Some newspapers, like *Le Monde*, removed their paywalls to facilitate access to news that was considered to be essential. Even though the public status of news is increasingly recognized, it would be premature to speak of the renaissance of the news business.

COVID-19 news consumption has also significantly contributed to the transnationalization of the public sphere. COVID-19 news confronted readers worldwide with the topic of how to combine loyalty towards fellow citizens with global solidarity, which is one of the core themes of the modern public sphere (Brunkhorst, 2005). Disasters and the emergency created by them tend to trigger solidarity in media spectators (Boltanski, 1999). One of the most curious rituals during the pandemic was the checking of country rankings of mortality rates that were not only updated daily but hourly by online news providers and vividly discussed on social media. Such rankings could, for instance, be used for normative assessments of the performance of populist or authoritarian governments by pointing out the mortality rates of countries like the United States or Brazil as deterrent examples. Countries were graded as measures of good and bad governments to inform world opinion about common standards of health policies, demand conformity and to ask for policy coordination and identify alleged deviators. The discussion of coordination measures and international solidarity to cope with a global health crisis involve states, scientists and entire populations. Focused attention on central government decision-making authority is required at nation-state level (for example, in a federal state like Germany, where regions have to be brought in line), at EU level and internationally. In the competition between regions and states, there was an upwards spiral of even harsher measures of lockdown, not of being more liberal. COVID thus triggered country-wide competition under vivid participation of audiences observing and assessing their crisis coping skills. Social control and sanctioning mechanisms do not, of course, apply directly, and negative world opinion imposed on one country can even strengthen domestic deviators and their *Sonderweg* (special path). In most cases, however, world public opinion secured conformity of state responses and outed the deviators with negative headlines. Sweden, for instance, which unlike most other countries did not impose a lockdown, was defined as a high-risk country by its European neighbours; precisely because it was deviating from international norms, it was spotlighted by the international press. The national *Sonderweg* consequently became a topic of domestic contestation, with national audiences attentively following how the international press covered the country. Swedish governmental officials and experts were contacted by journalists worldwide to defend their position, some of whom even appeared on late-night shows[50] in the United States.

The COVID-19 pandemic brings to the fore the case for learning about complexity and global interconnectedness. It is an instructive case of what it is like to live in a world without exit options. The pandemic focused world attention and triggered a global affectedness, a feeling of being together in the same boat, armed with only insufficient policy tools. If there is no exit from world society, this inevitably weakens the positions of those political actors who base their programmes on the promise of such an exit. At the same time, it strengthens the position of those who discuss global solutions to shared problems and provide common good formulae for a better future. There is thus a potential to enhance the willingness of international cooperation and to strengthen international law, international organizations and international human rights. Regional cooperation schemes, such as the EU, are best equipped to make use of such opportunities. In the Europe of free movement, the sudden closure of borders was experienced as a major rupture in travel routines and everyday cross border exchanges of European citizens (Recchi and Favell, 2019). The common market strengthened, however, the resilience forces of citizens; goods continued to travel freely, production chains, for instance in car manufacturing, were not interrupted, and large-scale unemployment could be prevented.

From resilience to resistance: escaping the 'tyranny of privacy'

In Chapter 4, I elaborated on how the notion of privacy, as related to exclusive intimate relationships, has a high *public* value in societies that are saturated by media and publicness. Intimacy is commonly perceived as something we actively search or yearn for, not as something that is imposed on us by higher authority. It arises from the longing of the public individual to withdraw, at least temporarily, from public life in order to find an angle for the identification of the self. By imposing isolation on us, and forcing us into retreat to intimate life, the pandemic meant for many people an experience of excesses of privacy. Intimacy has a high value only if it is self-chosen. Through the imposed intimacy of the pandemic, our private life became a cage from which we wished to escape. This expectedly leads to a reappraisal of publicness, which again supports the emergence of a political movement to restore it.

In the history of the modern public sphere, publicness has always been superior in the hierarchy of values of how to conduct a good life and gain recognition in society. Privateness not only remained more unstable and fragile, depending on public recognition. It was also suspected of becoming pathological, in the sense that excesses of intimacy had to be avoided, or even required public intervention. The 'tyranny of intimacy' threatened to be conducive to the 'fall of public man' (Sennett, 1977). During COVID-19, this 'tyranny of intimacy' became an existential experience endured by many, but it was also taken as a larger symptom for an unsustainable imbalance between publicness, privacy and intimacy. There is only a short distance between resilience and resistance, and the type of political mobilization that followed is an important element of public sphere renewal.

To understand the conditions for political mobilization during the pandemic, the Internet gives us many cues for such escape mechanisms from the 'tyranny of privacy', even during normal, non-pandemic times. Instead of individual escapes in the form of entertainment, or other substitute functions of publicness, such escapes can also trigger renewal, and more fundamentally, include individuals in a process of radically rethinking their own place in the public sphere. The COVID-19 pandemic, in this sense, can be interpreted as an invitation for individuals to take back control of their public lives against the 'tyranny of intimacy' imposed by digitalization. This might sound rather euphoric, but it is still important to notice how the radical rethinking of the conditions of the public sphere is no longer an intellectual exercise but a central survival strategy for digital citizens. The design of the digital public sphere becomes a collective task.

The many moments that can trigger such a rethinking of the conditions of publicness during the pandemic are often related to the experiences of quite severe restrictions of civic rights and individual freedom. States did indeed implement harsh measures of public sphere surveillance, for example in the form of tracking techniques like the anti-COVID spread apps, which allowed public health authorities to monitor mobility and public gatherings. This was often done in collaboration with social media giants such as Google and Apple, already specialized in the surveillance of their users. 'Stop COVID' contact-tracing apps were meant to control the movements of persons who may have been in contact with an infected person. The COVID-19 Digital Green Certificate, or 'Green Pass', allowed state authorities and private providers of services to discriminate between vaccinated and non-vaccinated people, and to grant privileged rights and access to holders of COVID passports. Such discriminatory measures were publicly supported once the majority of citizens were vaccinated and claimed back their rights of free movement. At the same time, authoritarian state measures nourished new fears, resulting in the anti-vaxxers' movement and an atmosphere of growing mistrust on social media around civil rights arguments, combined with a plethora of insinuations about the potential health risks of the new vaccines (Broniatowski et al, 2020).

Fake news and conspiracies as a form of protest

The fear that states would enforce far-reaching surveillance measures, however, was not only (and not even dominantly) expressed by civil rights groups or data protection supervisors. The mobilization of fear instead became a project of populist opposition parties, who amplified the voices of the anti-vaxxer rebels. Resistance during the pandemic took the dominant form of an appropriation of civil rights and liberties discourse by populist parties and their leaders.

During the COVID-19 lockdowns, a new bottom-up resistance could emerge which, instead of 'fear through fake news', built on the widespread 'fear of fake news' and of insufficiencies in our knowledge. The protesters mistrusted the 'official truth' and expressed their fear of being misled by science and government. Basically, the protesters saw themselves as 'enlightened and critical citizens' escaping victimization by state propaganda. The critical argument of 'fake news' as manipulated opinion is thus turned against government and science. Official governmental experts and scientists working for public health authorities were suspected of disinforming or withholding information, selecting only partial and biased evidence to legitimize state authority. It is interesting to note that protesters adopt here traditional arguments of the left to detect authoritarian tendencies of government, suspected of controlling information flows in a way to intimidate electorates, or to play with their fears through biased information about risks.

The global pandemic offered, in this sense, an opportunity for populist parties and their leaders to rethink their relationship with truth. Most populists would not go so far as to accuse journalists or scientists of being 'fake news producers' (even though some populist leaders, like Trump or Bolsonaro, regularly did so); they rather point at the necessary selective use of scientific knowledge on which to base political decisions. Hence, populists learn to use an epistemic critique against authoritarian decisions by government, which, by default, is based on insufficient data and partial information. The 'fake news' argument that is used by liberals and leftists against the populists is thus turned around, accusing governments of disseminating biased information and fearmongering. The vocabulary of left-liberal political mobilization in their struggle against the 'big brother state' is adapted by a bottom-up resistance movement that defines itself as 'popular': a form of self-protection of the ordinary people who confront power and big industry manipulation.

In order to explain why resistance in the global pandemic predominantly took the form of conspiracy theories, we need to understand the transmutations of populism as a political force that redefined its agenda from being mostly anti-liberal to becoming a defender of civil rights and liberties, and of 'alternative truth'. It would be misleading to assume that populist parties and leaders who make use of these strategies are simply post-factual. On the contrary, they insist on scientific reasoning and knowledge that are mobilized in the form of alternative facts and often supported by the authoritative voice of counter-experts. These strategies often are successful in creating a wider resonance, precisely because they include larger publics in scientific disputes. Even questions of immunology were suddenly discussed controversially in broader public debates. The combination of protest with an epistemic critique of science was also effective in empowering users to question the authority of experts and government. The message was that the distinction between truth and falsity is blurred and should therefore be questioned by critically minded ordinary citizens.

'Fake news' and conspiracies, in this sense, are part of the legitimacy contestation of the public sphere, not outside it. They are an element of mediatized debates and are used for public attention management by political contestants, who adapt to media logics through the use of a scandalizing language, exaggerations or false allegations of intent. Such forms of 'fake news' 'weaponization' can be found, for instance, on YouTube channels run by political influencers (Michailidou et al, 2022). The popularity of such channels might be explained by the fact that those who watch them are not simply consumers but people who see themselves as critically engaged citizens, keeping abreast of the news. The video material presented is often based on 'alternative scientific stories' backed by the authority of 'alternative experts' who report 'alternative knowledge'. Followers are made to believe that they get privileged access to truth. The videos often imitate a journalistic style, claiming to reveal exclusive facts that have been kept secret by others. The factual claims raised in the videos are typically combined with accusations against 'official truth' and 'official science', which is seen as ideological and manipulated by power. This mixture of factual and normative claims provides ready-made argumentative structures for the protesters, who often stage their protests as 'acts of Enlightenment' against authoritarian government, and their manipulation of truth. Street protest is staged as a revolt against restrictions of freedom and the alleged manipulation of the minds of the people by the holders of power. At the same time, protesters are empowered as public opinion leaders who spread myths, disinformation and half-truths through their presence in the streets, but also through the videos, texts or memes that relate to their protest action: COVID has been bred in a laboratory, the pandemic is a 'plot by elites', the measures taken are part of panic mongering by the government.

Adherents of conspiracy theories, therefore, are not simply passive social media users, whose minds have been brainwashed. An encounter with conspiracy theories activates them and increases their readiness to mobilize. Against all objections, the conspirators usually are the last to be modest in expressing their opinion and often seek opportunities to spread their 'alternative facts'. It has been observed that conspiracy theories have a religious impulse in the sense that those who adhere to them often display a missionary attitude to actively contribute to the spread of their convictions (Franks et al, 2013). For the adherents of conspiracies, however, this is not a question of faith, but of Enlightenment and criticism. The reference to conspiracies is for them an element of the political struggle against manipulation and authoritarianism by states and industries.

In most European countries (though not outside of Europe), 'fake news' and conspiracy resistance is a form of non-partisan, grassroots mobilization. Political parties like the National Front in France, the AfD in Germany and Lega in Italy might support anti-lockdown protesters, but their leaders would seldom stand behind their confusing claims. 'Fake news' and conspiracies rarely originate in populist movements and parties. Confusion triggered by conspiracies might help these parties, but it would be too risky for their leaders to openly support those who spread the misleading narratives. In most cases, the origin of conspiracies and 'fake news' remains, in fact, unclear, or, in itself, mythical and conspiratorial (for example, the alleged spread of conspiracies by Russian lie labs, or the influence of the QAnon movement). Conspiracies and 'fake news', however, do not need a mastermind who invents them and places them strategically in public debates. They need amplifiers who vaguely refer to them as a reference point in public debates. This can only be successful if the participants themselves, at least in appearance, stick to the rules of public debate. For instance, they do not ground their claims in transcendental authority or superstition but rather seek explanation, often providing evidence and justification while subscribing to the principles of freedom of expression. Alternative news is not meant to be fact-free but based on alternative facts and alternative science. The anti-COVID lockdown resistance movement, in fact, is very clever in that it appropriates public sphere vocabulary. It adds a new element to the mobilization of conspiracy theories by linking them to a civil rights discourse in defence of liberal values, free society and the construction of a potential threat to state authoritarianism and 'sanitary dictatorship', as Italian philosopher Giorgio Agamben (2020) labels it. This also includes allegations of censorship whenever conspirators encounter debate regulations and fact-checking by moderators.

To understand how 'fake news' and disinformation can become a tool of public sphere criticism, we first need to acknowledge that individuals are not just victimized or manipulated by misinformation. The reference to 'fake news' can be used for political empowerment of collectives in their intention to oppose government, and to re-politicize political choices. This is an important corrective to the fake news debate, which often treats misplaced and wrong information as a mental health issue related to the 'irrational' behaviour of individuals who need to be cured of a disease and who are victimized by the conspirators and their abusive forms of language (Hendricks and Vestergaard, 2018). At the collective level, such individual consumption behaviour of 'fake news' is then seen as creating 'dangerously inaccurate beliefs', a form of 'emotional contagion' or 'collective conspiracy ideation' (Ravenelle et al, 2021). Such a 'medical approach' to conspiracy theories externalizes and individualizes the problem: the adherents of conspiracies are victimized, and their irrationality must be cured and corrected. The medical approach to 'fake news', however, cannot explain how fake news mobilization can empower a political opposition and be turned into resistance of government.

The post-factual democracy is said to be distinguished by the politicization of facts, not opinions (Hendricks and Vestergaard, 2018: 104). However, why should facts not be politicized, and is the contestation of science necessarily a symptom of post-democracy? Instead of focusing on conspiracy theories as an exceptional case for the emergence of a new post-democratic order and the dysfunctional public sphere, an account should be given of the politicization of facts as part of the democratic game that encompasses science and knowledge production. Protesters do not relate to 'fake news' as a form of revolt against the democratic order but are driven by the desire to sustain and restore democracy in the pandemic.

Therefore, it is not by coincidence that conspiracy theories proliferate in times of uncertainty. Conspiracies claim back control over politics that is lost in a world of disorder. Understanding conspiracies as a form of resistance points to a double function they can play in protest movements: first, conspiracy theories underlie a plot that explains political causes and effects. Despite all the disorder and uncertainty that distinguishes a moment of crisis, the protesters assume that there are political agents who actually have a plan and, even though secretly, keep control. For the political logics at play, it does not matter much whether this calculation of political intent is correct or not. What matters is that these agents can be targeted and opposed. The formation of a political opposition becomes possible, despite disorder and confusion. The protesters' message is that the world is not irrational, but that there are human forces at work, and there are logics which operate and explain things in a certain way. The second function of conspiracies in democracy is that the democratic majority can have a plan, too. Even though they might not know the best recipe of what to do in the pandemic, they can warn of the wrong recipes and reach certainty by fighting them. The salience of conspiracies, in this sense, is an invitation to intensify the struggle over the detection of truth and not abandoning it, as is insinuated by the critics of post-truth politics.

By engaging in 'fake news' and conspiracies, publics, in other words, engage in fact-finding and critical assessment of scientific knowledge and expertise. They do not outrightly reject expertise but learn to use it, to question and contest it with what they perceive as counter-expertise. Against epistemic uncertainty, conspiracy theories construct a non-contingent world for the protesters, where causalities apply and responsibilities can be attributed. They offer schemes of interpretation and collective action frames that facilitate political mobilization. Conspiracy-based social movements are successful as alternative providers of facts and knowledge in a situation of epistemic uncertainty, when publics request and seek information. They are movements which occupy a cognitive space in society.

'Fake news' and conspiracies as a form of public sphere criticism, however, are a double-edged sword. On the one hand, they drive radicalized forms of street protests, and are thus highly effective in generating public visibility. On the other hand, the chosen forms of protests are deeply divisive, and ultimately self-exclusive. Conspiracies do not polarize society, as is often assumed by public observers of social media debates, such as Cass Sunstein (2018); they rather marginalize their adherents and contribute to the exclusion of their voice of protest. Even though conspirators enter public sphere contestation and adapt to media logics, their presence as equal players is not recognized. The anti-lockdown resistance movement had little chance to build coalitions or gain public support. Instead, their decision to ignore the lockdown or reject the vaccine became individualized, privatized, radicalized or even criminalized. Their appropriation of protest ultimately strengthened the public sphere resilience of a silent majority, which did not fear state surveillance, but conspirators. The protesters were visible, but not popular. Instead, their radicalized forms of actions became part of public perceptions of risk during the pandemic. Like the virus that had to be defeated, resistance also became a nuisance that blocked society from recovery. Public sphere functioning was ultimately supported, its normative script confirmed, and rationality and the authority of science reinstalled.

'Fake news' and conspiracies as a key element of political campaigning during the pandemic must therefore be interpreted as a symptom of the marginalization of the protest, not its strength. Instead of a broad resistance movement, the anti-lockdown and anti-vaccination protests scared people off, contributing to the formation of consensus with restrictive government. Opinion polls show regular support of global citizens for science and states to contain the pandemic, and a widespread demand for getting vaccinated.[51] The surveillance apps stood for a private deal that individuals entered into with the benign state as a common effort to overcome the public health crisis: I agree to use the app and you give me back my rights to conduct a public and professional life. The app gives permission to leave the forced privacy and to reinstall public life. The use of surveillance techniques to control the spread of COVID, in this sense, was not imposed by the state, but passed through the critical eye of the public sphere. Public authorities did not restrict critical discussions but rather opened a broad forum of debate through all available media channels, including intellectuals, journalists, experts, political parties and corporate actors and many local citizen initiatives that discussed the limits of surveillance and the possibilities of its legitimate use. The fear of state authoritarianism became a global public concern, which is also reflected in the close attention journalists paid to cases of abuse of power, and interferences into press freedom by foreign governments (such as the debates about Hungary and Poland).

The exploration of public sphere resilience in post-pandemic democracies is a task for future research. The evidence selected here should suffice as a first, though not as yet systematic confirmation of my thesis that the manifestations of resistance against COVID-19 restrictions in many European countries should not, as is commonly assumed, be taken as an indicator of enhanced polarization and new salience of value conflicts (Eigmüller and Trenz, 2020). Populations in Europe were not polarized but rather united by consensus, solidarity and support of the authority of science and government. The pandemic was a moment of public sphere resilience, not resistance. The choice of the resilient majorities, nonetheless, was political in the sense of investing in strategies of trust and solidarity in a situation of emergency, instead of the culture of mistrust of the protesters and their fundamental opposition to politicians, scientists and the 'mainstream media'. Instead of opposing political camps, the resilient majorities and resisting minorities stand for different cultures of trust and mistrust in democratic politics. As such, they mutually conditioned each other: the radicalized forms of protest of the few strengthened the resilience of the many, and the marginalization of the few fuelled the anti-lockdown protests. The often spontaneous and radicalized protest actions were readily amplified by the mass media, which explains their salience but not their overall impact. Rather, on the contrary, there is evidence that the high media visibility of the protest has contributed to its marginalization: the resisting minorities' attempts to reoccupy the empty streets were observed with suspicion and reservation by the resilient majorities and strengthened trust in science and government.

More than a return to an authoritarian state, it should be explored how the COVID-19 crisis has led to the revival of responsible statehood. This is the rediscovery of the public in the form of a state that takes responsibility for shared problems (Dewey, 1927). Again, we find evidence of a new alliance of statehood with science, which redefines its authority, not as a form of dominance over society, but as a creative force of society in a collective effort to face global problems. If states take back control, they often do this through coordinated efforts and regulatory frameworks that include international organizations and the use of international law instruments, as well as various partnerships with industries and civil society. New state regulation is meant to supplement and support evolving forms of self-regulation. For civil society, there are good reasons to enter such new partnerships as an opportunity to regain state authority over unbound capitalist markets. During the pandemic, massive interventions of states in economic production and distribution became consensual. At the same time, states, in conjunction with the EU, granted huge amounts of money and benefits to individuals who became victims of global hazards. People experienced their life chances suddenly being bound back to state services. States, and not the economy, guaranteed survival. States also made an effort to rule the media and to channel public communication. Providers of news and Internet platforms quickly adapted and implemented the new safety measures agreed on in consultation with states to protect people from the infodemic. Social media political communication turned from being anarchic (which it possibly never was), to being channelled, rule based and controlled by self-regulating users, providers, moderators and, ultimately, the state authority.

States, then, also became the last resort of trust for people who endured the negative consequences of the pandemic. States expanded their protective hands over the body of people, but equally so over the market, as private business needed protection and all too readily accepted entering into state assistance programmes. Only states guarantee employment and allow small enterprises to survive. States buy time for society and the market to adapt to fundamental change. People trust states as a guarantor of survival, but this new demand for state protection against immediate life risks and hazards can also be turned into a chance to re-establish the idea of responsible government in response to the evident dysfunctions of markets.

Future research should further elaborate on the nexus between resilience and resistance, which, as the pandemic suggests, can be transitory in the way that initial practices of resilience are replaced by forms of resistance, as dissatisfaction, fear and public unease grow during lockdown but can also be conditional and mutually reinforcing in the way that certain manifestations of resistance become part of public risk perceptions, trigger fears and overall strengthen the resilience of the majorities. Resistance during the pandemic is multifaceted, relating to anti-lockdown protests, as well as the mobilization of economically deprived people and minorities. In the same way, resilience is framed differently because forms of civic engagement to cope with economic uncertainties, unemployment or political repression require different types of action. Resilience, last but not least, must be seen as a political choice, not supplementing but opposing ongoing and parallel forms of resistance, which, as the pandemic has shown, are not always progressive and can be deeply reactionary.

6

Conclusion: Beyond Post-democracy

Where did we get to, and where do we go from here?

This book has departed from the expression of disbelief in the verdict that the contemporary world is entering a new phase of post-democracy. It has not questioned the symptoms of the malfunctioning of our contemporary democracies but its forms of diagnosis. Democracies, the starting assumption goes, cannot predict their own failure without at the same time reconfirming their commitment to democratic principles. Democracies cannot discontinue forms and practices of democratization. Such an account focuses on democracy as a 'state of mind', and not simply an institutional form. Democracy shapes people's expectations about government and is a motivation for people to apply critical standards to assess governments' performance and their legitimate use of power. As such, democracy remains intrinsically related to the modern public sphere, which sets the conditions for the validation of the claims of legitimacy raised by the holders of political power and of criticism of those who contest power. We can establish non-democratic forms and practices of political authority, and many governments and states in the contemporary world would try to do so, but we cannot seek the legitimation of the exercise of political authority over others without recurring to democratic norms and principles. Democracy is a normative claim of validity (*Geltungsanspruch*) that is raised in public legitimation struggles whenever political subjects use communicative tools to support or challenge the holders of political power and confront them with the expectation that they will act in their common interest. This goes beyond the formal account of the establishment of 'real-existing democracies', pointing at a process of institutionalization that was triggered after the First World War in what is called the 'first wave of democratization' (Huntington, 1991). My argument throughout this book has been that democracies are insufficiently described in terms of their 'real' existence. Before democracies materialize, they exist in the political visions and ideals of the people who challenge the holders of power with claims for rights and political participation. The French and American revolutions allowed, above all, a new imagination of society and the emergence of political subjects who might still have had only a few rights as citizens but learned to raise claims of inclusion through the mass media to share their visions, and engage society in a process of self-emancipation.

Modern societies dreamt of democracy long before they became democratic. Democracies did not simply replace the ancien régime at one point of time in history but slowly eroded authoritarian state forms from within. Even under authoritarian conditions, such as in Germany, a democratic mindset slowly took root and resonated with the power holders' concessions to the people's will (Richter, 2020). Such a democratic mindset translates into many everyday practices that reshaped public and private life before democracies could be installed. Not coincidentally, the rise of a democratic mindset in early modernity simultaneously demarcates the birth of sociology as a new discipline that specializes in the study of the self-organization of society. Modernization and democratization are cognates, even though they did not always go hand in hand. Against the claims raised by the proponents of postmodernity and post-democracy, there is no convincing evidence that this intrinsic bond between democracy and modernity is broken (Wagner, 2020). This does not, of course, exclude changes in practices and institutional forms of democracy. As long as modern societies continue, we can describe such transmutations of democracy, which are of genuine sociological concern.

In developing my argument about the resurgence of democracy, I contended that a critical perspective of contemporary media is not exclusive to media and communication scholarship but is deeply inscribed in practices of media usage and, as such, involves various segments of audiences and critical publics. The question of whether digital and global media violate the foundational principles of the modern public sphere is of public interest and is not simply an academic research agenda. The alleged effects of media disruptions and corruption on contemporary democracy drive a critical discourse that involves society and allows different forms of engagement. I applied two yardsticks for the identification of public sphere disruptions: (1) adherence of citizens, collective actors and the media to democratic norms and procedures; and (2) deficits of the performance of the available media and communication infrastructures. In the first case, the indicator for public sphere disruptions would be a validity test of its normative underpinnings. In the second case, the indicator would be the detection of various malfunctions of the media that do not comply and often systematically deviate from its guiding norms and principles. The identification of public sphere disruptions, therefore, is either a question of the validity of public sphere principles, or it is question of the functioning of communication infrastructures and media institutions that support such principles. The public sphere would become redundant, or even collapse, if democratic norms and procedures no longer hold valid. The public sphere would become self-defeating if democratic norms can no longer be put into practice. A post-democracy would break the constitutive linkage of the public sphere to a democratic community of citizens and rely on a set of norms and communication infrastructures that are fundamentally different from the ones established by the free press and independent media.

There is the paradox, however, that in order to apply these yardsticks for the identification of violations of public sphere principles or dysfunctions of media performances, we need to rely on these very principles, postulate their validity, and run critical tests of media performance. The normative template of the public sphere is needed, if we wish to understand how such norms are inscribed into social and political practices, guiding the interactions between media, political institutions and audiences. The analytical or scientific identification of public sphere disruptions, in this sense, can only be perceived as an operation of the democratic public sphere in the way it opens a process of critical judgement and reflexivity. I therefore introduced the public sphere not only as a contribution to a normative theory of democracy but also as a key concept of the theory of self-constitution, self-organization and self-legitimation of modern society (Eder, 2013; O'Mahony, 2013; Trenz, 2016).

Such an ideational-historical perspective of the co-evolution of the modern public sphere and society was found to be useful for the assessment of the claim that contemporary society is entering a new age of post-democracy. My argument was that such post-accounts of modernity, truth and democracy deliver yet another critical vision of society. The alarming empirical evidence of contemporary media and public sphere disruptions can only be interpreted beyond the normative template of public sphere criticism; they do not exist outside or independently of the realm of democratic politics. More specifically, the identification of media malfunctions requires the recoupling to public sphere infrastructures and the re-validation of public sphere principles and procedures. In the diagnosis of post-democracy, there is thus good reason to look beyond the measurement of the performance of democracies and the ranking of 'real-existing democracies'. As I was trying to show in this book, people all over the world still dream of democracy, and this is not only during deep sleep but as a daydream that continues to inspire political aspirations and agency. Democratic principles are held alive by governments and institutions, as well as by ordinary people in their criticism of endured injustice and dominance. Likewise, the normative validity of democratic principles is put to the test by critical media scholars, whose democratic imagination is seemingly intact, despite the undeniable erosion of democratic institutions and constitutions in many parts of Europe and the world.

If contemporary democratic societies show multiple signs of exhaustion, they still lack alternative imaginings of how a post-democratic political order should be legitimized. On the contrary, public sphere criticism all over Europe is still informed by the vision of an inclusive society based on democratic institutions of self-government, which has not lost its appeal for the vast majority of the population. In this book, I have collected evidence for democratic movements in Western societies that still dream of democracy – not necessarily and always in the form of revolutionary movements of resistance, but in everyday practices of democratic participation against democratic malfunctions, and the often-personal experiences of disruptions of the media and the public sphere. Such practices of public sphere resilience do not simply look back on the good old days of a well-functioning and integrated public sphere that supported national democracy. They are often forward looking and contribute to the reformulation of the public good in such a way as to face the new challenges of globalization and digitalization and take collective responsibility. The focus of this book was on European movements of public sphere resilience, which often promote a transnational agenda of debate and occupy local, national and transnational spaces of democratic renewal. It would be the task for other researchers to write the history of democratic movements in non-Western societies, as it would be to trace processes of public sphere resilience and resistance in authoritarian regimes. Selected evidence from very different places such as China, or the Islamic world, point at the growing relevance of public sphere struggles in response to state surveillance, control of media and restrictions of freedom of expression. Authoritarian regimes continue to be notoriously more unstable than established democracies in safeguarding the legitimacy of government, which cannot purely rely on economic performance and output. They are not only confronted with requests for compliance with standards of democracy in their international relations but regularly face protests and resistance from their own repressed populations. The diagnosis of post-democracy would be sheer mockery of the efforts of such movements and citizens in authoritarian regimes, who often risk their life to stand for democratic principles. If the claim for post-democracy is also meant to apply to the political visions and ideologies of a future world, it is even harder to see what should come after democracy. Democracy is *in vogue*, precisely because there are no remaining political ideologies.

If democracy has proven superior over all the different 'isms' that have shaped 20th-century political mobilization, one of the last remaining 'isms' that haunts contemporary democratic politics is populism. I have discussed populism in different chapters of this book, locating it always as part of democracy and public sphere contestation, and not taking it as a syndrome of post-democracy. Yet, while populism abides by democratic principles, for instance in the way it re-values the 'rule of the people', it also needs to be understood that it misconfigures democracy in important ways and disrupts the public sphere of democratic will formation. Populism contributes to the conundrum of contemporary public spheres, and populist leaders often flirt with anti-liberal ideas.

Several observers have compared populism to a parasite that weakens the democratic body (Urbinati, 2014; Müller, 2016). It claims majorities through democratic procedures but, at the same time, redefines the majoritarian will of the people in a substantial and not procedural way. The claim for populist representation of the people constantly shifts between democracy and authoritarianism. This is what Nadia Urbinati (2019) describes as the 'unresolvable paradox' of populism: it claims to represent the majority of the people in democracy but cannot sustain such a majority by democratic means. It can, of course, win democratic elections and, in some cases, even build large majorities through the charisma of its leaders, but once in power, it cannot go back and become a minority again, without ceasing to be populist. Unlike the verdict of Ernesto Laclau (2005), the populist demand, therefore, is not the democratic demand per se, but rather a disfiguration of democracy (Urbinati, 2014). By excluding the possibility of losing majorities, it displays an intrinsic authoritarianism. Populism, in short, has a totalitarian tendency, as I have described in the demands of Brexiteers for popular representation in a referendum that disempowers the will of the losing minority.

Whether and under what conditions the parasite of populism can be lethal is not a question of clinical tests, but of democratic experiments, which Western and non-Western democracies are currently undergoing. Established democracies in Europe, which were the focus of my studies, have built resilience capacities over time to lower the risk of fatality after infection. I conclude, therefore, with some confidence, that the populist challenge will remain internal to democracy and not transmute it into something completely different. My focus on public sphere resilience, in this sense, is meant to open another perspective on the parasite of populism, which, if not killing its host, might strengthen the body's defences. At the same time, I cannot categorically exclude the possibility of an authoritarian shift as a result of democracy's internal struggle with populism. When Ralf Dahrendorf (2003) observed the emerging populist phenomenon some 20 years ago, he still assumed that populism would remain largely oppositional and that populists, once in power, would automatically turn again into democrats. If the authoritarian option was not yet on the table at the beginning of the millennium, there is less reason to be confident in the self-healing capacities of democracies in our contemporary world. Democracy could succeed populism, for instance, in the way populist parties in some countries have not been re-elected and have accepted their minority role in opposition. Yet, what comes after populism could, indeed, be a new authoritarianism (Wieviorka, 2018). Populism is transitory in the way it either returns to democracy or becomes authoritarian. The authoritarian shift is an empirical possibility, and there are several candidates in our contemporary Western world that would stand for it.

For a long time, many sociologists and political scientists have held the belief that democratic development paths are directional. T.H. Marshall (1950) famously described the expansion of citizenship and rights as an institutionalized class struggle that included ever larger parts of the population in national welfare states. In international relations, as well, democracies set the standards for legitimate statehood, as the number of democratic nation states increased through several waves of democratization that, despite all the authoritarian backlash, marked 20th-century history (Diamond, 1994). For the year 2000, political scientists could report that democratic states, for the first time, outnumbered authoritarian states. Democracy, in short, was meant to be a success story. There was no way back from democracy to authoritarianism, except for some local and transitory backlash.

In this book, I did not argue in support of this emphatic account of democracy as a story of triumph, but neither did I oppose it. The idea was rather to relate such accounts of democracy as a success to the parallel and co-existing accounts of democracy as failure, and to treat both as symptoms of the functioning of public spheres. Democracies observe and critically scrutinize themselves. Such accounts can be rewarding to the degree that democratic regimes can sometimes convince their citizens that they live in the best of all democracies. However, these are accounts of critical self-reflection and, all too often, their conclusions, are rather chastening, confronting citizens with the permanent malfunctioning of democratic institutions and their own insufficiencies as democratic citizens, pursuing the common interest. A democracy that is reduced to complacency and self-appraisal, therefore, is more exceptional than a democracy that constantly engages in self-criticism. Without their critical impetus, democracies would indeed herald the 'end of history'. By following this line of thought, the new vogue of post-democracy in academic writing should be interpreted as a continuation of the tradition of public sphere criticism, not as its point of rupture. Many critical thinkers, who are riding the vogue, simply wish to pour cold water on the eternal optimists who praised democracy's victory in the aftermath of the fall of communism. The prophets of post-democracy might no longer be forward looking into democracy's bright future, but their critical view is meant to confirm and put to the test the validity of democratic principles, and not simply reject it. Their accounts might sometimes be more depressing than refreshing, but still their alarming voice can rejuvenate democratic public spheres.

In short, there is evidence that the critical apparatus of the democratic public sphere remains intact despite the gloomy diagnosis of post-democracy. Public sphere criticism has never been limited to the assessment of compliance with democratic norms. Apart from putting public actors to the test, public sphere criticism also comprises the continuous questioning of democracy, and the search for new and better justifications for why democracy is the preferred, or even the best, form of government. To provide such justifications, democracies need to look beyond daily 'politics' and 'policies', and reflect on their own past and future, confronting themselves meanwhile with other forms of political authority and scrutinizing the validity of its underlying rules, principles and constitution. If democracies persist, this does not mean that societies are necessarily going to become more democratic; it only means that they continue to hold democratic principles valid as standards for critical assessment of their own insufficiencies. Degrees of inclusiveness, participation and freedom can then indeed be used as indicators to aid in the ranking of states and societies on a scale from authoritarian to fully democratic. Such rankings, however, do not simply provide an objective measurement of democratic performance; they are, above all, used as templates of critical discourse in international relations. As such, the survival of democracy not only depends on institutional performance but on the continuation of critical discourse and the mobilization of democratic demands that are raised collectively against potential violators of democratic principles.

Instead of a rescue plan: the self-corrective mechanisms of public sphere resilience

As democracies do not develop in a clear direction, nor do they undergo deep ruptures. My main argument in this book was that any form of diagnosis of democratic decline would be, at the same time, the entry point for a process of democratic reform. By following this line of thought, the debate about the future of democracy can be de-dramatized. Democracies do transform; they are conflictual, and they might also be disordered or disrupted. They are drama, for sure, but they are not a tragedy. The drama keeps the democrats alive and constantly brings in new actors who sometimes enrich the plot and fill it with new tensions, while, at other times, they just slow the action down, making audiences feel bored and inattentive, or as 'bad actors' launch a frontal attack on democracy (Chambers and Kopstein, 2022). The legitimacy of such actors, however, continues to be scrutinized by critical publics. To the degree in which strategies and tactics of agents to build or destroy the public sphere still count, the audiences' consumption choices and differentiated responses still matter. This audience is clearly wrongly understood as an entity that reacts in a unitary way, either trusting or mistrusting, supporting or opposing government, paying attention or turning away from politics. Attitudes and levels of audience attention alter continuously, as well as levels of engagement of the citizens and collectives that constitute democracy, and that can sometimes (or most of the time) be passive receivers or consumers of content, and other times engage with content, re-interpret it and use it for the articulation of their concerns. Instead of talking of audiences (a term often used to study media effects), I have proposed that public sphere research should return to the original notion of the *public* as ongoing encounters facilitated by discourse (Warner, 2002). Such publics do not speak in one language to one people, as the chimera of a nationally unified public sphere wants us to believe. In contemporary societies, such an idea of *the public* as a unified people becomes outright anti-democratic and is used to suppress the plurality of opinions and life projects that distinguish the modern public sphere. Publics are instead defined by the articulation of critique that asks to be put to a test of public scrutiny. Public criticism builds on argumentative exchanges, and not on the aggregated attention of audiences. Differentiated and even segmented publics can play this critical card efficiently and find innovative ways of digital media use to reconnect with government.

If publics differentiate, they do not disappear but, on the contrary, multiply. Through digitalization and globalization, publics become omnipresent. This, in turn, has given rise to increasing concerns with the protection of privacy and the colonization of the private sphere by public monitors. In this book, I have called attention to the effects of a privacy trap that consists of the illusionary retreat to privacy by citizens who are primarily identified as 'users' of various apps, and who seek protection in their private homes from the perils of public exposure. The privacy of the digital sphere, however, is illusionary, as these apps are principally used for public activities. They enable users to connect to a social world, to place themselves on the market or to form their political opinion. Along with enhanced privacy protection, the digital public sphere, therefore, is conducive to the rediscovery of the value of publicity and a return of the political in the form of new publics that discover shared problems. The political protests against 'surveillance capitalism' have a potential to turn loose forms of public sphere resilience into resistance. 'Surveillance' is, at the same time, a very old topic of public sphere criticism that can be turned against states and markets. The newly re-politicized publics target globalized and digitalized forms of political power, for example in the ways new public management has contributed to the disconnection of governance from popular democracy (Box et al, 2001). More often, however, the data protection and privacy movements seek alliances with states and international organizations against unbound market forces. I predicted, therefore, that the open struggle over regulation of the digital public sphere might lead to the revival of both civil society and states as new ordering forces of the emerging digital society. The rebalancing of privacy and publicity is a task of public government that reconnects to the public sphere, which does not need to be reinvented due to its always having been there, adapting its forms of criticism to the digital communication infrastructures and affordances.

My empirical outlook in this book was restricted to the analysis of three public sphere resilience movements that fight media and democracy disruptions in creative ways while tackling the challenge of surveillance, of populism and post-truth politics. By raising this new research agenda of public sphere resilience, my proposal is not to disregard the drama of current public sphere disruptions that shape contemporary media landscapes and have favoured democratic backlash. Without negating the possibility of a failure of democracy, I nonetheless conclude that the diagnosis of post-democracy is premature and unsubstantiated. Democracy's future remains hard to predict, but also, historically speaking, democratic societies have always occupied an open experimental space and are distinguished as a form of political authority that constantly questions and redefines its own legitimation requirements. Being involved in such democratic experiments shapes individual attitudes but also collective mindsets. What counts is not only active or passive participation and engagement in democratic practices but also a sort of meta-reflection about the success and failure of the democratic experiment. The account of post-democracy is evidence for the capacity of the contemporary public sphere, despite its internal differentiation and fragmentation, to continue producing such meta-reflections about the conditions of democracy and its realization. We can call this the continuation of the great narrative of democracy, which includes a critical assessment of its desired and undesired effects, of its successes and failures and of causality and shared responsibility. Democracy is a self-propelling process that is fuelled by inherent and ceaseless critique. The diagnosis of post-democracy does not discontinue this practice of criticism. It can only exist as a form of self-diagnosis of democracies which critically puts to the test the validity and applicability of their normative parameters.

Understanding public sphere functions and malfunctions and mapping disruptions and resilience is an ongoing research programme that is combined with a programme of critique of the public sphere, media and democracy. The conclusion of this book can therefore only be presented in the form of an ongoing discussion. I hope that I have convinced with the argument that, despite the current talk of public sphere disruptions and demise, public sphere theory is still highly topical and has actually gained in relevance for the critical understanding of the linkage between contemporary media and democracy. We need to explore contemporary public sphere transformations to understand digital infrastructures, the reach and effects of new media communications, and the many ways society creatively engages in critical discourse. We need to map these often very fragmented moments of democratic bouncing back, document how they take shape in experimental forms and understand what effects such corrective and countervailing forces have on democratic processes, political institutions and people's attitudes and opinions.

My intention in this book has not been to design a rescue plan for the democratic public sphere and for the project of liberal democracy to which the public sphere project seems to be intrinsically related.[1] By pointing at the self-corrective mechanism of public sphere resilience, one could argue that the public sphere does not need to be rescued. Disrupted public spheres can only bounce back. Does this mean, then, that the public sphere and liberal democracy are in the process of building immunity against the perils of digitalization and globalization?

In the diagnosis of post-democracy, the complacency of liberals after the fall of communism is often mentioned, ignoring for a long time the signs of deep democratic crisis and the erosion of the liberal world order (Zielonka, 2018). Yet, the complacency of liberals is not the complacency of public sphere scholars, who have never stopped criticizing, and for whom the bourgeois public sphere has always been in deficit. By emphasizing the silent processes of public sphere resilience, I rather wish to supplement the prevailing political science view on democracy and the public sphere as a struggle that is always dramatic and marked by a few moments of mobilization that decide its collective destinies (Tilly, 1978). From this perspective of democracy as a struggle, our times are seen as exceptional and distinguished by a new polarization that either leads to the end of democracy or its heroic rescue. In this book, another metaphor has been introduced for the public sphere and democracy, not as a struggle, but as a play. Thus, the martial political science language is replaced by a sociological emphasis on creativity, skills and practices. Citizens do not express their preferences for democracy in the form of a dramatic choice that wins over competing alternative but are socialized in democracies and have internalized their values.

I have tried to avoid re-telling the story of public sphere history as progress. Still, the reader might argue that my account of countervailing public sphere forces is somehow optimistic, as it does not really foresee rupture. There can be no end to the story, as we cannot imagine a point where public criticism stops. Does this mean that we are urged to believe that the public sphere is immortal? I would respond to this objection that public sphere theory has always meant to be a theory of society, and not just a normative theory of democracy.[2] Theories of society typically explain social change and processes of structuration over time, but what is hard to see is how a theory of society should be able to address the death of the social. We can, of course, imagine societal breakup, but we cannot meaningfully integrate it into our explanatory framework. Sociology could of course analyse what happens to society when narratives of change are increasingly driven by apocalyptic scenarios. If societies describe themselves increasingly in terms of decay, they invest at the same time in enhanced and accelerated criticism. As long as this form of societal self-description continues, the linkage between (modern) society and the public sphere persists. A society without a public sphere could not even engage in apocalyptic thinking. By opening a critical view to post- (modern, democratic, liberal) society, sociologists can therefore only renew the theory of the public sphere as a theory of society and not discontinue it.

Critical reviewers of my approach could interpret my emphasis on the mechanisms of public sphere resilience as a defence of the liberal project of democracy. Two questions arise here: First, *does the liberal project need to be rescued?* For the different movements that were the focus of my attention in this book, the rescue of the democratic project is rather a side product of critical engagement for privacy protection, quality of information or social and ecological justice, and not the main concern. Their forms of civic engagement and practices of resilience do not much resemble a recovery plan of the liberal project designed by some heroic democrats to avert the imminent threat of post-democracy. Even though these movements do not decide to rescue the liberal project, they still contribute to its renewal in important ways (Kavada, 2021). As progressive social movements, these actors firmly believe in the value of collective action, the possibilities of change from below, and of pragmatic and incremental reform that is guided by their commitment to the common good, social equality and justice (della Porta, 2021).

Beyond the focus on social mobilization and the role of new democratic actors, progressive social movements need to be discussed in relation to the critical publics that sustain them and replicate the validity of the critical standards of democracy. I have argued that social progressivism is inscribed in the democratic public sphere, which is why the liberal project, even if not explicitly supported, cannot easily be dismissed by critical publics. Progressive social movements are not the exception but the rule in a modern public sphere that constantly produces new knowledge to address social problems and achieve collectively set goals. Sociologically speaking, modern societies that are held together by the communicative links of the public sphere can only learn; they cannot deny knowledge, ignore validity claims or give up cognitive capacities of critique. Modern societies, in the words of Klaus Eder (1999: 195), 'learn how to learn' but cannot stop learning. Collective learning through critical engagement can be called progressive, but it includes the possibility that societal development is collectively interpreted as regression. The paradox is that such an interpretation of democratic regression or decline cannot exist independently from the progressive template, but only convinces in the act of reconfirming and renewing the validity of democratic principles in the light of new critical insights and counterfactual evidence. Progressive social movements, therefore, do not need to reinvent narratives for future post-democratic political struggles. The democratic project remains their distant utopia, even though their daily criticism is often driven by a deep scepticism of the possibilities of its realization.

The second hot question that is debated in contemporary public spheres is *whether the liberal project deserves to be rescued*. Do we, as scholars of democracy, blend out all the insufficiencies of the liberal public sphere and of privately owned media on which it is built? Should we pay more systematic attention to the victims of liberalism, the privileges of the elites and the processes of structural exclusion of minorities? Should we develop more empathy with the suffering that people are undergoing in the name of freedom and reason, and take the concerns of ordinary people, who opt for illiberal values, more seriously? My approach was not meant to exclude critical scholarship of any kind, but rather to encourage the engagement in political struggles for the enhancement of democracy. By routinely combining analytical and normative-evaluative dimensions in the study of contemporary media, its modes of production, content and effects, contemporary media scholars remain deeply involved in the programme of constant renewal of the public sphere through the mechanism of public criticism. My argument is simply that the public sphere is still the only place where we can bring forward such a critique of liberalism and make it effective. Public sphere criticism is essentially about putting the performance of liberal democracy to the test, identifying its shortcomings and blaming those responsible. Public spheres are facilitators of trust, as well as mistrust, in a democracy and its institutions. Democratic citizens will always find many reasons to be concerned and to mistrust their political representatives. At times, they might even despair or fear the end of democracy. However, whenever they search for signs of hope, or ask for reform, they do so within the normative framework established by the modern public sphere, not beyond it.

Notes

Preface

[1] So, for instance, Freedom House (2019) 'Media Freedom – A Downward Spiral' (https://freedomhouse.org/report/freedom-and-media/2019/media-freedom-downward-spiral); Freedom House (2021) "Democracy under Siege' (https://freedomhouse.org/report/freedom-world/2021/democracy-under-siege).

[2] American journalists run the website Newspaper Death Watch to collect evidence of American newspapers that have closed since 2007 (http://newspaperdeathwatch.com/).

[3] See, for instance, the annual Reuters Institute Digital News Report (https://reutersinstitute.politics.ox.ac.uk/sites/default/files/2020-06/DNR_2020_FINAL.pdf) and the State of the News Media Annual report published by the Pew Research Center (https://www.pewresearch.org/topics/state-of-the-news-media/).

[4] See, for instance, the Freedom in the World Index (https://freedomhouse.org/report/freedom-world) or the Human Freedom Index developed by the Cato Institute (https://www.cato.org/human-freedom-index/2020).

[5] Post-truth politics, nationalism and the (de-)legitimation of European integration, funded by the Erasmus plus Programme of the European Union and coordinated by the University of Iceland (2019–23) (https://ams.hi.is/is/projects/post-truth-politics/).

[6] *Javnost – The Public*, 28(1) and (2) (2021). Reclaiming the Public Sphere in a Global Health Crisis, edited by Hans-Jörg Trenz, Annett Heft, Michael Vaughan and Barbara Pfetsch.

Chapter 1

[1] The German author, Eva Menasse, in her acceptance speech of the renowned Ludwig-Borne-Preis, received in 2019 (Vom Verschwinden der Offentlichkeit: https://www.deutschlandfunk.de/gesellschaftsdebatte-vom-verschwinden-der-oeffentlichkeit.1184.de.html?dram:articleid=453426) (the quotation is my own translation).

[2] Berlusconi as a prime Minister of Italy between 1994 and 2013 and owner of major Italian TV-channels paired privatization of television with entrepreneurial control over public opinion.

[3] Eva Menasse in endnote 1.

[4] Eva Menasse in endnote 1.

[5] In an intervention at the 50th World Economic Forum on 24 January 2020 (https://www.youtube.com/watch?v=eOsKFOrW5h8&t=10s).

[6] See https://www.wired.com/story/artificial-intelligence-yuval-noah-harari-tristan-harris/

Chapter 2

[1] For those readers who are interested in the development of the concept, major reference work is available: Hartmut Wessler (2019) provides a systematic reconstruction of Habermas'

work on media. Slavko Splichal (2012) points to some of the difficulties of distinguishing basic concepts like public–private, publicness, publicity and public sphere in light of the challenges of digitalization and transnationalization of the public sphere. Within the discipline of sociology, a major reference work is Patrick O'Mahony's (2013) ground-breaking contribution to the sociology of the public sphere. Apart from providing a summary account of the history of the concept, this book sketches a theory of the modern public sphere as a theory of society that can be formulated out of the synthesized accounts of normative and social theory. For more engaged readers who want to consult the classical authors, a one-volume textbook and a three-volume collection of key readings about public sphere theory stretching over several centuries has been published by Jostein Gripsrud et al (2010a, 2010b). For German readers, the volume by Pöttker (2001) containing key texts by the classics in media and public sphere theory and, most recently, a special journal issue about the new structural transformation of the public sphere are available (Seeliger and Sevignani, 2021).

[2] I will refer in the following to the English edition (Habermas, 1989).

[3] As this was also later developed in Habermas' oeuvre, especially in the *Theory of Communicative Action* (1985).

[4] The so-called agonistic model of democracy has completely reversed this relationship. It claims that political debates by default rely on group distinctions (like proponents and opponents, both of whom are bound by strong identities), and that the positioning of groups in political debates forms their political identities. Any political confrontation takes the shape of an Us versus Them distinction (Mouffe, 2000: 31–5). This is not a public sphere theory in the proper sense, since it fails to consider the binding force of discourse through a free and inclusive exchange of arguments, nor does it foresee the possibility that discursive structures develop over time in such a way as to filter arguments and condense meaning and understanding. While public sphere theory allows us to conceptualize social evolution, the notion of agonistic democracy, if taken literally, would reduce politics to identitarian confrontations with no exit.

[5] The objective world and the social world are external to actors. In the theory of communicative action, Habermas (1985) further distinguishes the subjective world, which is internal but can still be put to the test in public communications: actors also need to convince others that they are sincere, and the sincerity of their intentions can be challenged by others.

Chapter 3

[1] These latter aspects are covered by a broad literature. For an overview, see Cammaerts (2015).

[2] Glenn Greenwald, 'The Death Spiral of Establishment Journalism' (https://www.alternet.org/2013/10/glenn-greenwald-death-spiral-establishment-journalism/).

[3] See https://reutersinstitute.politics.ox.ac.uk/sites/default/files/2019-06/DNR_2019_FINAL_0.pdf (last accessed 25 October 2021).

[4] This is what Karl Mannheim in his classic treatise describes as the 'utopian mentality' (Mannheim, 2013 [1936]).

[5] In 2010 Facebook through private consulting firm Cambridge Analytica collected personal data belonging to millions of users without their prior consent to be used mainly for political advertising.

[6] https://research.fb.com/data/

[7] https://www.wired.com/2005/12/google-7/

Chapter 4

[1] https://techpolicyinstitute.org/wp-content/uploads/2020/02/Prince_Wallsten_How-Much-is-Privacy-Worth-Around-the-World-and-Across-Platforms.pdf

[2] Hanno Rauterberg, 'Unfrei frei', *Die Zeit*, 7 November 2019.

3   The so-called 'Network for Academic Freedom', see https://www.netzwerk-wissenscha ftsfreiheit.de/en/home-2/.

4   As, for instance, in media literacy research, see Humprecht et al (2020).

Chapter 5

1   'Facebook to Consider Public Interest before Removal of Posts Violating Guidelines', *The Guardian*, 24 October 2016 (https://www.theguardian.com/technology/2016/oct/ 24/facebook-public-interest-removal-posts-violating-guidelines).

2   Lim (2020: 1) talks in this regard of Facebook's business model as based on a 'dogmatic personal identity economics'. Anti-Facebook campaigns would then, however, be symptomatic of the same transition from identity politics to personal identity economics.

3   https://www.statista.com/chart/16959/share-of-the-internet-that-is-porn/

4   https://www.spiegel.de/gesundheit/sex/diese-zwei-studierenden-haben-ein-feministisc hes-porno-startup-gegruendet-a-9f421d2a-f954-4539-97c4-s5d7266620fb7

5   William Davies, 'What's Wrong with WhatsApp?', *The Guardian*, 2 July 2020 (https:// www.theguardian.com/technology/2020/jul/02/whatsapp-groups-conspiracy-theor ies-disinformation-democracy).

6   William Davies, in endnote 5.

7   The Corporate Europe Observatory published a highly instructive dossier on the role of the big industries in the fight against the copyright directive, drowning out critical voices with very powerful lobbying, while, at the same time, supporting public mobilization that backs their cause. See https://corporateeurope.org/en/2018/12/copyright-direct ive-how-competing-big-business-lobbies-drowned-out-critical-voices

8   Donald Trump's executive order against social media companies signed on 28 May 2020, for instance, was justified as follows: "We're here today to defend free speech from one of the gravest dangers it has faced in American history. … A small handful of powerful social media monopolies control the vast portion of all private and public communications in the United States" (https://www.npr.org/2020/05/28/863932758/stung-by-twitter-trump-signs-executive-order-to-weaken-social-media-companies?t=1592731338948).

9   Cory Doctorow (2013) 'More Than 130 European Businesses Tell the European Parliament: Reject the #Copyright Directive', EFF: Electronic Frontier Foundation (https://www.eff.org/de/deeplinks/2019/03/more-130-european-businesses-tell-europ ean-parliament-reject-copyrightdirective).

10   https://www.coe.int/en/web/freedom-expression/internet-governance

11   https://quantifiedself.com/

12   https://theconversation.com/facebooks data-lockdown-is-a-disaster-for-academic-rese archers-94533

13   https://research.fb.com/data/

14   https://ec.europa.eu/digital-single-market/en/tackling-online-disinformation

15   https://www.coe.int/en/web/digital-citizenship-education

16   To define the new 2.0 populism in relation to the restriction of communicative spaces for the raising of representative claims might be useful also in distinction to 'old populism', which was rather interested in amplifying the populist claims and occupying the whole public sphere infrastructure for populist mobilization (Revelli, 2019).

17   The question of whether populism should be considered as a 'corrective' or as a 'threat' to democracy is discussed extensively in the literature (Kaltwasser, 2012; Mudde, 2012; Müller, 2016).

18   Think of the way Donald Trump refused to recognize the result of the 2020 elections. The will of the people cannot lose in elections. It is either confirmed, or the elections are claimed to be fraudulent. See Pérez-Curiel et al (2021).

[19] For the case of the Austrian *Kronen Zeitung* as one of Europe's most powerful newspapers, see de Wilde et al (2013). For the case of the 'tabloidization of the Brexit campaign, see Zappettini (2021).

[20] The table is adapted from Galpin and Trenz (2022).

[21] This section is based on research carried out in the framework of the Eurochallenge project at University of Copenhagen between 2015 and 2018. I would like to thank Verena Brändle and Charlotte Galpin for the permission to reproduce some of the material published in Brändle et al (2018a and b; 2021) and Galpin and Trenz (2022).

[22] All quotations in this section, if not stated differently, are taken from the Manifesto of the Sardines, and translated by the author (https://www.fanpage.it/politica/il-manifesto-del-popolo-delle-sardine-cari-populisti-avete-tirato-la-corda-ora-si-e-spezzata).

[23] In the words of Mattia Santori, one of the founding members (https://www.panorama.it/news/sardine-storia-movimento-nome-lega-salvini).

[24] Danilo Magli quoted in the *Daily Star*, 2 December 2019 (https://www.thedailystar.net/backpage/news/tens-thousands-march-against-far-right-italy-1834483).

[25] As described in the classical treatise by Elias Canetti (1984).

[26] https://www.theguardian.com/environment/live/2019/mar/15/climate-strikes-2019-live-latest-climate-change-global-warming

[27] These are non-corroborated figures provided by #FridaysforFuture (https://fridaysforfuture.org/). As protest tends to be sporadic and situational, it is not exactly clear what distinguishes membership and support, and how individuals can connect to the movement.

[28] The representation of the future generation has also been discussed within political and moral philosophy (Ekeli, 2005). #FridaysforFuture is an avant-garde movement that translates moral philosophy into political claims and, as such, gives important impulses to the reformulation of democratic theory.

[29] Greta Thunberg at the opening of the UN's Climate Action Summit of 24 September 2019 (https://www.un.org/development/desa/youth/news/2019/09/greta-thunberg/).

[30] As in the case of Greta Thunberg on Twitter, who mentions the personal attacks against her by Donald Trump only in a side note as 'hilarious', and turns to science again in her next sentence (https://www.vox.com/energy-and-environment/2019/9/26/20882958/greta-thunberg-climate-change-trump-attacks-right-wing).

[31] https://www.ouest-france.fr/societe/gilets-jaunes/gilets-jaunes-environnement-emploi-precarite-impots-voici-leurs-revendications-6099353

[32] Luc Rouban (2019) Les gilets jaunes, une transition populiste de droite. https://hal-sciencespo.archives-ouvertes.fr/hal-03501707

[33] https://www.reuters.com/article/us-france-protests-future/no-leader-lots-of-anger-can-frances-yellow-vests-become-a-political-force-idUSKBN1O51ON

[34] https://metropolitiques.eu/Gilets-jaunes-regards-de-jeunes-de-banlieue.html

[35] https://www.facebook.com/giletsjaunescatholiques/

[36] As reported by Reuters: https://www.reuters.com/article/us-france-protests-future/no-leader-lots-of-anger-can-frances-yellow-vests-become-a-political-force-idUSKBN1O51ON

[37] https://newrepublic.com/article/152853/ugly-illiberal-anti-semitic-heart-yellow-vest-movement

[38] Among the many, see, for example, Mudde (2012); Anselmi and Morrisey (2017); Norris and Inglehart (2019); Urbinati (2019).

[39] https://www.theguardian.com/politics/2020/feb/14/anti-populism-politics-why-champions-of-civility-keep-losing

[40] https://www.theguardian.com/politics/2020/feb/14/anti-populism-politics-why-champions-of-civility-keep-losing

41 A first version of this section was co-authored with Annett Heft, Michael Vaughan and Barbara Pfetsch (Trenz et al, 2020, 2021). I wish to thank my co-authors for their permission to reuse parts of our joint paper.

42 Information given by the Centers for Disease Control and Prevention in 2021.

43 https://en.unesco.org/sites/default/files/critical_role_press_media_councils_covid19.pdf

44 https://www.un.org/en/coronavirus/covid-19-journalists-biggest-story-their-lifetime

45 https://www.dw.com/en/coronavirus-anger-foments-violence-against-journalists/a-53383927

46 https://en.ejo.ch/media-economics/the-economic-impact-of-covid-19-on-europ ean-media-in-2020

47 See the World Press Freedom Index 2020 (https://rsf.org/en/2020-world-press-free dom-index-entering-decisive-decade-journalism-exacerbated-coronavirus).

48 European Commission (EC) (2020) 'Tackling COVID-19 Disinformation: Getting the Facts Right', JOIN(2020), 8 final, 10 June (https://eur-lex.europa.eu/legal-content/ EN/TXT/?uri=CELEX%3A52020JC0008).

49 Frankfurter Rundschau on 10 April 2020 (https://www.fr.de/kultur/gesellschaft/juer gen-habermas-coronavirus-krise-covid19-interview-13642491.html)

50 Thanks to Ally McCrow-Young for this observation.

51 For a selection of global public opinion polls, see https://www.ipsos.com/en/public-opin ion-covid-19-outbreak

Chapter 6

1 See Forestal (2022) for such a rescue plan that combines the collective imagination of a better Internet with the blueprints of a participatory approach to democratic politics. Her built democratic digital environments resemble more the 'lost community' than the open public sphere. With this, she shares a nostalgia for bounded and durable spaces, undoubtedly driving the experts, advocates and many critical citizens who have taken up the fight for the digital future of democracy.

2 See my further explications of public sphere theory as a contribution to the cognitive sociology of modern society in Trenz (2021).

References

Adorno, T.W. (2001) *The Culture Industry: Selected Essays on Mass Culture*, London: Routledge.

Adorno, T.W. and Horkheimer, M. (2002) *Dialectic of Enlightenment*, Stanford: Stanford University Press.

Agamben, G. (2020) *A che punto siamo*, Milan: Feltrinelli.

Agamben, G., Badiou, A., McCuaig, W., Bensaid, D., Brown, W., Nancy, J.L. et al (2011) *Democracy in What State?*, New York: Columbia University Press.

Aigrain, P. (2012) *Sharing: Culture and the Economy in the Internet Age*, Amsterdam: Amsterdam University Press.

Alemanno, A. (2018) 'How to Counter Fake News? A Taxonomy of Anti-fake News Approaches', *European Journal of Risk Regulation*, 9(1): 1–5.

Alexander, J. (2006) *The Civil Sphere*, Oxford: Oxford University Press.

Alexander, J.C., Breese, E.B. and Luengo, M. (2016) *The Crisis of Journalism Reconsidered*, Cambridge: Cambridge University Press.

Altheide, D.L. (1997) 'The News Media, the Problem Frame, and the Production of Fear', *The Sociological Quarterly*, 38(4): 647–68.

Alvares, C. and Dahlgren, P. (2016) 'Populism, Extremism and Media: Mapping an Uncertain Terrain', *European Journal of Communication*, 31(1): 46–57.

Andersen, K. (2020) 'Realizing Good Intentions? A Field Experiment of Slow News Consumption and News Fatigue', *Journalism Practice*, 16(5): 848–63.

Anderson, B. (1991) *Imagined Communities: Reflections on the Origins and Spread of Nationalism*, London: Verso.

Andrejevic, M. (2018) '"Framelessness", or the Cultural Logic of Big Data', in M.S. Daubs and V. Manzerolle (eds) *Mobile and Ubiquitous Media*, Brussels: Peter Lang, pp 251–67.

Anselmi, M. and Morrisey, L.F. (2017) *Populism: An Introduction*, London: Routledge.

Antoniades, A. (2003) 'Epistemic Communities, Epistemes and the Construction of (World) Politics', *Global Society*, 17(1): 21–38.

Arendt, H. (1967) 'Truth and Politics', *The New Yorker*, 4 February. Available from: https://www.newyorker.com/magazine/1967/02/25/truth-and-politics

Arendt, H. (1998) *The Human Condition* (2nd edn), Chicago: University of Chicago Press.

Armingeon, K. and Guthmann, K. (2014) 'Democracy in Crisis? The Declining Support for National Democracy in European Countries, 2007–2011', *European Journal of Political Research*, 53(3): 423–42.

Arvanitakis, L. and Fredriksson, M. (2016) 'Commons, Piracy and the Crisis of Property', *tripleC: Communication, Capitalism and Critique*, 14(1). Available from: https://www.triple-c.at/index.php/tripleC/article/view/680

Aytac, U. (2022) 'Digital Domination: Social Media and Contestatory Democracy', *Political Studies*, 0(0). Available from: https://doi.org/10.1177/00323217221096564

Bail, C.A., Argyle, L.P., Brown, T.W., Bumpus, J.P., Chen, H., Hunzaker, M.B.F., et al (2018) 'Exposure to Opposing Views on Social Media Can Increase Political Polarization', *Proceedings of the National Academy of Sciences*, 115(37): 9216–21.

Balibar, E. (2014) *Equaliberty: Political Essays*, Durham: Duke University Press.

Balme, C.B. (2014) *The Theatrical Public Sphere*, Cambridge: Cambridge University Press.

Beck, U., Giddens, A. and Lash, S. (1994) *Reflexive Modernization: Politics, Tradition and Aesthetics in the Modern Social Order*, Stanford: Stanford University Press.

Beck, U. (2006) *Cosmopolitan Vision*, Cambridge: Polity Press.

Becker, L. and Vlad, T. (2009) 'News Organizations and Routines', in K. Wahl-Jorgensen and T. Hanitzsch (eds) *The Handbook of Journalism Studies*, London: Routledge, pp 59–72.

Becker, M. (2019) 'Privacy in the Digital Age: Comparing and Contrasting Individual versus Social Approaches towards Privacy', *Ethics and Information Technology*, 21(4): 307–17.

Bell, D. (1962) *The End of Ideology: On the Exhaustion of Political Ideas in the Fifties*, Cambridge, MA: Harvard University Press.

Bennett, C.J. and Raab, C.D. (2017) *The Governance of Privacy: Policy Instruments in Global Perspective*, London: Routledge.

Bennett, W.L. and Pfetsch, B. (2018) 'Rethinking Political Communication in a Time of Disrupted Public Spheres', *Journal of Communication*, 68(2): 243–53.

Bennett, W.L. and Segerberg, A. (2013) *The Logic of Connective Action: Digital Media and the Personalization of Contentious Politics*, Cambridge: Cambridge University Press.

Benson, R. and Neveu, E. (2005) *Bourdieu and the Journalistic Field*, Oxford: Wiley.

Bentele, G. and Nothhaft, H. (2010) 'Strategic Communication and the Public Sphere from a European Perspective', *International Journal of Strategic Communication*, 4(2): 93–116.

Bentham, J. (1838) *The Works of Jeremy Bentham, Published under the Superintendence of his Executor, John Bowring*, 11 vols. Vol 2, chapter 2, 'Of Publicity'. Edinburgh: William Tait. Available from: https://oll.libertyfund.org/title/bentham-works-of-jeremy-bentham-11-vols

Berger, P.L. and Luckmann, T. (1966) *The Social Construction of Reality: A Treatise in the Sociology of Knowledge*, Anne Arbor, MI: Doubleday.

Berglez, P. (2008) 'What Is Global Journalism?', *Journalism Studies*, 9(6): 845–58.

Berlo, D. (1960) *The Process of Communication: An Introduction to Theory and Practice*, New York: Holt, Rinehart and Winston.

Bian, J., Guo, Y., He, Z. and Hu, X. (eds) (2019) *Social Web and Health Research: Benefits, Limitations, and Best Practices*, Berlin: Springer International Publishing.

Bickerstaff, K., Lorenzoni, I., Jones, M. and Pidgeon, N. (2010) 'Locating Scientific Citizenship: The Institutional Contexts and Cultures of Public Engagement', *Science, Technology, & Human Values*, 35(4): 474–500.

Bieler, A. (2011) 'Labour, New Social Movements and the Resistance to Neoliberal Restructuring in Europe', *New Political Economy*, 16(2): 163–82.

Blackman, L. and Walkerdine, V. (2017) *Mass Hysteria: Critical Psychology and Media Studies*, London: Macmillan Education.

Blatterer, H., Johnson, P. and Markus, M.R. (2010) *Modern Privacy: Shifting Boundaries, New Forms*, Basingstoke: Palgrave Macmillan.

Blokker, P. (2011) 'Pragmatic Sociology: Theoretical Evolvement and Empirical Application', *European Journal of Social Theory*, 14(3): 251–61.

Blokker, P. (2014) 'The European Crisis and a Political Critique of Capitalism', *European Journal of Social Theory*, 17(3): 258–74.

Boczek, K. and Koppers, L. (2020) 'What's New about Whatsapp for News? A Mixed-Method Study on News Outlets' Strategies for Using WhatsApp', *Digital Journalism*, 8(1): 126–44.

Bode, C. (2019) 'Totalitarianism by Consent: Orwell, Huxley, and Capitalism in the Stage of Corporate Surveillance', in B. Wasihun (ed) *Narrating Surveillance: Überwachen erzählen*, Baden-Baden: Ergon-Verlag, pp 21–42.

Boehme-Neßler, V. (2020) *Digitising Democracy: On Reinventing Democracy in the Digital Era – A Legal, Political and Psychological Perspective*, Berlin: Springer International Publishing.

Bohman, J. (2000) *Public Deliberation: Pluralism, Complexity, and Democracy*, Cambridge, MA: MIT Press.

Boltanski, L. (1999) *Distant Suffering: Morality, Media and Politics*, Cambridge: Cambridge University Press.

Boltanski, L. (2011) *On Critique: A Sociology of Emancipation*, Oxford: Wiley.

Boltanski, L. and Thévenot, L. (1999) 'The Sociology of Critical Capacity', *European Journal of Social Theory*, 2(3): 359–78.

Boltanski, L. and Thévenot, L. (2006) *On Justification: Economies of Worth*, Princeton: Princeton University Press.

Bossetta, M., Dutceac Segesten, A. and Trenz, H.-J. (2017) 'Engaging with European Politics through Twitter and Facebook: Participation beyond the National?', in M. Barisone and A. Michailidou (eds) *Social Media and European Politics*, Basingstoke: Palgrave, pp 53–76.

Bourdieu, P. (2005) 'The Political Field, the Social Science Field, and the Journalistic Field', in R. Benson and E. Neveu (eds) *Bourdieu and the Journalistic Field*, Cambridge: Polity, pp 29–47.

Box, R.C., Marshall, G.S., Reed, B.J. and Reed, C.M. (2001) 'New Public Management and Substantive Democracy', *Public Administration Review*, 61(5): 608–19.

Brändle, V.K., Galpin, C. and Trenz, H.-J. (2018a) 'On the Frontline: Brexit as Bereavement', *Discover Society*, 9 January. Available from: https://archive.discoversociety.org/2018/01/09/on-the-frontline-brexit-as-bereavement/

Brändle, V.K., Galpin, C. and Trenz, H.-J. (2018b) 'Marching for Europe? Enacting European citizenship as Justice during Brexit', *Citizenship Studies*, 22(8): 810–28.

Brändle, V.K., Galpin, C. and Trenz, H.-J. (2021) 'Brexit as "Politics of Division": Social Media Campaigning in the Aftermath of the Referendum', *Social Movement Studies*, 21(1–2): 234–51.

Brighenti, A.M. (2010) *Visibility in Social Theory and Social Research*, Basingstoke: Palgrave Macmillan.

Broersma, M. (2013) 'A Refractured Paradigm: Journalism, Hoaxes and the Challenge of Trust', in C. Peters and M. Broersma (eds) *Rethinking Journalism: Trust and Participation in a Transformed News Landscape*, London: Routledge, pp 28–44.

Broniatowski, D.A., Jamison, A.M., Johnson, N.F., Velasquez, N., Leahy, R., Restrepo, N.J., et al (2020) 'Facebook Pages, the "Disneyland" Measles Outbreak, and Promotion of Vaccine Refusal as a Civil Right, 2009–2019', *American Journal of Public Health*, 110(3): 312–18.

Brown, M.B. (2009) *Science in Democracy: Expertise, Institutions, and Representation*, Cambridge, MA: MIT Press.

Brubaker, R. (2017) 'Why Populism?', *Theory and Society*, 46: 357–85.

Brunkhorst, H. (2005) *Solidarity: From Civic Friendship to a Global Legal Community*, Cambridge, MA: MIT Press.

Bruns, A., Enli, G., Skogerbo, E., Larsson, A.O. and Christensen, C. (eds) (2015) *The Routledge Companion to Social Media and Politics*, London: Routledge.

Bruns, A. and Nuernbergk, C. (2019) 'Political Journalists and Their Social Media Audiences: New Power Relations', *Media and Communication*, 7(1): 198–212.

Calhoun, C. (ed) (1992) *Habermas and the Public Sphere*, Cambridge, MA: MIT Press.

Cammaerts, B. (2015) 'Social Media and Activism', in R. Mansell and P. Hwa (eds) *The International Encyclopedia of Digital Communication and Society*, Oxford: Wiley-Blackwell, pp 1027–34.

Canetti, E. (1984) *Crowds and Power*, New York: Farrar, Straus and Giroux.

Canniffe, E. (2008) *The Politics of the Piazza: The History and Meaning of the Italian Square*, Aldershot: Ashgate.

Canovan, M. (2005) *The People*, Oxford: Wiley.

Cappella, J.N. and Jamieson, K.H. (1997) *Spiral of Cynicism: The Press and the Public Good*, Oxford: Oxford University Press.

Carey, J.W. (1975) 'A Cultural Approach to Communication', *Communication*, 2(2): 1–22.

Carey, J.W. (1992) *Communication as Culture: Essays on Media and Society*, London: Routledge.

Carpentier, N., Schrøder, K.C. and Hallett, L. (2013) *Audience Transformations: Shifting Audience Positions in Late Modernity*, London: Routledge.

Casero-Ripollés, A. (2020). 'Impact of Covid-19 on the Media System: Communicative and Democratic Consequences of News Consumption during the Outbreak', *Profesional de la información*, 29(2). Available from: https://doi.org/10.3145/epi.2020.mar.23

Castells, M. (1996) *The Rise of the Network Society: The Information Age*, Oxford: Blackwell.

Castells, M. (2009) *Communication Power*, Oxford: Oxford University Press.

Castells, M. (2018) *Rupture: The Crisis of Liberal Democracy*, Oxford: Wiley.

Castro Seixas, E. (2021) 'War Metaphors in Political Communication on Covid-19', *Frontiers in Sociology*, 5. Available from: https://doi.org/10.3389/fsoc.2020.583680

Chambers, S. and Kopstein, J. (2022) 'Wrecking the Public Sphere: The New Authoritarians' Digital Attack on Pluralism and Truth', *Constellations* 16. Available from: https://doi.org/10.1111/1467-8675.12620

Chamorel, P. (2019) 'Macron versus the Yellow Vests', *Journal of Democracy*, 30(4): 48–62.

Chouliaraki, L. (2010) 'Global Representations of Distant Suffering', in N. Coupland (ed) *The Handbook of Language and Globalization*, Chichester: Wiley-Blackwell, pp 608–24.

Cinalli, M., Trenz, H.-J., Brändle, V.K., Eisele, O. and Lahusen, C. (2021) *Solidarity in the Media and Public Contention over Refugees in Europe*, London: Routledge.

Cohen, J. and Fung, A. (2021) 'Democracy and the Digital Public Sphere', in L. Bernholz, H. Landemore and R. Reich (eds) *Digital Technology and Democratic Theory*, Chicago: University of Chicago Press, pp 23–61.

Coleman, G. (2014) *Hacker, Hoaxer, Whistleblower, Spy: The Many Faces of Anonymous*, London: Verso.

Collins, J. (2019) 'The Facts Don't Work: The EU Referendum Campaign and the Journalistic Construction of Post-truth Politics', *Discourse, Context and Media*, 27: 15–21.

Connolly, H. (2010) *Renewal in the French Trade Union Movement: A Grassroots Perspective*, Brussels: Peter Lang.

Connolly, H. and Antoni, A. (2021) 'We All Stand Together (or Do We?): The Messy Process of Building and Maintaining Solidarity in the "Gilets Jaunes" Movement', Paper presented at the European Group for Organization Studies (EGOS) conference, Amsterdam, 8–10 July.

Conti, N. and Memoli, V. (2015) 'The Emergence of a New Party in the Italian Party System: Rise and Fortunes of the Five Star Movement', *West European Politics*, 38(3): 516–34.

Cook, T.E. (2005) *Governing the News: The News Media as a Political Institution*, Chicago: University of Chicago Press.

Corcuff, P. (2021) *La grande confusion: Comment l'extrême-droite gagne la bataille des idées?*, Paris: Textuel.

Couldry, N. (2012) *Media, Society, World: Social Theory and Digital Media Practice*, Cambridge: Polity.

Crouch, C. (2004) *Post-democracy*, Cambridge: Polity.

Crouch, C. (2020) *Post-democracy after the Crises*, Oxford: Wiley.

Curran, J. (ed) (2011) *Media and Society*, London: Bloomsbury Academic.

Dahlberg, L. (2015) 'Expanding Digital Divides Research: A Critical Political Economy of Social Media', *The Communication Review*, 18(4): 271–93.

Dahlgren, P. (2005) 'The Internet, Public Spheres, and Political Communication: Dispersion and Deliberation', *Political Communication*, 22(2): 147–62.

Dahlgren, P. (2012) 'Public Intellectuals, Online Media, and Public Spheres: Current Realignments', *International Journal of Politics, Culture, and Society*, 25(4): 95–110.

Dahlgren, P. (2013) *The Political Web: Media, Participation and Alternative Democracy*, Basingstoke: Palgrave Macmillan.

Dahrendorf, R. (2003) 'Acht Anmerkungen Zum Populismus', Eurozine. Available from: www.eurozine.com/acht-anmerkungen-zum-populismus

De Mateo, R., Bergés, L. and Garnatxe, A. (2010) 'Crisis, What Crisis? The Media: Business and Journalism in Times of Crisis', *tripleC*, 8(2): 251–74. Available from: https://www.triple-c.at/index.php/tripleC/article/view/212

De Vreese, C.H. (2004) 'The Effects of Strategic News on Political Cynicism, Issue Evaluations and Policy Support: A Two-Wave Experiment', *Mass Communication and Society*, 7(2): 191–213.

De Wilde, P., Michailidou, A. and Trenz, H.-J. (2013) *Contesting Europe: Exploring Euroscepticism in Online Media Coverage*, Colchester: ECPR Press.

De Wilde, P., Koopmans, R., Merkel, W. and Zürn, M. (2019) *The Struggle over Borders: Cosmopolitanism and Communitarianism*, Cambridge: Cambridge University Press.

Decker, B.A. (2007) 'Violence and the Private: A Girardian Model of Domestic Violence in Society', *University of Pennsylvania Journal of Law and Social Change*, 11(15): 105–29.

Della Porta, D. (2005) 'Globalizations and Democracy', *Democratization*, 12(5): 668–85.

Della Porta, D. (2012) 'Critical Trust: Social Movements and Democracy in Times of Crisis', *Cambio*, 2(4): 33–43.

Della Porta, D. (2021) 'Communication in Progressive Movement Parties: Against Populism and Beyond Digitalism', *Information, Communication & Society*, 24(10): 1344–60.

Della Porta, D., Fernández, J., Kouki, H. and Mosca, L. (2017) *Movement Parties against Austerity*, Oxford: Wiley.

Delmas, C. (2018) 'Is Hacktivism the New Civil Disobedience?', *Raisons Politiques*, 69(1): 63–81.

Dewey, J. (1927) *The Public and Its Problems*, Chicago: Gateway Books.

Diamond, L.J. (1994) 'Towards Democratic Consolidation', *Journal of Democracy*, 5(3): 4–14.

Diamond, L. and Plattner, M.F. (2012) *Liberation Technology: Social Media and the Struggle for Democracy*, Baltimore: Johns Hopkins University Press.

Donsbach, W. and Patterson, T.E. (2004) 'Political News Journalists: Partisanship, Professionalism, and Political Roles in Five Countries', in F. Esser and B. Pfetsch (eds) *Comparing Political Communication: Theories, Cases, and Challenges*, Cambridge: Cambridge University Press, pp 251–70.

Dubois, E. and Blank, G. (2018) 'The Echo Chamber Is Overstated: The Moderating Effect of Political Interest and Diverse Media', *Information, Communication & Society*, 21(5): 729–45.

Duerr, G.M.E. (2015) *Secessionism and the European Union: The Future of Flanders, Scotland, and Catalonia*, Lanham: Lexington Books.

Durkheim, É. (1964) *The Division of Labour in Society*, New York: Free Press.

Durkheim, É. (1973) *On Morality and Society: Selected Writings*, ed R.N. Bellah, Chicago: University Chicago Press.

Dutton, W.H. and Reisdorf, B.C. (2019) 'Cultural Divides and Digital Inequalities: Attitudes Shaping Internet and Social Media Divides', *Information, Communication & Society*, 22(1): 18–38.

Dyer-Witheford, N. and Matviyenko, S. (2019) *Cyberwar and Revolution: Digital Subterfuge in Global Capitalism*, Minneapolis, MN: University of Minnesota Press.

Eastham, K., Coates, D. and Allodi, F. (1970) 'The Concept of Crisis', *Canadian Psychiatric Association Journal*, 15(5): 463–72.

Eder, K. (1985) *Geschichte als Lernprozess: Zur Pathogenese politischer Modernität in Deutschland*, Frankfurt am Main: Suhrkamp.

Eder, K. (1999) 'Societies Learn and Yet the World Is Hard to Change', *European Journal of Social Theory*, 2(2): 195–215.

Eder, K. (2006) 'The Public Sphere', *Theory, Culture & Society*, 23(2–3): 607–11.

Eder, K. (2013) 'Struggling with the Concept of the Public Sphere', in A. Salvatore, O. Schmidtke and H.-J. Trenz (eds) *Rethinking the Public Sphere through Transnationalizing Processes: Europe and Beyond*, Basingstoke: Palgrave Macmillan, pp 25–55.

Eder, K., Giesen, B., Schmidtke, O. and Tambini, D. (2002) *Collective Identities in Action: A Sociological Approach to Ethnicity*, Aldershot: Ashgate.

Eder, K., Hellmann, K.-U. and Trenz, H.-J. (1998) 'Regieren in Europa jenseits öffentlicher Legitimation? Einer Untersuchung zur Rolle von politischer Öffentlichkeit in Europa', *Politische Vierteljahresschrift*, 29: 321–43.

Eder, K. and Trenz, H.-J. (2006) 'Prerequisites of Democracy and Mechanisms of Democratisation', in B. Kohler-Koch (ed), *Debating the Democratic Legitimacy of the European Union*, Lanham: Rowman & Littlefield, pp 165–81.

Eigmüller, M. and Trenz, H.-J. (2020) 'Werte und Wertekonflikte in einer differenzierten EU', in A. Grimmel (ed) *Die neue Europäische Union: Zwischen Integration und Desintegration*, Baden-Baden: Nomos, pp 33–56.

Eisenegger, M., Udris, L. and Ettinger, P. (2019) *Wandel der Öffentlichkeit und der Gesellschaft: Gedenkschrift für Kurt Imhof*, Wiesbaden: Springer.

Ekeli, K.S. (2005) 'Giving a Voice to Posterity: Deliberative Democracy and Representation of Future People', *Journal of Agricultural and Environmental Ethics*, 18(5): 429–50.

Engler, S., Brunner, P., Loviat, R., Abou-Chadi, T., Leemann, L., Glaser, A. et al (2021) 'Democracy in Times of the Pandemic: Explaining the Variation of COVID-19 Policies across European Democracies', *West European Politics*, 44(5–6): 1077–102.

Eribon, D. (2013) *Returning to Reims*, Cambridge, MA: MIT Press.

Eriksen, E.O. (2007) 'Conceptualising European Public Spheres: General, Segmented and Strong Publics', in J.E. Fossum and P. Schlesinger (eds) *The European Union and the Public Sphere: A Communicative Space in the Making?*, Abingdon: Routledge, pp 23–43.

Esser, F., Stępińska, A. and Hopmann, D.N. (2017) 'Populism and the Media: Cross-national Findings and Perspectives', in T. Aalberg, F. Esser, C. Reinemann, J. Strömbäck and C.H. de Vreese (eds) *Populist Political Communication in Europe*, London: Routledge, pp 365–80.

Ferree, M.M., Gamson, W., Gerhards, J. and Ruchts, D. (2002) 'Four Models of the Public Sphere in Modern Democracies', *Theory and Society*, 31(3): 289–324.

Flaxman, S., Goel, S. and Rao, J. (2016) 'Filter Bubbles, Echo Chambers, and Online News Consumption', *Public Opinion Quarterly*, 80(1): 298–320.

Fletcher, R. and Nielsen, R.K. (2017) 'Are News Audiences Increasingly Fragmented? A Cross-national Comparative Analysis of Cross-platform News Audience Fragmentation and Duplication', *Journal of Communication*, 67(4): 476–98.

Forestal, J. (2021) *Designing for Democracy: How to Build Community in Digital Environments*, Oxford: Oxford University Press.

Fossum, J.E. (2019) 'Can Brexit Improve Our Understanding of "Wicked Problems"? Reflections on Policy and Political Order', *European Policy Analysis*, 5(1): 99–116.

Fossum, J.E. and Schlesinger, P. (eds) (2007) *The European Union and the Public Sphere: A Communicative Space in the Making?*, London: Routledge.

Foster, C. and Frieden, J. (2017) 'Crisis of Trust: Socio-economic Determinants of Europeans' Confidence in Government', *European Union Politics*, 18(4): 511–35.

Foucault, M. (2002) *Archaeology of Knowledge*, London: Routledge.

Franks, B., Bangerter, A. and Bauer, M. (2013) 'Conspiracy Theories as Quasi-religious Mentality: An Integrated Account from Cognitive Science, Social Representations Theory, and Frame Theory', *Frontiers in Psychology*, 4(424). Available from: https://doi.org/10.3389/fpsyg.2013.00424

Fraser, N. (1992) 'Rethinking the Public Sphere: A Contribution to the Critique of Actually Existing Democracy', in C. Calhoun (ed) *Habermas and the Public Sphere*, Cambridge, MA: MIT Press, pp 109–42.

Fraser, N. (2007) 'Transnationalizing the Public Sphere: On the Legitimacy and Efficacy of Public Opinion in a Post-Westphalian World', *Theory, Culture & Society*, 24(4): 7–30.

Freiling, I., Krause, N.M., Scheufele, D.A. and Brossard, D. (2021) 'Believing and Sharing Misinformation, Fact-Checks, and Accurate Information on Social Media: The Role of Anxiety during COVID-19', *New Media & Society*, 25(1): 141–62.

Friedland, L., Hove, T. and Rojas, H. (2006) 'The Networked Public Sphere', *Javnost – The Public*, 13(4): 5–26.

Frisch, M. (1967) *Öffentlichkeit als Partner*, Frankfurt am Main: Suhrkamp.

Frischlich, L., Schttao-Eckrodt, T., Kuhlfeldt, K. and Clever, L. (2020) 'Fueling the Infodemic? Consuming Alternative and Non-professional News during the Corona Crisis', DemoRESILdigital Whitepaper 1. Available from: https://osf.io/asz64/?pid=6up8y

Fuchs, C. (2014a) 'Critique of the Political Economy of Informational Capitalism and Social Media', in C. Fuchs and M. Sandoval (eds) *Critique, Social Media and the Information Society*, London: Routledge, pp 51–65.

Fuchs, C. (2014b) 'Social Media and the Public Sphere', *Journal for a Global Sustainable Information Society*, 12(1): 57–101.

Fuchs, C. (2016) *Critical Theory of Communication: New Readings of Lukács, Adorno, Marcuse, Honneth and Habermas in the Age of the Internet*, London: University of Westminster Press.

Fuchs, C. (2021) 'The Digital Commons and the Digital Public Sphere: How to Advance Digital Democracy Today', *Westminster Papers in Communication and Culture*, 16(1): 9–26.

Fuchs, C. and Sandoval, M. (eds) (2014) *Critique, Social Media and the Information Society*, London: Routledge.

Fukuyama, F. (1999) *The Great Disruption*, New York: Touchstone.

Galpin, C. and Trenz, H.-J. (2019) 'Participatory Populism: Online Discussion Forums on Mainstream News Sites during the 2014 European Parliament Election', *Journalism Practice*, 13(7): 1–18.

Galpin, C. and Trenz, H.-J. (2022) 'Struggling over Democracy: Social Media as a Test Ground for Anti-populist Campaigning', University of Birmingham and Scuola Normale Superiore, Unpublished Manuscript.

Garfinkel, H. (1967) *Studies in Ethnomethodology*, Englewood Cliffs, NJ: Prentice-Hall.

Gaus, D. (2011) 'The Dynamics of Legitimation: Why the Study of Political Legitimacy Needs More Realism', RECON Online Working Paper 2011/15. Available from: https://www.sv.uio.no/arena/english/research/publi cations/arena-working-papers/2011/wp-08-11.pdf.

Gelin, M. (2019) 'The Misogyny of Climate Deniers', *The New Republic*, blog post. Available from: https://newrepublic.com/article/154879/misog yny-climate-deniers

Gerbaudo, P. (2019) *The Digital Party: Political Organisation and Online Democracy*, London: Pluto Press.

Gerbaudo, P. (2022) 'From Individual Affectedness to Collective Identity: Personal Testimony Campaigns on Social Media and the Logic of Collection', *New Media & Society*, 0(0). Available from: https://doi.org/10.1177/14614448221128523

Gerhards, J. (1994) 'Politische Öffentlichkeit: Ein system- und akteurstheoretischer Bestimmungsversuch', in F. Neidhardt (ed) *Sonderheft der Kölner Zeitschrift für Soziologie und Sozialpsychologie: Öffentlichkeit und soziale Bewegungen*, Opladen: Westdeutscher Verlag, pp 77–105.

Gerhards, J. (2000) 'Europäisierung von Ökonomie und Politik und die Trägheit der Entstehung einer europäischen Öffentlichkeit', in M. Bach (ed) *Sonderheft 40 der Kölner Zeitschrift für Soziologie und Sozialpsychologie: Die Europäisierung nationaler Gesellschaften*, Opladen: Westdeutscher Verlag, pp 277–305.

Gerhards, J. and Neidhardt, F. (1991) 'Strukturen und Funktionen moderner Öffentlichkeit: Fragestellungen und Ansätze', in S. Müller-Dohm and K. Neumann-Braun (eds) *Öffentlichkeit, Kultur, Massenkommunikation: Beiträge zur Medien- und Kommunikationssoziologie*, Oldenburg: Universitätsverlag, pp 31–90.

Gerhards, J. and Schäfer, M.S. (2010) 'Is the Internet a Better Public Sphere? Comparing Old and New Media in the US and Germany', *New Media & Society*, 12(1): 143–60.

Giddens, A. (1994) *Beyond Left and Right: The Future of Radical Politics*, Cambridge: Polity Press.

Giddens, A. and Sutton, P.W. (2021) *Sociology*, Cambridge: Polity Press.

Giesen, B. (1993) *Die Intellektuellen und die Nation: Eine deutsche Achsenzeit*, Frankfurt am Main: Suhrkamp.

Giesen, B. (2004) *Triumph and Trauma*, Boulder, CO: Paradigm Publishers.

Gil de Zúñiga, H., Ardèvol-Abreu, A. and Casero-Ripollés, A. (2021) 'WhatsApp Political Discussion, Conventional Participation and Activism: Exploring Direct, Indirect and Generational Effects', *Information, Communication & Society*, 24(2): 201–18.

Gitlin, T. (1998) 'Public Sphere or Public Sphericules', in J. Curran (ed) *Media, Ritual and Identity*, London: Routledge, pp 168–74.

Goffman, E. (1959) *The Presentation of Self in Everyday Life*, Garden City, NY: Doubleday.

Greengard, S. (2015) *The Internet of Things*, Cambridge, MA: MIT Press.

Gripsrud, J. (2000) 'Tabloidization, Popular Journalism and Democracy', in C. Sparks and J. Tulloch (eds) *Tabloid Tales*, Lanham: Rowman & Littlefield, pp 285–300.

Gripsrud, J., Moe, H., Molander, A. and Murdoch, G. (eds) (2010a) *The Public Sphere: Four Volume Set*, London: Sage.

Gripsrud, J., Moe, H., Molander, A. and Murdock, G. (eds) (2010b) *The Idea of the Public Sphere: A Reader*, Lanham: Lexington.

Gripsrud, J. and Weibull, L. (2010) *Media, Markets & Public Spheres: European Media at the Crossroads*, Bristol: Intellect.

Groshek, J. and Tandoc, E.C. (2017) 'The Affordance Effect: Gatekeeping and (Non)reciprocal Journalism on Twitter', *Computers in Human Behavior*, 66: 201–10.

Gubrium, A. and Harper, K. (2016) *Participatory Visual and Digital Methods*, London: Routledge.

Guiraudon, V., Ruzza, C. and Trenz, H.-J. (eds) (2015) *Europe's Prolonged Crisis: The Making or the Unmaking of a Political Union*, Basingstoke: Palgrave Macmillan.

Gurstein, M. (2007) *What Is Community Informatics (and Why Does It Matter)?*, Milan: Polimetrica.

Habermas, J. (1974) 'The Public Sphere. An Encyclopedia Article (1964)', *New German Critique*, 3: 49–55.

Habermas, J. (1975) *Legitimation Crisis*, Boston: Beacon Press.

Habermas, J. (1985) *The Theory of Communicative Action: Reason and the Rationalization of Society*, Boston: Beacon Press.

Habermas, J. (1989) *The Structural Transformation of the Public Sphere: An Inquiry into a Category of Bourgeois Society*, Cambridge, MA: MIT Press.

Habermas, J. (1990) *Die Moderne, ein unvollendetes Projekt: Philosophisch-politische Aufsätze 1977–1990*, Stuttgart: Reclam.

Habermas, J. (1990 [1962]) *Strukturwandel der Öffentlichkeit: Untersuchungen zu einer Kategorie der bürgerlichen Gesellschaft*, Frankfurt am Main: Suhrkamp.

Habermas, J. (1993) 'Further Reflections on the Public Sphere', in C. Calhoun (ed), *Habermas and the Public Sphere*, Cambridge, MA: MIT Press, pp 421–61.

Habermas, J. (1995) 'Reconciliation through the Public Use of Reason: Remarks on John Rawls's Political Liberalism', *The Journal of Philosophy*, 92(3): 109–31.

Habermas, J. (1996) *Between Facts and Norms: Contributions to a Discourse Theory of Law and Democracy*, Cambridge: Polity Press.

Habermas, J. (2001) *The Postnational Constellation: Political Essays*, Cambridge: Polity.

Habermas, J. (2009) 'Hat die Demokratie noch eine epistemische Dimension? Empirische Forschung und normative Theorie', in J. Habermas (ed) *Philosophische Texte Band 4: Politische Theorie*, Frankfurt am Main: Suhrkamp, pp 87–139.

Habermas, J. (2021). 'Ueberlegungen Und Hypothesen Zu Einem Erneuten Strukturwandel Der Politischen Oeffentlichkeit', in M. Seeliger and S. Sevignani (eds) *Leviathan Sonderband 37 (Ein neuer Strukturwandel der Oeffentlichkeit)*, pp 470–500.

Habermas, J. (2022) 'Reflections and Hypotheses on a Further Structural Transformation of the Political Public Sphere', *Theory, Culture & Society*, 39(4): 145–71.

Haleva-Amir, S. and Nahon, K. (2016) 'Electoral Politics on Social Media', in A. Bruns, G. Enli, E. Skogerbo, A. Larsson and C. Christensen (eds) *Routledge Companion to Social Media and Politics*, New York: Routledge, pp 471–87.

Halford, S. and Savage, M. (2010) 'Reconceptualizing Digital Social Inequality', *Information, Communication & Society*, 13(7): 937–55.

Hall, K. (2020) 'Public Penitence: Facebook and the Performance of Apology', *Social Media + Society*, 6(2): 2056305120907945.

Hall, P.A. and Lamont, M. (2013) *Social Resilience in the Neoliberal Era*, Cambridge: Cambridge University Press.

Hall, S. (1973) 'Encoding and Decoding in the Television Discourse', Centre for Cultural Studies, University of Birmingham, selected working papers, vol 2: 386–98.

Hall, S. (2001) 'Foucault: Power, Knowledge and Discourse', in M. Wetherell, S. Taylor and S.J. Yates (eds) *Discourse Theory and Practice: A Reader*, London: Sage, pp 72–81.

Hallin, D.C. and Mancini, P. (2004) *Comparing Media Systems: Three Models of Media and Politics*, Cambridge: Cambridge University Press.

Hamdaoui, S. (2021) 'A "Stylistic Anti-populism": An Analysis of the Sardine Movement's Opposition to Matteo Salvini in Italy', *Social Movement Studies*, 21(4): 436–51.

Hanitzsch, T. (2016) 'Das journalistische Feld', in M. Löffelholz and L. Rothenberger (eds) *Handbuch Journalismustheorien*, Wiesbaden: Springer, pp 281–93.

Harcup, T. (2015) *Journalism: Principles and Practice*, Thousand Oaks: Sage.

Helles, R. and Ørmen, J. (2020) 'Big Data and Explanation: Reflections on the Uses of Big Data in Media and Communication Research', *European Journal of Communication*, 35(3): 290–300.

Helles, R., Ørmen, J., Radil, C. and Jensen, K.B. (2015) 'Media Audiences: The Media Landscapes of European Audiences', *International Journal of Communication*, 9: 299–320.

Hendricks, V.F. and Vestergaard, M. (2018) *Reality Lost: Markets of Attention, Misinformation and Manipulation*, Cham: Springer International Publishing.

Hermans, L. and Drok, N. (2018) 'Placing Constructive Journalism in Context', *Journalism Practice*, 12(6): 679–94.

Hjarvard, S. (2008) 'The Mediatization of Society: A Theory of the Media as Agents of Social and Cultural Change', *Nordicom Review*, 29(2): 105–34.

Hjarvard, S. (2013) *The Mediatization of Culture and Society*, London: Routledge.

Holten, R.J. (1987) 'The Idea of Crisis in Modern Society', *The British Journal of Sociology*, 38(4): 502–20

Hooghe, L. and Marks, G. (2018) 'Cleavage Theory Meets Europe's Crises: Lipset, Rokkan, and the Transnational Cleavage', *Journal of European Public Policy*, 25(1): 109–35.

Hoye, J.M. and Monaghan, J. (2018) 'Surveillance, Freedom and the Republic', *European Journal of Political Theory*, 17(3): 343–63.

Humprecht, E., Esser, F. and Van Aelst, P. (2020) 'Resilience to Online Disinformation: A Framework for Cross-national Comparative Research', *The International Journal of Press/Politics*, 25(3): 493–516.

Huntington, S. (1991) *The Third Wave: Democratization in the Late Twentieth Century*, Norman: University of Oklahoma Press.

Huntington, S. (1993) 'The Clash of Civilizations?', *Foreign Affairs*, 72(3): 22–49.

Ignatow, G. (2020) *Sociological Theory in the Digital Age*, London: Routledge.

Inglehart, R. (2003) 'How Solid Is Mass Support for Democracy: And How Can We Measure It?', *PS: Political Science and Politics*, 36(1): 51–7.

Isin, E. and Ruppert, E (2020) *Being Digital Citizens*, Lanham: Rowman & Littlefield.

Iyengar, S. and Simon, A.F. (2000) 'New Perspectives and Evidence on Political Communication and Campaign Effects', *Annual Review of Psychology*, 51(1): 149–69.

Jääsaari, J. and Hildén, J. (2015) 'From File Sharing to Free Culture: The Evolving Agenda of European Pirate Parties', *International Journal of Communication*, 9: 870–98.

Jackson, S.J., Bailey, M., Welles, B.F. and Lauren, G. (2020) *#HashtagActivism: Networks of Race and Gender Justice*, Cambridge, MA: MIT Press.

Jacobs, R.N. and Townsley, E. (2011) *The Space of Opinion: Media Intellectuals and the Public Sphere*, Oxford: Oxford University Press.

Jardine, E. (2017) 'Privacy, Censorship, Data Breaches and Internet Freedom: The Drivers of Support and Opposition to Dark Web Technologies', *New Media & Society*, 20(8): 2824–43.

Jenkins, H. (2014) 'Participatory Culture: From Co-creating Brand Meaning to Changing the World', *Marketing Intelligence Review*, 6(2): 34–9.

Jenkins, H., Purushotma, R., Weigel, M., Clinton, K. and Robison, A.J. (2009) *Confronting the Challenges of Participatory Culture: Media Education for the 21st Century*, Cambridge, MA: MIT Press.

Jenkins, H., Thorburn, D. and Seawell, B. (2004) *Democracy and New Media*, Cambridge, MA: MIT Press.

Jensen, K.B. (2012) 'Introduction: The State of Convergence in Media and Communication Research', in K.B. Jensen (ed) *A Handbook of Media and Communication Research: Qualitative and Quantitative Methodologies* (2nd edn), Abingdon: Routledge, pp 1–20.

Johnson, W. (2015) *Disrupt Yourself: Putting the Power of Disruptive Innovation to Work*, New York: Gildan Media.

Jones, E. and Papaconstantinou, G. (2020) 'Foreword', in G. Papaconstantinou, *Whatever It Takes*, Newcastle upon Tyne: Agenda Publishing, pp xiii–xiv.

Jünger, J. and Fähnrich, B. (2019) 'Does Really No One Care? Analyzing the Public Engagement of Communication Scientists on Twitter', *New Media & Society*, 22(3): 387–408.

Kahan, D.M. (2017) 'Misconceptions, Misinformation, and the Logic of Identity-Protective Cognition', Cultural Cognition Project Working Paper Series No. 164, Yale Law School, Public Law Research Paper No 605, Yale Law & Economics Research Paper No 575. Available from: https://ssrn.com/abstract=2973067 or http://dx.doi.org/10.2139/ssrn.2973067

Kaltwasser, C.R. (2012) 'The Ambivalence of Populism: Threat and Corrective for Democracy', *Democratization*, 19(2): 184–208.

Kant, I. (1991 [1784]) 'An Answer to the Question: "What Is Enlightenment?"', in H.S. Reiss (ed) *Kant: Political Writings*, Cambridge: Cambridge University Press, pp 54–60.

Kant, I. (2000 [1790]) *Critique of the Power of Judgment*, Cambridge: Cambridge University Press.

Katz, E. and Lazarsfeld, P.F. (1966) *Personal Influence: The Part Played by People in the Flow of Mass Communications*, New York: Free Press.

Kavada, A. (2021) 'Progressive Social Movements', *IPPR Progressive Review*, 27(4): 344–53.

Kavada, A. and Poell, T. (2021) 'From Counterpublics to Contentious Publicness: Tracing the Temporal, Spatial, and Material Articulations of Popular Protest through Social Media', *Communication Theory*, 31(2): 190–208.

Keating, M. (1996) *Nations against the State: The New Politics of Nationalism in Quebec, Catalonia and Scotland*, Basingstoke: Palgrave Macmillan.

Keen, A. (2012) *Digital Vertigo: How Today's Online Social Revolution Is Dividing, Diminishing and Disorienting Us*, London: Constable.

Kepplinger, H.M., Geiss, S. and Siebert, S. (2012) 'Framing Scandals: Cognitive and Emotional Media Effects', *Journal of Communication*, 62(4): 659–81.

Kim, Y. and Zhou, S. (2020) 'The Effects of Political Conflict News Frame on Political Polarization: A Social Identity Approach', *International Journal of Communication*, 14: 937–58.

Klein, A., Koopmans, R., Trenz, H.-J., Klein, L., Lahusen, C. and Rucht, D. (2003) *Bürgerschaft, Öffentlichkeit und Demokratie in Europa*, Opladen: Leske + Budrich.

Klein, B., Meier, L.M. and Powers, D. (2017) 'Selling Out: Musicians, Autonomy, and Compromise in the Digital Age', *Popular Music and Society*, 40(2): 222–38.

Klein, D. and Wueller, J. (2017) 'Fake News: A Legal Perspective', *Journal of Internet Law*, Available from: https://ssrn.com/abstract=2958790

Koltay, T. (2011) 'The Media and the Literacies: Media Literacy, Information Literacy, Digital Literacy', *Media, Culture & Society*, 33(2): 211–21.

Koselleck, R. (1973) *Kritik und Krise: Eine Studie zur Pathogenese der bürgerlichen Welt*, Frankfurt am Main: Suhrkamp.

Krämer, B. (2014) 'Media Populism: A Conceptual Clarification and Some Theses on Its Effects', *Communication Theory*, 24(1): 42–60.

Krastev, I. (2014) *Democracy Disrupted: The Politics of Global Protest*, Philadelphia: University of Pennsylvania Press.

Kress, G.R. (2003) *Literacy in the New Media Age*, London: Routledge.

Kriesi, H., Grande, E., Lachat, R., Dolezal, M., Bornschier, S. and Frey, T. (2008) *West European Politics in the Age of Globalization*, Cambridge: Cambridge University Press.

Kriesi, H.P., Lavenex, S., Esser, F., Matthes, J., Bühlmann, M. and Bochsler, D. (2013) *Democracy in the Age of Globalization and Mediatization*, Basingatoke: Palgrave.

Laclau, E. (2005) *On Populist Reason*, London: Verso.

Lahusen, C. (2020) 'Enlightened Trust: A Conceptual Framework of Analysis for the Examination of Trust and Distrust in Governance', EUHorizon2020-Projekt 'Enlightened Trust: An Examination of Trust and Distrust in Governance – Conditions, Effects and Remedies' (EnTrust), Grant Agreement No. 870572. Work-Package 1: The theoretical and normative underpinnings of trust/distrust. Deliverable 1.2.

Lane, J.E. (2009) 'Political Representation from the Principal–Agent Perspective', *Representation*, 45(4): 369–78.

Lang, A. (2013) 'Discipline in Crisis? The Shifting Paradigm of Mass Communication Research', *Communication Theory*, 23(1): 10–24.

Lasswell, H.D. (1948) 'The Structure and Function of Communication in Society', in L. Bryson (ed) *The Communication of Ideas,* New York: Harper and Row, pp 37–51.

Latour, B. (1999) *Pandora's Hope*, Cambridge, MA: Harvard University Press.

Latour, B. (2005) *Reassembling the Social: An Introduction to Actor-Network-Theory*, Oxford: Oxford University Press.

Laurell, C. and Sandström, C. (2017) 'The Sharing Economy in Social Media: Analyzing Tensions between Market and Non-market Logics', *Technological Forecasting and Social Change*, 125: 58–65.

Lee, O.E.-K. and Kim, D.-H. (2018) 'Bridging the Digital Divide for Older Adults via Intergenerational Mentor-Up', *Research on Social Work Practice*, 29(7): 786–95.

Lee, T.-T. (2005) 'The Liberal Media Myth Revisited: An Examination of Factors Influencing Perceptions of Media Bias', *Journal of Broadcasting & Electronic Media*, 49(1): 43–64.

Levendusky, M. (2013) *How Partisan Media Polarize America*, Chicago: University of Chicago Press.

Levmore, S. and Nussbaum, M.C. (2010) *The Offensive Internet: Speech, Privacy, and Reputation*, Cambridge, MA: Harvard University Press.

Lim, E. (2020) 'The Protestant Ethic and the Spirit of Facebook: Updating Identity Economics', *Social Media and Society*, 6(2): 1–8.

Lindgren, S. (2017) *Digital Media & Society*, Los Angeles, CA: Sage.

Lindgren, S. and Linde, J. (2012) 'The Subpolitics of Online Piracy: A Swedish Case Study', *Convergence*, 18(2): 143–64.

Lippmann, W. (1927) *The Phantom Public*, New York: Macmillan.

Livingstone, S., Bober, M. and Helsper, E.J. (2005) 'Active Participation or Just More Information?', *Information, Communication & Society*, 8(3): 287–314.

Livingstone, S.M. (2005) *Audiences and Publics: When Cultural Engagement Matters for the Public Sphere*, Bristol: Intellect.

Luhmann, N. (1992) 'Die Beobachtung der Beobachter im politischen System', in J. Wilke (ed) *Öffentliche Meinung: Theorie, Methoden, Befunde*, Freiburg: Alber, pp 77–86.

Luhmann, N. (2000) *The Reality of the Mass Media*, Stanford: Stanford University Press.

Lupton, D. (2014) *Digital Sociology*, London: Routledge.

Lück, J., Wessler, H., Wozniak, A. and Lycarião, D. (2016) 'Counterbalancing Global Media Frames with Nationally Colored Narratives: A Comparative Study of News Narratives and News Framing in the Climate Change Coverage of Five Countries', *Journalism*, 19(12): 1635–56.

Mair, P. (1998) 'Representation and Participation in the Changing World of Party Politics', *European Review*, 6(2): 161–74.

Mair, P. (2013) *Ruling the Void: The Hollowing of Western Democracy*, London: Verso.

Mancini, P. (2012) 'Media Fragmentation, Party System, and Democracy', *The International Journal of Press/Politics*, 18(1): 43–60.

Manin, B. (1997) *The Principles of Representative Government*, Cambridge: Cambridge University Press.

Mannheim, K. (2013 [1936]) *Ideology and Utopia*, London: Routledge.

Manow, P. (2008) *Im Schatten des Königs: Die politische Anatomie demokratischer Repräsentation*, Frankfurt am Main: Suhrkamp Verlag.

Manow, P. (2020) *(Ent)demokratisierung der Demokratie*, Berlin: Suhrkamp.

Marichal, P.J. (2012) *Facebook Democracy: The Architecture of Disclosure and the Threat to Public Life*, Burlington: Ashgate.

Marquardt, J. (2020) 'Fridays for Future's Disruptive Potential: An Inconvenient Youth between Moderate and Radical Ideas', *Frontiers in Communication*, 5(48). Available from: https://doi.org/10.3389/fcomm.2020.00048

Marres, N. (2017) *Digital Sociology: The Reinvention of Social Research*, Oxford: Wiley.

Marshall, T.H. (1950) *Citizenship and Social Class*, Cambridge: Cambridge University Press.

Marwick, A.E. (2013) *Status Update: Celebrity, Publicity, and Branding in the Social Media Age*, New Haven, CT: Yale University Press.

Mazzoleni, G. (2003) 'The Media and the Growth of Neo-populism in Contemporary Democracies', in G. Mazzoleni, S. Julianne and B. Horsfield (eds) *The Media and Neo-populism*, Westport: Praeger, pp 1–20.

Mazzoleni, G. (2008) 'Populism and the Media', in D. Albertazzi and D. McDonnell (eds) *Twenty-First Century Populism: The Spectre of Western European Democracy*, Houndmills: Palgrave Macmillan, pp 49–64.

McChesney, R.W. (2013) *Digital Disconnect: How Capitalism Is Turning the Internet against Democracy*, New York: New Press.

McChesney, R.W. (2016) 'Journalism Is Dead! Long Live Journalism? Why Democratic Societies Will Need to Subsidise Future News Production', *Journal of Media Business Studies*, 13(3): 128–35.

McChesney, R.W. and Pickard, V. (2013) *Will the Last Reporter Please Turn out the Lights: The Collapse of Journalism and What Can Be Done to Fix It*, New York: New Press.

McCombs, M. (1981) 'The Agenda-Setting Approach', in D.D. Nimmo and K.R. Sanders (eds) *Handbook of Political Communication*, Beverly Hills, CA: Sage.

McGuigan, J. (2005) 'The Cultural Public Sphere', *European Journal of Cultural Studies*, 8(4): 427–43.

McKeon, M. (2006) *The Secret History of Domesticity: Public, Private, and the Division of Knowledge*, Baltimore: Johns Hopkins University Press.

McNair, B. (2000) *Journalism and Democracy*, London: Routledge.

McNair, B. (2006) *Cultural Chaos: Journalism, News and Power in a Globalised World*, London: Routledge.

McNair, B. (2009) 'The Internet and the Changing Global Media Environment', in A. Chadwick and P.N. Howard (eds) *Routledge Handbook of Internet Politics*, London: Routledge, pp 217–29.

McNair, B. (2017) *Fake News: Falsehood, Fabrication and Fantasy in Journalism*, London: Routledge.

McNair, B., Hibberd, M. and Schlesinger, P. (2002) 'Public Access Broadcasting and Democratic Participation in the Age of Mediated Politics', *Journalism Studies*, 3(3): 407–22.

McNamara, K. (2009) 'Publicising Private Lives: Celebrities, Image Control and the Reconfiguration of Public Space', *Social & Cultural Geography*, 10(1): 9–23.

Mead, G.H. (2015 [1932]) *Mind, Self, and Society: The Definitive Edition*, Chicago: University of Chicago Press.

Mede, N.G. and Schäfer, M.S. (2020) 'Science-Related Populism: Conceptualizing Populist Demands toward Science', *Public Understanding of Science*, 29(5): 473–91.

Meikle, G. (2016) *Social Media: Communication, Sharing and Visibility*, London: Routledge.

Mény, Y. and Surel, Y. (2002) 'The Constitutive Ambiguity of Populism', in Y. Mény and Y. Surel (eds) *Democracies and the Populist Challenge*, London: Palgrave Macmillan, pp 1–21.

Merkel, W. (2018) 'Challenge or Crisis of Democracy', in W. Merkel and S. Kneip (eds) *Democracy and Crisis*, Cham: Springer, pp 1–29.

Michailidou, A. (2016) '"The Germans Are Back": Euroscepticism and Anti-Germanism in Crisis-Stricken Greece', *National Identities*, 19(1): 91–108.

Michailidou, A. and Trenz, H.-J. (2013) 'Mediatized Representative Politics in the European Union: Towards Audience Democracy?', *Journal of European Public Policy*, 20(2): 260–77.

Michailidou, A. and Trenz, H.-J. (2015) 'The European Crisis and the Media: Media Autonomy, Public Perceptions and New Forms of Political Engagement', in H.-J. Trenz, C. Ruzza and V. Guiraudon (eds) *Europe in Crisis: The Unmaking of Political Union?*, Basingstoke: Palgrave Macmillan, pp 232–50.

Michailidou, A. and Trenz, H.-J. (2021) 'Rethinking Journalism Standards in the Era of Posttruth Politics: From Truth Keepers to Truth Mediators', *Media, Culture and Society*, 43(7): 1340–9.

Michailidou, A., Trenz, H.-J. and Eike, E. (2022) 'Journalism, Truth and the Restoration of Trust in Democracy: Tracing the EU "Fake News" Strategy', in M. Conrad, G. Hálfdanarson, A. Michailidou, C. Galpin and N. Pyrhönen (eds) *Europe in the Age of Post-truth Politics: Populism, Disinformation and the Public Sphere*, Basingstoke: Palgrave, pp 53–75.

Michailidou, A., Trenz, H.-J. and De Wilde, P. (2014) *The Internet and European Integration: Pro- and Anti-EU Debates in Online News Media*, Opladen: Barbara Budrich Publisher.

Mill, J.S. (1998 [1861]) *On Liberty and Other Essays*, Oxford: Oxford University Press.

Moffitt, B. (2016) *The Global Rise of Populism: Performance, Political Style, and Representation*, Stanford: Stanford University Press.

Moffitt, B. (2018) 'The Populism/Anti-populism Divide in Western Europe', *Democratic Theory*, 5(2): 1–16.

Mouffe, C. (2000) *The Democratic Paradox*, London: Verso.

Mudde, C. (2012) *Populism in Europe and the Americas: Threat or Corrective for Democracy?*, Cambridge: Cambridge University Press.

Mudde, C. (2021) 'Populism in Europe: An Illiberal Democratic Response to Undemocratic Liberalism (The Government and Opposition/Leonard Schapiro Lecture 2019)', *Government and Opposition*, 56(4): 577–97.

Muldoon, J. (2022) *Platform Socialism: How to Reclaim Our Digital Future from Big Tech*, London: Pluto.

Murray, I., Plagnol, A. and Corr, P. (2017) ' "When Things Go Wrong and People Are Afraid": An Evaluation of Group Polarisation in the UK Post Brexit'. Available from: https://ssrn.com/abstract=3041846 or http://dx.doi.org/10.2139/ssrn.3041846

Müller, J.W. (2011) *Contesting Democracy: Political Ideas in Twentieth-Century Europe*, New Haven, CT: Yale University Press.

Müller, J.W. (2016) *What Is Populism?*, Philadelphia, PA: University of Pennsylvania Press.

Müller, J.W. (2019) *Furcht und Freiheit: Für einen anderen Liberalismus*, Berlin: Suhrkamp.

Nassehi, A. (2019) *Muster: Theorie Der Digitalen Gesellschaft*, München: C.H. Beck.

Nassehi, A. (2002) 'Politik des Staates oder Politik der Gesellschaft. Kollektivität als Problemformel des Politischen', in K.-U. Hellmann and R. Schmalz-Bruns (eds) *Niklas Luhmanns politische Soziologie*, Frankfurt a. M: Suhrkamp, pp 38–59.

Neidhardt, F. (1994a) 'Die Rolle der Publikums: Anmerkungen zur Soziologie politischer Öffentlichkeit', in H.U. Derlien, U. Gerhard and F.W. Scharpf (eds) *Systemrationalität und Partialinteresse: Festschrift für Renate Mayntz*, Baden-Baden: Nomos, pp 315–28.

Neidhardt, F. (1994b) *Öffentlichkeit, öffentliche Meinung, soziale Bewegungen*, Opladen: Westdeutscher Verlag.

Neumann, R., Just, M. and Crigler, A.N. (1992) *Common Knowledge: News and the Construction of Political Meaning*, Chicago: University of Chicago Press.

Newman, N., Levy, D. and Nielsen, R. (2015) 'Reuters Institute Digital News Report 2015: Tracking the Future of News', Reuters Institute for the Study of Journalism.

Newman, S. (2022) 'Post-truth, Postmodernism and the Public Sphere', in M. Conrad, G. Hálfdanarson, A. Michailidou, C. Galpin and N. Pyrhönen (eds) *Europe in the Age of Post-truth Politics: Populism, Disinformation and the Public Sphere*, Basingstoke: Palgrave Macmillan, pp 13–30.

Nielsen, R.K., Fletcher, R., Newman, N., Brennen, J.S. and Howard, P. (2020) 'Navigating the "Infodemic": How People in Six Countries Access and Rate News and Information about Coronavirus', Report published by the Reuters Institute for the Study of Journalism, Available from: https://reutersinstitute.politics.ox.ac.uk/infodemic-how-people-six-countries-access-and-rate-news-and-information-about-coronavirus

Nieto-Galan, A. (2016) *Science in the Public Sphere: A History of Lay Knowledge and Expertise*, London: Routledge.

Noelle-Neumann, E. (1974) 'The Spiral of Silence: A Theory of Public Opinion', *Journal of Communication*, 24(2): 43–51.

Norris, P. (1996) 'Does Television Erode Social Capital? A Reply to Putnam', *PS: Political Science & Politics*, 29(3): 474–80.

Norris, P. (2020) 'Closed Minds? Is a "Cancel Culture" Stifling Academic Freedom and Intellectual Debate in Political Science?', HKS Working Paper No RWP20–025. Available from: https://ssrn.com/abstract=3671026 or http://dx.doi.org/10.2139/ssrn.3671026

Norris, P. and Inglehart, R. (2019) *Cultural Backlash and the Rise of Populism: Trump, Brexit, and Authoritarian Populism*, Cambridge: Cambridge University Press.

O'Connor, J. (1981) 'The Meaning of Crisis', *International Journal of Urban and Regional Research*, 5(3): 301–29.

O'Mahony, P. (2013) *The Contemporary Theory of the Public Sphere*, Bern: Peter Lang.

O'Mahony, P. (2021) 'Habermas and the Public Sphere: Rethinking a Key Theoretical Concept', *European Journal of Social Theory*, 24(4): 485–506.

O'Riordan, T., McGowan, A.H., Cutter, S., Hamann, R. and Lahsen, M. (2020) 'Reframing Sustainability in the Emergent Age', *Environment: Science and Policy for Sustainable Development*, 62(6): 2–7.

Offe, C. (2015) *Europe Entrapped*, Oxford: Wiley.

Ojala, M. (2017) 'The Making of a Global Elite: Global Economy and the Davos Man in the Financial Times 2001–2011', PhD Thesis, University of Helsinki. Available from: http://urn.fi/URN:ISBN:978-951-51-2600-9

Olsen, E.D.H. and Trenz, H.-J. (2014) 'From Citizens' Deliberation to Popular Will Formation? Generating Democratic Legitimacy in Transnational Deliberative Polling', *Political Studies*, 62(1): 117–33.

Ott, B.L. and Mack, R.L. (2020) *Critical Media Studies: An Introduction*, Oxford: Wiley.

Owen, G. and Savage, N. (2015) 'The Tor Dark Net', GCIG Paper No. 20, Series: Global Commission on Internet Governance Paper Series. Available from: https://www.cigionline.org/publications/tor-dark-net?source=post_page

Pang, A., Hassan, N.B.B.A. and Chong, A.C.Y. (2014) 'Negotiating Crisis in the Social Media Environment: Evolution of Crises Online, Gaining Credibility Offline', *Corporate Communications: An International Journal*, 19(1): 96–118.

Papacharissi, Z. (2002) 'The Virtual Sphere: The Internet as a Public Sphere', *New Media & Society*, 4(1): 9–27.

Papacharissi, Z. (2009) 'The Virtual Sphere 2.0: The Internet, the Public Sphere, and Beyond', in A. Chadwick and P.N. Howard (eds) *Routledge Handbook of Internet Politics*, London: Routledge, pp 230–45.

Papacharissi, Z. (2010) *A Private Sphere: Democracy in a Digital Age*, Cambridge: Cambridge University Press.

Papacharissi, Z. (2015) *Affective Publics: Sentiment, Technology, and Politics*, Oxford: Oxford University Press.

Pariser, E. (2011) *The Filter Bubble: What the Internet Is Hiding from You*, London: Penguin.

Parsons, T. (1951) *The Social System*, London: Routledge.

Patterson, T.E. (2011) *Out of Order: An Incisive and Boldly Original Critique of the Mews Media's Domination of America's Political Process*, New York: Knopf Doubleday Publishing Group.

Pérez-Curiel, C., Domínguez-García, R. and Velasco-Molpeceres, A.M. (2021) 'High-quality Journalism in the Face of Donald Trump's Theory of Electoral Fraud: The Information Strategy of the Media in the 2020 US Presidential Election', *Profesional de la información*, 30(6). Available from: https://doi.org/10.3145/epi.2021.nov.19

Perry, S.L. (2021) 'Banning Because of Science or in Spite of It? Scientific Authority, Religious Conservatism, and Support for Outlawing Pornography, 1984–2018', *Social Forces*, 100(3): 1385–414.

Perry, S.L. and Whitehead, A.L. (2020) 'Porn as a Threat to the Mythic Social Order: Christian Nationalism, Anti-pornography Legislation, and Fear of Pornography as a Public Menace', *The Sociological Quarterly*, 63(2): 316–36.

Peters, B. (2008) *Public Deliberation and Public Culture: The Writings of Bernhard Peters, 1993–2005*, ed H. Wessler, Basingstoke: Palgrave Macmillan.

Pfetsch, B. (2018) 'Dissonant and Disconnected Public Spheres as Challenge for Political Communication Research', *Javnost – The Public*, 25(1–2): 59–65.

Picard, R.G. (2010) *Value Creation and the Future of News Organizations: Why and How Journalism Must Change to Remain Relevant in the Twenty-First Century*, Lisbon: Media XXI.

Pitkin, H.F. (1967) *The Concept of Representation*, Berkeley, CA: University of California Press.

Pollak, J. (2013) 'Political Representation and the Common Good: A Fragile Relationship', in S. Puntscher Riekmann, A. Somek and D. Wydra (eds) *Is There a European Common Good?*, 1, Baden-Baden: Nomos Verlagsgesellschaft mbH & Co. KG, pp 156–73.

Poos, L. (2020) 'Lessons from Past Pandemics: Disinformation, Scapegoating, and Social Distancing', Brookings, Techtank, blog post. Available from: https://www.brookings.edu/blog/techtank/2020/03/16/lessons-from-past-pandemics-disinformation-scapegoating-and-social-distancing

Putnam, R.D. (1995a) 'Bowling Alone: America's Declining Social Capital', *Journal of Democracy*, 6(1): 65–78.

Putnam, R.D. (1995b) 'Tuning In, Tuning Out: The Strange Disappearance of Social Capital in America', *PS: Political Science & Politics*, 28(4): 664–83.

Pörksen, B. (2018) *Die große Gereiztheit: Wege aus der kollektiven Erregung*, Munich: Carl Hanser Verlag.

Pöttker, H. (2001) *Öffentlichkeit als gesellschaftlicher Auftrag: Klassiker der Sozialwissenschaften über Journalismus und Medien*, Konstanz: Universitätsverlag Konstanz.

Rall, D.N. (2019) 'Rage – Beyond the Point of Boiling Over', *M/C Journal*, 22(1). Available from: https://doi.org/10.5204/mcj.1517

Rampp, B., Endreß, M. and Naumann, M. (2019) *Resilience in Social, Cultural and Political Spheres*, Wiesbaden: Springer.

Räsänen, M. and Nyce, J.M. (2013) 'The Raw Is Cooked: Data in Intelligence Practice', *Science, Technology & Human Values*, 38(5): 655–77.

Ravenelle, A.J., Newell, A. and Kowalski, K.C. (2021) '"The Looming, Crazy Stalker Coronavirus": Fear Mongering, Fake News, and the Diffusion of Distrust', *Socius*, 7: https://doi.org/10.1177/2378023121 1024776.

Recchi, E. and Favell, A. (2019) *Everyday Europe: Social Transnationalism in an Unsettled Continent*, Bristol: Policy Press.

Reckwitz, A. (2020) *Society of Singularities*, Cambridge: Polity.

Reiman, C. (2012) *Public Interest and Private Rights in Social Media*, The Hague: Elsevier Science.

Resende, G., Melo, P., Sousa, H., Messias, J., Vasconcelos, M., Almeida, J. et al (2019) '(Mis)Information Dissemination in WhatsApp: Gathering, Analyzing and Countermeasures', New York: ACM Press. https://doi.org/10.1145/3308558.3313688

Reuter, C., Hartwig, K., Kirchner, J. and Schlegel, N. (2019) 'Fake News Perception in Germany: A Representative Study of People's Attitudes and Approaches to Counteract Disinformation', in *Proceedings of the International Conference on Wirtschaftsinformatik (WI)*, Siegen: University of Siegen, 1069–83. https://doi.org/10.26083/tuprints-00020795

Reveley, J. (2013) 'Understanding Social Media Use as Alienation: A Review and Critique', *E-Learning and Digital Media*, 10(1): 83–94.

Revelli, M. (2019) *The New Populism: Democracy Stares into the Abyss*, London: Verso.

Reviglio, U. and Agosti, C. (2020) 'Thinking Outside the Black-Box: The Case for "Algorithmic Sovereignty" in Social Media', *Social Media + Society*, 6(2): 2056305120915613.

Rey, P.J. (2012) 'Alienation, Exploitation, and Social Media', *American Behavioral Scientist*, 56(4): 399–420.

Rheingold, H. (1994) *The Virtual Community: Surfing the Internet*, London: Minerva.

Richey, L.A. (2016) '"Tinder Humanitarians": The Moral Panic around Representations of Old Relationships in New Media', *Javnost – The Public*, 23(4): 398–414.

Richter, H. (2020) *Demokratie: Eine deutsche Affäre*, Munich: Beck.

Ritzi, C. (2021) 'Libration im Öffentlichkeitsuniversum: Anziehung und Kräfteausgleich in der Digitalen Kommunikationsstruktur', in *Leviathan* Sonderband 37, Ein neuer Strukturwandel der Öffentlichkeit, 298–319.

Roberts, J.A. and David, M.E. (2020) 'The Social Media Party: Fear of Missing Out (FoMO), Social Media Intensity, Connection, and Well-Being', *International Journal of Human–Computer Interaction*, 36(4): 386–92.

Rosanvallon, P. (2008) *Counter-democracy: Politics in an Age of Distrust*, Cambridge: Cambridge University Press.

Ross, B. and Stacie Renfro, P. (2010) 'Emotion, Media, and the Global Village', in K. Doveling, C. von Scheve and E.A. Konjin (eds) *The Routledge Handbook of Emotions and Mass Media*, London: Routledge, pp 181–94.

Rossini, P. (2020) 'Beyond Incivility: Understanding Patterns of Uncivil and Intolerant Discourse in Online Political Talk', *Communication Research*, 49(3): 399–425.

Rouban, L. (2019) *La matière noire de la démocratie*, Paris: Presses de Sciences Po.

Rucht, D. (2019) 'Jugend auf der Straße Fridays for Future und die Generationenfrage', WZB Mitteilungen, 165. Available from: https://bibliothek.wzb.eu/artikel/2019/f-22359.pdf

Rudesill, D.S., Caverlee, J. and Sui, D. (2015) 'The Deep Web and the Darknet: A Look Inside the Internet's Massive Black Box (October 20, 2015)'. Woodrow Wilson International Center for Scholars, STIP 03, October 2015, Ohio State Public Law Working Paper No. 314. Available at SSRN: https://ssrn.com/abstract=2676615 or http://dx.doi.org/10.2139/ssrn.2676615

Ruiz, C., Domingo, D., Micó, J.L., Díaz-Noci, J., Meso, K. and Masip, P. (2011) 'Public Sphere 2.0? The Democratic Qualities of Citizen Debates in Online Newspapers', *The International Journal of Press/Politics*, 16(4): 463–87.

Ryan, M. (2001) 'Journalistic Ethics, Objectivity, Existential Journalism, Standpoint Epistemology, and Public Journalism', *Journal of Mass Media Ethics*, 16(1): 3–22.

Salvatore, A. (2013) 'New Media, the "Arab Spring," and the Metamorphosis of the Public Sphere: Beyond Western Assumptions on Collective Agency and Democratic Politics', *Constellations*, 20(2): 217–28.

Samuelsson, K., Barthel, S., Colding, J., Macassa, G. and Giusti, M. (2020) 'Urban Nature as a Source of Resilience during Social Distancing amidst the Coronavirus Pandemic', *Landscape and Urban Planning*, Preprint DOI: 10.31219/osf.io/3wx5a

Sartori, G. (1998) *Homo videns: Televisione e post pensiero*, Rome: Laterza.

Saunders, R. (2020) *Bodies of Work: The Labour of Sex in the Digital Age*, Basingstoke: Palgrave.

Saward, M. (2010) *The Representative Claim*, Oxford: Oxford University Press.

Schlesinger, P. (2020) 'After the Post-public Sphere', *Media, Culture & Society*, 42(7–8): 1545–63.

Schlesinger, P. and Doyle, G. (2015) 'From Organizational Crisis to Multiplatform Salvation? Creative Destruction and the Recomposition of News Media', *Journalism*, 16(3): 305–23.

Schmitter, P (2015) 'Crisis and Transition, But Not Decline', *Journal of Democracy*, 26(1): 32–44.

Schoenfeld, A.C., Meier, R.F. and Griffin, R.J. (1979) 'Constructing a Social Problem: The Press and the Environment', *Social Problems*, 27(1): 38–61.

Scholl, A. (2019) 'Ideologiekritik und Kontingenz(Erfahrung) am Beispiel Fake News: Der Beitrag des Radikalen Konstruktivismus', in S. Sevignani (ed) *Ideologie, Kritik, Öffentlichkeit*, Frankfurt a.M.: Westend, pp 46–64.

Seeliger, M. and Sevignani, S. (eds) (2021) *Ein Neuer Strukturwandel der Öffentlichkeit* (Leviathan Sonderband 37), Baden-Baden: Nomos.

Sennett, R. (1977) *The Fall of Public Man*, Cambridge: Cambridge University Press.

Sevignani, S. (2015) *Privacy and Capitalism in the Age of Social Media*, London: Routledge.

Shannon, C.E. and Weaver, W. (1949) *A Mathematical Model of Communication*, Urbana, IL: University of Illinois Press.

Shaw, J. (2020) *The People' in Question: Reflections on the Relationship between Citizenship and Constitutions*, Bristol: Bristol University Press.

Shils, E. (1966) 'Privacy: Its Constitution and Vicissitudes', *Law and Contemporary Problems*, 31(2): 281–306.

Smith, D. (2015) 'Not Just Singing the Blues: Dynamics of the EU Crisis', in H.-J. Trenz, C. Ruzza and V. Guiraudon (eds) *Europe in Crisis: The Unmaking of Political Union?*, Basingstoke: Palgrave Macmillan, pp 23–43.

Snyder, L.L. (2003) *The New Nationalism*, Ithaca: Cornell University Press.

Somers, M.R. (1993) 'Citizenship and the Place of the Public Sphere: Law, Community, and Political Culture in the Transition to Democracy', *American Sociological Review*, 58(5): 587–620.

Sonntag, A. (2012) 'Grilles de perception et dynamiques identitaires dans l'espace européen du football "Le projet FREE"', *Politique européenne*, 36(1): 85–192.

Sorensen, R. (2003) *A Brief History of the Paradox: Philosophy and the Labyrinths of the Mind*, Oxford: Oxford University Press.

Spilker, H.S. (2017) *Digital Music Distribution: The Sociology of Online Music Streams*, London: Routledge.

Splichal, S. (2012) *Transnationalization of the Public Sphere and the Fate of the Public*, New York: Hampton Press.

Splichal, S. (2016) 'Publicness, Publicity', in K.B. Jensen, E.W. Rothenbuhler, J.D. Pooley and R.T. Craig (eds) *The International Encyclopedia of Communication Theory and Philosophy*, Oxford: Wiley, pp 1–9.

Splichal, S. (2018) 'Publicness–Privateness: The Liquefaction of "The Great Dichotomy"', *Javnost – The Public*, 25(1–2): 1–10.

Spohr, D. (2017) 'Fake News and Ideological Polarization: Filter Bubbles and Selective Exposure on Social Media', *Business Information Review*, 34(3): 150–60.

Stanyer, J. (2013) *Intimate Politics: Publicity, Privacy and the Personal Lives of Politicians in Media Saturated Democracies*, Oxford: Wiley.

Starr, P. (2019) 'How Neoliberal Policy Shaped the Internet – and What to Do about It Now', The American Prospect. Available from: https://prospect.org/power/how-neoliberal-policy-shaped-internet-surveillance-monopoly

Steininger, C. (2007) *Markt und Öffentlichkeit*, Leiden: Wilhelm Fink.

Stephany, A. (2015) *The Business of Sharing: Making It in the New Sharing Economy*, Basingstoke: Palgrave Macmillan.

Stier, S., Bleier, A., Lietz, H. and Strohmaier, M. (2018) 'Election Campaigning on Social Media: Politicians, Audiences, and the Mediation of Political Communication on Facebook and Twitter', *Political Communication*, 35(1): 50–74.

Streeck, W. (2014) *Buying Time: The Delayed Crisis of Democratic Capitalism*, London: Verso.

Strydom, P. (1999) 'Triple Contingency: The Theoretical Problem of the Public in Communication Societies', *Philosophy & Social Criticism*, 25(2): 1–25.

Strydom, P. (2000) *Discourse and Knowledge: The Making of Enlightenment Sociology*, Liverpool: Liverpool University Press.

Strydom, P. (2011) *Contemporary Critical Theory and Methodology*, London: Routledge.

Staab, P. (2019) *Digitaler Kapitalismus: Markt und Herrschaft in der Ökonomie der Unknappheit*, Berlin: Suhrkamp Verlag.

Sui, D., Caverlee, J. and Rudesill, D. (2015) *The Deep Web and the Darknet: A Look inside the Internet's Massive Black Box*, Washington: The Wilson Center.

Sunstein, C.R. (2009) *Going to Extremes, How Like Minds Unite and Divide*, Oxford: Oxford University Press.

Sunstein, C.R. (2018) *#Republic: Divided Democracy in the Age of Social Media*, Princeton, NJ: Princeton University Press.

Süssenguth, F. (2015) 'Die Organisation des digitalen Wandels: Zur Funktion von Digitalisierungssemantiken in Wirtschaft, Medien und Politik', in F. Süssenguth (ed) *Die Gesellschaft der Daten*, Bielefeld: Transcript Verlag, pp 93–122.

Taddeo, M. (2017) 'Data Philanthropy and Individual Rights', *Minds and Machines*, 27(1): 1–5.

Tandoc, E.C. (2014) 'Journalism is Twerking? How Web Analytics Is Changing the Process of Gatekeeping', *New Media & Society*, 16(4). Available from: https://doi.org/10.1177/1461444814530541

Taylor, P. and Harris, J. (2007) *Critical Theories of Mass Media: Then and Now*, Maidenhead: Open University Press.

Taylor, S.H., DiFranzo, D., Choi, Y.H., Sannon, S. and Bazarova, N.N. (2019) 'Accountability and Empathy by Design: Encouraging Bystander Intervention to Cyberbullying on Social Media', *Proceedings of the ACM on Human–Computer Interaction*, 3(CSCW): article 118.

Terranova, T. (2000) 'Free Labor: Producing Culture for the Digital Economy', *Social Text*, 18(2): 33–58.

Terzis, G. (ed) (2014) *Mapping Foreign Correspondence in Europe*, London: Routledge.

Till, K.E. (2005) *The New Berlin: Memory, Politics, Place*, Minneapolis, MN: University of Minnesota Press.

Tilly, C. (1978) *From Mobilization to Revolution*, New York: McGraw.

Torgerson, D. (1999) *The Promise of Green Politics: Environmentalism and the Public Sphere*, Durham, NC: Duke University Press.

Trenz, H.-J. (2005) *Europa in den Medien: Die europäische Integration im Spiegel nationaler Öffentlichkeit*, Frankfurt: Campus Verlag.

Trenz, H.-J. (2009a) 'Digital Media and the Return of the Representative Public Sphere', *Javnost – The Public*, 16(1): 33–46.

Trenz, H.-J. (2009b) 'European Civil Society: Between Participation, Representation and Discourse', *Policy and Society*, 28(1): 35–46.

Trenz, H.-J. (2009c) 'In Search of a European Public Sphere: Between Normative Overstretch and Empirical Disenchantment', in I. Salovaara Moring (ed) *Manufacturing Europe: Spaces of Democracy, Diversity and Communication*, Gothenburg: Nordicom, pp 35–52.

Trenz, H.-J. (2015) 'The Public Sphere', in G. Mazzoleni (ed) *The International Encyclopedia of Political Communication*, Oxford: Wiley-Blackwell, pp 1362–73.

Trenz, H.-J. (2016) *Narrating European Society: Toward a Sociology of European Integration*, Lanham: Rowman and Littlefield.

Trenz, H.-J. (2021) 'Öffentlichkeitstheorie als Erkenntnistheorie Moderner Gesellschaft', edited by M. Seeliger and S. Sevignani. *Leviathan Sonderband* 37 (Ein neuer Strukturwandel der Oeffentlichkeit): 385–405.

Trenz, H.-J. (2023) 'Democracy in the digital public sphere: disruptive or self-corrective?', *Communication Theory*, qtad009, https://doi.org/10.1093/ct/qtad009

Trenz, H.-J. and Eder, K. (2004) 'The Democratizing Dynamics of a European Public Sphere: Towards a Theory of Democratic Functionalism', *European Journal of Social Theory*, 7(1): 5–25.

Trenz, H.-J., Guiraudon, V. and Ruzza, C. (2015) *Europe's Prolonged Crisis: The Making or the Unmaking of a Political Union*, Basingstoke: Palgrave Macmillan.

Trenz, H.-J, Heft, A., Vaughan, M. and Pfetsch, B. (2020) 'Resilience of Public Spheres in a Global Health Crisis', Weizenbaum Series, 11. Berlin: Weizenbaum Institute for the Networked Society – The German Internet Institute. Available from: https://doi.org/10.34669/wi.ws/11

Trenz, H.-J., Heft, A., Vaughan, M. and Pfetsch, B. (2021) 'Resilience of Public Spheres in a Global Health Crisis', *Javnost - The Public*, 28(2): 111–28.

Urbinati, N. (2013) 'The Populist Phenomenon', *Raisons politiques*, 51(3): 137–54.

Urbinati, N. (2014) *Democracy Disfigured*, Cambridge, MA: Harvard University Press.

Urbinati, N. (2019) *Me the People: How Populism Transforms Democracy*, Cambridge, MA: Harvard University Press.

Urbinati, N. and Warren, M.E. (2008) 'The Concept of Representation in Contemporary Democratic Theory', *Annual Review of Political Science*, 11: 387–412.

Uscinski, J.E., DeWitt, D. and Atkinson, M.D. (2018) 'A Web of Conspiracy? Internet and Conspiracy Theory', in A. Dyrendal, D.G. Robertson and E. Asprem (eds) *Handbook of Conspiracy Theory and Contemporary Religion*, Leiden: Brill, pp 106–30.

Vaidhyanathan, S. (2018) *Anti-Social Media: How Facebook Disconnects US and Undermines Democracy*, Oxford: Oxford University Press.

Valentino, N.A., Banks, A.J., Hutchings, V.L. and Davis, A.K. (2009) 'Selective Exposure in the Internet Age: The Interaction between Anxiety and Information Utility', *Political Psychology*, 30(4): 591–613.

van Dijck, J. (2014) 'Datafication, Dataism and Dataveillance: Big Data between Scientific Paradigm and Ideology', *Surveillance & Society*, 12(2): 197–208.

van Dijck, J. and Poell, T. (2013) 'Understanding Social Media Logic', *Media and Communication*, 1(1): 2–14.

van Dijck, J. and Poell, T. (2015) 'Social Media and the Transformation of Public Space', *Social Media + Society*, 1(2): https://doi.org/10.1177/2056305115622.

van Dijk, J. and Beek, A. (2009) *The Perspective of Network Government: The Struggle between Hierarchies, Markets and Networks as Modes of Governance in Contemporary Government*, Innovation and the Public Sector. Ebook Volume 14: ICTs, Citizens and Governance: After the Hype!, Amsterdam: IOS Press. Available from: http://ebooks.iospress.nl/volumearticle/7975

van Dijk, J.A.G.M. (2012a) 'Digital Democracy: Vision and Reality', *Innovation and the Public Sector*, 19: 49–62.

van Dijk, J.A.G.M. (2012b) 'The Evolution of the Digital Divide: The Digital Divide Turns to Inequality of Skills and Usage', in J. Bus, M. Crompton, M. Hildebrandt and G. Metakides (eds) *Digital Enlightenment Yearbook*, Amsterdam: IOS Press, pp 57–75.

Vasilopoulou, S. (2016) 'UK Euroscepticism and the Brexit Referendum', *The Political Quarterly*, 87(2): 219–27.

Veneti, A., Jackson, D. and Lilleker, D.G. (2019) *Visual Political Communication*, Basingstoke: Palgrave Macmillan.

Vetulani-Cęgiel, A. and Meyer, T. (2020) 'Power to the People? Evaluating the European Commission's Engagement Efforts in EU Copyright Policy', *Journal of European Integration*, 43(8): 1025–43.

Vie, S. (2014) 'In Defense of "Slacktivism": The Human Rights Campaign Facebook Logo as Digital Activism', *First Monday*, 19(4–7). Available from: https://doi.org/10.5210/fm.v19i4.4961

Viehmann, C., Ziegele, M. and Quiring, O. (2020) 'Gut informiert durch die Pandemie? Nutzung unterschiedlicher Informationsquellen in der Corona-Krise', *Media Perspektiven*, 10–11: 556–77.

Von Beyme, K. (2017) *From Post-democracy to Neo-democracy*, Berlin: Springer.

Wagner, P. (2008) *Modernity as Experience and Interpretation: A New Sociology of Modernity*, Cambridge: Polity Press.

Wagner, P. (2020) 'Is There a Crisis of European Democracy? The Political Condition of Our Time', *Journal of the British Academy*, 8(1): 53–61.

Wahl-Jorgensen, K., Williams, A., Sambrook, R., Harris, J., Garcia-Blanco, I., Dencik, L., et al (2016) 'The Future of Journalism', *Digital Journalism*, 4(7): 809–15.

Wallace, P. (2016) *The Psychology of the Internet*, Cambridge: Cambridge University Press.

Walsh, J.P. (2020) 'Social Media and Moral Panics: Assessing the Effects of Technological Change on Societal Reaction', *International Journal of Cultural Studies*, 23(6): 840–59.

Walzer, M. (2002) 'Passion and Politics', *Philosophy & Social Criticism*, 28(6): 617–33.

Warner, M. (2002) *Publics and Counterpublics*, New York: Zone Books.

Weale, A. (2019) *The Will of the People: A Modern Myth*, Oxford: Wiley.

Webster, J.G. and Ksiazek, T.B. (2012) 'The Dynamics of Audience Fragmentation: Public Attention in an Age of Digital Media', *Journal of Communication*, 62(1): 39–56.

Weigmann, K. (2018) 'The Genesis of a Conspiracy Theory: Why Do People Believe in Scientific Conspiracy Theories and How Do They Spread?', *EMBO Reports*, 19(4). Available from: https://doi.org/10.15252/embr.201845935

Weingart, P. (1999) 'Scientific Expertise and Political Accountability: Paradoxes of Science in Politics', *Science and Public Policy*, 26(3): 151–61.

Wessler, H. (2019) *Habermas and the Media*, Cambridge: Polity.

Wiederhold, B. (2020) 'Using Social Media to Our Advantage: Alleviating Anxiety during a Pandemic', *Cyberpsychology, Behavior, and Social Networking*, 23(4): 197–8.

Wieviorka, M. (2018) 'Le populisme et après', Hypotheses. Available from: https://wieviorka.hypotheses.org/950

Wildavsky, A. (1988) *Searching for Safety*, New Brunswick, NJ: Transaction Books.

Wilkinson, E. (2017) 'The Diverse Economies of Online Pornography: From Paranoid Readings to Post-capitalist Futures', *Sexualities*, 20(8): 981–98.

Wodak, R. and Boukala, S. (2015) 'European Identities and the Revival of Nationalism in the European Union', *Journal of Language & Politics*, 14(1): 87–109.

Wollebæk, D., Karlsen, R., Steen-Johnsen, K. and Enjolras, B. (2019) 'Anger, Fear, and Echo Chambers: The Emotional Basis for Online Behavior', *Social Media + Society*, 5(2): https://doi.org/10.1177/205630511982.

Wynn, E. and Hult, H.V. (2020) 'Platforms and the Public Sphere', *AMCIS 2020 Proceedings*, 4. Available from: https://aisel.aisnet.org/amcis2020/philosophical_is/philosophical_is/4

Yates, S. and Lockley, E. (2018) 'Social Media and Social Class', *American Behavioral Scientist*, 62(9): 1291–316.

Zappettini, F. (2021) 'The Tabloidization of the Brexit Campaign: Power to the (British) People?', *Journal of Language and Politics*, 20(2): 277–303.

Zielonka, J. (2018) *Counter-revolution: Liberal Europe in Retreat*, Oxford: Oxford University Press.

Zuboff, S. (2019) *The Age of Surveillance Capitalism: The Fight for a Human Future at the New Frontier of Power*, London: Profile.

Index

References to tables appear in **bold** type. References to endnotes show both the page number and the note number (222n4).